THE TRIATHLETE'S TRAINING BIBLE

3rd Edition

JOE FRIEL

VELO press

BOULDER, COLORADO

The Triathlete's Training Bible, Third Edition
Copyright © 2009 by Joe Friel

1830 North 55th Street
Boulder, Colorado 80301-2700 USA
303/440-0601 · Fax 303/444-6788 · E-mail velopress@competitorgroup.com

Distributed in the United States and Canada by Publishers Group West

Library of Congress Cataloging-in-Publication Data
Friel, Joe.
  The triathlete's training bible / Joe Friel.—3rd ed.
  p. cm.
  Includes bibliographical references and index.
  ISBN 978-1-934030-19-6 (pbk. : alk. paper)
1. Triathlon—Training.   I. Title.
GV1060.73.F74 2009
796.42'57—dc22
                          2009000097

For information on purchasing VeloPress books, please call 800/234-8356 or
visit www.velopress.com.

Cover design by Erin Johnson
Cover photo © Tim De Frisco
Interior design by Erin Johnson
Illustrations by Charlie Layton, chapters 12 and 13 and pages 37, 94, 116, 118, and 323
Composition by Eclipse Publishing Services

09 10 11 / 10 9 8 7 6 5 4 3 2 1

To Team Friel—
Joyce, Kim, and Dirk

CONTENTS

FOREWORD

I have been racing triathlons for more than half of my life. One would think that after so many years of training and racing, I would have learned how to train and race and would understand all of the elements it takes to be consistently at my peak in the sport. But the trials and tribulations of triathlon continue for me to this day.

Joe Friel's *The Triathlete's Training Bible* contains all of the information a triathlete needs, whether he or she is a novice, a budding junior, at the top of his or her age group, or competing at the elite level. Unlike the single disciplines of swimming, biking, and running, the combination of all three strengthens almost all of the muscles in your body. Feeling healthy and fit enhances all aspects of your life.

The Triathlete's Training Bible is the most comprehensive triathlon book I have read. It is formatted in such a way that you can find detailed information on any question of immediate concern. What should you do the week before the race? Find the answer in Chapter 10. What types of foods are best for all of the demands you put on your body? Turn to Chapter 16. What distance are you planning to race? See Chapter 9. A key chapter for me is Chapter 4 on training intensity and fighting fatigue. Joe leaves no rock unturned. More than twenty-five years of racing, coaching, and analyzing every tidbit of pertinent information on fitness are compacted into this one book.

Only a handful of people can claim to swim, bike, and run, whether it is a one-hour sprint-distance triathlon or a twelve-hour Ironman. Training for three sports is more time consuming than just preparing for a 10-kilometer running race. Because we must juggle work, family, and numerous other affairs in our busy lives, triathletes need to use their time to train wisely. *The Triathlete's Training Bible* is your coach. It will maximize the limited training time you have in order to prepare you to race at an optimal level.

For those of you who are constantly striving to improve your performance, this book will lead you in the right direction. Keep tri-ing!

—*Wesley Hobson*

1997–1998 USA Triathlon national team member, 1992 U.S. Olympic Center male triathlete of the year, 1997 U.S. national sprint champion, and 1992–1993 world championship bronze medalist

PREFACE TO THE THIRD EDITION

It's been over ten years since I wrote the first edition of *The Triathlete's Training Bible*. During that decade a lot has changed, prompting me to revisit the book. Most of the changes are additions, and so it has grown considerably larger, just as the sport has grown in the past ten years. When I sat down to write *The Triathlete's Training Bible* in 1997, the USA Triathlon Federation had 16,212 licensed members. The sport was still in its infancy. In 2007, as I started this revision, USAT had more than 100,000 members.

The sport has grown in a way that none of us who were there in the early days could ever have imagined. It is now mainstream. When I wrote *The Triathlete's Training Bible*, I knew of only five other books on the topic. Now major book stores have a section of their shelves just for triathlon. There are several other indications that triathlon has gone mainstream. Fictional characters on television shows are triathletes. Celebrities do triathlons. When you tell someone you ride a bike, the first thing they'll ask is if you're a triathlete. When your neighbors see you heading out for your daily bike and run, they no longer think you're a wacko; they know you're a triathlete. Websites devoted to triathlon were practically nonexistent ten years ago. Now there are thousands. What a remarkable change we've experienced in such a short time.

This growth has caused the sport of triathlon to change in other ways as well. Ten years ago, the average triathlete was more knowledgeable when it came to training, nutrition, equipment, and racing. Of course there was a lot less information to be aware of back then. In the past ten years there has been an explosion not only of training information but also of training technology. Power meters were pretty much unheard of in 1997, and GPS devices for training and accelerometers existed only in our imaginations.

Our knowledge of every aspect of training has grown. Physiology and nutrition have led the way, with sports psychology lagging just a bit behind. As a result, how we should train and eat is much better defined than it was in 1997. But I'm afraid a result of this explosion of information and technology is that triathletes are more confused now than ever. That's why I felt a need to revise *The Triathlete's Training Bible*.

I've grown as a coach in the past ten years. In the early days, I could keep up with almost every new development that came down the pike—wheels, running shoes, sports-nutritional products, goggles, wetsuits, bike frames, skill techniques, races, websites, books, and on and on. Now I find that it's impossible. I have to focus my attention on just a few things at at time, the ones I find are most important. As a result, I now know more about fewer things. I've tried to describe these things in the latest edition of this book.

While every chapter has new material added, the greatest number of additions have been made in the chapters devoted to the intensity of training (Chapter 4), skills (Chapter 12), strength (Chapter 13), and nutrition (Chapter 16). You can also go to my website—trainingbible.com—for ongoing updates to many of the concepts found here.

As always, I hope that my book proves helpful to your pursuit of the triathlon life-style. If it does (or even if it doesn't), feel free to send me an e-mail at jfriel@trainingbible.com and tell me about it. I attend many races throughout the season and would enjoy talking with you about your triathlon experience. Hearing from those who benefit from my books is always a great pleasure and gives meaning to what is otherwise a solitary and tedious activity.

I wish you all the best for your training and racing!

—Joe Friel
Boulder, Colorado

ACKNOWLEDGMENTS

I am indebted, as always, to the triathletes who have read *The Triathlete's Training Bible* and given me their suggestions for making it a more useful tool. Much of what you will find amended and added here came from questions asked by those who had read previous editions.

I also want to thank the staff at VeloPress, my publisher, who have continued to support my ideas for books and create products that get better every year. Special thanks go to Renee Jardine, associate publisher, for championing my idea for this format and for continuing to support my writing projects. Thanks also to Dave Trendler, marketing manager, for getting the word out whenever I give a training bible–based talk.

Three athletes whom I have coached agreed to allow me to use their experiences in this book: Ryan Bolton, Justin Daerr, and Marlene Zuhl. Thank you.

Nate Koch, P.T., A.T.C., director of rehabilitation at Endurance Rehabilitation in Scottsdale, Arizona, who assesses all of my coaching clients, reviewed the section in Chapter 5 on physical assessment and offered suggestions. Thanks, Nate.

And, of course, I am grateful to my loving wife, Joyce, who after 43 years of marriage continues to support my passion for sports science by putting up with my 4 A.M. writing sessions and late evenings at the computer. Thanks, sweetheart.

PART 1

THE SELF-TRAINED ATHLETE

Multisport is a huge challenge, one that is greatly simplified by hiring a coach. While training under the watchful eye of a good coach often makes for effective use of limited workout time, it's not an option that everyone wants or can afford. Self-training is far more common, and often just as effective. After all, no one knows you as well as you do. There are, however, many pitfalls to self-training. The obvious one has to do with knowledge of the scientific principles of training. Less obvious, but no less important, is the wisdom of training: having a systematic approach, developing a philosophy of training, fully understanding and accepting the importance of consistency, creating a determined and purposeful attitude, and committing to a well-defined mission. Before the physical training begins, these mental attributes need to be explored. The successful self-trained athlete is first and foremost wise.

SMART TRAINING

Many dedicated endurance athletes don't need to be told what to do—they need to be told what not to do.
—SCOTT TINLEY, PROFESSIONAL TRIATHLETE

MULTISPORT IS BOTH amazingly simple and incredibly complex. Its simplicity is apparent to anyone who has ever enjoyed swimming, riding a bike, or running. All are easily accomplished by children, and it often takes only a little practice for people of all ages to advance to higher levels. Finishing a short-course triathlon or duathlon is achievable by almost anyone who dabbles in the sport. Multisport's complexity becomes apparent as soon as the novice decides to improve performance. Questions immediately arise, such as, Should I do all three sports each day? How long should I work out? Why am I tired all the time? What should I eat?

The experienced multisport competitor also has questions, but these are born of a higher level of understanding of the intricacies of the sport. Seasoned athletes ask, How can I predict a fitness peak? What's the best way to blend workouts for maximum fitness gains without overtraining? Is there a way to speed recovery so I can train hard more frequently? In fact, it appears that the more experienced the athlete, the more complex the training issues become.

While it's the purpose of this book to answer such questions, understand that there is not one and only one answer for each. Because of individual differences, there are as many ways to train for multisport as there are triathletes and duathletes. Yet there is much that athletes—regardless of experience, age, gender, and natural ability—have in common. All rely on the same fuel sources, all have the same number of bones and muscles that are put together in the same manner, and all have nervous systems that operate in the same way.

It is when it comes to the specifics of training that each athlete is unique. There are individual motivations for racing, different genetic capabilities, varied time constraints, and unique goals. Since the spectrum of such possibilities is wide, the key to success in multisport does not come from following a one-size-fits-all training regimen. If that were so, this book could cover the topic in a few pages.

Success in multisport racing comes from understanding two aspects of training: the commonly accepted principles of training and your own exceptional needs. What this means is that training is both science and art. The promising athlete is one who understands the training aspects and blends this knowledge into a systematic training program.

SYSTEMATIC TRAINING

Multisport training is much like putting a jigsaw puzzle together. To the novice in either endeavor, the many pieces of the puzzle can be overwhelming. What comes first? It's like the old saying "you can't see the forest for the trees." If the details of jigsaw-puzzle solving, just like multisport training, get in the way of seeing the big picture, wasted effort and time are a certainty. It will take far longer to get to the end result of a completed puzzle, and there is a great possibility that you'll give up early in the process.

The way to solve any puzzle is to have a system, which is nothing more than a set of guidelines to get you organized. An elaborate or complex system isn't needed; a simple one will work just as well. The less time you have available to put the puzzle together, the more critical the system becomes. For the puzzle, you could start with these guidelines to simplify the task and make efficient use of time:

- Spread the pieces out on the table so all are seen.
- Put pieces of similar colors together in groups.
- Start by putting the edge pieces together.
- Work only one section at a time.
- Position completed sections relative to the finished product.
- Try to connect the finished sections.
- Protect the finished sections so they aren't broken up by the wind or the family cat.

The most important aspect of a jigsaw-puzzle system is to keep the picture of the finished puzzle on the box lid where it is visible. You have to know what the finished product is supposed to look like. Without the picture in front of you, the task would be an immense one; it would take far longer to complete the puzzle and you would continually have doubts about your progress.

Anyone who has ever worked on a complex jigsaw puzzle knows that it takes a long time. Working straight through to completion could be an all-night ordeal, and if you decided to tackle it that way, puzzle burnout would be likely. By the time you finished putting the puzzle together, you wouldn't want to see it again or even think about doing another one for a long, long time. To prevent burnout, you would need to take longer than a night to do the puzzle, and you would need to take frequent breaks. While most of the breaks would be short, it would be best if some of them were quite long. That way, every time you came back to the puzzle, you would start with renewed enthusiasm and heightened creativity.

Suppose researchers in fact did a study and found that people who took breaks became better at putting together jigsaw puzzles than people who stayed up all night long doing them. Such a study would add some science to the puzzle-solving project. Here, science is really nothing more than methodically determining a way of acting that works. Without a methodology, the task of putting a puzzle together—or training for multisport—is a random activity based largely on luck.

So that's the science, but where does the art of a training system come in? Art is the aspect of training in which you learn to better understand yourself as an individual. To use the puzzle analogy one last time: Art, or the ability to make creative decisions based on intuition and experience, plays a role because

- Not everyone's puzzle is the same—some have big puzzles, and others have small ones;
- Certain areas of the picture are fuzzy;
- Some pieces of the puzzle are more important than others;
- Pieces may get lost or broken along the way and need to be replaced;
- Some people have precious little time to work on their puzzles;
- The part of the puzzle you are working on at any given time is part of a bigger picture that also needs solving;
- Others may tell you what a bad job of puzzle solving you are doing;
- The puzzle may not be coming along as well as you had hoped, as it is taking longer to solve than you anticipated;
- Some sections of the puzzle can seem monotonous and frustrating.

This book will help you devise a personal training system employing both science and art. The science part is easy to describe; the art of training can be described, but it is learned only by doing. The system you devise will differ from those of your training partners. It won't duplicate the system used by the pro athlete you most admire. It will work only for you. For any system to work you must have confidence in it, derived from understanding the "whys" and "hows." But you must also remain open-minded, as no system is foolproof, and no one has all the answers.

PHILOSOPHY OF TRAINING

Because it is critical to success in multisport, the art of training needs a firm foundation. The way to establish that foundation is with a personal training philosophy. Although you have probably never thought about it, you already have one. Every athlete does, since training decisions must be made every day, and the answers spring from an underlying personal philosophy. For example, your training philosophy is reflected in the decisions you make when you

- Feel tired, but have a hard workout planned;
- Can't decide which workout to do;
- Are afraid you will lose your fitness while taking time off;
- Know your competition is doing more than you are;
- Dread doing a certain workout;
- Feel like your training partners are going too fast;
- Know your weaknesses, but prefer working on your strengths;
- Sense you can do only one more interval;
- Think you could do more, but you are not sure;
- Have a bad race;
- Seem to have lost fitness.

If your philosophy is "More is better—always train as hard as I can," you will answer these questions in a certain way. In fact, this philosophy of training is quite common in multisport and is the leading cause of breakdown from illness, injury, burnout, and over-training. By adopting a philosophy that is more moderate, you can avoid such problems and see improvements in your racing performance.

A person with a completely different training philosophy would answer the same questions very differently. Suppose, for example, someone took the following statement as his or her basic training philosophy: An athlete should do the least amount of the most specific training that brings continual improvement. What does this mean? Let's examine the key parts to better understand it.

Least amount implies that less is better. It may sound counterintuitive for endurance training, but most successful athletes support the notion that small fitness gains made over a long time are better than quick fitness changes over a short time. We all know that "too much, too soon" leads to breakdown, yet for some reason we keep doing it.

Most specific has to do with how daily workouts benefit triathlon- and duathlon-specific fitness, which is the ultimate goal of training. Each and every workout should have a purpose, whether it's to improve fitness, maintain fitness, or recover. Getting the balance of these three factors right is the key to success.

Continual improvement has to do with taking a long-term approach to training. Making gradual workout changes from week to week produces fitness that stays with you longer and ultimately allows you to reach a higher level than making big changes does. Your body is prepared to handle changes of a bit more than 10 percent at a time. Doing more than what you are physically capable of absorbing is worse than simply wasting effort, as it often leads to breakdown.

The idea of placing limits on training is a scary thought for some. Many athletes are so used to existing on the edge of overtraining that it seems a natural state. Such athletes can seem as addicted as drug users. Those who abuse training are not becoming better athletes, but they can't bring themselves to change. That is the way addictions are. Changing your personal training philosophy means taking a risk by trying something new and different, but the potential rewards are great.

CONSISTENT TRAINING

Consistent training, not extreme training, is the way to attain the highest possible fitness. Illness, injury, burnout, and overtraining can cause training breakdown, and extended or frequent downtime from such problems inevitably results in a loss of fitness and the need to rebuild by returning to previous levels of training. Multisport athletes who experience these problems with some regularity seldom achieve their potential in the sport.

Consistency must serve as the ultimate standard in all training decisions. It results from following a philosophy such as the one described above, emphasizing the least amount of the most specific training that brings continual improvement. The key is to strive for moderation in training while resting at regular intervals.

MODERATION AND CONSISTENCY

Your body has limits when it comes to endurance, strength, and speed, and you should seldom test them. By generally staying within those limits, while stretching yourself just a little in a well-designed training program, you can avoid breakdowns and ensure consistent training results. Aim to finish workouts feeling as though you could have done more. For example, when there is only one interval left in you, and digging deep is the only way to complete it, stop. Don't do it.

The time to abandon a workout is when it is perceived as very hard, your speed has decreased noticeably, or your technique has changed. For athletes with a strong work ethic, this is difficult to do. For this reason, many successful athletes have coaches; training under the watchful eye of an objective person whose emotions are not linked to the workout can help you to avoid breakdowns. Self-coaching requires you to think objectively and unemotionally. Although this is possible to do, it is difficult for many of us. A self-coached athlete is often unsure whether to continue or stop. Doubt is a good reason to discontinue the session. When in doubt, leave it out.

Hard workouts progress through a "discomfort-hurt-agony" sequence. Be assured that there is nothing beneficial about reaching the "agony" stage. There are benefits achieved at the "hurt" level, but beyond that, the risk of injury and overtraining rises dramatically. There is no scientific evidence to support the need for supreme effort in training, but there is a great deal that supports the notion of moderate stress as beneficial.

The hardest workouts should occur sparingly throughout the year. Especially in the few weeks immediately preceding a major race, you will need to be judicious. That is because it only takes a short time to reach ceiling levels of the extreme components of fitness. As you will see in a later chapter, a season should include only three or four of these major events. Training at the highest intensities year-round is ultimately detrimental to performance.

During the times of the year when you are not doing intense, race-specific training, it is best to devote your workouts to building or maintaining endurance and strength, recovering from a race or race season, or refining your skills.

REST AND CONSISTENCY

Intellectually, multisport athletes know they should rest, but emotionally they fear that taking an appropriately timed break, even for a couple of days, will lead to a loss of fitness. Few fully appreciate the physiological benefits that accrue during rest, especially while asleep. But it is while we are sleeping that the body releases growth hormone to repair damage from the day's training stress. Sleep enables the body to shore up any of the systems weakened by training. Without adequate sleep, fitness is lost regardless of how intense or how long an athlete's workouts are. When the intensity and duration of training increase, rest must also increase to maintain balance in the body. Besides sleep, rest includes regular easy training days, days off from training altogether, frequent recovery weeks, and extended breaks from training at the end of a race season.

There is no scientific evidence to support the idea that appropriate breaks in training will lead to a loss of fitness. There is, however, a mountain of research showing that frequent rest is beneficial to fitness. A well-rested triathlete looks forward to workouts, enjoys doing them, feels sharp and in control during training sessions, and grows stronger afterward. The chronically tired triathlete drags through workouts only by the force of extreme willpower, performs sluggishly, recovers poorly, and derives little benefit. You will not improve without adequate rest.

TRAINING LESSONS

I was once asked to talk on the most important lessons I had learned in nearly three decades of coaching. It was a good exercise, as it required me to summarize my coaching philosophy and highlight the most important points. Some of what I've learned may not make sense at first to a dedicated endurance athlete. But trust me, these lessons came from years of working with athletes just like you. Here are my guidelines for multisport athletes. Bear them in mind as you read through this book and learn to create your own personalized training plan.

LESSON #1: HAVE A CLEAR GOAL

Most athletes think they have goals. Few really do. What most call goals are actually wishes. They are vague desires for grand achievements that are poorly defined. These also often include the word "faster." When first starting a coaching program for an athlete,

Training for endurance sports involves taking risks. Some of the risks you take may even be life threatening, but you can minimize them by taking certain precautions.

Cycling carries a high amount of risk because of the reliance on the machine and because of the distances a triathlete must ride on the open road in training. To minimize the danger, avoid heavily trafficked areas whenever possible, and always wear a helmet. Ride only with safe groups, not with people who run stop signs, ride in between traffic, or generally ignore traffic laws. Never take undue risks on steep descents while riding. And before every ride, test your brakes, check the quick releases to make sure they are tight, examine the tires to see if they have any cuts or show signs of too much wear, and tighten any loose bolts.

Swimming can also be risky, particularly if you train in open water. Never swim in open water alone. Always swim with a partner, and ideally, with a kayak "spotter." Kayakers often volunteer for organized group training swims in open water. Similarly, if there is no lifeguard present for a pool swim, make sure you train with a partner.

Running on open roads requires safety precautions similar to those you would take in cycling. Avoid heavily trafficked roads. If you run within an hour of dawn or dusk, wear reflective material. Be aware of whether the sun will be in drivers' eyes, making it difficult for them to see you. As for which side of the road to run on, it is your choice—there are no laws saying you must run on one side or the other. (This is a contrast to cycling, as cyclists must ride in the direction of traffic, as close as practicable to the right.) I prefer to run against traffic so I can see what's coming toward me, but if you do so, be aware of drivers about to turn onto the road you are on, because they may not be looking in your direction when they enter the intersection. Finally, run only with safe groups who respect traffic laws.

Also, whether you are cycling, swimming, or running, if you experience any unusual physical conditions, such as chest pain, radiating arm or neck pain, an unusually high or erratic heart rate, joint soreness, back pain, unusual muscle or tendon discomfort, or blood in the urine, be sure to inform your doctor right away. Such conditions should also cause you to stop the workout immediately. Let's have a safe and successful season.

I help them turn their wishes into goals by asking questions such as *How much? When? Where? Is this goal a good stretch for you? Is it realistic?* Another good question to ask in order to better define one's goals is *How will you know if this season was successful?* We do talk about dreams when I ask *What is the greatest accomplishment you'd like to achieve as a triathlete?* Long-term dreams can eventually become goals. Knowing precisely what you want is critical to success in triathlon just as it is in life. Goal setting is discussed in greater detail in Chapter 7.

LESSON #2: DETERMINE WHAT STANDS BETWEEN YOU AND YOUR GOAL

A good goal will stretch your limits. Pushing yourself to reach that goal obviously requires that you improve some aspect of yourself, and you need to identify whatever that "something" is. Instead of training randomly by doing what you've done in the past, what your training partners want to do, or the workouts some pro does, you should isolate and improve the quality you are lacking. This is kind of an engineer's way of looking at training, but it works. I call it "fixing the limiters." You'll find more on this in Chapter 6.

LESSON #3: PLANNING IS NECESSARY TO ACHIEVE A BIG GOAL

This may sound boring, but planning is at the heart of training, especially when your goals are big ones. I know you may have heard good athletes say that they don't plan and do quite well anyway. I'd wager they really are following a plan, but it's not in writing. The plan is in their heads. Good athletes don't become good by training randomly, and you won't either. This book is essentially about planning. Chapter 7 provides the details on how to map out a seasonal plan. Chapter 8 covers race-week planning, and Chapter 9 discusses race-day planning.

LESSON #4: MEASURE PROGRESS TOWARD YOUR GOAL

There's nothing worse than thinking you are making good progress toward achieving your goal and later finding out on race day that you are not physically ready. Had you known earlier that you weren't improving as expected in some aspect of fitness, you might have had time to correct it by changing your training. There are many ways to assess fitness progress. Chapter 5 addresses some of these.

LESSON #5: DO ONLY THE TRAINING NECESSARY TO ACHIEVE YOUR GOAL

This training philosophy, though noted above, is worth repeating. When I was a much younger athlete, I thought my success depended on training as much as possible. That approach led to frequent injury, overtraining, illness, and burnout. It took me many years to figure out what I should be doing—only the training that was necessary to achieve my goals. Once I cut out the excessive stuff, I got better as an athlete. This book will return again and again to the theme of identifying what is important and then doing only that.

LESSON #6: MENTAL FITNESS IS AS IMPORTANT AS PHYSICAL FITNESS

Chapter 2 discusses mental toughness. I believe the key mental skill is confidence. Of all the factors I consider when talking to the athletes I coach, this is the most important. What I look for in athletes is a quiet, "can-do" attitude. This is the common denominator

Professional athletes typically sleep ten to twelve hours a day, breaking this down into eight- to ten-hour nights with one or two daily naps. You may not be a pro or have time for naps, but the more training volume and intensity you do, the more rest you need.

Quality of sleep is another concern. Having difficulty going to sleep, or waking up frequently throughout the night, cuts into the benefits derived from sleep. Here are some tips for improving sleep quality:

- Go to bed at a regular time every day, including weekends and the nights before races.
- As bedtime approaches, unwind slowly by reading, going for a short walk, or engaging in light conversation.
- Sleep in a darkened room that is 60 to 64 degrees Fahrenheit and well ventilated.
- Use a comfortable bed and pillow.
- Take a warm bath before retiring.
- Drink herbal tea to promote relaxation.
- Try to sleep only when feeling tired.
- Progressively contract and relax your muscles to induce total-body relaxation.

Also, avoid stimulants such as coffee, caffeinated tea, and cola in the last few hours before going to bed. Salt and refined sugar may even cause sleep problems for some. Although alcohol is a depressant that may help you fall asleep, it can also interfere with sleep patterns, causing you to wake early.

Besides herbal tea, other foods that may help induce sleep are turkey, tuna fish, cottage cheese, and milk, since they're high in sleep-inducing L-tryptophan. Avoid eating a large meal right before going to bed, but don't go to bed hungry.

Happy dreams.

for all of the best athletes I have known. A great deal of self-doubt is a sure sign of someone who is incapable of achieving high goals regardless of physical ability.

LESSON #7: SKILL IS CRITICAL TO ATHLETIC SUCCESS

In endurance sports, with the possible exception of swimming, athletes tend to downplay or even disregard technique. Most athletes, including elites, have lots of room for improvement in their sport-specific skills. As skills improve, less energy is wasted, which means you can go faster with the same effort because your movements are more economical. Skills and economy are discussed in Chapter 12.

LESSON #8: TRAIN FOR THE UNIQUE DEMANDS OF THE GOAL RACE

Every race is unique. The principal factor is race distance, such as sprint- or Ironman-distance. Beyond this are other, less obvious factors: A course may be over hilly, rolling, or flat terrain; the water may be rough or calm; there are wetsuit and non-wetsuit swims, hot and cold temperatures, courses with lots of turns or very few turns, off-road and road courses, morning and afternoon start times, races in which you will use a disk wheel and those in which you will not, and a multitude of other variables. Your training, as you get closer to race day, should take on more and more of the unique characteristics of the race you are preparing for. In Chapter 10, you will learn how to write a race plan that takes key variables into consideration: Learn to take charge of the factors you can control, and learn how to deal with those you can't.

LESSON #9: RECOVERY IS JUST AS IMPORTANT AS HARD WORKOUTS

Training is composed of two elements: hard work and recovery. One without the other makes for an ineffective program. I've found that most triathletes have no problem at all with the hard work part. In fact, they seem to thrive on it. Where most need help is with recovery. Left to their own devices, most triathletes will work too hard and rest too little. And since it is during rest that the body adapts and becomes fitter, training overly hard and resting too little is counterproductive. Chapter 11 takes a closer look at recovery.

LESSON #10: FOCUS YOUR LIFESTYLE ON SUCCESS

The bigger your triathlon goals are relative to your abilities, the more things in your life that must be focused on achieving your goals. If your goal is to complete a sprint-distance race, you can afford to be a bit sloppy with nutrition, sleep, stress, training partners, friends, stretching, equipment, workout analysis, and strength work and still do well. But if your goal is to win a national championship or qualify for Ironman Hawaii, you will need to get everything in your life pointed at triathlon success. Since the people who ask me to coach them are aiming for big goals, I spend a lot of time helping them focus their lifestyles on success. Chapters 13 through 16 address most of these issues.

It's worth adding to this list one last bit of advice—have fun. This may seem obvious, but some athletes are so focused on achieving the right numbers in their logs that they've forgotten why they got involved in the sport in the first place. They've taken the fun out of it. Many of the pros I talk to are amazed at how much training time age groupers do on top of working 50 to 60 hours per week, raising a couple of kids, getting them to soccer practice, taking care of the landscaping, doing volunteer work, and myriad other responsibilities. By comparison, the pros have it easy; they train 30 to 40 hours per week with a few naps sprinkled in. But they also tell me that if it ever stops being fun they will quit racing and get a real job. Fun is the reason we participate in triathlon. Smile more. Frown less.

ATTITUDE

I saw the Ironman for the first time on television in 1982, when Julie Moss fell and crawled across the finish line. Everyone in the room was all choked up. People were crying and cheering. I thought, "This is incredible."
—MARK ALLEN, PROFESSIONAL TRIATHLETE

IN FEBRUARY 1982, ABC's *Wide World of Sports* program covered the fifth Hawaii Ironman and, unintentionally, established mainstream recognition for the fledgling sport of triathlon, and also the attitude of an entire generation of triathletes.

That summer, repeated broadcasts of the dramatic finish riveted sports-hungry Americans to their television sets. A freckle-faced, red-haired former waitress from Carlsbad, California, named Julie Moss had a big lead going into the run. Moss, a strong swimmer and cyclist, soon found herself losing ground to a quickly closing Kathleen McCartney. Near the end of the marathon, Moss was reduced to walking, and with the finish line in sight she began to wobble. Then she fell and struggled to her feet while refusing assistance that would have disqualified her. Finally she crawled on hands and knees to "stay low where no one could bother me," she later said. Just short of the finish line McCartney passed Moss to win. Twenty-nine seconds later Julie Moss reached the finish line to take second.

Moss's dramatic finish, played out repeatedly on the American sports program, brought an explosion of interest in the Ironman. That year, a second race was held in October, which allowed those from the northern states to train in the summer instead of the winter. The second 1982 race swelled to more than 900 entrants from the 580 who had competed only eight months earlier (the annual race is now held every October). In 1983, there were thousands of applicants, causing Ironman officials to set a limit of 1,500 and establish the qualifying and lottery system for entry that is in use today.

The television coverage of Moss's finish did more than promote the growth of the Ironman—it also established a stereotype of the triathlete as a mix of crazy, macho, and heroic. And it gave the impression that triathlons are "gruelathons." These initial images attracted people to the sport who favored the extremes of training—either massive swim, bike, and run volumes, or minimal training to enhance the mental tenacity required to deal with extreme suffering.

The first triathletes really weren't crazy; they actually had a lot going for them mentally, if not scientifically. Their greatest mental attribute was a "can-do" attitude. Show them a challenge, no matter how big, and they knew it was not only doable but something at which they could excel. Most came to triathlon with a strong background in one or two of the three disciplines and soon became passably proficient in the others due to their mental tenacity.

Today, many people, especially juniors, come to the sport as multisport athletes first and foremost. Their attitudes differ from those of their predecessors in the sport. For one thing, the new triathletes and duathletes are more willing than the earlier ones to listen to science and pay attention to the needs of their bodies. What they sometimes lack, however, is the swashbuckling, never-say-quit attitude of the original multisport athletes. While their more moderate mindset may be an advantage for long-term success, some degree of relentless motivation is required to conquer big challenges like the triathlon and duathlon. The trick is to balance a determined attitude with a purposeful approach.

Several years ago, as the story goes, scientists at the National Aeronautics and Space Administration (NASA) developed an interest in the bumblebee. The lab folks reckoned that the little insect held some secrets of flight that might provide answers to questions about operating in space. After all, they asked, how could such small wings produce efficient lift for a relatively large and hairy torso? And how could a round body, and a flight position that violated so many principles of aerodynamics, move so effectively through the air? Indeed, there was much to learn from the little hummer.

So the scientists set about studying the bumblebee to discover its flying secrets. As scientists always do, they hypothesized about, scrutinized, examined, dissected, measured, timed, filmed, observed, compared, quantified, thought about, and debated the bumblebee. After weeks of study they came to one conclusion: Bumblebees are not capable of flight.

Fortunately, no one told the bumblebee. The silly insects go right on believing that flight is normal for them, despite what the best minds in the scientific world know as fact.

We can learn a lot from the bumblebee. The single most critical piece of the multisport puzzle is believing in yourself and your capacity to succeed. "If you think you can or think you can't," automobile manufacturer Henry Ford said, "you're probably right." The bumblebee thinks it can fly. Actually, the thought of anything else never even crosses its tiny mind. It just keeps on flying.

Then there's the racehorse. Have you ever been to the Kentucky Derby or another big horse race? The physiology of the equine athlete is similar to that of the human athlete, and the racehorse is trained in much the same manner as a runner. Racehorse trainers know they have a very valuable, carefully bred animal to train, and they use scientifically proven methods to make sure the owner gets the most out of his or her investment. They use heart rate monitors, interval and endurance training, periodization plans, and a diet designed to enhance performance.

Psychologically, however, racehorses differ a great deal from multisport athletes. They never question their training preparation. When it comes time for a workout designed by their trainer, they do it without wondering if it's enough. They don't go out in the morning and put in a few extra junk miles for "insurance." They don't worry and fret after a poor performance. Whether they succeed or not, life in the stable goes on as usual.

On Derby day, racehorses are nervous just as human athletes are; they know what is about to happen, but they don't magnify the tension by comparing themselves with the other horses ("Look at the legs on that stud!"). Instead, they are very purposeful. There is but one reason for everyday existence—to get faster. If the horse is physically strong and the trainer is smart, this happens.

If you are to succeed in multisport, the first thing you must do is believe in yourself just as the bumblebee does. Without this confidence, all the science in the world won't do you any good. Also, if this book is to help, you must have a purposeful, racehorse trust in your training. Continually second-guessing and changing your training direction after every race is a sure way to fail. Think like a bumblebee; train like a horse.

MISSION

In 1994, Dave "The Man" Scott had a bumblebee and racehorse year. Upon turning 40 years old, he decided to come out of retirement and take on the Hawaii Ironman following a five-year absence. This was going to be a daunting challenge.

Many triathlon and aging experts said his presence wouldn't be an issue; Scott was too old to compete head-to-head with men 10 to 15 years his junior. And besides, they pontificated, the Ironman had become more competitive since his swan song as runner-up to Mark Allen in 1989. This grueling event was not an old man's race. Better to stay comfortably in retirement than to risk losing badly and damaging his reputation as a six-time winner of the Hawaii Ironman and the undisputed King of Kona, they explained.

Like the bumblebee, Scott didn't listen to all the reasons why he didn't seem to have a chance. Instead, he did what the racehorse does—eat, sleep, and live in order to become faster. He went off to train alone for several weeks leading up to the race. He prepared for this greatest challenge of a long and storied career by staying away, both physically and emotionally, from the naysayers who would try to convince him he "couldn't fly."

On race day, Scott came out of the water near the front, moved up on the bike, and was strongly in second place late in the run. Nineteen miles into the marathon, he had closed the gap to within 11 seconds of race leader Greg Welch. But run as hard as he could, Scott couldn't narrow the lead any further. He crossed the finish line on Ali'i Drive in second place. Later he proclaimed it his "best race, ever."

That a 40-year-old "has-been" triathlete could come out of retirement and beat the best in the world, minus one, at the greatest challenge in the sport is nothing short of remarkable. Had Scott listened to the experts he would never have even attempted the comeback. But he didn't listen. He was on a mission.

Unlike Dave Scott, you may never have experts telling you that it can't be done. Maybe that's because you have surrounded yourself with supportive people and a positive atmosphere. If so, you are a wise and fortunate person. But your lack of negativity may also come from a different source—from living comfortably within your limits and never taking on a big challenge. Which is it?

What is it you want to achieve in multisport? Do you know? Can you put it in a few words? Can you write it down in such a way that it motivates and gives direction to training? Are you convinced it is possible? If so, you are a rare athlete. Unfortunately, most

Entering Ironman

There is no bigger challenge in triathlon than the Hawaii Ironman. Just getting in is perhaps the most formidable task. Attaining one of the coveted 1,500 spots by qualifying at a selected event provides many triathletes with a quest that may last for years.

An alternative is to enter through the lottery system. There are 200 lottery spots available each year. Considering there are typically about 5,000 applications for those entries, the chances are slim, but there is a chance. Here's how the lottery works:

1. There are 150 slots available to U.S. applicants. You must be a U.S. citizen to apply. Fifty slots are available to international applicants. To apply, go to the Ironman Web site at www.ironmanlive.com.
2. Of the 200 lottery slots, 125 are awarded to Ironman Passport Club members. So, joining increases your chances considerably. And club membership brings other benefits such as a quarterly newsletter, discounts on merchandise purchases, and free gifts.
3. Apply online by the end of February. You will be required to pay an application fee.
4. In mid-April, a computer at the Ironman organization picks the winners, and on May 1, the local newspapers and television stations of those selected are notified.
5. If you are one of the fortunate, all that remains is to complete one of the designated triathlons by the end of July to validate your lottery slot and establish your preparedness.

Good luck!

have only a vague idea of what they are doing in the sport and why they train a certain way. Often there is a nebulous notion of "getting faster." Seldom is there anything done to define and give direction to such wishes.

Most of us go through life never coming close to our limits and living only on wishes. Wishes are important; they're the start of great feats. Wishes grow into dreams when you are able to mentally "see" yourself accomplish the wish. Dreams turn into goals when a plan for attaining them is defined. Goals become a mission when unwavering self-belief and purposeful zeal are realized. Big challenges require mission status. The difference between a goal and a mission is attitude. Passionate commitment is self-evident in successful missions. With the proper attitude, almost anything is possible. What you believe, you will achieve.

COMMITMENT

Talk is cheap. It's easy to have big dreams and set high goals before the race season starts. The true test of commitment to better racing results is not in the talking, but in the doing. Commitment doesn't start with the first race of the season; it's all the things you do today to get stronger and faster and gain endurance. Real commitment means 365 days a year and 24 hours a day.

Ask the best athletes you know about commitment. Once you probe past all of the "aw, shucks" stuff you'll discover how big a role multisport plays in their lives. The better they are, the more you'll hear about their lives revolving around the sport. The most likely remark you will hear is that each day is arranged around training. It's a rare champion who fits in workouts randomly.

Racing to your potential can't be an on-again, off-again endeavor. It's a full-time commitment—a passion. Achieving the pinnacle of excellence requires living, breathing, eating, and sleeping triathlon every day. Literally.

The greater the commitment, the more life pivots around the basic three factors of training: eating, sleeping, and working out. Eating fuels the body for training and speeds recovery, replacing depleted energy and nutrient stores. Sleeping and working out have a synergistic effect on fitness. Each can cause the release of growth hormone from the pituitary gland. Growth hormone speeds recovery, rebuilds muscles, and breaks down body fat. By training twice daily and taking a nap, the dedicated athlete gets four hits of growth hormone daily, resulting in higher levels of fitness sooner.

In the final analysis, greater fitness is what we are all after. It's the product of three ingredients: stress, rest, and fuel. Table 2.1 shows how training, sleeping, and eating can be built into your day. This is not the final word on daily routines, but is intended only to offer suggested ways of fitting training into your day along with the many other activities. Notice that there are no three-a-day routines. Few, if any, amateur multisport athletes should train more than twice a day. Even two workouts can be too many for some.

	TWO WORKOUTS DAILY		ONE WORKOUT DAILY	
	WORK DAY	NO-WORK DAY	WORK DAY	NO-WORK DAY
6:00 am	Awake	Awake	Awake	Awake
:30	Workout 1	Eat	Workout	Eat
7:00	│	Stretch	│	Stretch
:30	│	Personal	│	Personal
8:00	Eat	│	Eat	│
:30	Shower	Workout 1	Shower	Workout
9:00	Work	│	Work	│
:30	│	│	│	│
10:00	│	│	│	│
:30	│	Eat	│	│
11:00	│	Shower	│	│
:30	Eat	Nap	│	Eat
12:00 pm	Nap	Stretch	Eat	Shower
:30	Work	Personal	Nap	Nap
1:00	│	Eat	Work	Personal
:30	│	Personal	│	│
2:00	│	│	│	│
:30	│	Workout 2	│	│
3:00	Eat	│	│	│
:30	│	│	Eat	Eat
4:00	│	│	│	Personal
:30	│	Eat	│	│
5:00	End work	Shower	End work	│
:30	Workout 2	Nap	Personal	│
6:00	│	Stretch	│	│
:30	Eat	Personal	Eat	Eat
7:00	Shower	│	Personal	Personal
:30	Personal	Eat	│	│
8:00	│	Personal	│	│
:30	Eat	│	│	│
9:00	To bed	To bed	To bed	To bed

This level of commitment may not be for you. In fact, there comes a point at which each of us has to check our "want to" against our "have to." You can't forsake your job, family, and other responsibilities for multisport. Even the pros must consider other aspects of life. Realistically, there are limits to passion; otherwise we'd soon alienate everyone who wasn't equally zealous and become one-dimensional bores.

What can you do to improve fitness and race performances, given the obvious constraints placed on training? Small changes in lifestyle are certainly possible and go a long way toward improving fitness. Balancing training and other responsibilities is hard to achieve, but shifting your daily activities by 10 percent in the direction of better fitness doesn't take much and brings noticeable improvement. How about committing to hitting the sack 30 minutes earlier each night so that you are more rested? Another small, daily change that can bring better results is healthier eating. Can you cut out 10 percent of the junk food you eat by replacing it with wholesome foods? What you put in your mouth is the stuff the body uses to completely rebuild and replace each muscle cell every six months. Do you want muscles made from potato chips, Twinkies, and pop? Or from fruits, vegetables, and lean meat? What can you change?

MENTAL TOUGHNESS

Why are Lance Armstrong, Tiger Woods, and Michael Jordan often referred to as being the greatest of all time in their respective sports? Is it due to genetics or opportunity? To nature or nurture? Are they "naturals" who were destined to succeed once they had the chance to appear on the playing field?

These are hard questions to answer because it's difficult to separate innate ability from hard work. But one thing we can certainly see in these three exemplary athletes is their dedication to improvement. Armstrong was well known for daily six-hour rides, repeated practice on key routes of the Tour de France, and weighing every bite of food that went into his mouth.

After Woods won the 1997 Masters Tournament by a record 12 strokes over second place, he set about improving his swing so he could be even better. After winning the four major tournaments on the PGA Tour in succession, the only man to ever do so, he again went back to work on improving his swing. And he has single-handedly changed the work ethic among pro golfers.

Michael Jordon was cut from his junior high school basketball team, which made him determined to prove himself. Never one to rest on his laurels, Jordan developed a reputation even at the pro level for his dedication to improvement, often staying after practice to work on his "weaknesses."

It would appear that hard work was a major component in the success of each of these athletes. But was it the main reason for their success? Recent research seems to indicate that it was. This research goes even farther by suggesting that it takes ten years of focused work on one's sport to reach the threshold of greatness. That was certainly true with Armstrong, Woods, and Jordan.

As a coach for three decades, I've seen essentially the same thing—athletes improve physiologically for about seven years. They continue to improve their race performances for at least another three years because they apply their experience, knowing what it takes in training, racing, and lifestyle to succeed. This timeline holds true regardless of the age at which an athlete starts training and competing.

I believe that the key to all of this hard work is more mental than physical. Being mentally tough, like triathletes in the early days of the sport, is what eventually produces high-level performance in athletes once they have achieved their physiological peak. What does it take to be mentally tough? There are four qualities I look for in athletes who say they want to perform at the highest levels: a desire to succeed, self-discipline, an attitude of believing in themselves, and patience (or perseverance). To evaluate whether you possess these qualities, ask yourself the questions that I ask athletes, which are included below.

DESIRE TO SUCCEED

- Can you train alone, or do you need to be with others to motivate you to complete hard sessions?
- Do you find a way to work out regardless of environmental conditions such as rain, snow, wind, heat, darkness, or other potential training interruptions?

I find that athletes who regularly train alone tend to have higher levels of mental toughness and a great desire to succeed. The same holds for those who train in the rain and cold, or who find a way to regularly train despite busy work schedules and family commitments.

DISCIPLINE

- Do you shape your training and lifestyle to fit your goals?
- How important to you are nutrition, sleep, periodization, goal setting, physical skills, attitude, health, and strength?
- Do your family and friends support you and your goals?

There are athletes who fit training into their lives as much as possible, and those for whom the daily workout is paramount and nearly everything else is secondary. I look for athletes who make workouts, diet, and rest a regular and reliable part of daily life. When those athletes are surrounded by a good support network, they're most likely to stick with a training program.

BELIEF IN SELF

- Do you go into a race with a success plan?
- Do you really believe you can succeed even when the conditions are not favorable?
- When it comes to racing, which do you think more about—the controllable variables or the uncontrollable variables?
- Do you accept occasional setbacks as necessary steps on the way to success, or as signs you simply can't do it?
- Do you believe you can, or question whether you can?

I have seen gifted athletes who didn't believe in their own potential, and I've seen those athletes defeated by physically weaker but mentally tougher competitors. If you don't truly believe that you can improve and win, it will be difficult for a coach to convince you otherwise.

PATIENCE AND PERSEVERANCE

- Are you in this for the long term?
- Do you need immediate success, or can you postpone it until the time is right, even if that is years in the future?
- Do you ever skip training for days or even weeks at a time and then try to get into shape quickly?

As discussed earlier, athletes continue to improve for about ten years, no matter what age they start training. Training to win is a long-term commitment that may have periods of seemingly no progress. Athletes need the patience to work steadily through those periods, knowing that improvement will come later.

My experience has been that if any one of these mental toughness qualities is lacking, the athlete will not achieve his or her lofty career goals. Few athletes have high levels of all these qualities. I've only coached one athlete who I felt had exceptional overall mental toughness. He became a Team USA Olympian.

Mental toughness is perhaps where the nurturing part of the success equation is most evident. Some athletes seem to have internalized these qualities at an early age. Others have not. What makes the difference? It is probably hundreds of seemingly insignificant interactions that take place on a daily basis from birth through the formative years, experiences that we don't exactly know how to identify or instill.

Perhaps the best thing you could do to improve your mental toughness is to work with a sports psychologist much the same as you would work with a coach. Sports psychology is a rapidly growing field, and it is becoming increasingly common for athletes at all competitive levels to seek the services of such professionals.

FROM LAB TO REAL WORLD

The availability of training information is greater now than at any other time in the history of sport. Scientific journals, scholarly periodicals, popular magazines, newspaper reports, training books, clinics by professional athletes and coaches, Web sites, Internet newsgroups and discussions, and television programs widely disseminate a cornucopia of physiological information. There is so much data that one of the greatest challenges facing the self-coached multisport athlete is sifting through all of it and then deciding how to blend the various bits of information worth keeping into a comprehensive training program.

The purpose of Part II is to simplify and "demystify" the scientific aspects of training by describing how and why a training program is organized, and especially the role of intensity in training. Intensity is probably the least understood component of preparation for multisport racing.

For the reader who has little interest in science or theory, this part of *The Triathlete's Training Bible* may present a challenge. But a base of understanding about how to organize training—and why to organize it in that way—will help you to develop an effective personal training program and greater race fitness.

THE SCIENCE OF TRAINING

3

It is not a matter of how much you train, but of how you train.

—RICK NILES, TRIATHLON COACH

THE MULTISPORT ATHLETE'S body is made up of structures and systems that may be measured and quantified. Scientists now know quite a bit about the workings of the muscles, bones, and internal organs, for example. They have discovered much about the chemistry and mechanics of the cardiovascular and respiratory systems, and they know much more about the immune system than they did even two or three decades ago. The rate at which this type of knowledge continues to grow is staggering. In the 1980s, science learned more about the human athlete than in the previous eight decades combined.

Few of us question the notion that science provides tremendous insight into how to physically and psychologically improve multisport performance. So it appears that science holds all of the answers for better racing, right? Well, actually it doesn't. The best scientists in the world can take a group of the most fit athletes into a state-of-the-art lab, test, poke, prod, measure, analyze, and predict how they will do in a race—and fail miserably. Labs are just not the real world of racing, where many individual variables beyond the ken of the scientist escape quantification.

For all of our technology, exactly how the athlete's body performs under race conditions remains largely a mystery. Unfortunately, when it comes to contributing anything extraordinary to the training and techniques of athletes, science has a poor track record. It works best when scientists step out of the lab to observe the performances of elite athletes who have made a breakthrough, and then explain why they were successful. Take the high jump, for example. For decades, most high jumpers used a rolling technique in which the arm and leg on one side of the body went over the bar first, followed by the other arm and leg with the belly facing down. Then in the late 1960s, a college jumper named Dick Fosbury revolutionized the event by clearing the bar head first with his belly pointing up. Soon other jumpers were adopting this technique and quickly pushing the world record up. Later, the "Fosbury Flop," as it was called, was painstakingly analyzed by scientists, who explained that the flop worked better than the older technique because the athlete's center of gravity remained under the bar instead of over it, thus requiring less vertical lift.

The world of sport is replete with such stories of science later explaining what athletes previously discovered, such as Bjorn Borg's two-handed backhand in tennis; Jan Boklov's "V" style in ski jumping; the "skate" technique of cross-country skiing popularized by Jim Koch; Frank Shorter's altitude training; and the bicycle aero bars developed by Boone Lennon.

Science is seldom on the leading edge, and it is far from perfect. Research studies all too often have design flaws, and even the biases of those doing the investigation may shade the conclusions. That's just the way life is: Nothing is 100 percent guaranteed. Science is not perfect, but until something better comes along—and unless you are one of those rare athletes who discovers a groundbreaking technique by accident—it's the best thing we have going for us.

If you have been a multisport athlete for a while, think back to the first year you did triathlons or duathlons. All you had to do was train more and you could chop several minutes off your time. The second year, the same strategy worked, but the gains weren't as great. By the third year, you were probably scratching your head and looking for answers. The more you learned, the more you discovered you didn't know. One answer led to half a dozen new questions. So you turned to the experts—the scientists, coaches, and elite athletes. On big-picture issues, you probably found there was some general agreement, although there were dissenters as well. The more complex your questions became, the more confusing the answers were. Scientist X says this, while coach Y says that, and athlete Z says something altogether different. What do you do?

Unfortunately, there is no sure-fire solution to this quandary. That's why training is both a science and an art. Every athlete is an experiment, in a sense, because every athlete brings a different set of strengths and weaknesses, both mental and physical, to the sport. You have to find what works best for you. A variety of sources of training information can help with this quest, but don't expect easy answers. Science is one source, and it is probably the one most likely to present solutions that fit a broad range of athletes. Nevertheless, you would be missing out on a lot of helpful information if you only looked to science for guidance. Always keep the limitations of science in mind. It cannot provide you with answers to big questions such as how to train. Science is best at finding solutions to small questions, such as those having to do with recovery, hydration, overtraining, and illness. The problem often has to do with how research experiments are designed. A six- to twelve-week research project must, of necessity, allow little time for adaptation. What would have happened had a given study continued for a year, or a decade? Research also stifles individual uniqueness in order to find out what works for most people most of the time. Perhaps you don't fit the mold. Science can help you improve as an athlete, but be skeptical. Remember the bumblebee (Chapter 2).

Coaches and elite athletes are also helpful sources. A little skepticism is healthy here, also. Observe them, listen to what they have to say, compare them with each other and with science, ask questions, experiment, and then decide for yourself. As Yogi Berra said, "You can observe a lot by watching."

TRAINING STRESS

In order to bring positive changes, physical stress to the body is necessary. That is why we train. Stress can be changed by manipulating three elements of training: workout frequency, workout duration, and workout intensity. Volume and workload provide a method for quantifying that stress.

FREQUENCY

How often you work out is the most basic element of training. Novice multisport athletes typically work out five or six times each week. Such a frequency is appropriate for their level, and improvement will occur rapidly, probably in the range of 10 to 15 percent after a few weeks. An Olympic hopeful might work out twelve to eighteen times in a week. That's also appropriate, but it may only result in a 1 or 2 percent gain.

Studies for single-sport athletes have found that training three to five times a week brings the greatest benefit for the time invested and that additional workouts have diminishing returns. In other words, a few weekly workouts will produce the bulk of your fitness, and anything beyond about five weekly sessions is "icing on the cake." This is an example of the "80-20 rule" at work: Eighty percent of the desired results come from 20 percent of the work required to realize a 100 percent gain. If you are an elite triathlete or duathlete trying to realize your racing potential, that last 20 percent of potential gain is worth the extra work, since competition is quite close at the top and rewards are few.

Frequency varies throughout the season. Early in the training year, you should gradually increase the frequency of your workouts in order to add stress. Just prior to and during the race season, you will want to decrease the frequency to allow more time for recovery.

DURATION

Swimming, cycling, and running workouts are often referred to in terms of the distance covered in miles, kilometers, yards, or meters. Another method of referring to duration, and the one generally used in this book, is the elapsed time of the workout, including warm-up, cool-down, and the recovery periods within an interval workout.

Workout length varies considerably from day to day. Some workouts are long to build greater endurance, while others are short to allow for more emphasis on higher intensities, or to promote recovery. A general rule of thumb is that the longest workouts should be about the same duration as, or slightly longer than, that discipline's leg of the longest race you will compete in. There are obvious exceptions at both ends of the race-duration spectrum. For example, it's not wise when training for an Ironman to go the full race distance in all three disciplines in a single workout, but training at twice sprint-distance duration can be beneficial.

Early in the season, the higher-intensity workouts are done on low-duration days, but as the most important races approach, long duration and high intensity are occasionally combined. This gradually prepares the body for the specific stresses of racing.

INTENSITY

Since frequency and duration are easy to measure, we often refer to them in describing a training regimen. Workout intensity is somewhat more difficult to quantify but in many ways better defines a training session or race, especially for sprint- and Olympic-distance events.

High-intensity training is powerful medicine. Too much, too frequently, and you wind up sick, injured, burned out, or overtrained, and on the sidelines watching. Too little intensity in training, and you are off the back in races and unlikely to achieve high goals. Chapter 4 explains how to measure intensity, determine your individual intensity zones, and use them wisely in training. Pay close attention to the intensity of training. If you get this part wrong, it doesn't matter what else you may be doing right.

VOLUME

The terms "volume" and "duration" are often confused; they aren't interchangeable. Duration is the time or distance of a given workout, whereas volume is the combination of duration and frequency. In other words, volume is the total of all durations for a given period, such as a week. So if an athlete runs three times in a week (frequency) for an hour each time (duration), the running volume for that week is three hours.

WORKLOAD

The combination of all three stress elements—frequency, duration, and intensity—is referred to as "workload." An athlete who trains frequently with long durations and high intensity is training at a high workload. Infrequent, short-duration workouts done at a low intensity produce a low workload. By manipulating the three elements, workloads may be designed to fit every athlete's needs. It's important to understand that what may be an appropriate workload for one athlete may not be appropriate for another. Generally, several years of experience, a high level of fitness, and youth favor high workloads, but there are exceptions. Determining the appropriate workload for your own regimen is part of the art of training, although science can help you make an informed decision. Experience and cautious trial and error can also be the basis for workload decisions.

PRINCIPLES OF TRAINING

Although science has not produced any detailed, guaranteed training plans for multisport, or any other sport, it has developed a set of guidelines from which we can take direction in the quest for peak performance. The following training principles are generally accepted throughout the world of athletics, but exceptions have also been noted. Understanding and applying these concepts will help you design a solid training program based in proven techniques.

PROGRESSIVE OVERLOAD

Milon of Croton became the strongest man in ancient Greece, winning the Olympic wrestling contest five times, according to Greek mythology. The stories of this great athlete told how he achieved his strength: Every day, Milon would hoist a calf above his head and carry it around the stable. As the calf grew, so did Milon's strength, until he could eventually carry the full-grown cow. The training principle Milon was using—progressive overload—is still the basis of athletic training today.

Overloading the body with progressively increasing stress appears straightforward: Lift more, run farther, swim faster, ride harder, and your fitness will improve. Unfortunately, it's not quite that simple. The confounding element is that the body's cells are sensitive. They do indeed respond and grow stronger, but only when the proper amount of stress is applied followed by rest. Theoretically, there is a threshold, or level, of stress that is appropriate for the improvement of every cell. Too much stress applied too soon and the cell is considerably weakened and struggles for days, perhaps weeks, merely to recover.

Training builds up fitness by first tearing it down. Following a stressful workout, one in which the workload was high, you are in worse shape than before you started, as evidenced by reduced performance if you try to repeat the workout immediately. If the workload was appropriate and rest follows, the body will respond in a few hours or a couple of days, and you'll be slightly more fit. This principle is called "overcompensation" and is illustrated in Figure 3.1.

Repeated overcompensation leading to increased fitness results from applying the correct overloads at the right times. It's doubtful that Milon's calf grew at just the right rate to allow for recovery and the perfect progressive overloads. But the novice triathlete or duathlete doesn't need a calf-level load; almost any low-level stress provides an overload. The more fit an athlete becomes, the more difficult it is to apply just the right load of stress, since the highly fit athlete has a narrowed overload threshold. Being close to one's fitness potential means there is little room for error.

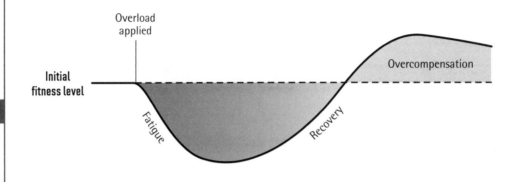

FIGURE 3.1

Effect of Training
Overload

Each physiological system of the body responds to an overload at a unique rate. For example, muscle strength improves quickly compared to aerobic endurance. Even within a given system there are varying speeds of adaptation, since the cells don't all respond at the same rate. In the cardiovascular system, for example, blood plasma increases significantly with a week of high workload, but the capillaries that carry the blood to the muscles take years of training to fully develop.

Knowing what the optimal workload is, and when to apply it, is one more aspect of the art of training discussed earlier. Science can point the way, but you must determine through trial and error what is appropriate for you. Erring on the side of too little rather than too much is the key to consistency.

SPECIFICITY

Fitness is specific to training. In other words, you won't reach peak triathlon or duathlon fitness by jumping rope, doing aerobics, or rock climbing. High levels of triathlon fitness require swimming, cycling, and running. Some improvement may result from crossover into other endurance activities, primarily benefits to the heart and lungs and their related structures, but this is minimal considering all that is necessary for multisport fitness.

For the best results, the training stress must follow two maxims. First, it should have a pattern of joint and muscle coordination that is specific to the sport. Second, the exercise must place specific duration and intensity stresses on specific muscles. For example, running and cross-country skiing appear quite similar, since many of the same muscles are used in almost the same manner. Yet scientific studies have shown that there is no relationship between the aerobic capacities of running and cross-country skiing. Aerobic capacity is one measure of endurance fitness. Someone trained for skiing, but who never runs, is likely to have a high aerobic capacity when skiing, but not when running. To achieve peak fitness for running, you must run.

Does this mean you should never do anything except swim, bike, and run? No. There are good reasons to include other activities, especially during a period of preparation many weeks or months before racing begins. These reasons may include mental breaks from the exercise routine, bad weather, injury avoidance, recovery, and the development of the most basic fitness elements. But consider all such exercise a supplement to, and not a substitute for, multisport training.

REVERSIBILITY

Fitness is always changing and is never stagnant. Right now your race-specific physiology is either improving or deteriorating, depending on what you have done recently in your training. Don't take this to mean that you must train hard every day, since it's during rest that fitness improves. Even during periods of extended rest, as when building to a peak, physical conditioning improves if the right amount of stress is applied at the right times.

The problem comes when a pattern of consistent, fitness-producing training is interrupted, preventing stresses of adequate magnitude to produce an overload. Training interruptions can result not only from illness, injury, burnout, and overtraining, but also from job, family, and other obligations. When consistency is broken by one of these, the body's systems begin to slip back to previous conditioning levels. For the endurance athlete, noticeable losses of fitness are evident within two weeks of the cessation of workouts. By three weeks, many of the elements crucial to race performance significantly erode. Each system has its own rate of decline. For example, aerobic fitness declines faster than anaerobic conditioning. Strength, however, remains relatively constant for about four weeks, although power declines by up to 14 percent in the same amount of time, according to one study. Interestingly, highly conditioned athletes lose their fitness at a faster rate than the less-conditioned, probably because they have more to lose. Table 3.1 lists changes that commonly occur during a period without training.

So it appears that two to three weeks of inactivity result in significant losses of fitness, especially of the critical endurance components necessary for success in multisport. The time required to regain previous levels depends on how intensive and extensive the downtime was. It has been my experience that a very fit athlete can count on the return to competitive form taking about twice as long as the duration of the break.

INDIVIDUALITY

From the training principles discussed so far, it may appear that science has everything neatly measured and packaged. It isn't so. The problem is that research results are based on averages within given groups of subjects. What the reported conclusions don't usually tell us is that some subjects responded quite well, but others failed to improve much at all. One study, for example, looked at the response of aerobic

TABLE 3.1

Changes
Resulting from
3 Weeks of Not
Training

MEASURE OF FITNESS	CHANGE
Aerobic capacity (VO$_2$max)	–8%
Heart stroke volume (blood pumped per beat)	–10%
Submaximum heart rate (beats per minute)	+4%
Blood plasma volume	–12%
Muscle capillary density	–7%
Oxidative enzymes	–29%
Blood insulin at rest	+17–120%
Blood lactate during exercise	+88%
Lactate threshold	–7%
Use of fat for fuel during exercise	–52%
Time to fatigue (minutes)	–10%

Note: Adapted from R. L. Wilber and R. J. Moffatt "Physiological and Biochemical Consequences of Detraining in Aerobically Trained Individuals," *Journal of Strength Conditioning Research* 8(1994): 110.

capacity to a standard exercise protocol. The average improvement was 14 percent, but one subject boosted his aerobic capacity by only 4 percent while another saw a whopping 40 percent increase.

The most important principle to remember is that we're all individuals when it comes to training. Some of us are slow responders, what bodybuilders call "hard gainers," and others are fast responders. Given the same workouts, the same number of weeks of training, and the exact same starting fitness levels, it's unlikely that two athletes will achieve the same degree of performance. This difference is most likely a result of genetics.

This is why triathletes and duathletes cannot simply duplicate the training programs of others. No matter how good the program is, it can't meet everyone's needs to the same extent. Not only will the physiological responses to a shared program vary, but since each athlete has unique strengths and weaknesses, what one person really needs to work on the most, the other may already have in abundance.

Keep in mind, however, that the various fitness parameters of all multisport athletes theoretically may be represented by a bell-shaped curve as illustrated in Figure 3.2. In the middle of the curve are those who are "average" for any specific performance measure. To the left of center are those who are low in the quality; those to the right end are high in it. Chances are good that you fall into the average group in any particular area of physiology. But don't count on it. Knowing yourself is an important tenet of training.

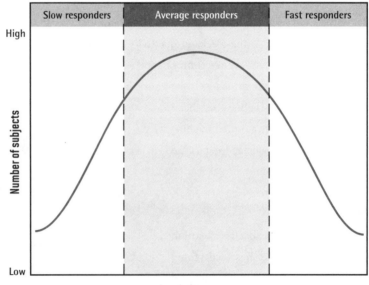

FIGURE 3.2

Theoretical
Response Curve

PEAKING

Coming to a fitness peak at just the right times in the season is the ultimate reason for training. Creating that moment when racing seems effortless makes months of hard work and sweat worthwhile. Yet few athletes ever experience such a fitness high. Even fewer know how to create it.

Most multisport athletes believe that peaking is as simple as reducing the workload for a few days before a big race. There's more to it than that. In fact, such a "taper" will not produce a true fitness peak: The athlete is unlikely to be rested, let alone near the apex of his or her potential.

When a true peak comes about, you will experience several physical changes that combine to create a performance that borders on astonishing. These changes include increased leg power, reduced lactic acid production, increased blood volume, a greater red blood cell concentration, and increased fuel storage. Top these physical transformations with sharper mental skills such as concentration, confidence, and motivation, and you are truly in top race form. All of this, and no illegal drugs are needed.

There are three elements of physical preparation to balance in the last two to three weeks before your highest priority races—fatigue, fitness, and form. Fatigue is a measure of workload. If intensity or volume has recently been high, then fatigue will be elevated.

But when fatigue is high, fitness will also be high. High-intensity and long-duration training produce fatigue and fitness simultaneously—hard workouts make you tired but also make you more fit. Sadly, fatigue increases more rapidly than fitness, so three hard workouts in three days will produce a lot of fatigue but only a tiny increase in fitness. Fitness is best measured in weeks, whereas fatigue is usually measured in days.

Form, which measures how rested you are, is also one of the key elements during the peaking process. You can have high form—that is, be well rested (have low fatigue)—without high fitness. In other words, fitness can be low from too much rest. That's not a good thing when you are trying to peak for a race. It is a bit of a balancing act to reduce fatigue, maintain fitness (or allow only a slight decrease), and increase form so that you are peaked and ready to race.

In triathlon, the peaking process is complicated further by the variety of sports. For example, running requires a longer taper than cycling does, but the cycling taper should be longer than the swimming taper. There are other elements to consider, such as the length of the race (long races require long tapers), how fit you are (high fitness requires long tapers), how easily injured you are (injury-prone athletes need longer tapers), and how old you are (older athletes need longer tapers).

Brief interludes of peak performance can be mapped out weeks in advance if an athlete is willing to train in a highly structured manner and then cut back on training for several days. The problem is that few serious multisport triathletes are willing to reduce

Anatomy of a Peak

For perfect race readiness at the right time, you need to mix two key elements—intensity and rest. Here's how: Starting two to three weeks before your most important race, do a short, race-intensity workout that simulates the conditions of the race every third or fourth day. Gradually make these workouts shorter as you progress through the peaking period, so that your weekly volume is dropping and you get more rest.

Volume should drop rather rapidly. To maintain fitness, your intensity must be at least heart rate zone 3 (see Chapter 4) or moderately hard. The two or three days of low-intensity, low-duration workouts between these race simulations are the key to erasing fatigue and elevating form. They should also get shorter as peaking progresses.

The week of the race is the time to emphasize rest but still maintain a degree of intensity. Put the long workouts on hold and instead do three or four workouts in which you complete several 90-second intervals at race intensity or at least heart rate zone 3, with 3-minute recoveries. Five days before the race, do five of these 90-second efforts. Four days before, do four times 90 seconds. This pattern continues throughout the week.

The easiest day of race week should be two days before the race. This is usually best as a day off, but for the high-volume athlete it may be a short and easy ride or swim. The day before should also include some race-like intensity within a very brief session—for example, a 15-minute swim followed later in the morning by a combination workout including a 30-minute bike ride and a 15-minute run. Include a few short efforts at race intensity or higher. You should feel rested, strong, and ready to race!

their training for that long for fear of losing fitness. Many have become so familiar with the feeling of chronic fatigue that even a small reduction in training feels like a lot.

In the past fifteen years there have been numerous scientific studies of the peaking process. The following concepts have emerged from this research and are applicable to peaking for a triathlon or duathlon.

Taper 10–21 Days. The exact length of the taper depends on two elements: how fit you are coming into it, and the nature of the race for which you're peaking. If you have a great base of fitness—meaning endurance, strength, and speed skills are at high levels—taper longer than if your fitness level in these abilities is low. The more unfit you are, the more important it is to continue training and creating higher levels of fitness until perhaps as little as ten days before the big race. Since it takes about ten days to realize the full benefits of a given workout, training with a high workload beyond the tenth day prior to the event is unlikely to produce additional fitness.

Deciding how fit you are is a subjective call. If you err, make it on the side of allowing too much taper time.

Again, the longer the race is for which you are tapering, the longer the taper should be. An Ironman-distance race needs a longer taper than a sprint-distance event. This, in part, is to allow adequate time for accumulated fatigue and possible muscle damage to completely improve.

Reduce Volume. If you're tapering for 21 days, reduce each week's volume by about 20 percent of the previous week. A two-week taper involves cutting back on volume by about 30 percent each week. For a ten-day taper, cut volume by 50 percent for the entire period.

Maintain Frequency. In reducing volume, you are better off cutting back on the number of hours you train each day than decreasing the number of weekly workouts. Greatly reducing how often you swim, ride, or run can cause a loss of "feel." You may not seem as smooth and comfortable in the movements of the sport as you normally do. It's probably best to keep a minimum of two or three workouts in each sport weekly during the taper period.

Maintain Intensity. High-intensity training is the most potent stimulus for both improving and maintaining fitness. A race-intensity workout every 72 to 96 hours is all the stimulus needed at this point in the season to peak your fitness. These workouts could be a tune-up race on the weekend or combined swim-bike-run workouts that simulate a portion of the race. It's also a good idea to focus on your greatest weakness for the target race. For example, if climbing is what you are most worried about, do a hill workout. The intensity of these key workouts should closely simulate the effort you expect in the race.

Otherwise, Train Easily. All other workouts should be easy enough to allow for recovery. Work on swim skills, ride in the small chainring, and run slowly. Keep these workouts on the short side. By taking it easy you will come into the peaking, race-effort workouts fully rested. Rest is the key to greater fitness at this time, both because it allows the body to absorb the stress you have been placing on it, and because it prepares you for more intense workouts when the time is right.

Such a peaking process should be done only two or three times in a season. Each of these peaks could last a few weeks, perhaps two or three at most, if you are doing a race or simulation each week and an intense workout between races. Eventually there will be an erosion of aerobic fitness necessitating a return to more endurance training. At that point the buildup to the next peak begins.

PERIODIZATION

Scientific conclusions and concepts are the easy part; putting it all together into an effective training plan that brings you into peak form for the most important races is where the rubber meets the road. Multisport success, or lack of it, is determined by how you blend the stresses of frequency, duration, and intensity into a comprehensive plan while also taking into consideration the training principles of progressive overload, specificity, reversibility, and individuality. Science alone cannot determine this for you presently because there are just too many variables. Consequently, at this point we begin to move away from hard-core science and into the realm of opinion.

TRAINING SYSTEMS

Whether they realize it or not, all athletes follow a training system of some type just by the mere fact that their workouts progress from day to day. The three most common training programs used by athletes are random, mixed, and periodization.

In random training the athlete does whatever he or she feels like doing every day. Little or no forethought goes into the decision, and the weather and training partners frequently dictate the workout. This method is common for the strictly recreational athlete who has no concern with performance beyond simply participating and finishing. Beyond resting for a couple of days beforehand, peaking for races is nonexistent, workouts are frequently too hard, and high levels of fitness are seldom achieved. Random training is common among novices and is appropriate at this level as the new multisport athlete explores the world of training. But if growth is to occur, this method must be abandoned after the first year.

Mixed training represents an improvement over random training as the athlete generally puts more thought into what to do on a daily basis. Training this way means doing all types of workouts, such as endurance, intervals, hills, and steady state, every week throughout the year. Rest breaks may or may not be planned. If they aren't routinely included, the mixed trainer is a candidate for overtraining. Even if rest is inserted, following such a program often leads to a belief that fitness must progress linearly throughout the season with the workouts becoming progressively harder every week, often resulting in a severe case of overtraining. Boredom, low motivation, and burnout are also common with this type of training, as each week can become pretty similar to the previous one. Although peaking is difficult with mixed training, many athletes perform well when training this way.

Periodization is a training concept in which the year is divided into periods; in each period the athlete focuses on improving a specific aspect of fitness while maintaining the gains made in previous periods. Periodization has become such a standard among serious athletes in all sports that it is often mistakenly referred to as a necessary principle of training. Even though it is quite effective in producing fitness peaks at the right times while preventing overtraining and burnout, it is not the only path to excellence. Training by following the concepts of periodization is, however, the most likely way known today to achieve athletic success.

PERIODIZATION THEORY

In the late 1940s, Soviet sports scientists discovered that they could improve athletic performance in their athletes by varying the training stresses throughout the year rather than maintaining a constant training focus as in mixed training. This finding led to dividing the year into multiweek periods with the stresses changing in some way with each new period. The East Germans and Romanians further developed this concept by establishing goals for the different periods, and the system of "periodization" was born.

In the 1960s, Tudor Bompa, Ph.D., on the faculty of the Romanian Institute of Sport, so refined the concept that he became known as the "father of periodization." This system was so effective that Eastern bloc countries dominated world competition for three decades by using it. Bompa's seminal work, *Theory and Methodology of Training*, introduced Western athletes to this training system in the early 1980s. A decade earlier, however, a handful of European and American athletes studied the training methods of their Eastern bloc competitors, adopted periodization, and challenged the superiority of Soviet, East German, and Romanian athletes.

Periodization means more than simply dividing the year into periods. It carefully employs the training principles discussed earlier. The basic premise of all periodization programs is that training should progress from the general to the specific (principle of specificity), and it should emphasize the unique needs of the athlete (principle of individuality). For example, early in the season an athlete needing greater cycling strength may work with weights to develop general fitness. Later in the season, as the first important races approach, this athlete should spend more time riding in the hills while simulating race intensities, and less time working with weights. Figure 3.3 illustrates this concept.

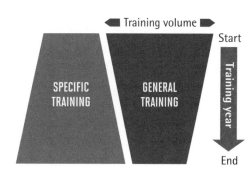

FIGURE 3.3

Training Progression

Of course, periodization also goes well beyond simply training more specifically throughout the year. It also involves arranging the workouts in such a way that elements of fitness achieved in an earlier phase of training are maintained (principle of reversibility) while new ones are addressed and gradually improved (principle of progressive overload). Small changes are introduced into workouts, typically during three- to eight-week periods. The targeted physiological system gradually becomes more fit with such a pattern of change and is then maintained as a new system is targeted.

Figure 3.4 shows how the training year is divided into periods, and Figure 3.5 represents a theoretical development of fitness as a result.

While following a periodization plan as outlined in this book may help you to achieve your racing goals, it is not perfect. Regardless of the system used, the training plan you develop is only a guide. It is more like a road map than a scientific formula. There is not just one way to reach your destination; many routes are possible. Flexibility and a willingness to change are paramount for success.

FIGURE 3.4

Periods of Yearly
Training

Macrocycle	TRAINING YEAR								
Mesocycle	Preparation					Competition		Transition	
	General preparation			Specific preparation		Pre-comp	Competition	Transition	
	Prep	Base 1	Base 2	Build 1	Build 2	Peak	Race	Transition	
Microcycle	1	2	3	4	5	6	7	8	Weeks 9–42	43 44 45 46	47 48 49 50 51 52

PERIODIZATION ALTERNATIVES

Figure 3.5 illustrates what is known as "linear" or "classic" periodization. With this model you start the season in the Base period, focusing primarily on the volume of training by doing long and frequent workouts at a low intensity. This creates a high level of aerobic endurance fitness. Then in the Build period you decrease volume by doing long sessions less frequently while increasing the intensity of your training. This improves muscular endurance and anaerobic endurance (described in detail in Chapter 6). All of the training suggestions in this book are based on this linear periodization model. While it is the easiest to understand and the most common way of organizing the training season for endurance athletes, it is not the only model. Two others that are common in triathlon are "undulating" periodization and "reverse linear" periodization.

UNDULATING PERIODIZATION

Figure 3.6 shows how this model works. Essentially, volume and intensity rise and fall alternately as the season progresses. For example, an athlete could pair high-volume biking with high-intensity running one week, and then do high-volume running and high-intensity biking the next. The variety can help to maintain motivation. Research has

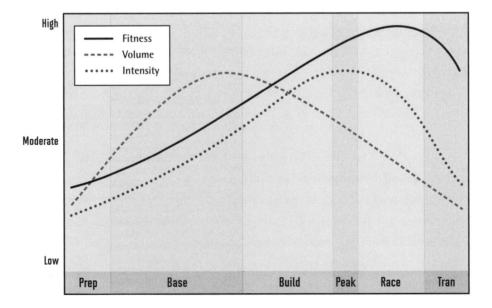

FIGURE 3.5

Effect of
Periodization
on Fitness

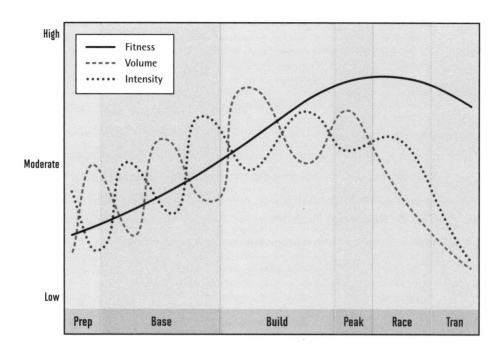

FIGURE 3.6

Undulating
Periodization

shown that weightlifters using this model make significant improvements in strength performance. Research is lacking for endurance sports, however.

REVERSE LINEAR PERIODIZATION

Figure 3.7 shows just the reverse of the model shown in Figure 3.5—intensity is high in the Base period, and volume reaches a high point in the Build period. This model works best with long-course triathletes. High intensity and low volume early in the season boost

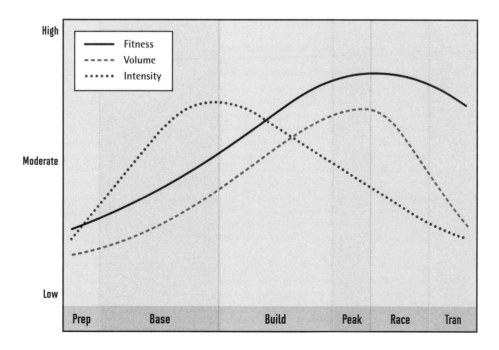

FIGURE 3.7

Reverse Linear
Periodization

aerobic capacity (VO$_2$max), and lower-intensity, longer workouts later on develop aerobic endurance. This combination has the potential to bring you into excellent fitness for long events such as Ironman- and half-Ironman-distance races. It may not be as effective for shorter races.

The periodization platform you choose should be one that you understand and are committed to. Linear periodization is generally the easiest model to understand and put into place, and it is still the model used by most athletes around the world, regardless of their levels of performance. The other models have very little established research behind them, and training guidelines are therefore lacking. Trying to create and follow such a plan would involve a lot of trial and error and would likely result in uneven performances. With linear periodization, you will know you are following a well-researched, proven plan for success.

INTENSITY

*Simply put, the most profound training
responses will occur when you train faster.*
—RICK NILES

MULTISPORT ATHLETES often place great em-
phasis on volume and pay scant attention to intensity. That's too bad, since it is intensity,
rather than volume, that has the potential to lift fitness to the highest levels. For example,
in a 1995 study of runners in Germany, four weeks of increased intensity—while volume
held constant—produced significant performance gains, but four weeks of increasing volume as intensity remained unchanged led to performance stagnation. In this study, fitness
was measured as time to exhaustion in a steady treadmill run, and speed at approximate
15-kilometer and marathon paces. All three measures significantly improved after four
weeks of high intensity, but high volume improved only the marathon pace—and by a
slight margin at that.

This is not to say that training volume is unimportant or that low mileage is the way
to achieve peak performance. For every athlete there is a correct blend of volume and
intensity that must be discovered, largely through trial and error. This is the principle of
individualization described in the previous chapter. Later chapters will help you to determine an appropriate volume and intensity to include in training. For now, however, our
purpose is to better understand intensity in training.

FIGHTING THE CAUSES OF FATIGUE

"Fitness" is a somewhat elusive term. What does it mean to be "fit"? The truth is, fitness
means different things to different people, and it is best defined in terms of the activity
for which one is preparing. For example, a bodybuilder may be just as fit as a marathon

runner, only in a different way. When it comes to endurance events such as triathlons and duathlons, fitness is the ability to resist or delay fatigue at a desired speed. Reduced fatigue means faster race times at the same effort. So for the purposes of this book, we'll define fitness in terms of limiting fatigue.

The reason we train, then, is to reduce the effects of fatigue that accompany race-like effort. That sounds simple enough, but to complicate things, there are at least three physiological causes of fatigue that slow the endurance athlete:

- Accumulation of hydrogen ions in the muscles and blood
- Depletion of carbohydrate-based fuel stored in the muscles (glycogen) and blood (glucose)
- Failure of the muscles' contractile mechanisms

A scientifically based training program improves fitness by stressing the systems associated with these causes of fatigue. The following is a brief summary of how training improves resistance to each.

BUILDUP OF HYDROGEN IONS

To produce energy for movement, the muscles primarily use fat and carbohydrate for fuel. When carbohydrate—the sugar-based fuel source—breaks down, lactic acid is produced in the muscles. As this lactic acid seeps out of the muscle cell and into the blood and surrounding body fluids, hydrogen ions are released, and the resulting salt is called lactate. The amount of hydrogen ions and lactate increases as the intensity of the exercise increases. At low levels of production, the body efficiently removes and recycles them. Even while you are reading this page, hydrogen ions and lactate are appearing in your blood and rapidly being removed.

The level of exertion at which the body shifts from aerobic (light breathing) to anaerobic (labored breathing) is marked by such rapid hydrogen and lactate production that the body can't keep up with their removal. The hydrogen ions are actually the real concern, but measuring lactate is an indirect way of knowing how much hydrogen is present. As lactate begins to accumulate in the blood, the hydrogen ions interfere with energy production and muscular contractions, thus causing fatigue. This type of fatigue occurs in very short, high-intensity races such as sprint triathlons, and then only during near-maximal efforts such as a finishing kick or a short hill climb.

This is not a major cause of fatigue in most multisport races. If, however, you compete primarily in short events, it may be a limiter for you. In longer events, if you surge powerfully or climb a hill going deeply anaerobic, you will experience short-term fatigue in the same manner. The way to improve both the body's ability to remove the hydrogen ions and your tolerance for acidity is to perform short, high-intensity efforts followed by long recoveries. The specifics of this type of training will be discussed in later chapters. The anaerobic endurance workouts in Appendices B, C, D, and E will improve your resistance to this type of fatigue.

DEPLETION OF FUEL

Fat is the primary source of fuel at low levels of effort like the type you would experience during a long, slow bike ride. As the exercise becomes more intense, the body increasingly turns to carbohydrate for fuel, and fat usage diminishes (see Figure 4.1). Carbohydrate is stored in the muscles and liver as glycogen and is available in the blood as glucose. At any given moment, a well-nourished athlete has between 1,500 and 2,000 calories of stored glycogen and glucose available for use, depending on body size and fitness level, with about 75 percent of this in the muscles. While competing in an Olympic-distance race (1,500-meter swim, 40 km bike, 10 km run), a triathlete may burn 1,000 calories per hour, with about 650 of them coming from carbohydrate. It is easy to see that at this rate, the stored glucose and glycogen may be depleted before the athlete reaches the finish line. If he or she does not replace it during the race with a sports drink, the likely result will be a "DNF" (did not finish).

Fuel depletion is a critical cause of fatigue for the multisport athlete that must be addressed in training. If you set out to do a moderately hard workout at the highest level of aerobic intensity *without going deeply anaerobic,* you will find an effective way to teach the body to conserve glycogen and glucose while becoming more proficient at using fat for fuel. In addition, by training at paces similar to what is expected in races, you will teach your muscles to work more economically, thus sparing precious carbohydrate. Your diet may also have an effect on the ratio of fat and carbohydrate used. This is discussed further in Chapter 16.

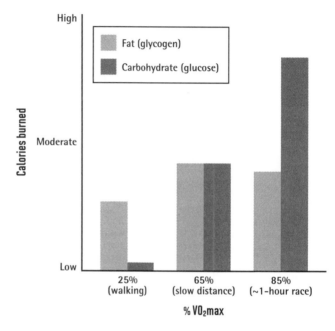

FIGURE 4.1

Relative Contribution of Fat and Carbohydrate to Exercise Fuel

FAILURE OF MUSCLES

The exact mechanism that results in the failure of muscles to continue contractions is unknown, but it is probably related either to chemical failure at the point where the nervous system connects with the muscles or to a protective mechanism in the central nervous system meant to prevent muscular damage.

Exercising at high intensities may fortify the body against muscle failure by training the nervous system to call on more of its muscles for endurance activities. More fast-twitch muscles are recruited at higher levels of intensity, such as those reached in intervals, than at lower levels of intensity, such as those maintained in long, slow workouts. Fast-twitch muscles contract quickly and need a long time to recover. They are best for sprinting, but by training at a moderately high effort, some of these muscles take on the characteristics of slow-twitch, or endurance, muscles, allowing the athlete to continue exercising longer.

UNDERSTANDING INTENSITY

Intensity is a measure of how hard your body works in training, and science has established important benchmarks that help pinpoint individual intensity levels. Even if you don't delve into the testing required to establish your physiological makeup, it helps to have a basic understanding of the measures of intensity and how they are used.

LACTATE THRESHOLD

Lactate threshold (LT) is also sometimes called anaerobic threshold. Lactic acid is produced from the breakdown of carbohydrate and becomes lactate that builds up in the blood, a chain reaction that ultimately interferes with muscle contraction. The level of intensity at which accumulation of lactate begins is called the "lactate threshold." This is a critical event. An analogy may help convey this important concept.

Imagine slowly pouring water into a paper cup that has a hole in the bottom, allowing the water to run out as fast as it goes in. This is what happens to lactate in the blood at low levels of exertion. By pouring faster, there comes a rate at which the water goes in faster than it goes out, and so the cup begins to fill. This is similar to what happens with lactate in your bloodstream during exercise of increasing intensity. The point at which the water first begins to accumulate is analogous to the LT. You may have also seen the term "anaerobic threshold" used to describe this concept.

By swimming, cycling, or running at or near the LT, muscular endurance training improves the body's ability to process lactate while also teaching the muscles to conserve precious glycogen and glucose fuel sources. In addition, the muscles' contractile mechanisms become more resistant to fatigue. The result of this type of training is an increase in your speed at and near LT. Later on you will learn the details of how to do these workouts.

Lactate threshold also serves as an intensity "landmark." Exercising below LT, or working aerobically, is relatively easy and may be continued for hours, depending on an athlete's fitness level. But the duration of the workout or race must be greatly reduced when exercising above LT, or exercising anaerobically. We can easily describe how intense the workout is in relation to LT just as we did by using the terms "aerobic" and "anaerobic." The next section offers a system for categorizing intensity into zones based on LT, and Chapter 5 describes how you can determine your lactate threshold.

While all of this may sound simple and straightforward, your LT remains, at best, an estimate, even when it's determined in a lab by scientists using state-of-the-art equipment and procedures. One reason we are unable to pinpoint LT is that it is a moving target. It drifts down during workouts as a result of weariness and increasing body temperature. It can even vary on a daily basis because of fatigue, variations in diet, and changing environmental conditions. This is yet another reason why training is as much art as science.

AEROBIC THRESHOLD

Lactate threshold is a critical intensity level for the endurance athlete, especially one who focuses on racing Olympic- and sprint-distance races. Aerobic threshold is the other critical threshold for triathletes racing at all distances, but especially at Ironman distance. It occurs at a much lower intensity than LT does.

Aerobic threshold is important for the Ironman athlete because such a long-distance event is raced at about this intensity, particularly for the athlete who finishes roughly in the range of 10 to 13 hours. Ironman triathletes finishing faster than about 10 hours will race well above aerobic threshold, and those taking more than about 13 hours will stay below the aerobic threshold throughout the event.

You will recall that the LT is marked by the accumulation of acid in the body. As we will discuss in the next section, one way to determine your LT is to measure your lactate production in a lab or clinic. Your aerobic threshold is less precisely measured but is physiologically marked by a slight increase in the depth of breathing accompanied by a sense of moderate-effort intensity.

In terms of heart rate, aerobic threshold occurs at the lower end of what I call zone 2. But your heart rate at aerobic threshold will probably vary from one sport to another according to how fit you are for each. For example, if you are a strong cyclist with years of riding behind you, your aerobic threshold may be well into the zone 2 heart rate. But if you've just started swimming seriously, that threshold may be somewhere in zone 1.

Your aerobic threshold in a given sport will also vary from day to day based on how well rested you are. When you are fresh, your aerobic threshold will be found at a higher intensity than when you are fatigued. Because aerobic threshold is something of a moving target, it can be easy to push past it by working out according to heart rate zones only, without paying attention to signs of fatigue. To truly stay below or at your aerobic threshold, paying close attention to your effort is just as important as watching your heart rate monitor (the same is true with LT, but the intensity there is so great that fatigue will usually keep you from overdoing it). The next section of this chapter discusses how to determine effort.

Training in the aerobic threshold zone is perfect for building basic aerobic endurance. This is why aerobic threshold is the dominant intensity during the Base period when developing such fitness is a primary focus. A good portion of each week's training in the Base period should be devoted to zone 2. In the Build period, short-course triathletes should include regular (but less frequent) workouts in zone 2 to maintain aerobic endurance. Long-course athletes will continue to do such workouts frequently in the Build period, since this comes close to simulating the intensity at which they will race.

INTENSITY ZONES

Energy production from fat and carbohydrate, and the efficient conservation of fuel, is at the heart of training for multisport. Each workout you do during the year contributes to, or detracts from, this purpose. When you vary the three stresses of training—frequency, duration, and, especially, intensity—certain benefits accrue. Below I describe the six workout intensity zones referred to in this book (regardless of the measuring technique), a summary of what each involves, and their benefits. All zone 5 intensities are anaerobic; zones 1 through 4 are aerobic.

Recovery (Zone 1). As the name implies, zone 1 sessions are the easiest workouts, and the ones that help fit and experienced athletes rejuvenate the body following hard workouts or periods of difficult training. Intensity is quite low, well below the LT. Inexperienced athletes, or those with low fitness levels, generally recover sooner by not training, rather than by exercising easily. This is the intensity most often used during the recovery periods in an interval workout.

Extensive Endurance (Zone 2). Long endurance workouts are common at this intensity. Aerobic endurance is built and eventually maintained by exercising at this "conversational" effort. Lactate production is low enough to allow extensive, although comfortable, training sessions to the limits of the athlete's aerobic endurance and slightly beyond. Slow-twitch endurance muscles become stronger and more capable of using oxygen to produce energy while learning to conserve glycogen and glucose. Triathletes competing in longer events spend more time in zone 2 than in any other level of intensity.

Intensive Endurance (Zone 3). At this slightly higher intensity, lactate production rises above the previous levels as more fast-twitch muscles are called upon to support the work of the slow-twitch muscles. Training in this zone is employed primarily in the early Preparation or Base period, and after that is avoided in favor of the next intensity level.

Threshold (Zones 4 and 5a). Other than extensive endurance, threshold intensity is perhaps the most important training zone for the multisport athlete. This effort brings the athlete to just below or slightly above the LT, so long durations at this intensity are measured in minutes, not hours. Since work is now maximally aerobic, the slow-twitch muscles and energy-production systems are highly stressed. A significant portion of the work is now occurring anaerobically, and improvements accrue in lactate tolerance and removal as well as in fast-twitch muscle conversion to slow-twitch characteristics. Two zone designations are used here to distinguish efforts above and below LT.

Anaerobic Endurance (Zone 5b). Intensity now exceeds the LT, and so intervals are common with this type of training. Fast-twitch muscles contribute greatly to the work at this level, which stimulates their growth and development. The body's ability to tolerate and remove lactate is also stressed. A high volume of anaerobic endurance training is the most likely cause of overtraining in the serious athlete, so it must be approached with caution and followed by extended recovery.

Power (Zone 5c). Power training has limited value for multisport athletes, with the possible exception of those who are greatly lacking in the capacity to develop muscle mass or recruit fast-twitch muscles when speed is needed. Duration at this intensity is a matter of seconds, and maximal effort is required to realize a benefit. Power workouts use only a few short, explosive intervals separated by long recoveries. Two or more days of recovery are often necessary following one of these sessions, as damage to muscle tissue is likely.

Figure 4.2 illustrates how these six intensity zones can be combined into an annual training program. This is meant only as an example of mixing intensities to build fitness. The actual blend you will use will depend on your individual strengths and weaknesses and the types of races you are training for. In Chapters 7, 8, and 9, you will learn how to make these decisions.

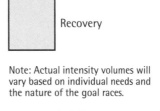

Note: Actual intensity volumes will vary based on individual needs and the nature of the goal races.

FIGURE 4.2

Relative Contributions of Training Intensities to Annual Training Volume

MEASURING INTENSITY

How do you know which intensity zone you are in? Because heart rate monitors are now so common, endurance athletes have come to think of the heart as the best—and perhaps only—indicator of intensity. Such an exaggerated emphasis on heart rate has caused many to forget that it is not the heart rate that limits performance in races and training. As previously explained, fatigue occurs mostly in the muscles, not the cardiovascular system. The beating of the heart is merely one way to peek into the body to see what is happening. At best, heart rate is an indirect measure of intensity, and not a very sensitive one. There are others that should also be used whenever possible to quantify how intensely you are swimming, biking, or running. Just as with heart rate, each method has shortcomings. By employing two or more methods every time you work out, however, you will learn how to accurately gauge intensity and reap the desired training benefits.

PACE

In the "old" days of triathlon (circa 1980), training intensity was based primarily on pace. Pace is emphasized less now, which is too bad because it is an effective measure that can provide useful information. For the experienced athlete, pace is still, in fact, the best gauge of swimming intensity. For cycling it has less benefit. Tables 4.1 and 4.2 provide standards for the seven training zones described above for swimming and running.

TABLE 4.1

Estimated
Swimming Zones

TIME 1,000M/YDS	ZONES (BY 100M/YD PACE IN MIN:SEC)						
	ZONE 1	ZONE 2	ZONE 3	ZONE 4	ZONE 5A	ZONE 5B	ZONE 5C
9:35–9:45	1:13+	1:09–1:12	1:04–1:08	1:01–1:03	:58–1:00	:54–:57	:53–max
9:46–9:55	1:15+	1:11–1:14	1:06–1:10	1:02–1:05	:59–1:01	:55–:58	:54–max
9:56–10:06	1:16+	1:12–1:15	1:07–1:11	1:03–1:06	1:00–1:02	:56–:59	:55–max
10:07–10:17	1:17+	1:13–1:16	1:08–1:12	1:04–1:07	1:01–1:03	:57–1:00	:56–max
10:18–10:28	1:18+	1:14–1:17	1:09–1:13	1:05–1:08	1:02–1:04	:58–1:01	:57–max
10:29–10:40	1:20+	1:15–1:19	1:10–1:14	1:06–1:09	1:03–1:05	:58–1:02	:57–max
10:41–10:53	1:22+	1:17–1:21	1:12–1:16	1:08–1:11	1:05–1:07	1:00–1:04	:59–max
10:54–11:06	1:23+	1:19–1:22	1:13–1:18	1:09–1:12	1:06–1:08	1:01–1:05	1:00–max
11:07–11:18	1:24+	1:20–1:23	1:14–1:19	1:10–1:13	1:07–1:09	1:02–1:06	1:01–max
11:19–11:32	1:26+	1:21–1:25	1:15–1:20	1:11–1:14	1:08–1:10	1:03–1:07	1:02–max
11:33–11:47	1:28+	1:23–1:27	1:17–1:22	1:13–1:16	1:10–1:12	1:05–1:09	1:04–max
11:48–12:03	1:29+	1:24–1:28	1:18–1:23	1:14–1:17	1:11–1:13	1:06–1:10	1:05–max
12:04–12:17	1:32+	1:26–1:31	1:20–1:25	1:16–1:19	1:13–1:15	1:07–1:12	1:06–max
12:18–12:30	1:33+	1:28–1:32	1:22–1:27	1:17–1:21	1:14–1:16	1:08–1:13	1:07–max
12:31–12:52	1:35+	1:30–1:34	1:24–1:29	1:19–1:23	1:16–1:18	1:10–1:15	1:09–max
12:53–13:02	1:38+	1:32–1:37	1:26–1:31	1:21–1:25	1:18–1:20	1:12–1:17	1:11–max
13:03–13:28	1:40+	1:34–1:39	1:28–1:33	1:23–1:27	1:20–1:22	1:14–1:19	1:13–max
13:29–13:47	1:41+	1:36–1:40	1:29–1:35	1:24–1:28	1:21–1:23	1:15–1:20	1:14–max
13:48–14:08	1:45+	1:39–1:44	1:32–1:38	1:27–1:31	1:23–1:26	1:17–1:22	1:16–max
14:09–14:30	1:46+	1:40–1:45	1:33–1:39	1:28–1:32	1:24–1:27	1:18–1:23	1:17–max
14:31–14:51	1:50+	1:44–1:49	1:36–1:43	1:31–1:35	1:27–1:30	1:21–1:26	1:20–max
14:52–15:13	1:52+	1:46–1:51	1:39–1:45	1:33–1:38	1:29–1:32	1:23–1:28	1:22–max
15:14–15:42	1:56+	1:49–1:55	1:42–1:48	1:36–1:41	1:32–1:35	1:25–1:31	1:24–max
15:43–16:08	1:58+	1:52–1:57	1:44–1:51	1:38–1:43	1:34–1:37	1:27–1:33	1:26–max
16:09–16:38	2:02+	1:55–2:01	1:47–1:54	1:41–1:46	1:37–1:40	1:30–1:36	1:29–max
16:39–17:06	2:04+	1:57–2:03	1:49–1:56	1:43–1:48	1:39–1:42	1:32–1:38	1:31–max
17:07–17:38	2:09+	2:02–2:08	1:53–2:01	1:47–1:52	1:43–1:46	1:35–1:42	1:34–max
17:39–18:12	2:13+	2:05–2:12	1:57–2:04	1:50–1:56	1:46–1:49	1:38–1:45	1:37–max
18:13–18:48	2:18+	2:10–2:17	2:01–2:09	1:54–2:00	1:50–1:53	1:42–1:49	1:41–max
18:49–19:26	2:21+	2:13–2:20	2:04–2:12	1:57–2:03	1:53–1:56	1:44–1:52	1:43–max
19:27–20:06	2:26+	2:18–2:25	2:08–2:17	2:01–2:07	1:56–2:00	1:48–1:55	1:47–max
20:07–20:50	2:31+	2:22–2:30	2:12–2:21	2:05–2:11	2:00–2:04	1:52–1:59	1:51–max
20:51–21:37	2:37+	2:28–2:36	2:18–2:27	2:10–2:17	2:05–2:09	1:56–2:04	1:55–max
21:38–22:27	2:42+	2:33–2:41	2:22–2:32	2:14–2:21	2:09–2:13	2:00–2:08	1:59–max
22:28–23:22	2:48+	2:38–2:47	2:27–2:37	2:19–2:26	2:14–2:18	2:04–2:13	2:03–max
23:23–24:31	2:55+	2:45–2:54	2:34–2:44	2:25–2:33	2:20–2:24	2:10–2:19	2:09–max
24:32–25:21	3:02+	2:52–3:01	2:40–2:51	2:31–2:39	2:25–2:30	2:15–2:24	2:14–max

Based on a 1,000-meter or 1,000-yard time trial.

TABLE 4.2

Estimated
Running Zones

| TIME | | ZONES (BY 100M/YD PACE IN MIN:SEC) | | | | | | |
5 KM	10 KM	ZONE 1	ZONE 2	ZONE 3	ZONE 4	ZONE 5A	ZONE 5B	ZONE 5C
14:15	30:00	6:38+	5:52–6:37	5:27–5:51	5:09–5:26	4:59–5:08	4:37–4:58	4:36–max
14:45	31:00	6:50+	6:02–6:49	5:37–6:01	5:18–5:36	5:07–5:17	4:45–5:06	4:44–max
15:15	32:00	7:02+	6:13–7:01	5:47–6:12	5:27–5:46	5:16–5:26	4:53–5:15	4:52–max
15:45	33:00	7:13+	6:23–7:12	5:56–6:22	5:36–5:55	5:25–5:35	5:01–5:24	5:00–max
16:10	34:00	7:25+	6:33–7:24	6:06–6:32	5:45–6:05	5:34–5:44	5:10–5:33	5:07–max
16:45	35:00	7:36+	6:43–7:35	6:15–6:42	5:54–6:14	5:42–5:53	5:18–5:41	5:17–max
17:07	36:00	7:48+	6:54–7:47	6:25–6:53	6:03–6:24	5:51–6:02	5:26–5:50	5:25–max
17:35	37:00	8:00+	7:04–7:59	6:34–7:03	6:12–6:33	6:00–6:11	5:34–5:59	5:33–max
18:05	38:00	8:11+	7:14–8:10	6:44–7:13	6:21–6:43	6:09–6:20	5:42–6:08	5:41–max
18:30	39:00	8:23+	7:24–8:22	6:53–7:23	6:30–6:52	6:17–6:29	5:50–6:16	5:49–max
19:00	40:00	8:34+	7:35–8:33	7:03–7:34	6:39–7:02	6:26–6:38	5:58–6:25	5:57–max
19:30	41:00	8:46+	7:45–8:45	7:12–7:44	6:48–7:11	6:35–6:47	6:06–6:34	6:05–max
19:55	42:00	8:58+	7:55–8:57	7:22–7:54	6:57–7:21	6:44–6:56	6:14–6:43	6:13–max
20:25	43:00	9:09+	8:05–9:08	7:31–8:04	7:06–7:30	6:52–7:05	6:22–6:51	6:21–max
20:50	44:00	9:21+	8:16–9:20	7:41–8:15	7:15–7:40	7:01–7:14	6:31–7:00	6:30–max
21:20	45:00	9:32+	8:26–9:31	7:51–8:25	7:24–7:50	7:10–7:23	6:39–7:09	6:38–max
21:50	46:00	9:44+	8:36–9:43	8:00–8:35	7:33–7:59	7:18–7:32	6:47–7:17	6:46–max
22:15	47:00	9:56+	8:47–9:55	8:10–8:46	7:42–8:09	7:27–7:41	6:55–7:26	6:54–max
22:42	48:00	10:07+	8:57–10:06	8:19–8:56	7:51–8:18	7:36–7:50	7:03–7:35	7:02–max
23:10	49:00	10:19+	9:07–10:18	8:29–9:06	8:00–8:28	7:45–7:59	7:11–7:44	7:10–max
23:38	50:00	10:31+	9:17–10:30	8:38–9:16	8:09–8:37	7:53–8:08	7:19–7:52	7:18–max
24:05	51:00	10:42+	9:28–10:41	8:48–9:27	8:18–8:47	8:02–8:17	7:27–8:01	7:26–max
24:35	52:00	10:54+	9:38–10:53	8:57–9:37	8:27–8:56	8:11–8:26	7:35–8:10	7:34–max
25:00	53:00	11:05+	9:48–11:04	9:07–9:47	8:36–9:06	8:20–8:35	7:43–8:19	7:42–max
25:25	54:00	11:17+	9:58–11:16	9:16–9:57	8:45–9:15	8:28–8:44	7:52–8:27	7:51–max
25:55	55:00	11:29+	10:09–11:28	9:26–10:08	8:54–9:25	8:37–8:53	8:00–8:36	7:59–max
26:30	56:00	11:40+	10:19–11:39	9:36–10:18	9:03–9:35	8:46–9:02	8:08–8:45	8:07–max
26:50	57:00	11:52+	10:29–11:51	9:45–10:28	9:12–9:44	8:54–9:11	8:16–8:53	8:15–max
27:20	58:00	12:03+	10:39–12:02	9:55–10:38	9:21–9:54	9:03–9:20	8:24–9:02	8:23–max
27:45	59:00	12:15+	10:50–12:14	10:04–10:49	9:30–10:03	9:12–9:29	8:32–9:11	8:31–max
28:15	60:00	12:27+	11:00–12:26	10:14–10:59	9:39–10:13	9:21–9:38	8:40–9:20	8:39–max

Based on a time from a 5 km or 10 km running race (not triathlon split).

It used to be that if you wanted to run at a given pace there was only one way to do it. You would go to a measured course, such as a track, convert the goal pace into 400-meter or 200-meter splits, and start running. Of course, you wouldn't find out until you completed a split whether you were on pace or not. And then while running you'd have to do the math to figure out just how off target your pace was and how much to speed up or slow down. Experienced runners developed the ability to gauge exactly how fast they were going based on perceived exertion.

Fortunately, technology has made pace training more precise. A wristband GPS device can determine your position, pace, and distance using satellite technology. GPS, short for Global Positioning System, is accurate to within as little as 3 meters, depending on the device you use and how strong of a signal it receives.

Another useful device is the accelerometer. This electromechanical sensor measures movement changes—accelerations—to record pace and distance. For runners it comes with a small "pod" that fastens to your shoe. The accelerometer is built into the pod along with a small transmitter that wirelessly relays the data to a wristwatch where your pace and other information is displayed.

Some devices include other features as well, such as a heart rate monitor, and the capability to download the data to your computer for analysis. Neither a GPS nor an accelerometer is cheap, but prices vary considerably based on the features and functions included.

So which device is right for you? If you run in places where the sky is often blocked out by tall trees or buildings, then an accelerometer is the way to go. The accelerometer is also useful if you run frequently on treadmills. But if you switch shoes for your runs, or don't want to add a tiny amount of weight to your shoe, then the GPS option is better.

The key with using any such device for training is to think of it only as a tool to help you train more precisely. If you try to "beat" the device, or spend all of your time looking at your wrist rather than paying attention to how you feel, it will detract from, rather than enhance, your running enjoyment and performance.

RATING OF PERCEIVED EXERTION (RPE)

The experienced athlete has a well-developed ability to assess level of exertion based strictly on sensations emanating from the body's many systems. Perceived exertion is one of the best indicators of intensity, and it is used by all athletes, whether they are consciously aware of it or not. In fact, after years of training, many pros don't even wear heart rate monitors while training and instead rely on a combination of pace and perceived exertion.

Perceived exertion is quantifiable using the Borg Rating of Perceived Exertion (RPE) scale, which scientists frequently use to determine the levels their test subjects reach. Many coaches and athletes also rely on RPE as the supreme gauge of effort. Borg's RPE is applicable to any sport. It's based on a scale of 6 to 20, with 6 representing no exertion at all and 20 signifying a maximum, all-out effort with absolutely nothing held in reserve. The scale of 6 to 20 was chosen because this range corresponds to the heart rates experienced by a moderately fit, young to middle-aged person, as each number is 10 percent of a typical heart rate for that perceived exertion. In other words, a score of 6 (resting) should parallel a heart rate of about 60 beats per minute, and 20 (maximum) should indicate a pulse of 200. In reality, these numbers seldom equate so nicely, since heart rates vary considerably at different exertion levels for different individuals.

To use the Borg RPE scale, give an honest appraisal of the feeling of exertion you experience while working out, and assign it a number on the scale (see Table 4.3). As you increase or decrease the pace, your RPE will also change, reflecting greater or lesser stress. The main problem athletes encounter when using RPE is their own tendency to underestimate their exertion level to appear tough or brave. Moral value judgments should not accompany effort assessments. It should be a cold, scientific endeavor.

TABLE 4.3

Borg Rating of Perceived Exertion (RPE) and Training Zones

	ZONE	RPE	DESCRIPTION
		6	
1	Recovery	7	Very, very light
		8	
		9	Very light
2	Extensive endurance	10	
		11	Fairly light
		12	
3	Intensive endurance	13	Somewhat hard
		14	
4	Threshold	15	Hard
5a	Threshold	16	
5b	Anaerobic endurance	17	Very hard
		18	
5c	Power	19	Very, very hard
		20	

HEART RATE

In the 1980s, the introduction of the wireless heart rate monitor brought a profound change in the way athletes in all endurance sports trained. Since intensity could not be directly measured, volume was generally considered the key to race fitness. Using the monitor taught us that by varying intensity across a broad spectrum of heart rates, great benefits were possible. We learned how to improve recovery by using the monitor to slow down. The monitor also taught us that more intense workouts were often possible. The monitor not only allowed us to accurately determine intensity, but also to measure progress and gauge effort in a long race such as the Ironman.

At first the heart rate monitor was a "gee whiz" toy. It was fun to see what happened to heart rate under varying conditions, but the numbers didn't really mean much. By the late 1980s, some coaches and athletes were starting to get a handle on effective ways to employ heart rate monitoring in training. Today nearly all multisport athletes have heart rate monitors, and most are fairly sophisticated in their use.

The problem is that heart rate–based training has become so pervasive that athletes too often believe that heart rate is the determining factor in how they train and race. Too many have become slaves to their heart rate monitors and do not use other tools for measuring intensity as much as they could. Heart rate is but one window into how your body is doing. It may give you a better perspective on the exercising body, but this is not the only perspective that is worthwhile. Relying on it to the exclusion of all other measures of intensity can be as detrimental to your training as not having any gauge of effort at all.

When used intelligently, however, the heart rate monitor can improve fitness and race performance. Sometimes low motivation, high enthusiasm, competition, loss of focus, and poor judgment get in the way of smart training. In these instances the heart rate monitor is like having a coach along for the workout. With a good working knowledge of heart rate, skill in using other intensity measures, and a little common sense resulting from experience, you can use a monitor to help determine whether you're working too hard or not hard enough, if recovery is complete, and how your fitness is progressing. Later chapters will address these issues in detail.

Just as with most of the other measures of intensity discussed above, heart-rate training zones are best tied to the standard of lactate threshold. Often maximum heart rate is used as an estimate of LT, but that presents some problems. Attempting to achieve the highest heart rate possible in a workout requires extremely high motivation. In addition, for some individuals, exercising at such intensity may not be safe. Your true LT is a better indicator of what the body is experiencing and is highly variable from one athlete to the next. For example, your lactate threshold heart rate (LTHR) may occur at 85 percent of maximum heart rate while another athlete's may be found at 92 percent. If both of you train at 90 percent of maximum, one is deeply anaerobic and working quite hard, but the other is cruising along, primarily in aerobic zones. Using the percentage of maximum heart rate to define your workout goal just isn't as precise as using zones based on LTHR. Finding your LTHR requires some effort, but don't let that scare you away. It's actually a simple procedure and is described in Chapter 5.

Just as with LT, heart rate zones vary by sport, since there are differences in the amount of muscle used and the effects of gravity among the different sports. For most triathletes, LTHR is highest for running and lowest for swimming, with cycling in between. Lactate production also varies with the activity. This means that each sport must have its own set of heart rate values. Tables 4.4 and 4.5 provide heart rate training zones for cycling and running. Swimming is not included because training with a heart rate monitor is problematic in the water. Pace and RPE are the best measures of intensity for swimming.

POWER

Put simply, power is the ability to apply muscular strength. More precisely, it can be defined as

$$Power = force \times distance \div time$$

On the bike, if you are able to increase the gear size while your cadence remains constant, your power goes up. Your power also increases if you are able to turn the cranks faster with the same gear size. Currently it's not feasible to directly measure power in swimming or running, although the day may come when it is, probably sooner for running. Many multisport athletes, however, are now using power to govern, measure, and analyze cycling intensity. Given that the bike leg is the longest leg of a race, a power meter is a worthwhile investment.

Power is more closely related to performance than any other measure discussed here, and it is therefore an excellent indicator of training workload. The more power you can generate aerobically, the more likely you are to get good results in races. For example, according to one study, the amount of power generated during a 2-minute test is a better indicator of time trial ability on the bike than aerobic capacity (VO_2max) is.

I require every triathlete I work with to use a power meter. Why? I know athletes are more likely to achieve their race goals by training—and racing—with power than without. I've seen it happen with every athlete I've coached since power meters hit the market several years ago.

Heart rate monitors are great by themselves, but they're even more beneficial when they can work in conjunction with power. With a power meter, an athlete can compare heart rate to watts (the unit of measure for most power meters, named after James Watt, who invented the steam engine in 1769). Instead of just relying on how he or she feels, the athlete has objective information for establishing intensity.

Power meters remove most of the guesswork that goes into training and racing. For example, many athletes don't consider a work interval to be "started" until their heart rate reaches the targeted level. With a power meter, the interval starts as soon as the power hits the targeted zone—which means right away.

Heart rate monitors teach athletes to focus on the heart, but the muscles are really the key to fitness. This is particularly true when doing intervals. It can be very challenging to get the intensity right in the first minute or so of the first few intervals in a workout. Heart rate can't be relied upon, as it is low and takes the first couple of minutes to rise. But a power meter identifies your intensity level precisely and immediately.

Using a power meter in a long race such as an Ironman is almost like cheating. When everyone else is fighting the wind, flying downwind, or guessing how hard to go when climbing, the triathlete with a power meter is just rolling along at the prescribed power. He or she will produce the fastest possible bike portion of the race—leaving enough energy for the best possible run—because the optimal target power has been determined through training and then followed closely during the race. While something similar can be done with heart rate, there are some confounding factors, such as cardiac drift, the acute effect of diet, and the heart's slow response on hills.

Power meters also provide a highly accurate profile of how fitness changes throughout the season. I test the athletes I coach regularly using a combination of heart rate and power. Without this information I really wouldn't know for sure whether they were making progress. I'd just be guessing.

TABLE 4.4

Cycling Heart
Rate Zones

Find your lactate threshold heart rate (bold) in the "Zone 5a" column.
Read across to left and right for training zones.

ZONE 1	ZONE 2	ZONE 3	ZONE 4	ZONE 5A	ZONE 5B	ZONE 5C
Recovery	Extensive endurance	Intensive endurance	Subthreshold	Super-threshold	Anaerobic capacity	Power
90–108	109–122	123–128	129–136	**137**–140	141–145	146–150
91–109	110–123	124–129	130–137	**138**–141	142–146	147–151
91–109	110–124	125–130	131–138	**139**–142	143–147	148–152
92–110	111–125	126–130	131–139	**140**–143	144–147	148–153
92–111	112–125	126–131	132–140	**141**–144	145–148	149–154
93–112	113–126	127–132	133–141	**142**–145	146–149	150–155
94–112	113–127	128–133	134–142	**143**–145	146–150	151–156
94–113	114–128	129–134	135–143	**144**–147	148–151	152–157
95–114	115–129	130–135	136–144	**145**–148	149–152	153–158
95–115	116–130	131–136	137–145	**146**–149	150–154	155–159
97–116	117–131	132–137	138–146	**147**–150	151–155	156–161
97–117	118–132	133–138	139–147	**148**–151	152–156	157–162
98–118	119–133	134–139	140–148	**149**–152	153–157	158–163
98–119	120–134	135–140	141–149	**150**–153	154–158	159–164
99–120	121–134	135–141	142–150	**151**–154	155–159	160–165
100–121	122–135	136–142	143–151	**152**–155	156–160	161–166
100–122	123–136	137–142	143–152	**153**–156	157–161	162–167
101–123	124–137	138–143	144–153	**154**–157	158–162	163–168
101–124	125–138	139–144	145–154	**155**–158	159–163	164–169
102–125	126–138	139–145	146–155	**156**–159	160–164	165–170
103–126	127–140	141–146	147–156	**157**–160	161–165	166–171
104–127	128–141	142–147	148–157	**158**–161	162–167	168–173
104–128	129–142	143–148	149–158	**159**–162	163–168	169–174
105–129	130–143	144–148	149–159	**160**–163	164–169	170–175
106–129	130–143	144–150	151–160	**161**–164	165–170	171–176
106–130	131–144	145–151	152–161	**162**–165	166–171	172–177
107–131	132–145	146–152	153–162	**163**–166	167–172	173–178
107–132	133–146	147–153	154–163	**164**–167	168–173	174–179
108–133	134–147	148–154	155–164	**165**–168	169–174	175–180
109–134	135–148	149–154	155–165	**166**–169	170–175	176–181
109–135	136–149	150–155	156–166	**167**–170	171–176	177–182
110–136	137–150	151–156	157–167	**168**–171	172–177	178–183
111–137	138–151	152–157	158–168	**169**–172	173–178	179–185
112–138	139–151	152–158	159–169	**170**–173	174–179	180–186
112–139	140–152	153–160	161–170	**171**–174	175–180	181–187
113–140	141–153	154–160	161–171	**172**–175	176–181	182–188
113–141	142–154	155–161	162–172	**173**–176	177–182	183–189
114–142	143–155	156–162	163–173	**174**–177	178–183	184–190
115–143	144–156	157–163	164–174	**175**–178	179–184	185–191
115–144	145–157	158–164	165–175	**176**–179	180–185	186–192
116–145	146–158	159–165	166–176	**177**–180	181–186	187–193
116–146	147–159	160–166	167–177	**178**–181	182–187	188–194
117–147	148–160	161–166	167–178	**179**–182	183–188	189–195
118–148	149–160	161–167	168–179	**180**–183	184–190	191–197
119–149	150–161	162–168	169–180	**181**–184	185–191	192–198
119–150	151–162	163–170	171–181	**182**–185	186–192	193–199
120–151	152–163	164–171	172–182	**183**–186	187–193	194–200
121–152	153–164	165–172	173–183	**184**–187	188–194	195–201
121–153	154–165	166–172	173–184	**185**–188	191–195	196–202
122–154	155–166	167–173	174–185	**186**–189	190–196	197–203
122–155	156–167	168–174	175–186	**187**–190	191–197	198–204
123–156	157–168	169–175	176–187	**188**–191	192–198	199–205
124–157	158–169	170–176	177–188	**189**–192	193–199	200–206
124–158	159–170	171–177	178–189	**190**–193	194–200	201–207
125–159	160–170	171–178	179–190	**191**–194	195–201	202–208
125–160	161–171	172–178	179–191	**192**–195	196–202	203–209
126–161	162–172	173–179	180–192	**193**–196	197–203	204–210
127–162	163–173	174–180	181–193	**194**–197	198–204	205–211
127–163	164–174	175–181	182–194	**195**–198	199–205	206–212

Find your lactate threshold heart rate (bold) in the "Zone 5a" column.
Read across to left and right for training zones.

TABLE 4.5

Running Heart
Rate Zones

ZONE 1	ZONE 2	ZONE 3	ZONE 4	ZONE 5A	ZONE 5B	ZONE 5C
Recovery	Extensive endurance	Intensive endurance	Subthreshold	Super-threshold	Anaerobic capacity	Power
93–119	120–126	127–133	134–139	**140**–143	144–149	150–156
94–119	120–127	128–134	135–140	**141**–144	145–150	151–157
95–120	121–129	130–135	136–141	**142**–145	146–151	152–158
95–121	122–130	131–136	137–142	**143**–146	147–152	153–159
96–122	123–131	132–137	138–143	**144**–147	148–153	154–160
96–123	124–132	133–138	139–144	**145**–148	149–154	155–161
97–124	125–133	134–139	140–145	**146**–149	150–155	156–162
97–124	125–134	135–140	141–146	**147**–150	151–156	157–163
98–125	126–135	136–141	142–147	**148**–151	152–157	158–164
99–126	127–135	136–142	143–148	**149**–152	153–158	159–165
99–127	128–136	137–143	144–149	**150**–153	154–158	159–166
100–128	129–137	138–144	145–150	**151**–154	155–159	160–167
100–129	130–138	139–145	146–151	**152**–155	156–160	161–168
101–130	131–139	140–146	147–152	**153**–156	157–161	162–169
102–131	132–140	141–147	148–153	**154**–157	158–162	163–170
103–131	132–141	142–148	149–154	**155**–158	159–164	165–172
103–132	133–142	143–149	150–155	**156**–159	160–165	166–173
104–133	134–143	144–150	151–156	**157**–160	161–166	167–174
105–134	135–143	144–151	152–157	**158**–161	162–167	168–175
105–135	136–144	145–152	153–158	**159**–162	163–168	169–176
106–136	137–145	146–153	154–159	**160**–163	164–169	170–177
106–136	137–146	147–154	155–160	**161**–164	165–170	171–178
107–137	138–147	148–155	156–161	**162**–165	166–171	172–179
108–138	139–148	149–155	156–162	**163**–166	167–172	173–180
109–139	140–149	150–156	157–163	**164**–167	168–174	175–182
109–140	141–150	151–157	158–164	**165**–168	169–175	176–183
110–141	142–151	152–158	159–165	**166**–169	170–176	177–184
111–141	142–152	153–159	160–166	**167**–170	171–177	178–185
111–142	143–153	154–160	161–167	**168**–171	172–178	179–186
112–143	144–154	155–161	162–168	**169**–172	173–179	180–187
112–144	145–155	156–162	163–169	**170**–173	174–179	180–188
113–145	146–156	157–163	164–170	**171**–174	175–180	181–189
114–145	146–156	157–164	165–171	**172**–175	176–182	183–191
115–146	147–157	158–165	166–172	**173**–176	177–183	184–192
115–147	148–157	158–166	167–173	**174**–177	178–184	185–193
116–148	149–158	159–167	168–174	**175**–178	179–185	186–194
117–149	150–159	160–168	169–175	**176**–179	180–186	187–195
117–150	151–160	161–169	170–176	**177**–180	181–187	188–196
118–151	152–161	162–170	171–177	**178**–181	182–188	189–197
118–152	153–162	163–171	172–178	**179**–182	183–189	190–198
119–153	154–163	164–172	173–179	**180**–183	184–190	191–199
120–154	155–164	165–173	174–180	**181**–184	185–192	193–201
121–154	155–165	166–174	175–181	**182**–185	186–193	194–202
121–155	156–166	167–175	176–182	**183**–186	187–194	195–203
122–156	157–167	168–176	177–183	**184**–187	188–195	196–204
123–157	158–168	169–177	178–184	**185**–188	189–196	197–205
123–158	159–169	170–178	179–185	**186**–189	190–197	198–206
124–159	160–170	171–179	180–186	**187**–190	191–198	199–207
124–159	160–170	171–179	180–187	**188**–191	192–199	200–208
125–160	161–171	172–180	181–188	**189**–192	193–200	201–209
126–161	152–172	173–181	182–189	**190**–193	194–201	202–210
126–162	163–173	174–182	183–190	**191**–194	195–201	202–211
127–163	164–174	175–183	184–191	**192**–195	196–202	203–212
127–164	165–175	176–184	185–192	**193**–196	197–203	204–213
128–165	166–176	177–185	186–193	**194**–197	198–204	205–214
129–165	166–177	178–186	187–194	**195**–198	199–205	206–215
129–166	167–178	179–187	188–195	**196**–199	200–206	207–216
130–167	168–178	179–188	189–196	**197**–198	201–207	208–217
130–168	169–179	180–189	190–197	**198**–201	202–208	209–218
131–169	170–180	181–190	191–198	**199**–202	203–209	210–219
132–170	171–181	182–191	192–199	**200**–203	204–210	211–220

Unfortunately, power meters aren't cheap. But as with any technology, prices keep falling as the number of options increase. Eventually, just as with heart rate monitors, most multisport athletes will be training with power meters—and racing better because of them. Given the option of buying fast wheels or a power meter, the power meter is the better choice. There is more to be gained from having a powerful engine.

Training with power, just as training with pace, RPE, or a heart rate monitor, requires the use of training zones based on a personal standard. The next chapter describes how to determine your critical power zones.

LACTATE

If the LT is such an important phenomenon, why not simply measure blood lactate to gauge intensity? Until recently, it wasn't practical to check lactate levels in the real world of multisport athletes at the pool or on the road. The only equipment available required electricity; it was expensive and cumbersome, and better suited for lab use. Today, there are lactate-measuring devices and mail-in services available, making it possible to measure lactate from a drop of blood drawn from the finger or earlobe. Such testing is still rather sophisticated and is reliable only in the hands of an experienced technician or coach. I would not recommend this for the self-coached athlete.

Lactate measurement does not provide instantaneous feedback in the same way that power, pace, and RPE do, since it takes a minute or two, at best, to draw and analyze the blood. At a couple of dollars per analysis, frequent measurement, even with a portable analyzer, is impractical. So lactate measurement is best used in a testing situation. It can be used to confirm LT, measure improvement, determine economy of movement, or set up a bike for optimal efficiency, for example.

TRAINING TIME BY INTENSITY ZONE

How much time should you spend in each heart rate zone over the course of a season? This is a question often asked by athletes, and with good reason: Knowing the answer will lead to purposeful and effective training. Unfortunately, it's not an easy question to answer.

The intensity you should aim for in training depends on many different variables. The most important of these is the event for which you are training. There are tremendous differences between preparing for an Ironman-distance triathlon and a sprint-distance race. If we talk in terms of the five basic heart rate zones, it is obvious what our problem is. Preparing for a sprint requires a lot of training near and above the LT, but for an Ironman-distance race such an effort has no place in training. Ironman training requires a great deal of work around the aerobic threshold. Obviously one cannot train with the same intensities for both events.

It's not really possible to talk in general about how much time triathletes should spend over the course of the season in each zone, even if we look at each of the four common triathlon distances—sprint, Olympic, half-Ironman, and Ironman. The reason for this is that some people, for example, do a sprint-distance race in less than an hour, while others on the same course and on the same day do it in three hours or more. Regardless of distance, training for a three-hour event is a lot different from training for a one-hour event.

Keep this in mind as you look at Figure 4.3, which suggests what the distribution of training time by heart rate zone for an entire season might look like. The purpose of this figure is not to give you specific numbers to shoot for but rather to suggest how your training intensity should be generally distributed. Knowing how your intensity might be distributed by zone by the end of the season may help you make decisions about how hard to push yourself in workouts.

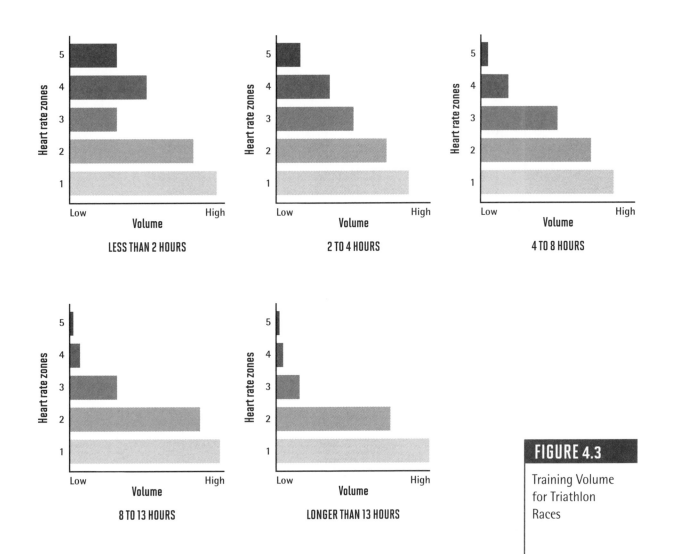

FIGURE 4.3

Training Volume for Triathlon Races

If we could create a distribution curve for most self-coached athletes, we would probably find that many of them spend a lot more time in the upper heart rate zones for the durations shown in Figure 4.3 than is advisable. Most athletes push themselves too hard in training. That's the reason injury, overtraining, illness, and burnout are so prevalent in triathlon.

MEASURING FITNESS

This is a good place to begin pulling together some of the intensity concepts in this chapter—aerobic threshold, heart rate, pace, and power. All of them come into play when determining whether you have done enough aerobic threshold training to consider that aspect of fitness complete.

To make this determination, you will compare heart rate to either power or pace, depending on the sport and your equipment, and see if the two are staying closely linked with little or no cardiac drift. Cardiac drift is the tendency of heart rate to rise even though power or pace remains steady. In an aerobically fit athlete it will be minimal. The following explains an advanced method that you may use to determine if your aerobic fitness is as good as it should be at the end of the Base period. This method is not for everyone. But if you are a serious athlete who enjoys analyzing training data, you can learn a lot about your fitness using this method.

On a bike with a power meter, complete an aerobic threshold ride, then upload the power meter's heart rate and power data to analysis software such as WKO+™, which is available at the Web site TrainingPeaks.com (see additional information on page 61, under "Form, Fitness, and Fatigue"). The software separates the aerobic threshold portion of the ride into two halves in order to compare the first half with the second half. For each half, it will divide average power by average heart rate to establish a ratio. It will then compare the results by subtracting the ratio from the first half of this portion of the ride from the ratio from the second half, and dividing the difference by the ratio from the first half. This produces a percentage of change in the power-to-heart-rate ratio from the first half to the second half of the aerobic threshold ride.

Here is an example of how power-to-heart-rate ratio percentage of change is calculated:

First half of aerobic threshold portion of ride
Power average: 180 watts
Heart rate average: 135 bpm
First-half power-to-heart-rate ratio: 1.33
Second half of aerobic threshold portion of ride
Power average: 178 watts
Heart rate average: 139 bpm
Second-half power-to-heart-rate ratio: 1.28

Calculating change

Second-half ratio minus first-half ratio: 0.05

The difference is then divided by the first-half ratio: 0.038

Power-to-heart-rate shift: 3.8 percent

If your power-to-heart-rate shift is less than 5 percent, as in the above example, the workout is said to be "coupled," meaning the power and heart-rate graph lines stay close to parallel, as shown in Figure 4.4. That's good. But if the shift in the power-to-heart-rate ratio is greater than 5 percent, the workout is "decoupled," as shown in Figure 4.5. Note that the two lines on this graph do not remain parallel for the entire aerobic threshold portion of the workout. That's not good.

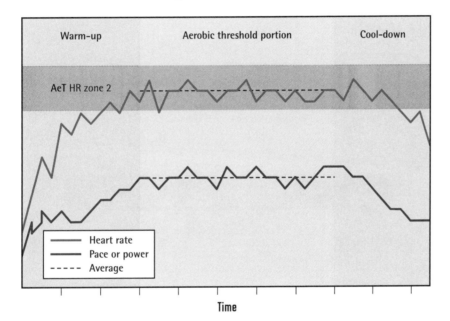

Note how heart rate remains parallel with pace or power.

There are two ways to do an aerobic threshold coupling workout on the bike. You can ride while keeping your heart rate steady to see what happens to your power, or you can maintain a steady power and see what your heart rate does. In the Base period, it's generally better to maintain a steady heart rate, while for the Build period you should keep power steady. To use the same calculation for running, substitute pace for power and aim to stay within that same 5 percent amount of drift.

When aerobic threshold rides at the race-duration goals in Table 4.6 remain coupled, I consider aerobic threshold fitness fully developed for that length of race and this primary goal of the Base period accomplished. When this happens, an athlete is ready to move on to more advanced training goals. The athlete does need to maintain aerobic threshold endurance even after it is developed, and this can be accomplished by doing such a workout about one-half as often as was necessary to create it in the first place. Note that being aerobically fit for a sprint-distance race does not mean you are also aerobically

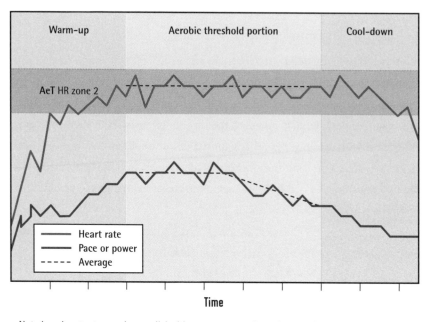

Note how heart rate remains parallel with pace or power for only part of the aerobic threshold portion of the workout. The decline in power indicates a lack of aerobic fitness for long durations.

RACE DISTANCE	BIKE (HEART RATE/POWER)	RUN (HEART RATE/PACE)
Sprint	1 hour	30 minutes
Olympic	2 hours	1 hour
Half-Ironman	3 hours	1.5 hours
Ironman	4 hours	2 hours

fit for longer-distance events, although, if you are aerobically fit for a longer race, you are certainly fit enough for shorter ones.

With a GPS device or accelerometer, this same procedure may be used for pace-based aerobic-threshold running workouts. Simply substitute pace for power in the procedure above, then use Table 4.6 to determine the duration goal for your aerobic threshold runs.

Determining coupling and decoupling is not possible for swimming as of this writing, as there is no way to accurately measure and analyze pace while swimming. I find that in the pool, heart rate monitors often have dead spots in the data stream due to poor transmission and reception in the water, which results in inaccurate heart rate information. That may well change soon with the rapid growth of digital technology.

Even if you don't have a power meter, GPS, or accelerometer, you can still do the aerobic threshold bike and run workouts using your trusty heart rate monitor. You will have to make decisions about your aerobic endurance fitness based strictly on perceived exertion; over time, the effort at aerobic threshold heart rate will seem to be getting easier.

FORM, FITNESS, AND FATIGUE

Although the previous discussion on periodization sounds very scientific, training based on periodization is largely a leap of faith. You simply trust that organizing your workouts in a certain way will produce peak readiness on race day. Along the way it is possible to take "snapshots" of your fitness every four weeks or so by doing field tests. But since the physiological changes are generally quite small—on the order of 1 percent—variables such as weather, the warm-up, or even a couple of cups of coffee can easily affect the results. So you are back to trusting your instincts when it comes to assessing whether you are fitter than you were a few weeks ago.

As mentioned above, though, for those who have power meters, that situation is changing for bike training. With new software designed by Hunter Allen and Andrew Coggan, it is possible to graph and manage the daily changes in your race preparation. This is the WKO+ software mentioned earlier, which is available at TrainingPeaks.com, and it is compatible with all power meters.

One of the most powerful features of WKO+ is its performance management chart, which allows you to track periodization and progress toward your race goals. Figure 4.6 is based on a screen shot of the chart for the early season for one of the athletes I coach. This a good example of the direction training technology is going. If you are serious about your race performance, you may want to consider downloading this software, as it will

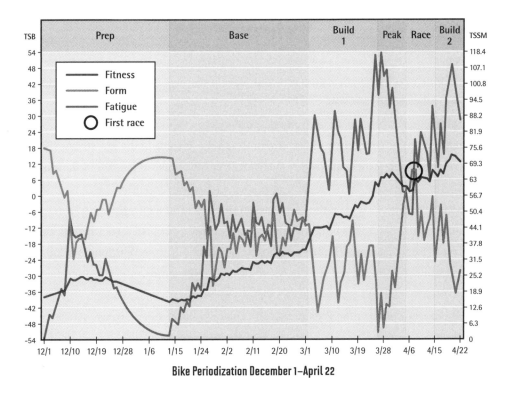

FIGURE 4.6

Performance Chart for Sample Athlete

allow you to keep a close eye on your progress. When you know exactly how your training is progressing, you can respond quickly when small periodization changes are necessary to stay on track toward your goals.

There are three aspects of training represented by the lines on the graph. All are derived from long, complicated formulas determined by certain power-based variables. These are called "normalized power," "intensity factor," and "training stress score" and reflect the intensity, duration, and frequency of your bike workouts. To learn more about these details, see Allen and Coggan's book *Training and Racing with a Power Meter* (VeloPress 2006).

The gray line on the chart represents *fatigue.* It closely approximates what you would subjectively describe after a few days of hard training. Notice the spikes and valleys. These indicate alternating hard and easy workout days. The spikes show increased training stress from long, high intensity and/or frequent bike workouts. The valleys represent short, easy rides or days off the bike.

The dark blue line is *fitness.* When this line rises, fitness is improving. Notice that it isn't a straight line. Fitness is never static; it is always changing, either positively or negatively. Also, fitness only increases in response to increases in fatigue. Fitness and fatigue go hand in hand. This makes sense, as being fatigued means you trained hard, and hard training produces greater fitness. Although a few days of extended rest are necessary every three or four weeks to prevent overtraining and burnout, you must be careful not to make the break too long, or too much fitness will be lost. The software allows you to monitor these changes. Effectively balancing rest and stress is tricky when it comes to fitness.

The light blue line represents *form,* which may also be described as race readiness. This use of the word "form" comes from late-nineteenth-century British horse racing when bettors would review a page of previous race results—a form—of the horses entered in a race. A horse was said to be "on form" when racing well.

Form rises when you back off from hard training to rest more. It falls when you train frequently with high intensity or long workouts. On the left side of the graph, you see a 0 (zero) in the center of the scale. When the lighter blue line is above this point, the athlete is "on form."

So now let's take a look at the early-season periodization for one of my athletes and see how it worked out. Along the fitness curve I've indicated his early-season periods: Prep, Base, Build, Peak, and Race (indicated with a circle). The second Build period following the Race period is the start of his return to hard training in preparation for the next A-priority race on his schedule.

As described earlier, the Prep period is a time when the athlete is just getting back into training following a break at the end of the previous season. In this case, it was December through early January. He had a family vacation planned for the last three weeks of this period and did not have a bike available. Here, since he wasn't riding, you can see the steady drop in both fatigue and fitness. Accompanying that drop is a rise in form. He was really rested—at least as far as the bike goes—but, of course, his bike fitness was rapidly declining.

In the Base period he returned to steady and consistent training. He spent time spent on the indoor trainer working on aerobic endurance, muscular force, and pedaling speed skills. The steady rise in fatigue and fitness, with a drop in form, all indicate that training was going as expected.

During the first Build period I began to increase the intensity of his training by including muscular endurance rides, made up primarily of intervals and tempo segments, while maintaining his three fitness abilities—endurance, force, and speed skills—established in the Base period. Both fatigue and fitness rose at a greater rate, and form dropped to a low point of the early season due to this increase in the training load. I made slight adjustments to stress and rest along the way as the chart revealed how he was responding to training.

In the short Peak period, he did just a couple of hard workouts with lots of rest between them. Notice how fatigue dropped dramatically while fitness decreased only slightly. The most important change to see here is the rapid rise in form, with an increase above the horizontal zero line mentioned above. At his first race, he was not only at a high level of fitness, he was also well rested. This was evident in his sense of being ready on race day and in his race performance. He was *on form.*

Following this first race of the season, he went on a mountain-biking vacation for a few days, and resumed hard training on his return. As you can see on the far right side, he was well on his way to the second peak of the season, which produced even better results.

HIGH-INTENSITY TRAINING IN THE REAL WORLD

The road to fitness generally takes one of two routes. For the multisport athlete with lots of time, high volume may bring excellent performances. Pro triathletes and duathletes typically train 25 to 30 or more hours per week. The downside of such training is the risk of injury and exhaustion leading to overtraining. To deal with this problem, those who make triathlon their occupation often train in blocks of time greater than the seven-day week. Nine- or ten-day "weeks" allow them to space the workouts and recover.

For the athlete with a full-time job, a family, a home to maintain, and myriad other responsibilities, such volume and calendar manipulations are not an option. High intensity scheduled around a seven-day week is—but it's not risk-free, as overtraining is just as likely, perhaps more so, when anaerobic workouts dominate the training routine in such a short period of time. There are limits to how many high-effort sessions an athlete can manage in a week without eventually breaking down.

For most multisport athletes, high-intensity training, when used intelligently, offers the possibility of a breakthrough in fitness. Most can do only three or four of these breakthrough efforts in a week; more may lead to overtraining, injury, illness, or burnout. The most important information you can learn about yourself as a serious triathlete is how many breakthroughs you can do in a week and how much recovery time is needed after them. Once you've determined this, planning a week of training is a snap.

PART III

TRAINING WITH A PURPOSE

How much time do you have available to train? After subtracting 40 hours for working and another 56 for sleeping from your 168-hour weekly allotment, you're left with 72. Of those remaining hours, more than half, perhaps 50, are accounted for in basic activities such as meal preparation, eating, personal care, home maintenance, transportation, and shopping for necessities. That leaves 22 "free" hours each week for most of us. According to John Robinson and Geoffrey Godbey in their 1997 book *Time for Life*, the average American spends 15 of those hours watching television and the remainder socializing with others, including family. Today, Americans spend much of their leisure time surfing the Internet, playing video games, or watching DVDs, all of which adds up to a lot of "screen time."

It's doubtful that you spend your 15 hours in these ways, because if you did, you wouldn't be competing in multisport events. After all, multisport does require a rather hefty time commitment. But more than likely, you don't have as many hours to train as you want, and the situation probably won't change in the foreseeable future. It's imperative, therefore, that you spend the time you do have available—whether it's 15 hours or 5—wisely, by doing workouts that have a direct and beneficial impact on race performance.

The purpose of the next two chapters is to help you determine exactly what your training needs are and the optimal ways to address them. Chapter 5 will show you how to determine your fitness and progress, and Chapter 6 examines the implications of the abilities and limiters discovered. With a solid understanding of personal training needs, you'll be ready for Part IV, to begin planning for better race performances.

ASSESSING FITNESS

The focus must be on individual workouts—
not on miles per week.

—MARK SISSON, AUTHOR OF
TRAINING AND RACING BIATHLONS

IN A WAY, TRAINING for triathlon or duathlon is similar to investing money. When you have a few spare dollars and want to increase them, you look for good investments. You consider several options and compare many factors, especially the potential rate of return and the risk of losing your money. The objective is to get the greatest growth possible with the lowest level of risk. Generally, these two factors—growth and risk—work in opposition. When the potential growth rate is high, so is the risk of losing everything. At low levels of growth, risk is minimal. The trick in investing is seeking a balance between growth and risk. To make that decision, you must understand yourself and your financial status quite well: How much money can you invest? How much risk are you willing to take? How much can you afford to lose?

Growth and risk play a similar role in multisport training. The precious resource you have to invest in training is time. The goal is to invest it wisely so that the fitness return you get is sizable. The greatest rate of growth comes from high-intensity, high-volume training. You could simply work out for an hour or two a day in each sport, including lots of intervals, hills, repetitions, and races. But this is also the riskiest combination, as the potential is high for injury, overtraining, illness, and burnout, all of which leave you with less fitness than when you started.

Just as with financial investing, it is important to understand your present fitness needs. The purpose of this chapter is to help you make wise training investments of your limited time so that you get a good growth rate while minimizing risk. Wise training investments also require knowing your fitness status:

- How much time do you have to invest in training?
- In which areas of multisport performance are you weakest?

- In which areas are you strongest?
- How intensely should you swim, bike, and run?
- Are you making progress toward fitness goals?

Knowing the answers to these questions makes training a simple process of devoting precious road and pool time to those needs that give you the greatest fitness return for your investment, while swimming, cycling, and running at appropriate intensities to keep your risk manageable.

One way to find the answers to these questions is to look at your race results. For example, if you've done the same race under similar conditions over several years, how do your times compare? Are you faster or slower now? Comparing your time splits with those of others in the same race category also reveals quite a lot. If you ranked fifth in the swim in your age group, eighth on the bike, and tenth on the run, you have a fair idea of which sports need the most work (cycling and especially running), and the least (swimming). Of course, these assessment methods assume that race conditions stay the same from year to year and that your age group was large enough to offer a good sample. This method also requires that you race often enough to measure progress, but there are few, if any, races in the winter in most parts of the country when many of your "investment" decisions must be made.

One way to resolve this dilemma is to periodically measure your fitness against a standard such as a graded exercise test or time trial. These aren't perfect gauges of fitness either, however, as conditions change. Many variables, such as the test venue, weather, warm-up procedures, and food and drink intake must be controlled. When testing is done carefully and regularly, the information gathered is invaluable.

PERSONAL PROFILE

The first step in making training decisions is to know yourself, especially your proficiencies and natural physical abilities. It's important that you are totally honest in these ranking exercises. The results will help you design your training program and must be based on reliable information.

Begin by scoring your swim, bike, and run proficiencies using the following scale. The score you choose for each sport is subjective and based on a long-term comparison with others in your race category or age group. A score of 5 means that you are among the best, 3 indicates average for your category, and 1 places you at the bottom of the category.

Compared with my race category, I'm among the . . .

Sport	Worst		Average		Best
Swimming	1	2	3	4	5
Biking	1	2	3	4	5
Running	1	2	3	4	5

Now complete and score the Natural Abilities Profile and the Mental Skills Profile on the following pages. Then go to the "Natural Abilities" section to find out what the results mean for your training.

SIDEBAR 5.1

Triathlete Natural Abilities Profile

DIRECTIONS

Read each statement below, decide if it applies to you, and check the true or false column accordingly. If unsure, go with your initial feeling.

T   F

___ ___ 1. I prefer to ride in a bigger gear with a lower cadence than most of my training partners.

___ ___ 2. The shorter the race, the better I perform.

___ ___ 3. As the intervals get shorter, I get better.

___ ___ 4. I'm stronger at the end of long workouts than my training partners.

___ ___ 5. I can squat and/or leg press more weight than most in my category.

___ ___ 6. I prefer long races.

___ ___ 7. I run and bike in the hills better than most in my age group.

___ ___ 8. I enjoy high-volume training weeks.

___ ___ 9. My running stride is short and quick.

___ ___ 10. I have always been better at sprints than at endurance.

___ ___ 11. In most sports, I've finished stronger than most others.

___ ___ 12. I'm more muscular than most triathletes of my age and sex.

___ ___ 13. I'm better at swimming in rough water than most others in my age group.

___ ___ 14. I prefer workouts that are short but fast.

___ ___ 15. I'm confident of my endurance at the start of long races.

Scoring: For each of the following statement sets, count the number of true statements to calculate your Force, Speed, and Endurance scores.

		Statement numbers	Score
FORCE	_____	(1, 5, 7, 12, 13)	Total _____
SPEED	_____	(2, 3, 9, 10, 14)	Total _____
ENDURANCE	_____	(4, 6, 8, 11, 15)	Total _____

SIDEBAR 5.2

Mental Skills
Profile

DIRECTIONS

Read each statement below and choose an appropriate answer from these possibilities:

1 = Never   2 = Rarely   3 = Sometimes
4 = Frequently   5 = Usually   6 = Always

____ 1. I believe my potential as an athlete is excellent.

____ 2. I train consistently and eagerly.

____ 3. When things don't go well in a race, I remain positive.

____ 4. In hard races I can imagine myself doing well.

____ 5. Before races I remain positive and upbeat.

____ 6. I think of myself more as a success than as a failure.

____ 7. Before races I'm able to erase self-doubt.

____ 8. The morning of a race I awake enthusiastically.

____ 9. I learn something from races when I don't do well.

____ 10. I can see myself handling tough race situations.

____ 11. I'm able to race at near my ability level.

____ 12. I can easily picture myself training and racing.

____ 13. Staying focused during long races is easy for me.

____ 14. I stay in tune with my exertion levels in races.

____ 15. I mentally rehearse skills and tactics before races.

____ 16. I'm good at concentrating as a race progresses.

____ 17. I make sacrifices to attain my goals.

____ 18. Before an important race I can visualize doing well.

____ 19. I look forward to workouts.

____ 20. When I visualize myself racing, it almost feels real.

____ 21. I think of myself as a tough competitor.

____ 22. In races I tune out distractions.

____ 23. I set high goals for myself.

____ 24. I like the challenge of a hard race.

____ 25. When the race becomes difficult I concentrate even better.

____ 26. In races I am mentally tough.

____ 27. I can relax my muscles before races.

____ 28. I stay positive despite late race starts, bad weather, poor officiating, etc.

___ 29. My confidence stays high the week after a bad race.

___ 30. I strive to be the best athlete I can be.

Scoring: Add up the numerical answers for each of the following sets of statements. Then score each mental skill according to the chart below.

		Statement numbers	Score
MOTIVATION	___	(2, 8, 17, 19, 23, 30)	Total ___
CONFIDENCE	___	(1, 6, 11, 21, 26, 29)	Total ___
THOUGHT HABITS	___	(3, 5, 9, 24, 27, 28)	Total ___
FOCUS	___	(7, 13, 14, 16, 22, 25)	Total ___
VISUALIZATION	___	(4, 10, 12, 15, 18, 20)	Total ___

Total	Ranking	Score
32–36	Excellent	5
27–31	Good	4
21–26	Average	3
16–20	Fair	2
6–15	Poor	1

NATURAL ABILITIES

Some people were born to be multisport athletes. Their parents blessed them with the physiology necessary to excel in swimming, biking, and running. Others were born to excel as soccer players, high jumpers, or pianists. Many of us have chosen to swim, bike, and run regardless of the genetic hand dealt to us. Passion for the sport means a lot and can overcome many physiological shortcomings. Success in any sport is determined by the right mix of three basic abilities:

• *Endurance:* The ability to resist fatigue
• *Force:* The ability to use muscular strength
• *Speed skills:* The ability to move body parts quickly and efficiently

The mix is different for different sports. An Olympic weightlifter, for example, must generate a tremendous amount of force, needs a fair amount of speed skills, and requires very little endurance. A pole vaulter needs tremendous speed skills, a moderate amount of force, and little endurance. A marathon runner doesn't need much force, but does need a little speed skills and great endurance. Because every sport is unique, every sport requires unique methods of training.

Triathlon and duathlon put a premium on endurance, but they also require force development for hills and rough open water along with speed skills for energy conservation at race pace. This unique combination of abilities is one of the reasons that triathlon and duathlon are such difficult sports for which to train. A multisport athlete can't just put in a lot of miles to develop huge endurance and disregard force and speed skills. It takes some mix of all three abilities to excel.

The Natural Abilities Profile you completed provides a snapshot of your individual capabilities for the three elements of fitness for multisport. A score of 4 or 5 for one of the abilities indicates a strength area. If all of your scores are 4 or 5, you undoubtedly have been a good athlete in many sports. A score of 3 or less indicates a weakness, one that may partly be due to heredity and partly to lack of training. You can't change your genes, but you can change your training, if necessary. That's what you will read about in the next chapter.

MENTAL SKILLS

Mental skills are the most neglected aspect of racing for serious triathletes at all levels. I've known talented athletes who, except for their lack of confidence, were capable of winning or always placing well, but were seldom contenders. Their heads held them back.

More than likely, you scored a 4 or 5 in the area of motivation on the Mental Skills Profile. I always see this in the athletes I coach. If you didn't, then it may be time to take a long look at why you train and race triathlon.

A highly motivated and physically talented triathlete who is confident, has positive thought habits, can stay focused during a race, and has the ability to visualize success is practically unbeatable. A physically talented athlete without these mental qualities hopes to finish in the middle of the pack.

If you are weak in this area, and you can work closely with a good sports psychologist, by all means do so. The next best thing would be to read a book by a top sports psychologist. In "References and Recommended Reading" I've included some books I have found helpful in improving mental skills. Some may be difficult to find, as they are out of print; try looking for them on Web sites that carry hard-to-find books, such as alibris.com.

MEDICAL EVALUATION

Before you start back into training for a new season, it's a good idea to have your doctor give you a complete physical exam. The older you become, the more important this is. It's most likely that nothing unusual will be found. Then again, your doctor may discover something important, such as skin cancer, high blood pressure, high cholesterol, or prostate or breast cancer. Conditions such as these are much easier to treat in their early stages than they are later on. Getting an annual physical exam is just a good preventative practice, whether someone is an athlete or not, but it is even more important for you as an athlete because you will be putting more stress on your body than the average person. Of course, your doctor will probably give you a clean bill of health.

I advise every athlete to make a preseason appointment with a physical therapist. Look for one who has experience working with endurance athletes. Some insurance plans allow you to go directly to a physical therapist without a doctor's prescription. If your health insurance does not cover such a visit to a physical therapy center, be prepared to pay $100 to $200 for a one-hour screening. What you will learn is well worth the cost.

The physical therapist will do a head-to-toe exam looking for potential injury sites due to lack of strength, limited flexibility, or physical imbalances. He or she can tell you how to modify your training to improve the condition or how to adjust equipment (such as running shoe orthotics) to allow for your unique weaknesses. Look for a therapist who can also do bike fits, and can then recommend adjustments including bike-shoe cleat spacers or a bike stem length change.

Everyone has physical imperfections. Common imperfections for triathletes are leg-length discrepancies; weak muscles that allow the body to move from side to side and rotate; tight muscles and tendons; muscle imbalances; limited range of motion in the joints; poor posture; and scoliosis. These may be hereditary, caused by a fall or other trauma to the body, or simply a result of the repetitive motions of swimming, biking, and running. The physical therapist can also suggest strengthening or stretching exercises to correct these imperfections.

You may wish to make an appointment with a lab for metabolic testing as well (see details below). This type of testing can provide you with information that will be valuable in designing your training program. Once you have the general health exam, the physical therapy exam, and the metabolic testing behind you, it will be time to evaluate yourself specifically for high-level cycling performance.

LAB TESTING

At least once each year, generally in the early Base period, I send my athletes to the lab for metabolic testing, sometimes called gas analysis. Athletes usually refer to this as a "VO_2max test," but it goes well beyond discovering your VO_2max. Most think this test reveals their potential for high-level performance. It does not tell you this any more than competing in a race shows your potential for future races. But this test does quantify your current level of fitness from many different angles.

Metabolic testing assesses your current fitness level, and such tests can also provide useful information about heart rate zones, bike power zones, run pace zones, how much fat and carbohydrate you use at various intensities, and how efficient your sport-specific skills are when swimming, pedaling a bike, or running, depending on the tested sport. Lab testing also helps establish your personal rating of perceived exertion (RPE) on a given scale (for example, a scale of 1 to 10, where 1 is easy and 10 is hard) so that you can think about effort more precisely in the future. All of this information will help fine-tune your training plan.

That's a lot to be gained from one test session that takes only about an hour to complete. If you are self-coached, the technician can help you make sense of the test results and may even offer suggestions on how to use the information to train more effectively.

All of this generally costs in the range of $100 to $200. Look for a facility that specializes in athlete testing, not one that caters to those at risk for heart disease or aging populations. These tests are becoming more readily available in health clubs, physical therapy centers, and bike, run and triathlon stores. Some coaches even provide such a service.

By repeating the test at the start of each major period of the season, especially the Base 1, Build 1, and Peak periods, you can closely monitor your training progress. These tests also serve as great motivators when you don't have a race scheduled for some time.

Once you have completed a physical assessment, you're ready to determine your current fitness level with a lengthy performance assessment.

PERFORMANCE TESTING

The best indicator of race fitness is racing. If you had a race every month or so and the course and weather never changed, performance testing might be unnecessary. Such is never the case, however, so to gauge your progress you must periodically measure your fitness in race-specific ways. When done correctly, testing can tell you if your training is working and provide clues as to weaknesses that need more attention. Testing also helps to locate your lactate threshold, which, as discussed in the previous chapter, is key to regulating workout intensity.

The trick is to make the tests dependable by repeating the procedures exactly the same way each time. Small variations in such areas as warm-up, weather, equipment, and eating all affect the measured results. One way to control such variables is to regularly have your testing done by a local sports medicine clinic or in a university laboratory, but the expense makes this impractical for most athletes. Self-testing with care and a high degree of precision is a reasonable alternative.

Besides having high dependability and repeatability, the tests used must also measure elements of fitness related to multisport success. Short-duration tests are preferable, so as not to leave you tired for several days afterward. Repeating the tests in each sport every three to six weeks during non-race periods of the year will keep you apprised of progress or lack thereof.

Two types of tests are recommended. The first is called a *graded exercise test* and involves monitoring heart rate and work output as the effort gradually rises until fatigue prevents further increases in effort. Graded exercise tests can be done throughout the year but are most effective early in the season during the Preparation period of training. The other type of test is a *short time trial* done at race intensity and measured as elapsed time. Time trials are best used to measure progress in the last several weeks before racing begins.

On the following pages you will find descriptions of graded exercise tests and time trials for swimming, biking, and running. Again, bear in mind that it's critical that the many potential variables, such as equipment and warm-up, are kept as constant as possible from one testing session to the next. Equipment selection and calibration are critical in bike and run graded exercise testing. If you don't have a CompuTrainer or other calibratable indoor trainer or a reliable treadmill, you're better off conducting these tests outdoors. Just be sure you do all subsequent tests in the same setting.

SWIM GRADED EXERCISE TEST IN POOL

TEST

Preparation

- An assistant is needed to record lap times, heart rates, and ratings of perceived exertion and to control recovery intervals. You will also need a pace clock near the pool. It's best to conduct the test when the pool is not crowded and the water relatively calm. If possible, use the same pool for retests. If not possible, the other pool should be the same length, either 25 meters or 25 yards.
- Do not eat for two hours before the test. It's generally best if the previous day was light exercise or a rest day.
- Warm up for 10–20 minutes before the test. Note in your log what the warm-up procedure was.
- If at any time you feel light-headed or nauseous, stop the test immediately. You are not looking for a maximum heart rate on the test, but it's necessary to attain a very high effort level.

Test

1. The test is a series of increasingly faster 100-meter/yard repeats with 20-second recovery intervals.

2. Swim the first repeat at a very slow speed and low effort, an RPE of about 7. Your assistant records the time for the repeat and monitors the 20-second recovery interval. As soon as you finish, determine how great the exertion was using the RPE scale below, look at the pace clock, count your pulse at the throat for 10 seconds, report this number to the assistant who records it alongside the repeat time, and prepare for the next sendoff on the assistant's command. It's a good idea to do a couple of practice repeats during the warm-up to become comfortable with the procedure. A heart rate monitor will make the test more accurate and may be used if the chest

RPE SCALE	
6	
7	Very, very light
8	
9	Very light
10	
11	Fairly light
12	
13	Somewhat hard
14	
15	Hard
16	
17	Very hard
18	
19	Very, very hard
20	

strap stays snugly positioned. Place this RPE scale where it can be seen at the end of each repeat.

3 On each subsequent repeat, increase the speed and effort slightly so that your repeat times get faster by increments of about 2–3 seconds.

4. The data collected will look something like this:

Time (sec.)	Heart Rate (beats/10 sec.)	RPE
88	15	7
86	16	8
84	18	10
82	20	12
79	23	13
77	25	15
74	26	17
72	27	19

TEST

BIKE GRADED EXERCISE TEST ON COMPUTRAINER

Preparation

• An assistant is needed to record information.

• Do not eat for two hours before the test. It's generally best if the previous day was light exercise or a rest day.

• Warm up for 10–20 minutes before the test. Note in your log what the warm-up procedure was.

• If at any time you feel light-headed or nauseous, stop the test immediately. You are not looking for a maximum heart rate on the test, but it's necessary to attain a very high effort level.

• Ride on the CompuTrainer for about 10 minutes at a light to moderate effort to warm up the equipment, and then calibrate. Reinsert Nintendo stereo jack into handlebar control unit.

• Set "Program" to "Road Races/Courses" program 70.

• Indicate a course of 10 miles' length (you won't use all of it).

• Input body weight plus bike weight.

• Turn "Drafting" off.

Test

1. Throughout the test you will maintain a predetermined power level (plus or minus 5 watts) as displayed on the television screen. Start at 50 to 100 watts and

increase by 20 watts every minute until you can no longer continue. Stay seated throughout the test. Shift gears at any time.

2. At the end of each minute tell your assistant how great your exertion is using the RPE scale (place this where it can be seen).

3. Your assistant records your power output level, exertion rating, and heart rate at the end of each minute and instructs you to increase power to the next level.

4. The assistant also listens closely to your breathing to detect when it first becomes labored. This point is marked as "VT" for ventilatory threshold.

5. Continue until you can no longer hold the power level for at least 15 seconds.

6. The data collected should look something like this:

RPE SCALE	
6	
7	Very, very light
8	
9	Very light
10	
11	Fairly light
12	
13	Somewhat hard
14	
15	Hard
16	
17	Very hard
18	
19	Very, very hard
20	

Power (watts)	Heart Rate (bpm)	RPE
100	110	9
120	118	11
140	125	12
160	135	13
180	142	14
200	147	15
220	153	17 VT
240	156	19
260	159	20

BIKE GRADED EXERCISE TEST ON ROAD

TEST

Preparation

- In a large parking lot or undeveloped housing area with finished streets that allow a circular course of about a half mile, locate landmarks such as light poles or place cones to indicate the course. Do not attempt this test if there is traffic or if parked cars block any portion of the course. It may be best to conduct this test early in the morning. Try to use the same course and bike for retests.

- An assistant with a stopwatch is needed to record lap splits and heart rates.

- Do not eat for two hours before the test. It's generally best if the previous day was light exercise or a rest day.

- Warm up for 10–20 minutes before the test. Note in your log what the warm-up procedure was.
- If at any time you feel light-headed or nauseous, stop the test immediately. You are not looking for a maximum heart rate on the test, but it's necessary to attain a very high effort level.

Test

1. Start the test at a very slow speed—13 to 15 mph. Every lap, increase speed by about 1 mph until you are eventually forced to stop because you can't go any faster. This may take 8 to 12 laps of the course.
2. Once the test starts, your assistant will record your time and your heart rate for each lap.
3. A few yards before passing by your assistant, call out your heart rate. The assistant will record this, along with your last lap split time in seconds. The data collected will look something like this:

Time (sec.)	Heart Rate (bpm)
120	117
110	123
104	128
99	124
92	139
88	144
82	149
76	152
71	155

TEST

RUN GRADED EXERCISE TEST ON TREADMILL

Preparation

- Use a treadmill that accurately displays speed and has a top speed exceeding your best 1-mile time or has variable incline. If the treadmill's top speed does not exceed your ability, set it at a sufficient grade to make the fastest speed quite difficult. Note this grade in your log.
- An assistant is needed to record information and operate the treadmill. He/she stands where he/she can easily reach the controls on the treadmill.
- Do not eat for two hours before the test. It's generally best if the previous day was light exercise or a rest day.
- Warm up for 10–20 minutes before the test. Note in your log what the warm-up procedure was.

- If at any time you feel light-headed or nauseous, stop the test immediately. You are not looking for a maximum heart rate on the test, but it's necessary to attain a very high effort level.

Test

1. Start at a slow speed such as 6 mph and increase by 0.2 mph every minute until you can no longer continue.
2. At the end of each minute tell your assistant how great your exertion is using the RPE scale (place this where it can be seen).
3. Your assistant records your speed, exertion rating, and heart rate at the end of each minute and increases the treadmill's speed to the next level (+0.2 mph).
4. The assistant listens closely to your breathing to detect when it first becomes labored, marking this point as "VT" for ventilatory threshold.
5. Continue until you can no longer hold the speed, and then slow the treadmill gradually until you are at a walking pace.
6. The data collected should look something like this:

RPE SCALE	
6	
7	Very, very light
8	
9	Very light
10	
11	Fairly light
12	
13	Somewhat hard
14	
15	Hard
16	
17	Very hard
18	
19	Very, very hard
20	

Speed (mph)	Heart Rate (bpm)	RPE
8.2	147	12
8.4	154	13
8.6	161	13
8.8	166	14
9.0	172	15
9.2	179	17 VT
9.4	182	19
9.6	185	20

RUN GRADED EXERCISE TEST ON TRACK

TEST

Preparation

- On a 400-meter or a 440-yard running track, locate both a starting mark and a half-lap mark.
- An assistant with a stopwatch is needed to record splits and heart rates.

- Do not eat for two hours before the test. It's generally best if the previous day was light exercise or a rest day.
- Warm up for 10–20 minutes before the test. Note in your log what the warm-up procedure was.
- If at any time you feel light-headed or nauseous, stop the test immediately. You are not looking for a maximum heart rate on the test, but it's necessary to attain a very high effort level.

Test

1. Start the test at a very slow speed—70 to 80 seconds for a half lap. Every half lap, slightly increase running speed until you are eventually forced to stop because you can't go any faster. This may take 6 to 10 full laps of the track.
2. Once the test starts, your assistant jogs back and forth across the track, meeting you at exactly the halfway point for each lap.
3 Two or three steps before passing by your assistant, call out your heart rate. The assistant will note this, call out your last half-lap split time in seconds, and record both numbers. Then pick up the pace slightly so that you run the next half lap about 3 to 5 seconds faster than the previous one. The data collected will look something like this:

Time (sec.)	Heart Rate (bpm)
78	127
75	132
70	137
66	143
61	149
57	153
52	159 VT
48	162

4. Both you and your assistant should pay close attention to your breathing. When it becomes labored for the first time (a lot of air being moved), the assistant should note the heart rate at that point on the data sheet. This is your "ventilatory threshold" (VT).

TEST

SWIM TIME TRIAL IN POOL

Preparation

- This test is conducted in a 25-yard or 25-meter pool. The only equipment needed is a stopwatch and possibly a heart rate monitor ("suspenders" may be necessary to keep the chest strap in place while swimming).

- Do not eat for two hours before the test. It's generally best if the previous day was light exercise or a rest day.
- Warm up for 10–20 minutes as if preparing for a race. Note in your log what the warm-up procedure was.
- If at any time you feel light-headed or nauseous, stop the test immediately. You are not looking for a maximum heart rate on the test, but rather the fastest time you can now swim.

Test

1. Immediately following the warm-up, swim 1,000 meters or yards at race effort. Start your stopwatch at the beginning of the time trial and stop it as you finish.
2. On finishing, count your pulse for 10 seconds. If you are using a heart rate monitor, this is not necessary.
3. Cool down or continue with the planned workout.
4. Determine your average 100 time by dividing your finish time by 10 and converting the time to minutes and seconds (17 minutes ÷ 10 = 1.7 = 1 minute, 42 seconds). Record the finish time, average 100 time, and heart rate in your training log for future reference.

BIKE TIME TRIAL ON ROAD

TEST

Preparation

- Find a flat, 5 km stretch of road that has no turns or stop signals and little traffic. Mark or note landmarks at the ends of this stretch of road. If 5 km is not convenient, any distance in the range of 2.5 to 4 miles may be used if the course remains constant from one test to the next.
- Wear a heart rate monitor and stopwatch.
- Do not eat for two hours before the test. It's generally best if the previous day was light exercise or a rest day.
- Warm up for 10 to 20 minutes as if preparing for a race. Note in your log what the warm-up procedure was.
- If at any time you feel light-headed or nauseous, stop the test immediately. You are not looking for a maximum heart rate on the test, but rather the fastest time you can now ride for 10 km.

Test

1. Immediately following the warm-up, ride 10 km at race effort. Ride 5 km out, turn around, and return to the starting point. Start your stopwatch at the beginning of the time trial and stop it as you finish.

2. On finishing, note your heart rate. If your heart rate monitor has an average function, note what it was later.

3. Cool down or continue with the planned workout.

4. Record the time, average, and highest heart rate observed in your training log for future reference.

As your fitness approaches your potential, changes in your results from one test to the next will become minimal, perhaps as little as 1 percent or less. At such times, your fitness may even appear to slide backward; this is usually due to the small variables that slip past you and affect the results. Even with the best testing, you must still listen to your body and assess your progress subjectively. Fitness testing is not perfect.

If you are new to racing, or have coronary risk factors such as a family history of heart disease, a high total-cholesterol-to-HDL ratio, high blood pressure, a heart murmur, or frequent dizziness or chest discomfort after exercise, you should only conduct such a test in a laboratory or clinic under the close supervision of a doctor.

CRITICAL POWER TESTS

If you have a power meter, establishing power-based training zones will allow you to make better use of the unit in training while also providing you with valuable comparison points for fitness throughout the season. If you also establish and periodically update a personal critical power profile as shown in Figure 5.1, you will also have a visual representation of how your performance is changing over time.

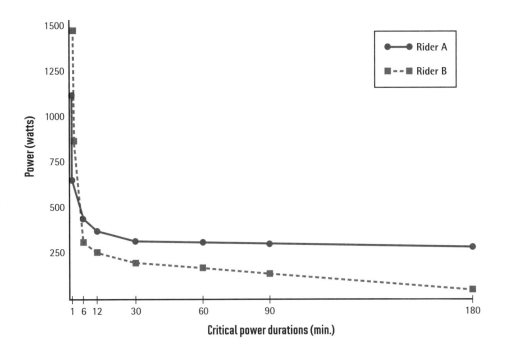

FIGURE 5.1

Critical Profiles of
Two Riders

As a multisport athlete, you will need to complete four time trials to establish a critical power profile, one each of 1, 6, 12, and 30 minutes. Each test is a maximum effort for the entire duration. It's best to spread these out over several days. Once your profile is established, you may want to update only certain critical power points along the curve in subsequent tests without completing the entire battery.

There is a learning curve associated with this testing. It's common to start out too fast on each of them and then fade near the end. It may take two or three attempts over a few days or even a few weeks to get the pacing right. To reduce the need for such continued testing, it's best to start each time trial test at a lower power output than you think is appropriate. This will pay off with fewer test failures. Begin such testing in the early Base period with at least one other battery of follow-up tests completed before beginning the Build period. (These periods are explained in Chapter 8.)

The longer durations of 60, 90, and 180 minutes may be estimated from the profile graph by extending the slope of the CP12 to CP30 line (see Figure 5.1). You may also get an estimation of the values for these extended data points with the use of a little math. To estimate 60-minute power, subtract 5 percent from your 30-minute average power result (see Table 5.1). For an approximation of 90-minute power, subtract 2.5 percent from the 60-minute power. Subtracting 5 percent from the 90-minute power figure estimates 180-minute power.

ZONE 1	ZONE 2	ZONE 3	ZONE 4	ZONE 5	ZONE 6	ZONE 7
Recovery	Aerobic	Tempo	Threshold	Aerobic capacity	Anaerobic capacity	Power
<56%	56–75%	76–90%	91–105%	106–120%	121–150%	>150%

TABLE 5.1

Power Zones Based on Percentages of CP60

Keep in mind that power points beyond 30 minutes are only estimates and may well be inaccurate. That's acceptable, because training with power is normally only recommended for shorter durations, as when doing intervals, hill repeats, sprints, or tempo efforts. Long, steady rides are best done using heart rate or perceived exertion to regulate intensity.

Once all of these power data points are established, you are ready to determine your critical power training zones as shown in Table 5.2.

TABLE 5.2

Critical Power
Zone Benefits and
Race Applications

DURATION	CP ZONES	FITNESS BENEFIT	RACE APPLICATION
12 sec.	CP0.2	Explosive power	Finishing sprint
			Short hill
			Start
1 min.	CP1	Lactate clearance	Fast starts
			Short climbs
6 min.	CP6	Velocity at VO$_2$max	Moderate-duration climbs
			Short, high-intensity segments
12 min.	CP12	Aerobic capacity (VO$_2$max)	Deeply anaerobic
30 min.	CP30	Lactate superthreshold	Long, steady efforts
60 min.	CP60	Lactate threshold	Short-duration race endurance
90 min.	CP90	Sublactate threshold	Moderate-duration race endurance
180 min.	CP180	Basic aerobic function	Long-duration race endurance

UNDERSTANDING TEST RESULTS

Regular testing is effective for measuring fitness changes, especially during the preparatory periods of training that precede important races. Each test provides unique indicators of progress. Time trials resemble the stresses of racing and are most effective in the last few weeks before racing, while graded exercise tests offer valuable insights earlier in the season. Of the two types of graded exercise tests for biking and running, those done on a CompuTrainer or on the treadmill are generally more comprehensive, since ratings of perceived exertion are possible and work output is more controllable than in tests conducted on the road or track. As previously mentioned, however, test repeatability is important, making calibration of equipment critical. If you are not confident of the future availability and accuracy of the equipment available to you, road and track tests are probably the better options.

Graded exercise tests and time trials provide information on three aspects of fitness: lactate threshold (LT), endurance, and velocity. Testing also provides insights into your potential for race performance by shedding light on such factors as your ability to control pace and cope with physical stress. In that sense, they can help to determine your readiness to race.

LACTATE THRESHOLD MEASUREMENT

Graded exercise tests are effective for estimating lactate threshold heart rate (LTHR) (bike and run), lactate threshold power (bike), and lactate threshold pace (swim). For the novice multisport athlete, or those who have been away from serious training for some time, improvement is evident in gradually rising heart rates at LT over the course of several weeks of spaced testing. For the experienced and fit athlete, advancing fitness is noted not in a higher heart rate at LT, but rather in faster pace, greater velocity, and greater power output at lactate threshold. Understand that LT is different for each sport and unique to the individual.

The first step in assessment, once testing is complete, is to estimate LTHR, power, and pace. This is done by observing the three related indicators of LT: RPE, ventilatory threshold (VT), and time above LT.

For the fit and experienced athlete, LT typically arrives when RPE is in the range of 15 to 17. You can get a rough indication of your LT by quickly noting the heart rates, power output, and paces that are within this range of exertion ratings. You can further refine your estimate of LT by noting your assistant's estimation of VT, or the point at which your breathing becomes labored. If this falls in the range of 15 to 17 RPE, it's probably close to your LT. In addition, an athlete will typically not be able to continue for more than 5 minutes once LT has occurred, so your LT is likely within the last five datapoints collected in the graded exercise test. On the CompuTrainer, with power used as an output measure, you can also estimate LT by multiplying the highest power achieved on the test by 0.85.

By comparing all of these indicators, you should now have an estimate of your LT for each sport. You can confirm these estimates by observing other indicators during workouts. The onset of an anaerobic state is marked by heavy breathing, for example, and the build-up of lactic acid is often marked by a burning sensation in the working muscles. Of course, the results of subsequent retests will also allow you to confirm or modify your LT estimate.

AEROBIC AND ANAEROBIC ENDURANCE MEASUREMENT

Graded exercise tests are valuable only as comparative tools. In other words, they show how you're doing in relation to your previous tests. The first time you complete this battery of tests, you establish standards, or baselines, against which to compare subsequent tests in order to determine your fitness progress. Greater endurance, both aerobic and anaerobic, results from producing greater outputs, such as velocity, with the same effort. This indicates that you are becoming more economical as a swimmer, cyclist, or runner, as less oxygen and fuel must be used to produce movement. Sparing fuel means better endurance.

Graphing allows you to easily compare the data from graded exercise tests. Using grid paper, create XY graphs for each test. Then, each time you are tested during the season, put the results on the appropriate graph. It is evident that your fitness has improved when the slope of retests moves to the right and more datapoints are collected at the upper end of a test. Now we'll learn how to analyze test results for different disciplines.

Swim Graded Exercise Test in Pool. Put swim repeat times on the horizontal axis, and pulse counts, multiplied by 6 to convert to beats per minute, on the vertical axis. Place

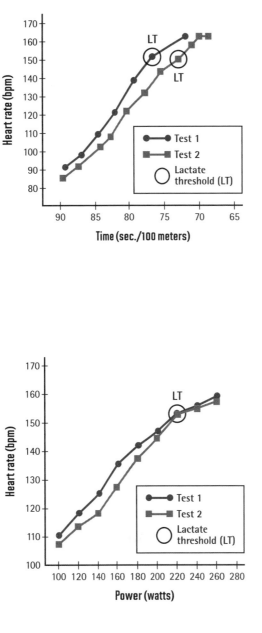

FIGURE 5.2

Two Swim Graded
Exercise Tests

FIGURE 5.3

Two Bike Graded
Exercise Tests on
CompuTrainer

the datapoints on these coordinates to create the graph. Figure 5.2 shows the results of two swim tests. Test 1 was done at the start of an eight-week training period; Test 2 shows progress at the end of that period. Notice that on Test 2, the slope of the line has moved to the right, indicating faster times at nearly the same heart rates, and therefore greater potential for endurance. Also note that LT remained constant at about 150 bpm, but that on Test 2 there are three datapoints beyond LT, instead of only two as on Test 1. This means that the individual has also improved anaerobic endurance.

Bike Graded Exercise Test on CompuTrainer. Graphing the results of a bike test done on the CompuTrainer compares heart rate (vertical axis) to power (horizontal axis). Figure 5.3 illustrates a situation that often occurs during the base-building period of the season, a time when the emphasis is on endurance and little training is devoted to anaerobic endurance. Notice how the lines are separated below LT, but converge above it.

Aerobic fitness improved as anaerobic fitness remained constant. As this athlete progresses to the intensity-building period of training, anaerobic endurance should improve, as noted by the test graphs separating at the upper end, and if aerobic endurance is maintained, the lines below LT should remain separated.

Run Graded Exercise Test on Treadmill. Figure 5.4 shows some of the unusual test results you may encounter in your training. Following a four-week training period, the test results indicate that this athlete has not improved aerobically. That result may in fact be accurate, but if the athlete feels as if his or her fitness has improved, and indeed, his or her running workouts seem to confirm this perception, the problem may be a treadmill that is not properly calibrated. That's common if you use health club treadmills that get many hours of use each day. Without reliable equipment, testing is best done on the roads or track. Such test results could also mean there have been unusual occurrences in your life in the hours or days before the test, such as poor sleep, a changed diet, or additional stresses.

Notice also that the final heart rate achieved is not as high on Test 2 as on Test 1, although an additional minute was run at the upper end. This kind of result sometimes leads athletes to mistakenly believe that they are in worse condition than they were in a previous test. The inability to achieve a near-maximum heart rate is fairly common, however, once an athlete has achieved a high level of fitness late in the season. Don't worry about it; any time you can swim, bike, or run faster than before at a lower heart rate, your fitness has improved.

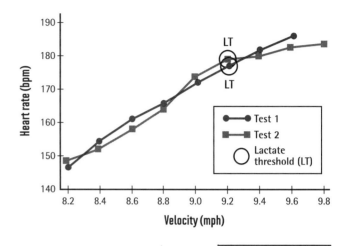

Two Run Graded Exercise Tests on Treadmill

CRITICAL POWER TESTS

The data gathered for the critical power tests should be graphed to produce a Power Profile as shown in Figure 5.5. The longer critical power durations may be estimated by extending the slope of the line for CP12 to CP30. This method provides rough estimations that may be a bit low or high, depending on your aerobic/anaerobic fitness balance. For example, in the early winter months, your aerobic fitness is probably relatively better than

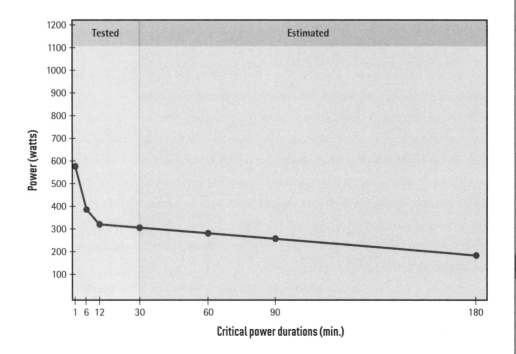

Power Profile for Hypothetical Rider

your anaerobic fitness. As a result, your CP12 may be lower than what would be found in the summer months, thus causing the extended slope of the line to be high on the right end. Follow-up tests done over the ensuing winter and spring months will help to correct this overestimation.

What should your Power Profile look like? That depends somewhat on the courses you race on. A short-duration race contested on a course with short, steep hills favors a rider with high CP1 and CP6 power, whereas a longer race with rolling hills and long, steady climbs favors those with high CP12 and CP30 power. In theory, those power zones that are trained in most frequently will tend to improve the most. So comparing your Power Profile with the course and race requirements of your most important races of the season can provide you with guidance for determining exactly how to train. And analyzing your Power Profile can also help guide you in choosing which races will play to your strengths. Chapter 4 provides greater detail on this issue.

MEASURING VELOCITY

In the final analysis, faster swim, bike, and run velocities are why we train. Short of racing, the best way to determine progress in this all-important area is with time trials. Race velocity is the primary focus of the intensity-building period of training in the last few weeks before important races. Time trials are used at the start of the Peak period and again every three to six weeks during the period. Once a period of frequent racing begins, testing is no longer necessary, as the races themselves provide important clues about fitness.

Don't expect great increases in velocity during the Peak period of training, especially if you are a seasoned triathlete or duathlete. A 5 percent improvement from one test to the next is considerable. Half or even less of that is a more reasonable expectation in a few weeks' time.

Your time trial results can be used as a gauge of what to expect in a race. Here's how to make a rough estimate for sprint- and Olympic-distance races. We know that as the distance doubles, pace slows about 5 percent. For example, if your 1.5-mile run time trial was done in 10 minutes (6:40 pace per mile), you could expect to run a 5 km (3.1 miles) at about a 7-minute pace (6:40 x 0.05 = 0:20; 6:40 + 0:20 = 7:00), or in a time of about 21:40. But, of course, during a triathlon, you'll have to run slower than you would in a running race, so expect to slow down approximately another 5 percent (7:20 pace, or about 22:45). As the distance doubles, expect your velocity in the race to diminish by about 10 percent. This system of prognosticating has limited value, especially as the distance increases by more than a factor of two, but it provides a rough estimate of what you might expect if you haven't raced for some time.

A better use of time trials is as a periodic indicator of progress in your ability to maintain a fast pace. Comparing past records of time trials at various points in the season from one year to the next is a good gauge of long-term improvement.

ASSESSMENT

Testing is of no value unless the information gained is used to improve your training or confirm that you are training in an appropriate manner. For example, you may learn from the graded exercise tests that you are steadily improving in swimming and running, but not in cycling. This should cause you to rethink what you're doing on the bike. Perhaps you need to ride more to improve the aerobic end of the graph, or start doing high-intensity training to boost the anaerobic side. In the same way, the time trials may indicate the need for a bigger change, such as incorporating more race-specific training into your program.

Periodic assessment of race performance and fitness is a valuable tool for multisport athletes and can help you learn how to train for steady improvement. But when you start doing these assessments, you will discover areas of weakness. The next chapter takes a closer look at how to go about correcting whatever is holding you back from better racing.

BUILDING FITNESS

*I train as a means to an objective, and that
objective is to race faster the next time than
I did the last time.*
—KAREN SMYERS, PROFESSIONAL TRIATHLETE

HAVE YOU EVER OBSERVED a house under construction for several weeks? If so, you know there's a well-defined order in which the many tasks of building are completed. First, the foundation is constructed of a durable material such as concrete. Great care is taken at this stage to ensure that the foundation is level, square, and stable. A haphazardly built foundation means the finished house will be of poor quality. Next, the wall and roof framing are put up. This goes quickly, and as it's done, the house begins to take shape. With just a little imagination, you can even picture what it will look like when done. Finally, after the plumbing and electrical systems are installed, walls are enclosed and the finish work begins. Windows, doors, cabinets, and floor covers appear, and a multitude of progressively smaller tasks are completed. Eventually, all the work is done, and if each stage of the construction was performed carefully, the house will provide shelter and a home for many years to come, with only minor maintenance necessary along the way.

It's remarkable how similar the paradigm of house building is to multisport fitness building. In triathlon and duathlon, training begins by first establishing a foundation of the most basic physical abilities, and then progresses to carefully constructing smaller, more refined aspects of fitness that match the "blueprint" requirements of racing. Building a solid base foundation takes years, but if it's done correctly, such fitness is easy to maintain. Too often, novice athletes want to speed up or even skip the foundation-building phase of training. Even experienced athletes are tempted to do this in order to get on with the intense training that produces final race shape. But just as with a poor house foundation, slighting the base-development period means a low-quality finished product. The stronger the base, the more solid and long-lasting the final fitness is.

On the other hand, developing only the foundation without ever doing the "finish work" means that one's race potential is never realized. A season of training must include all of the phases of construction at just the right times to bring a high level of race fitness when it's needed.

In the previous chapter you began developing the blueprints for a better race season by learning more about yourself. This chapter further develops the blueprint by helping determine exactly what is holding you back from better racing and discusses the tasks you need to accomplish in order to build multisport fitness. In Part Four, we'll finalize the blueprints as I show you how to organize your training so the tasks are completed in an order and to a magnitude that produces peak race fitness.

LIMITERS

In Chapter 5 you identified your strengths and weaknesses using the Natural Abilities Profile. At the bottom of the profile page you came up with a score for some of the factors related to multisport success. You also ranked your swimming, biking, and running proficiencies. A score of 3 or lower on any of these items indicates a weakness, while those scored as a 4 or 5 may be interpreted as strengths.

Let's examine just your weaknesses for a moment, as these are holding you back. Or are they? What if you gave yourself a score of 1 on swimming, but you race only in duathlons. Although swimming may indeed be a weakness for you, it is not limiting your race success in this case. That's an extreme example. But what if your endurance score was 3, and you concentrate on sprint-distance races? This would mean that endurance is not such a big deal for you; it is still a weakness, but it is not limiting your race performance. It's not a concern, unless, of course, you decide to train for a longer race. So some weaknesses hold you back, while others do not. If your endurance score was a 3 and you are struggling to finish half-Ironman and longer races, your weakness in endurance is definitely limiting your achievements. A force weakness is not a limiter unless you compete in hilly, windy, or rough-water events.

It's important to know which weaknesses are holding you back for the types of races you do. These race-specific weaknesses are your "limiters." You can work through plenty of examples of this principle as it pertains to your goals. This chapter focuses on the principle of improving your limiters in swimming, biking, and running in order to improve your race performance. Later chapters will address mental skills and other miscellaneous factors that may limit performance.

TRAINING BASIC ABILITIES

Before looking more closely at the concept of limiters, however, let's get a better understanding of the abilities required for successful multisport racing: endurance, force, and speed skills. These are the three basic abilities that will form the foundation of your training. Having a good grasp of what they are all about is important to both understanding your limiters and designing your training program.

You have probably noticed that some athletes seem to excel in long races, but are less competitive in short races, whereas others have just the opposite situation, excelling in sprints but becoming fatigued in longer events. Then there are riders who thrive in the hills, leading your training group every time the terrain goes vertical but struggling while riding into the wind on flat ground, and others who thrive on flat sections of the course but lag behind on the hills. What you're observing here are individual mixes of the three basic abilities of endurance, force, and speed skills resulting from a unique combination of genetics and training.

These basic abilities are crucial to optimal multisport performance. The experienced athlete must work on developing endurance, force, and speed skills at the beginning of every training season before progressing to the more advanced aspects of race fitness. In the first two or three years of a novice athlete's career, training must primarily consist of establishing these abilities and little else. Resist the temptation to take on high-effort workouts, such as fast-paced intervals, before your basic abilities are well established.

Think of fitness as represented by a triangle. The three basic abilities form the corners of the triangle (Figure 6.1). All are necessary to provide a solid foundation for racing. To design your training program, you need to understand how each ability fits into a broader picture and identify how you measure up in each area.

The various abilities related to multisport fitness are developed at different times of the year following a periodization plan, as described in Chapter 3. Figure 6.2 summarizes those periods in visual form, using the terms found in the following discussions about training.

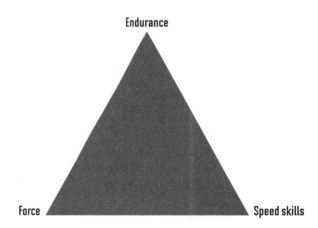

FIGURE 6.1

Basic Abilities Triangle for Triathlon Fitness

ENDURANCE

Endurance is the ability to delay the onset of fatigue and reduce its effects. Within the context of this book, when used by itself, endurance implies an aerobic level of exertion (heart rate zones 1–4). Endurance training develops slow-twitch muscle fibers. These are the ones that contract slowly but recover quickly. Working on endurance also improves

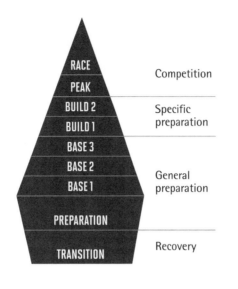

your ability to conserve the carbohydrate-based fuels glycogen and glucose while teaching your muscles to preferentially use fat for energy.

Endurance is specific to the event. On one hand, it's unlikely that you could complete an Ironman-distance race on sprint-distance training. On the other, the capacity to ride steadily for six hours is overkill for competing in short events.

For the novice multisport athlete, endurance is the key to improvement. Emphasize this ability above all others in the first year or two of training. The experienced athlete must rebuild and then maintain this vital ability each season. A high level of endurance takes years to mature.

As with the other abilities, endurance is best achieved by starting with general endurance training and then progressing to more race-specific workouts. This means that to build endurance, you will start by developing a sound cardiorespiratory system (heart, blood vessels, lungs, and blood) by engaging in a broad range of activities, crosstraining in such modes as cross-country skiing, rowing, and aerobics classes in addition to continuing your swimming, biking, and running. In the Prep and Base 1 periods, such workouts are done at low intensity, mostly in heart rate zones 1 to 3. Later, in the Base 2

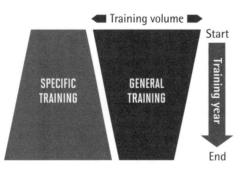

and 3 and Build periods, training becomes more specific as crosstraining is reduced or eliminated and workouts gradually begin simulating races, at first in terms of duration, and later in terms of intensity. Figure 6.3 illustrates this progression of general-to-specific training.

Endurance is improved not only by long swim, bike, and run workouts but also by consistent, chronic exposure to the activity. In other words, the weekly volume of training plays a role in the development of endurance, although not as great a role as individual workout duration. Great care is needed when increasing duration and volume, since the body is not capable of rapid change when it comes to endurance adaptations. Plan on taking months and even years, rather than days or weeks, to fully develop endurance.

FORCE

Force is the ability to overcome resistance. In multisport, force production relates to how well you do in rough water, on hills, and into the wind. It also plays a role in muscular economy. When slow-twitch muscles are strengthened, faster paces are produced at aerobic efforts, thus sparing carbohydrate-based glycogen and glucose.

Like the development of endurance, force development progresses from the general to the specific throughout the training year. It begins in the Prep and Base periods of the early season with weight training or other forms of general resistance work such as with stretch cords, body-weight exercises, and special equipment like the Vasa Trainer. By the end of Base 1, general body-strength development should be maximal, allowing you to begin more triathlon- and duathlon-specific force training in the pool and on the road. At this point, many young athletes stop lifting weights, since they are capable of easily maintaining strength with sport-specific training. Older athletes and many women, however, should continue general strength work throughout most of the remainder of the season, although at a reduced level, since they seem less capable of retaining their strength gains. Chapter 13 provides greater detail on general strength training in the weight room.

SPEED SKILLS

Speed skills are the ability to move effectively while swimming, biking, or running. They are a combination of technique and efficiency, and they determine how effective the arms and legs are when moving quickly. For example, in swimming this means having a hydrodynamic position in the water. In cycling and running, leg turnover rate is critical. Some portions of this ability may be genetic; in other words, you may have been born with certain muscle types, tendon attachment points, and limb lengths that favor effective movement in one or more of the sports. It's possible, however, to considerably improve speed skills.

Improving Technique

Technique is a nervous system function. It has nothing to do with how great your aerobic capacity and LT are. Breathing hard does not improve the functioning of the nervous system. Nor does fatigue. When it comes to improving technique, you must avoid both of these common side-effects of endurance training because they will prevent you from improving your biomechanics.

Maximizing Economy

Economy essentially refers to how much effort you're using when swimming, biking, or running at a given pace. By improving your economy and becoming more efficient, you can go faster with the same effort.

To run faster all you have to do is increase your leg turnover or lengthen your stride. In fact, running speed may be expressed as a formula using only these two variables:

$$\text{Run speed} = \text{stride rate} \times \text{stride length}$$

The same may be said for riding a bike fast, but now we use gear size instead of stride length:

$$\text{Bike speed} = \text{stroke rate} \times \text{gear size}$$

So to ride a bike fast, you can either turn the pedals around at a high rate, use a high gear, or do a little of both.

And it's no different for swimming:

$$\text{Swim speed} = \text{stroke rate} \times \text{stroke length}$$

That's all there is to it.

Well, actually, in the real world of triathlon there's more to it than just that. There are these other things that make up fitness called aerobic capacity (VO_2max), lactate threshold (LT), and economy. These markers of fitness make it possible to keep the cadence high, the stride or stroke long, and the gear high for a long time. Of these the most highly trainable for the fit athlete is economy.

Economy essentially refers to how much effort you're using when swimming, biking, or running at a given pace. By improving your economy you can go faster at the same effort. In this chapter I call this "speed skills"—one of the basic abilities of the training triad. In Chapter 12 we'll explore this ability in much greater detail.

Economy is largely determined by biomechanics—how efficiently you move the various body parts while swimming, biking, and running. This is a nervous system function. It does not have anything to do with how great your aerobic capacity and LT are. Since economy has nothing to do with these aerobic and anaerobic functions, it requires a different way of thinking when it comes to training. Breathing hard does not improve the functioning of the nervous system. Nor does fatigue. When it comes to improving speed skills you must avoid both of these common side effects of endurance training as they will prevent you from improving your biomechanics.

Improving biomechanics requires concentrating on making a few precise movement patterns and then taking a relatively long rest break before trying it again. After repeating this pattern several times, it's best to call it a day before fatigue sets in and you get sloppy. If you've ever tried to learn a skill-oriented sport—such as golf, tennis, or fly-fishing—you know what I mean. Once technique begins to break down you are no longer refining the skill—you're simply ingraining bad habits.

The downside of changing your biomechanics is that initially you will get slower or feel like you are working harder. This may last several weeks but will gradually turn around. When it does you will go faster at the same effort. Hang in there until then.

By regularly incorporating drills into swim, bike, and run workouts you can teach your muscles exactly when to contract and when to relax. This is true for both large and small muscles. When the muscles involved in forward movement are activated with precise harmony, economy improves and precious carbohydrate-based fuel is conserved. One study using Swedish runners found that economy continued to improve for 22 months after VO_2max had plateaued.

Are you already so economical that further work is unnecessary? That's doubtful. In the early 1980s, the American running legend Steve Scott improved his economy by a whopping 6 percent just before setting a world record for the mile. If an elite runner who already has excellent economy can improve by so much, imagine what the rest of us could do. A mere 1 percent enhancement in running economy could shave in the neighborhood of 20 to 30 seconds off of your 10 km time. Consider what a 6 or even a 10 percent improvement could mean for you. Several scientific studies have demonstrated that general technique and arm or leg turnover are trainable given the right types of workouts and consistency of purpose in training. However, it takes a long-term dedication to improving economy to realize the benefits. A brief experiment of only a few workouts just won't do it.

Speed-skills training begins in the Prep period and is maintained throughout the remainder of the season. Chapter 8 provides several workouts for improving speed skills, and Chapter 12 describes how to improve swimming, cycling, and running skills that ultimately lead to greater speed skills.

TRAINING ADVANCED ABILITIES

The basic abilities of endurance, force, and speed skills at the corners of the fitness triangle diagrammed in Figure 6.1 are only the foundation for our construction project. The sides of the triangle represent the wall and roof framing. In the parlance of endurance training, the framing is constructed of muscular endurance, anaerobic endurance, and power. These are the advanced abilities the athlete emphasizes in the later periods of

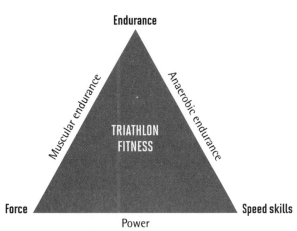

Endurance

Muscular endurance

Anaerobic endurance

TRIATHLON
FITNESS

Force

Power

Speed skills

FIGURE 6.4

Advanced
Racing Abilities
Triangle

training with only twelve weeks or so remaining until the most important races. Figure 6.4 shows how these abilities are situated in relation to the foundational abilities. Each advanced ability results from the development of the basic abilities on either end of it, but is further refined with training specific to that ability.

MUSCULAR ENDURANCE

Muscular endurance is the ability of the muscles to maintain a relatively high force load for a prolonged time period. It is a combination of force and endurance abilities. A high level of muscular endurance results from adaptation of the mechanical properties of the muscles to resist fatigue, an elevated LT, and tolerance of lactate that slowly accumulates at such intensities. Muscular endurance is a critical ability for the multisport athlete. Toward the end of each leg of a triathlon, an athlete with this ability is able to maintain a high pace. Muscular endurance for running is especially important because the run usually comes last in triathlon races and fatigue is cumulative throughout these events.

Muscular endurance work should begin in the Base 2 period with sustained efforts of several minutes in heart rate zone 3. Training gradually progresses by Base 3 to include mostly aerobic interval workouts in heart rate zones 4 and 5a. The work intervals lengthen but the recovery intervals remain quite short, about a third or fourth of the work-interval duration. By the Build periods, steady-state, nonstop efforts of 20 to 40 minutes in heart rate zones 4 and 5a are common. The effort of these workouts is much like "controlled" time trialing and is tremendously effective in boosting both aerobic and anaerobic fitness with little risk of overtraining. Throughout the Race period, muscular endurance is maintained.

ANAEROBIC ENDURANCE

As a blending of speed skills and endurance, anaerobic endurance is the ability to resist fatigue at very high efforts when arm or leg turnover is rapid. An athlete with excellent anaerobic endurance has good tolerance for lactate and performs well in short-distance events and head-to-head competitions with frequent speed surges. For the athlete who specializes in long-distance triathlons, such as half-Ironman events or longer, anaerobic endurance is of less importance.

There are two types of anaerobic endurance workouts. One is based on aerobic capacity–developing intervals done in heart rate zone 5b. At the start of the Build period of training, the experienced athlete training for shorter-distance events should phase into interval training to increase aerobic capacity. The intervals are 2 to 6 minutes long with recoveries, at first, approximately equal to the work interval for running and cycling, and somewhat shorter than the work interval for swimming. As the season progresses and fitness improves, the work-interval length is gradually decreased.

Shorter repetitions of 30 seconds to 2 minutes in duration at heart rate zone 5c in intensity are effective for developing the capacity to manage extremely high levels of lactate. Recovery intervals are two to three times the length of the work interval for lactate tolerance repetitions, with swimming having the shortest recoveries and running the longest. The idea is to produce a maximal effort that creates large amounts of lactic acid, recover, and then repeat the process several times. The early onset of fatigue from overly short recoveries will inhibit maximum effort and reduce lactic-acid production. For the fastest sprint-distance-race specialists, lactate-tolerance work in the Build 2 and Peak periods trains the body to remove lactate from the blood and reduce its fatiguing effects.

Anaerobic endurance training is quite stressful and should not be a part of the novice's regimen. In fact, there are very few multisport athletes who need this training at all. Those most likely to find it of benefit are the fastest sprint-distance racers, who may also be doing draft-legal events. Develop both speed skills and endurance with at least two years of training before regularly attempting these workouts. The likely result of too much anaerobic endurance work, too soon, is burnout and overtraining.

POWER

Power is the ability to apply maximum force quickly. It results from having high levels of the basic abilities of force and speed skills. Well-developed power, or a lack of it, is obvious on short, steep hills, in fast swim starts, and in sudden pace changes, such as when an athlete initiates a finishing sprint. For most multisport athletes this is seldom a limiter.

Since it includes both speed skills and force components, power depends on the nervous system to send strong signals, and on the muscles to contract maximally. For this reason, improvements in power come from short, all-out efforts followed by very long recovery intervals. These repetitions are quite brief—perhaps 8 to 12 seconds. Heart rate monitors are of no use in power training; use RPE, pace, or, on the bike, a power meter to gauge your progress.

Attempting to improve power when you are tired is counterproductive. Such training is therefore best done when you are rested, and early in a training session when your nervous system and muscles are most responsive.

Table 6.1 summarizes training approaches for the triathlon abilities.

LIMITERS AND RACING

Let's return to the discussion of limiters, previously defined as race-specific weaknesses. By now you should have a good idea of what your physical-ability limiters are. The basic abilities of endurance, force, and speed skills can usually be easily identified. The advanced

TABLE 6.1

Summary of
Triathlon Abilities

ABILITY	PERIOD*	FREQUENCY PER SPORT*	INTERVALS DURATION**	WORK	RECOVERY***	INTENSITY ZONES	BENEFIT	EXAMPLE
Endurance	Prep Base 1, 2, 3 Build 1, 2 Peak	1–2/week	20 min.–6 hrs.	N/A	N/A	1–3	Delay fatigue Build slow twitch Fuel economy	Swim 60 min. steady Bike 3 hrs. flat course Run 90 min.
Force	Base 2, 3 Build 1	1/week	4–60 min.	30–60 sec.	1:2	4–5b	Muscular strength Muscular economy	Swim with paddles Bike hills seated Run hilly course
Speed Skills	Base 1, 2, 3 Build 1, 2 Peak Race	1–2/week	1–6 min.	10–30 sec.	1:2–5	5a–5c	Arm/leg turnover Muscular economy	Swim 10x25 m on 1 min. Bike 12x30 sec. (90 sec. RI) Run 8x20 sec. (90 sec. RI)
Muscular Endurance	Base 2, 3 Build 1, 2 Peak Race	1/week	18–60 min. 20–40 min. steady state	6–12 min.	3–4:1	4–5a	Strength endurance Race–pace comfort Boost LT Lactate tolerance	Swim 6x400 m on 8 min. Bike 4x6 min. (2 min. RI) Run 20 min. steady state
Anaerobic Endurance	Build 1, 2 Peak Race	1/week	12–30 min. 3–12 min.	2–6 min. 30 sec.–2 min.	2:1–2 1:2–3	5b 5c	Elevate VO_2max Sustain high effort Lactate tolerance	Swim 6x200 m on 4 min. Bike 5x5 min. (5 min. RI) Run 5x400 m (400 m RI)
Power	Build 2 Peak Race	1/week	1–6 min.	10–30 sec.	1:2–3	5c	Muscular power Fast starts Climb short hills	Swim 12x25 m on 1 min. Bike 6x30 sec. on hill (60 sec. RI) Run 4x150 m (250 m RI)

* Varies with individual, period, and sport. **Applies to portion of workout that develops the ability. *** Work-interval-to-recovery-interval ratio (example: 3:1 means rest for 1 min. for every 3 min. of work time). Note: Recovery intervals typically are shortest for swimming and longest for running.

Abbreviations: LT = lactate threshold, m = meters, RI = recovery interval abilities are somewhat more difficult to recognize. But since the advanced abilities are based on the combination of the basic abilities, a weakness in the latter produces a weakness in the former. For example, if your endurance is weak, it will prevent both muscular endurance and anaerobic endurance from reaching their potential. If your endurance is good but your force is lacking, muscular endurance and power are negatively affected. Poor speed skills means low power and inferior anaerobic endurance.

As mentioned earlier, the types of races you do determine what strengths are needed and how your weaknesses limit you. Likewise, your strengths should guide your choice of races, as you can play to your strengths by selecting courses that will take advantage of your particular abilities. Matching your strengths to the demands of the event is critical for success. Let's examine how that works.

CHOOSING RACES

Races vary not only in course length but also in terrain. Matching your physical fitness to the demands of the most important events of your season produces the best results. The longer the race is, the more it favors the basic abilities. Conversely, the shorter the race, the more important the advanced abilities become. In preparing for an Ironman-distance race, endurance is paramount, but force is also necessary to deal with hills or even just undulating terrain and wind. Good fuel economy resulting from speed-skills training is also essential because it allows you to conserve energy. Muscular endurance plays a role, but training for anaerobic endurance and power is of questionable value.

In the same way, a sprint-distance race favors the advanced abilities, especially anaerobic endurance. That doesn't mean that endurance and force aren't needed; they just aren't needed to the same extent as the long- and ultra-course events. Speed-skills training is critical for short races, but muscular endurance also plays a role.

Sprint- and Ironman-distance races are easy to define in terms of the abilities needed. Race distances between these extremes demand a blending of basic and advanced abilities, with the half-Ironman favoring basic abilities and Olympic-distance events depending somewhat more on advanced abilities. Also, the faster you are as a competitor, the more likely it is that training the advanced abilities will benefit your performance.

So training for an important event means first deciding what is required for success, and then improving your limiters in those areas while also maintaining the necessary strengths.

SWIM, BIKE, AND RUN LIMITERS

Of course, you can have a limiter in one sport that may not be a limiter at all in another sport. For example, you may have developed a high level of muscular endurance for cycling from years spent in bike racing, but your muscular endurance for running is holding you back. Considering the three sports, the six abilities, and the most important races on your schedule, there are numerous possible combinations of limiters unique to you.

Before designing a training program, you will need to identify those limiters. This will involve doing some honest self-evaluation and making some important decisions. The next two chapters will explain how to prepare a training plan based on what you decide.

There are other ways to improve a limiter for swimming, biking, or running besides training with specific fitness abilities in mind. Table 6.2 offers a few "nontraining" suggestions to improve flagging proficiency in each sport. Chapter 12 will describe many of these in greater detail.

TABLE 6.2

Strategies to
Address Limiters

SWIMMING	CYCLING	RUNNING
Train with a masters swim team.	Lift weights, especially squats, step-ups, or leg presses.	Run with a group occasionally.
Take swimming lessons.	Ride shorter workouts more frequently.	Run shorter workouts more frequently.
Focus on form, not fitness, in workouts.	Ensure that your bike fits correctly.	Refine your running technique.
Attend a swimming camp.	Ride regularly with a group of multi-sport athletes.	Build running-specific leg strength with weights.
Swim shorter workouts more frequently.	Frequently ride a fixed-gear bike in the Base period.	Have your running gait analyzed by a coach.
Videotape your swim stroke and analyze it.	Improve your ability to spin smoothly.	Buy shoes that fit your exact structural needs.
Videotape a proficient swimmer and study his or her mechanics.	Buy "fast" equipment such as aero bars or disc wheels.	

RACE RESULTS AND LIMITERS

You probably already have a good sense of what your weakest sport is. If you are unsure, race results can help you decide. Look at your rankings from recent races. Do you see a pattern? For example, if finishing eighteenth in the swim, fourteenth in the bike leg, and sixth in the run is a typical ranking for you, then swimming is a primary limiter with cycling being second. You will probably want to improve your swimming.

But hold on: The decision may not be quite so simple. You also need to consider how much time you could gain by becoming a more proficient swimmer. Again, use your race results to determine this. If you could become a good enough swimmer to move up from eighteenth place in the swim to perhaps tenth, how much time would you gain? Examine the results to see what the time of the tenth-place athlete's swim was. Let's say you might gain a minute by devoting more training resources to swimming. A minute is a lot, so that would be good. But if you look at the bike times in the same way, you may find that by moving from fourteenth to tenth place you could save 2 minutes.

So while swimming may be your weakest sport, cycling is where you stand to shave the most time; from a risk/reward perspective, cycling is the sport to invest in. This doesn't mean you should ignore your weakness in swimming. You should still work to develop any limiters you have. It's just that by putting more of your resources into cycling you may reap a greater reward in future races.

Score each of the following racing abilities and miscellaneous factors on a scale of 1 to 5 using the following guidelines. Circle the selection that best describes you in relation to your competition.

1 = among the worst in my race category

3 = about the same as others in my race category

5 = among the best in my race category

Abilities/Techniques	Swim					Bike					Run				
Endurance	1	2	3	4	5	1	2	3	4	5	1	2	3	4	5
Force	1	2	3	4	5	1	2	3	4	5	1	2	3	4	5
Speed skills	1	2	3	4	5	1	2	3	4	5	1	2	3	4	5
Muscular endurance	1	2	3	4	5	1	2	3	4	5	1	2	3	4	5
Anaerobic endurance	1	2	3	4	5	1	2	3	4	5	1	2	3	4	5
Power	1	2	3	4	5	1	2	3	4	5	1	2	3	4	5
Technique	1	2	3	4	5	1	2	3	4	5	1	2	3	4	5

Miscellaneous Factors															
Time to train	1	2	3	4	5	1	2	3	4	5	1	2	3	4	5
Injuries	1	2	3	4	5	1	2	3	4	5	1	2	3	4	5
Health	1	2	3	4	5	1	2	3	4	5	1	2	3	4	5
Body strength	1	2	3	4	5	1	2	3	4	5	1	2	3	4	5
Flexibility	1	2	3	4	5	1	2	3	4	5	1	2	3	4	5
Mental skills	1	2	3	4	5	1	2	3	4	5	1	2	3	4	5
Nutrition	1	2	3	4	5	1	2	3	4	5	1	2	3	4	5
Body composition	1	2	3	4	5	1	2	3	4	5	1	2	3	4	5

OTHER LIMITERS

Besides the ability and proficiency limiters discussed in this and the previous chapter, there are other factors that may hold you back from achieving your race goals. One of the most critical is a lack of time to train. This is perhaps the most common limiter for multi-sport athletes, especially those who compete in long- and ultra-distance races. If this is a limiter for you, bear in mind when designing a program that specificity of training becomes increasingly important as the hours available to work out diminish. In other words, when time is scarce, your training must closely simulate racing, so as volume declines, workout intensity increases. The next chapter will help you decide how many hours you should expect to train in order to race successfully in different events.

Other common multisport limiters are poor swimming, biking, or running techniques; frequent injuries or poor health (discussed in Chapter 11); a general lack of muscular strength or flexibility (Chapter 13); unique age, gender, or experience needs (Chapter 14); and mediocre nutrition or excess body fat (Chapter 16). Before completing the Annual Training Plan in the following chapter, it may help to first read any of the chapters that relate to your particular limiters. Masters athletes, women, juniors, and novices should definitely read over Chapter 14 before starting an annual training plan.

FINAL ASSESSMENT

By now you should have established a clear idea of what your limiters are. Before starting to plan your season, let's summarize them. This will make the planning process more meaningful. Take a few minutes to complete the "Triathlete Assessment" form (Sidebar 6.2, page 103) before going to the next chapter.

PART IV

PLANNING

There are no "secrets" to success in athletics, regardless of what you may have heard. Although some elite athletes and coaches believe they have discovered the "latest, greatest way" to train, there is nothing new under the sun. Intervals of many types have been extensively used since the 1920s; fartlek training has been around for 90 years; periodization was born in the 1960s; long, slow distance was all the rage 30 years ago; tempo training was common in the early 1900s; and post–World War I athletes regularly recorded high volume. The list could go on. If you study the greatest endurance athletes of all time, you discover one inescapable fact: No two have trained in exactly the same way. In fact, the training methods of history's most talented swimmers, cyclists, and runners cover the spectrum of possibilities. Some trained only long and slow, while others favored sprint workouts; several employed long intervals, but many preferred a mix of regimens; a few found hill work effective, while others stayed only on flat ground. You name it, and someone's already done it.

No, there are no secrets when it comes to training. But there always have been, and probably always will be, five ingredients for success in sport:

1. *Purpose:* Know exactly what your goal is.
2. *Passion:* Have a burning desire to achieve it.
3. *Planning:* Determine how you'll go about achieving it.
4. *Perspiration:* Work hard, following your plan to achieve it.
5. *Perseverance:* Don't let anything get in the way of achieving it.

The purpose of the next three chapters is to help you with the third P—planning. In Chapter 7 you'll develop a one-year training plan. Chapter 8 describes how to lay out a week of training. And Chapter 9 provides examples of plans for races of different distances.

PLANNING A YEAR

7

Just as the farmer's field must lie fallow every winter, so does the human body, mind, and spirit need a rest, with time to reflect, recover, and rejuvenate.

—ROB SLEAMAKER, AUTHOR OF
SERIOUS TRAINING FOR SERIOUS ATHLETES

IN THIS CHAPTER YOU'LL DESIGN an annual training plan. The best time of year to do this is a few weeks following the end of your last race period of the preceding season, when you're ready to start preparing for the next season. If you're already well into the season, but have just purchased this book, it's still a good idea to plan for the rest of the year. Better late than never.

This chapter will take you through a simple six-step process of annual planning that will have you on the way to a better season before you even work up a sweat. It's amazing what having direction will do for your fitness. This will require some writing, so you'll need a pencil. Don't work in ink, as you'll undoubtedly need to make changes later. Make a copy of the blank Annual Training Plan Worksheet in Appendix A before starting to work, so you can reuse the form next year. Chapter 9 provides completed sample plans to give you an idea of how to proceed.

I have also designed a Web site (www.TrainingPeaks.com) that can greatly assist you with this process. In fact, the "VirtualCoach" on the site can actually design an annual plan for you once you've answered some basic questions.

While planning your season can lead to better race performance, there is a danger in following such a methodical process. Some athletes become so engrossed in creating the perfect plan that they forget about real life and fail to factor in their many variables. When they find they can't stick to the unrealistic plan, they feel like failures and get frustrated. Your purpose is not simply to write a plan, but to write a realistic plan that will help you race better than ever before. At the end of a successful season, you'll realize how important having a written plan was in achieving your goals.

Writing and following an annual training plan is similar to climbing a mountain. Before taking the first step it's a good idea to ask questions and do some planning: What equipment is needed? What's the likely weather? What routes are best? The answers to these and other questions will help you devise a plan to reach the summit. The plan will probably take into account your previous climbs on other mountains. You may also talk with others who have climbed this particular mountain to find out their experiences. They may advise you of problems you might encounter along the way so that you will be prepared to deal with them.

Finally, you decide on the route; estimate the required time; pack clothing, food, and all the equipment you will need; and start the arduous trek. While ascending the mountain, you'll stop occasionally to look at the peak and check your progress. Along the way, you may decide to change the route based on unexpected conditions, such as bad weather or obstacles. When you arrive at the summit, you're elated. Looking back down, you remember all of the challenges you had to overcome along the way. You may have had to deal with unexpected problems, but it was planning that gave you direction.

So it is with planning for a peak racing season. Planning is the master key to success. You will want to check your progress throughout the season. And you may run into unexpected problems or challenges and have to adjust your plan to deal with them. If you persevere, you will arrive at the peak—but in this case it is peak performance rather than an actual mountaintop.

Remind yourself throughout the remainder of this chapter that you are not writing an annual plan to impress anyone, or to simply feel organized. The purpose is to create a useful, dynamic, and realistic—there's that word again—guide for your training. In the coming months, you will refer to the plan regularly to make decisions about your training. The plan will help you to keep an eye on the goal and not get lost in just working out and going to races. A training plan is dynamic in that you will frequently modify it as new situations arise.

THE ANNUAL TRAINING PLAN

It's time to get started planning. As you complete the six steps presented in this chapter, you will:

1. Determine your goals for the upcoming season.
2. Establish objectives that will support your goals.
3. Establish your annual training hours.
4. Prioritize your planned races.
5. Divide your season into training periods.
6. Assign hours to each week of training.

In Chapter 8, you will complete the plan by assigning weekly workouts based on abilities. This probably sounds like a lot to accomplish. It is, but the system laid out here will make it easy to do. If any of the instruction here is unclear, refer to Chapter 9, where you'll find five annual training plans that encompass very different abilities, limiters, schedules, and season goals.

Notice that there are several parts to the Annual Training Plan (Appendix A). At the top left of the page are spaces for annual hours, season goals, and training objectives. The column on the left assigns a number to each week of the year. You should write in the date of the Monday of each week of the season. There are also columns to list the races, their priority levels ("Pri"), the specific period you will be working in each week (Base period, Build period, and so on), and the number of training hours for each week. You will use the small boxes down the right-hand side to indicate categories of workouts and abilities as listed at the top of the page. Chapter 8 will take you through this last part.

STEP 1: DETERMINE SEASON GOALS

Let's start with the destination. What racing goals do you want to accomplish this season? Perhaps you want to finish a half-Ironman-distance race, improve on your time in a particular race, or qualify for Ironman Hawaii. Studies have shown that clearly defined goals improve one's ability to achieve them. Just as the successful mountain climber always has the peak before him and knows exactly where he wants to go, you will have your season goals in mind to keep you on track. If you don't know where you want to go, by the end of the season you will have gone nowhere.

Don't get goals confused with dreams or wishes. Athletes often dream about what they want to accomplish. That's healthy. Without dreams there is no vision for the far-off future and no long-range incentives. Dreams can become realities, but the definition of a dream is that it is so big it will take longer than one season to accomplish. If you reasonably can achieve it this season, no matter how big it may seem, it's no longer a dream—it's a goal.

Let's be realistically optimistic. If you had trouble finishing Olympic-distance races last season, winning your age group at an Ironman is probably a dream, not a goal. "But," you say, "if you don't set high goals, you never achieve anything." That's true, but the problem with using dreams as annual goals is that since you know deep down you really aren't capable of achieving them this season, there's little commitment to the training required. A challenging goal will stretch you to the limits and may require you to take some risks, but you can imagine accomplishing it in the next few months. Ask yourself: "If I do everything right, can I achieve this goal this year?" If you can't even conceive of attaining it this year, making it a goal is just window dressing. If you can, it's a good goal. Otherwise, it's a dream. Hang on to it for the more distant future, establish this and the coming years' goals to lead you to it, and eventually the dream will become a goal.

There are four principles your goals should adhere to:

Principle 1. Your goal must be measurable. How will you know if you are getting closer to it? Businesspeople know if they are achieving their financial goals because they have a measurable way to gauge how close they are getting: They simply count their money. You also need to have measurable ways to gauge your progress. Rather than using vague phrases such as "get better" in your goal statement, you might specifically say, "I will complete Such-and-Such Race in less than 2:18."

Principle 2. Your goal must be under your control. A successful person doesn't set goals based on what other people might do. "Win my age group in the XYZ race" sounds like a measurable goal, but what if the world champion in your age group shows up? You have no control over who races, what kind of shape they're in, or whether they are "training through" or peaking for a given race. You only have a measure of control over yourself, your own training, and your own motivation. There are some goals that are obviously measurable, and yet on the cusp of your control. For example, qualifying for Ironman Hawaii certainly takes a major commitment on your part, and yet it is also determined by who shows up at the qualifier. You can improve how much control you have over such a goal by choosing particular races that suit your abilities, determining what finishing time you think it will take to qualify, probably based on results from previous years, and the like.

Principle 3. Your goal must stretch you. A goal that is too easy to achieve is the same as having no goal. "Finish the Stinkyville sprint-distance race" isn't much of a challenge for an experienced multisport athlete. But qualifying for the national championship may really stretch you.

Principle 4. Your goal must be stated in the positive. A major league baseball catcher once told his pitcher, "Whatever you do, don't throw it low and outside to this batter." Guess where the pitcher threw it? Home run. Your goal must keep you focused on what you want to happen, not what you want to avoid. What do you suppose happens to a triathlete who sets a goal such as, "Don't swim off course in the Podunkville triathlon"? Chances are the swim performance will be poor, because the athlete does not have a goal to focus on that emphasizes what he or she is supposed to do; it only says what not to do. In the same way, "Don't get a running injury," isn't as good a goal as "I will lower my risk of injury by running only when recovered." The latter tells you what to do rather than what not to do.

With few exceptions, the goal should also be racing-outcome oriented. For example, don't set a goal of climbing better. That's an objective, as we'll see shortly. Instead, commit to a certain bike split in a hilly race. A possible exception has to do with major obstacles that have held you back in the past, such as overtraining, injury, burnout, or health problems. While these aren't exactly race-specific, they may play a big part in your season's success and enjoyment.

After determining your first goal, you may have one or two others that are important to you. Give them the same consideration as you did the first goal. Stop at three goals so things don't get too complicated in the coming months. List all of your goals at the top of the Annual Training Plan.

EXAMPLES OF GOALS

- Break 2:30 at the national championship.
- Run 10 km in less than 40 minutes in the Boulder Peak Triathlon.
- Race for first in my age group in all A-priority races.
- Qualify for Ironman Hawaii with a sub-five-hour time at Half Vineman.
- Improve on my USA Triathlon national age-group ranking of 129 for last year.

STEP 2: ESTABLISH TRAINING OBJECTIVES

In the previous two chapters, you determined your strengths and weaknesses, and at the end of Chapter 6 you completed the "Triathlete Assessment" form. Look back at that form now to refresh your memory. What are your strengths and weaknesses?

Chapter 6 described the concept of limiters. These are the key race-specific weaknesses holding you back from being successful in certain events. Chapter 6 also explained that different abilities were required for different types of races. If you compared your weaknesses with the requirements for the races that interest you, you should know your limiters. For example, a long, hilly race requires good force for climbing hills and a high level of endurance. A weakness in either of these areas means you have a limiter that you must improve upon if you want to be successful in this type of race.

Read your first season goal. Do any of your weaknesses (score of 3 or lower on the Triathlete Assessment) present a limiter for this goal? If so, you will need to work specifically to improve that limiter for the coming season. Chapters 8 and 9 provide the details on how to do that.

Written objectives challenge you to improve a limiter by a certain time. They are specific and measurable tasks you must accomplish in order to achieve the season goal. There are several ways to measure the progress you have made toward meeting your objectives. Chapter 5 presented graded exercise tests and time trials, and you could repeat the ones that apply to your goals and supporting objectives periodically throughout the season to gauge your improvement. Low-priority races and workouts also serve as good progress indicators. Be specific in writing your training objectives, just as you were when writing your season goals. Setting a date for the completion of specific objectives can keep you on track, for example. Progress toward most objectives can be measured in some precise way, and the way you write the objective can specify this—for example, you might say that you will achieve a particular time in a 5 km run by a particular date. But sometimes you can only judge your progress subjectively. To gauge your progress toward improving a particular mental skill, for example, you may have to simply rely on your own sense of how much you have changed in that area. For example, do you feel that you are more confident or focused? Are you keeping a positive outlook? These are questions that only you can answer.

Timing of the objectives is critical to overall success. To accomplish your overarching goal, you must reach your training objectives by a certain point in the season, so be sure to set dates. Too late is as good as never when it comes to races.

By the time you are done with this part of the Annual Training Plan, you will probably have three to five training objectives listed. These are the short-term standards against which you will measure your progress toward goals. If they are appropriate to your limiters and accomplished on time, your goals should be within reach.

EXAMPLES OF LIMITERS AND TRAINING OBJECTIVES BY GOAL

Goal: Break 2:30 at the national championship.
Limiter: Bike muscular endurance.
Training Objectives:
1. Elevate LT power to 220 watts on graded exercise test by July 6.
2. Complete 4 x 10 km each under 15:15 with 5-minute recoveries by August 3.

Goal: Run 10 km in less than 40 minutes in the Boulder Peak Triathlon.
Limiters: Running speed skills and muscular endurance.
Training Objectives:
1. Run comfortably for 90 minutes at a cadence of 90 rpm by May 31.
2. Run a 10 km road race in 37:30 or faster by July 20.

Goal: Race for first in my age group in all A-priority races.
Limiter: Mental skills, especially confidence.
Training Objectives:
1. Read Mental Training for Peak Performance and complete all exercises by February 1.
2. Feel more confident and focused in spring races and group workouts.

Goal: Qualify for Ironman Hawaii with a sub-five-hour time at Half Vineman.
Limiters: Swim speed skills, bike force, run endurance.
Training Objectives:
1. Squat 250 pounds four times by January 5.
2. Complete a Total Immersion Swim Camp by February 1.
3. Feel stronger climbing hills by May 1.
4. Run 2 hours at an average pace of 7:30 following a 2-hour ride by June 22.

Goal: Improve on my USA Triathlon national age-group ranking of 129 for last year.
Limiter: Time available to train.
Training Objectives:
1. During Base period, complete longer workouts on weekend.
2. During Build period, schedule group interval workouts in my weekly calendar.
3. Throughout the season, swim with the 5:30 a.m. masters group.

STEP 3: SET ANNUAL TRAINING HOURS

The number of hours you train in the coming season—including swimming, cycling, running, weights, and crosstraining—determines a large part of your training workload. Too high an annual volume is likely to result in overtraining; too low and fitness is lost. Setting your annual training hours is one of the most critical decisions you will make about training.

Volume is best expressed in terms of hours rather than distance. Training with volume based on distance encourages you to repeat the same bike and run courses week after week. It also causes you to compare your time on a given course today with what it was last week, and to try to "beat" the previous time. While gauging progress periodically on standard courses can be effective, training this way day after day is counterproductive. Using time as a basis for training volume allows you to go wherever you want, so long as you finish within a given time. Your rides are more enjoyable because there is more variety and less concern about your speed or pace for that day.

To determine your annual hours, start by adding up the hours you have trained in the previous twelve months. For the coming season, a small increase in volume, in the range of 10 to 15 percent, may be necessary, particularly if you are training for a longer race this year than you have done in the past. If you have been training and racing successfully at the same distances for the past season or two, there is little reason to increase volume. There may even be seasons in which your annual hours must decrease because of greater responsibilities at work or lifestyle changes.

How do you determine annual hours if you haven't kept track of time in the past? Many athletes keep a record of the distances they have covered. If you have such a record, divide the totals by what you guess the average speeds were. For example, you may estimate that you swam 2,500 meters per hour, biked at 18 miles per hour, and ran 7 miles per hour on average for the year. If you have also crosstrained and lifted weights, estimate how many hours you have put into those activities in the past year. By adding all of the estimates together, you have a ballpark figure for your annual training hours.

Even without records of annual miles or hours trained, you may be able to come up with an estimate by simply guessing your average weekly volumes in each sport. That will give you a starting point.

Looking back over the past three years, you can probably see trends related to training volume. For example, did you race better in the high-volume years, or worse? Were you overtrained or undertrained at previous volume levels? There were undoubtedly other factors in your performance at those times, but this kind of analysis may help you to decide what your training volume should be for the coming season.

Table 7.1 offers general guidelines, presenting the annual hours typical of athletes by race distance and age. This is not a required volume. There are many athletes with years of racing experience who put in far fewer miles than those suggested here for their category and yet race quite well. Training volume is most effective for developing endurance. With endurance already established by years of training, the emphasis can be shifted away from volume and toward intensity.

You can produce better training results by carefully limiting the number of hours you train than by struggling through an overly ambitious volume. If you have a full-time job, a family, a home to maintain, and other responsibilities, be realistic—don't expect to train with the same volume as the pros. Training is their job.

If, however, you have not been competitive in the past, endurance is a limiter, and you fall well below the suggested annual hours for the longest races you have targeted for this season, consider increasing your volume to approach the lower figure in your race range, so long as this is not more than a 15 percent increase. Otherwise, if there are to be changes at all, keep increases in your annual hours from year to year in the range of 5 to 10 percent.

Many professional businesspeople have limitations imposed on their training time by travel and work responsibilities rather than inherent training capacity. If this is the situation you are in, base your estimate of annual training hours strictly on what is available.

Write your annual training hours at the top of the Annual Training Plan. Later you'll use that figure to assign weekly training hours. Note that although the total hours include recovery and crosstraining workouts, those are not broken out individually on the Annual Training Plan. You'll include those when you set up a weekly plan in Chapter 8.

STEP 4: PRIORITIZE RACES

For this step, a list of your planned races is needed. If the race schedule hasn't been published yet, go back to last year's race calendar and guess which days they'll be held on. Races usually stay on the same weekends from year to year. Later on, when the race dates are announced, you may need to make some changes. That's one reason for completing the plan in pencil or in electronic form.

On the Annual Training Plan, list all of the races you intend to do by writing them into the "Races" column in the appropriate rows by date. Remember that the date you indicate in the first column is the Monday of a given week, and the week includes the following Saturday and Sunday. This should be an inclusive list of tentative races, so list all that you *may* do, even if you're not sure now. You may decide later on not to do some of them, but for now assume you'll do all of them. Then categorize the races into A, B, and C priorities using the criteria below.

A-Priority Races

Pick out the two or three races—no more than this—that are most important to you this year. Two A races on the same weekend count as one race. The single greatest mistake

---

TABLE 7.1

Suggested Annual Training Hours

RACE DISTANCE	ANNUAL HOURS
Ironman	600–1200
Half-Ironman	500–700
Olympic	400–600
Sprint	300–500

Note: Juniors should limit their annual hours to 200–350.

I see self-coached athletes make is to schedule too many A-priority races in a season. This practically ensures that they will not reach a true peak of fitness. An A race isn't necessarily the one that gets the most press or has the biggest prize purse. It could be the Nowhereville Triathlon, but if you live in Nowhereville, that could be the big race of the year for you. The A-priority races are the most important on the schedule and all of your training will be designed around them. The purpose of training is to build and peak for these A races.

It's best that these races either be clumped together in two- or three-week blocks or widely separated by eight or more weeks. For example, two of the races may fall into a three-week period in May, with a non-race week between them, and the other one could be on a weekend in August. Then again, one may occur in May, one in July, and the other in September. The idea is that in order to come to a peak for each of these most important races, you will need a period of several weeks to rebuild race fitness. During this time between A races, you will still race, but you won't be in top form, because training volume and intensity has again increased. For most athletes, it's best for the single most important race of the year (the "Mother of All A Races") to be scheduled for the second half of the season, when fitness is likely the highest of the year.

If your A races aren't neatly spaced or grouped as described here, don't worry. Season priorities are not determined by the calendar, but rather by your goals. A schedule that doesn't conveniently space or group the races makes planning and coming to a peak much more difficult than one that follows this principle, and requires you to be more of an artist than a scientist. But it is not impossible to work with this kind of race season if it can't be helped.

In the "Pri" column write in "A" for all of your A-priority races. Remember, there should be no more than three of these.

B-Priority Races

These are important races but not as critical as the A races. You want to do well, but they are not the top priority. You'll rest for a few days before each of them, but you will not build to a peak for these. Select as many as six of these, and as with the A events, two B races on the same weekend count as one race. In the "Pri" column write in "B" for all of these races.

C-Priority Races

You now have up to nine weeks dedicated to either A or B races. That's a big chunk of the race season, and perhaps more than you will do. All other races on the list are C-priority. C races are done for experience, as hard workouts, as tests of progress, for fun or as tune-ups for A races. You will "train through" these races with no peaking and with minimal rest before each one. It's not unusual to decide at the last moment not to do one of these events. If your heart isn't in it, you're better off training that day—or resting.

Be careful with C races. They are the ones in which you are most likely to have a bad experience or go over the edge into a state of overtraining, since you may be tired or lack the motivation to perform well. They are also often done haphazardly or with confused incentives. There should be a reason for every race in your schedule, so decide before a C race what you want to get out of it. If unsure, consider not doing it. The more experienced you are as a multisport athlete, the fewer C races you should do. Conversely, juniors and novices should do several to gain experience.

Race priorities have nothing to do with how hard you push yourself in a given event. With few exceptions, your effort should always be high in races. You don't go all out in A races and loaf in C races. The main difference between A, B, and C races is in how you prepare for them. Your performance will probably be better in A races than in C races because you will come into them in better form, following a week or two of peak training and adequate recovery.

STEP 5: DIVIDE YEAR INTO PERIODS

Now that you know the times in the year when you want to be in top form (where the A-priority races are listed), you can assign periods. Periodization was described in Chapters 3 and 6. Figure 7.1 summarizes those discussions.

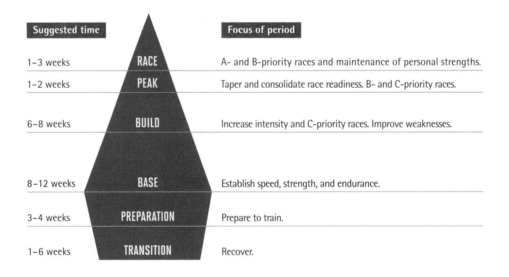

FIGURE 7.1

Using Training Periods to Peak at Preselected Times

Suggested time		Focus of period
1–3 weeks	RACE	A- and B-priority races and maintenance of personal strengths.
1–2 weeks	PEAK	Taper and consolidate race readiness. B- and C-priority races.
6–8 weeks	BUILD	Increase intensity and C-priority races. Improve weaknesses.
8–12 weeks	BASE	Establish speed, strength, and endurance.
3–4 weeks	PREPARATION	Prepare to train.
1–6 weeks	TRANSITION	Recover.

If you are a junior, master, or elite athlete, you should read the appropriate section in Chapter 14 before proceeding; you may need to alter the periodization routine described here based on the information in that chapter. There are also several factors that women should take into account before planning a season, and these are also addressed in Chapter 14.

Find your first A-priority race on the schedule, and in the "Period" column, write in "Race." This first Race period extends throughout your clumping of A races and could be as long as three weeks. Count (up the page) two weeks from Race and write in "Peak." If the A race is a sprint- or Olympic-distance event, work backward four weeks from Peak and write "Build 2." When training for an Ironman-distance race, you may omit the Build periods to concentrate on the most basic abilities for those who are new at that distance. Periodization for half-Ironman races also depends on your experience level. If you have done several races of this distance and are comfortable with them, continue to include the Build periods. Otherwise, omit the Build periods and concentrate on Base. Using weekly durations as indicated in Figure 7.1, do the same for Build 1, Base 3, Base 2, Base 1, Prep, and Transition. The first peak of the year is now scheduled.

Go to your second A race (or clumping of A races) and write in "Race" as you did above. Count backward two weeks and write in "Peak" again. Using the same criteria for race distances explained above, count back four weeks for Build 2 and another four for Build 1. Also include a "Transition" week immediately following the first Race period and before Build 1. When training for sprint- and Olympic-distance races, it may not be necessary to repeat the Base 3 period unless (1) you have had a long break from training after the first Race period, or (2) you sense your endurance or force has eroded.

It's unlikely that the Build-Peak period between your two Race periods will work out to exactly eleven weeks. Once you have the second Peak period and a Transition week scheduled, if you have six weeks remaining, plan on a three-week Build 2 period and a three-week Build 1 period. If there are seven weeks available, you could schedule a four-week Build 1 and a three-week Build 2, depending on your needs. Of course, if your next scheduled race is at the Ironman or half-Ironman distance, you may want to use Base 2 and Base 3 instead. In some schedules, there may be time for only one period, in which case it's probably best as a Build 1 or a Base 3, since these periods do a better job of helping you maintain your endurance, the most basic ability of multisport racing.

The one-week Transition after your first Race period allows for recovery and prevents burnout later in the season. A Transition period at this time always pays off with higher enthusiasm for training and greater fitness for late-season races. I have found that a Transition of five to seven days usually gives experienced and fit athletes enough time to recharge their batteries. Following the last Race period of the season, schedule a longer Transition period.

If this step in the planning process seems confusing, look ahead to Chapter 9, where you can see how it all comes together in five different case studies. Examples of easy and not-so-easy annual plans are provided.

STEP 6: ASSIGN WEEKLY HOURS

Throughout the season, there is a stair-step pattern of increasing and decreasing volume and intensity as you build to a peak. Figure 7.2 illustrates this. The purpose of this pattern is to ensure that endurance is maintained and to permit increases in intensity without overly stressing the body's systems.

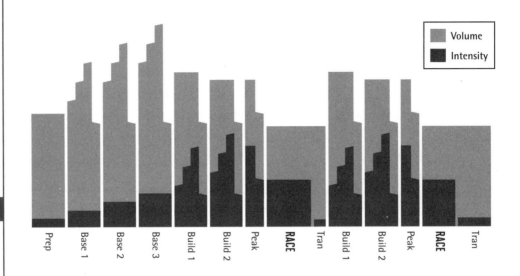

Prep | Base 1 | Base 2 | Base 3 | Build 1 | Build 2 | Peak | **RACE** | Tran | Build 1 | Build 2 | Peak | **RACE** | Tran

Volume
Intensity

FIGURE 7.2

Periodized Training Year

Now that you have an estimate of annual hours and have divided the year into periods, you are ready to assign weekly training hours. Find the annual hours column in Table 7.2. There, weekly hours are in half-hour increments. On the left-hand side of the table are all of the periods and the weeks. By reading across and down, determine the number of hours for each week and write those in under the "Hours" on the Annual Training Plan.

Congratulations! You've now completed the Annual Training Plan, with the exception of the swim, bike, and run workouts portion, which we will tackle in Chapter 8.

CHANGING THE ANNUAL TRAINING PLAN

Once you have created an Annual Training Plan, there are two common blunders you must avoid. The first is the more common—ignoring the plan and simply training as you always have. I hope that once you've put in the time to create a solid plan, one that will help produce your best race results ever, you won't disregard it. That would be a considerable waste of both your planning time and your training time. The second mistake is the opposite—to pay *too much* attention to the plan and not make changes when dictated by new circumstances. I'm not talking about circumstances like wanting to go on the group ride on a scheduled rest day. I mean those times when you realize that you are making inadequate progress, or you begin missing workouts because something unexpected has happened. Be realistic in these situations and adapt the plan as needed.

INADEQUATE PROGRESS

When you're not making the progress you had expected, you must make strategic changes in your plan. You'll know whether you're making progress because you will perform a test and compare the results with your training objectives as described earlier in Step 2.

TABLE 7.2

Weekly Training Hours

PERIOD	WEEK	ANNUAL HOURS																				
		200	250	300	350	400	450	500	550	600	650	700	750	800	850	900	950	1000	1050	1100	1150	1200
Prep	All	3.5	4.0	5.0	6.0	7.0	7.5	8.5	9.0	10.0	11.0	12.0	12.5	13.5	14.5	15.0	16.0	17.0	17.5	18.5	19.5	20.0
Base 1	1	4.0	5.0	6.0	7.0	8.0	9.0	10.0	11.0	12.0	12.5	14.0	14.5	15.5	16.5	17.5	18.5	19.5	20.5	21.5	22.5	23.5
	2	5.0	6.0	7.0	8.5	9.5	10.5	12.0	13.0	14.5	15.5	16.5	18.0	19.0	20.0	21.5	22.5	24.0	25.0	26.0	27.5	28.5
	3	5.5	6.5	8.0	9.5	10.5	12.0	13.5	14.5	16.0	17.5	18.5	20.0	21.5	22.5	24.0	25.5	26.5	28.0	29.5	30.5	32.0
	4	3.0	3.5	4.0	5.0	5.5	6.5	7.0	8.0	8.5	9.0	10.0	10.5	11.5	12.0	12.5	13.5	14.0	14.5	15.5	16.0	17.0
Base 2	1	4.0	5.5	6.5	7.5	8.5	9.5	10.5	12.5	12.5	13.0	14.5	16.0	17.0	18.0	19.0	20.0	21.0	22.0	23.0	24.0	25.0
	2	5.0	6.5	7.5	9.0	10.0	11.5	12.5	14.0	15.0	16.5	17.5	19.0	20.0	21.5	22.5	24.0	25.0	26.5	27.5	29.0	30.0
	3	5.5	7.0	8.5	10.0	11.0	12.5	14.0	15.5	17.0	18.0	19.5	21.0	22.5	24.0	25.0	26.5	28.0	29.5	31.0	32.0	33.5
	4	3.0	3.5	4.5	5.0	5.5	6.5	7.0	8.0	8.5	9.0	10.0	10.5	11.5	12.0	12.5	13.5	14.0	15.0	15.5	16.0	17.0
Base 3	1	4.5	5.5	7.0	8.0	9.0	10.0	11.0	12.5	13.5	14.5	15.5	17.0	18.0	19.0	20.0	21.0	22.5	23.5	25.0	25.5	27.0
	2	5.0	6.5	8.0	9.5	10.5	12.0	13.5	14.5	16.0	17.0	18.5	20.0	21.5	23.0	24.0	25.0	26.5	28.0	29.5	30.5	32.0
	3	6.0	7.5	9.0	10.5	11.5	13.0	15.0	16.5	18.0	19.0	20.5	22.0	23.5	25.0	26.5	28.0	29.5	31.0	32.5	33.5	35.0
	4	3.0	3.5	4.5	5.0	5.5	6.5	7.0	8.0	8.5	9.0	10.0	10.5	11.5	12.0	12.5	13.5	14.0	15.0	15.5	16.0	17.0
Build 1	1	5.0	6.5	8.0	9.0	10.0	11.5	12.5	14.0	15.5	16.0	17.5	19.0	20.5	21.5	22.5	24.0	25.0	26.5	28.0	29.0	30.0
	2	5.0	6.5	8.0	9.0	10.0	11.5	12.5	14.0	15.5	16.0	17.5	19.0	20.5	21.5	22.5	24.0	25.0	26.5	28.0	29.0	30.0
	3	5.0	6.5	8.0	9.0	10.0	11.5	12.5	14.0	15.5	16.0	17.5	19.0	20.5	21.5	22.5	24.0	25.0	26.5	28.0	29.0	30.0
	4	3.0	3.5	4.5	5.0	5.5	6.5	7.0	8.0	8.5	9.0	10.0	10.5	11.5	12.0	12.5	13.5	14.0	15.0	15.5	16.0	17.0
Build 2	1	5.0	6.0	7.0	8.5	9.5	10.5	12.0	13.0	14.5	15.5	16.5	18.0	19.0	20.5	21.5	22.5	24.0	25.0	26.5	27.0	28.5
	2	5.0	6.0	7.0	8.5	9.5	10.5	12.0	13.0	14.5	15.5	16.5	18.0	19.0	20.5	21.5	22.5	24.0	25.0	26.5	27.0	28.5
	3	5.0	6.0	7.0	8.5	9.5	10.5	12.0	13.0	14.5	15.5	16.5	18.0	19.0	20.5	21.5	22.5	24.0	25.0	26.5	27.0	28.5
	4	3.0	3.5	4.5	5.0	5.5	6.5	7.0	8.0	8.5	9.0	10.0	10.5	11.5	12.0	12.5	13.5	14.0	15.0	15.5	16.0	17.0
Peak	1	4.0	5.5	6.5	7.5	8.5	9.5	10.5	11.5	13.0	13.5	14.5	16.0	17.0	18.0	19.0	20.0	21.0	22.0	23.5	24.0	25.0
	2	3.5	4.0	5.0	6.0	6.5	7.5	8.5	9.5	10.0	11.0	11.5	12.5	13.5	14.5	15.0	16.0	17.0	17.5	18.5	19.0	20.0
Race	All	3.0	3.5	4.5	5.0	5.5	6.5	7.0	8.0	8.5	9.0	10.0	10.5	11.5	12.0	12.5	13.5	14.0	15.0	15.5	16.0	17.0

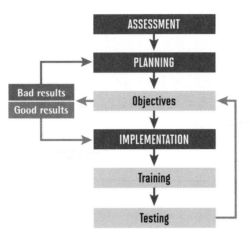

FIGURE 7.3

Planning and
Implementation
Model

The test could be a field test, a test conducted in a clinic, or a C-priority race. Figure 7.3 shows how to handle the results. Basically, you will compare them with your planned objectives and see if you are on track or not quite up to par. If your progress is good, you will continue following the plan. If you're not happy with your progress, you must reevaluate the plan and decide what must change.

What could need changing? It could be that you didn't spend enough time in the Base period and some of your basic abilities are lacking. This is the most common mistake athletes make—they can't wait to get to the hard training of the Build period, so they cut the Base period short. The solution is simply to go back to Base 3 for a few weeks to strengthen endurance, force, and speed skills. Of these, if you have made the Base period shorter than it should have been, poor endurance is the most likely problem.

Or it may be that your objectives, and perhaps even your goals, were set unrealistically high. This mistake is especially common among athletes who are in their first few years of triathlon. After you've had a chance to implement the plan and test your progress, it may become clear that you expected too much. Give some thought to revising your goals and objectives at this point.

Another common cause of poor progress is simply doing the wrong sort of training. The problem may be that you are spending too much time training your strengths while giving your limiters only lip service. As explained in Chapter 7, the focus of most of your training must be on those race-specific weaknesses—limiters—that are holding you back. The tendency among self-coached athletes is to spend more training time on what they are already good at than on their weaknesses. Realize that it is only by training in your limiters that you will obtain better results.

Doing too many group workouts can be a problem. If you are going along with the group, you may not be focusing on what you really need to focus on for that workout session. There are times when having training partners can be very beneficial, but group workouts are often detrimental, especially in the Base period. You may either be working too hard or too easy, depending on the skills and experience of your training partners. Look for partners who are of similar ability, and decide on a workout before starting. Unstructured group workouts tend to become "races." In the Build period this may be beneficial, but only if done in moderation. If your workout objectives are compatible with those of the group, then go ahead and take advantage of the camaraderie.

MISSING WORKOUTS—OR MORE

It happens to everyone. Your training is going well, you've been consistent, and you can tell that your fitness is progressing. Then your job throws you a curve ball and you have to miss a day or more of training. Or you catch a winter virus and don't train for four days while your body is fighting it off. Maybe your knee becomes inflamed and the doctor says no running or cycling for two weeks, or you decide you're too tired to train and need an extra day off. What should you do? Should you try to fit in the missed workouts at a later time by wedging them in between the others? Or do you just continue on as if nothing happened? How will this affect your race preparation? Here is how to handle such dilemmas.

Missing Three or Fewer Days

For downtime of just a few days, continue training with no adjustments. The worst thing you can do is to try to fit in the lost workouts. That will not only set you up for poor training quality due to accumulated fatigue but increase the potential for a breakdown, such as an overuse injury, an illness, or the early stages of overtraining.

Missing Four to Seven Days

If you've missed more than a few days, some rearranging is required. You'll need to readjust your workouts for up to two weeks, but you won't be able to do all of the missed workouts plus those originally planned over that time period. You'll need to be selective. The most important workouts to retain are the ones related to your limiters. Reorganize your schedule so that you can do most of those, although that may mean skipping some of the workouts that maintain your strengths. Be sure to include easy days just as you would normally do in training. Don't try to cram more hard training into fewer days.

Missing One to Two Weeks

If you miss one or two weeks of training, step back one mesocycle and omit an entire chunk of the training you had planned to do in the future, rather than trying to merge the lost workouts into your existing plan. For example, say you missed two weeks of training in Build 2. When ready to train normally again, go back to Build 1 for two weeks and do the appropriate workouts. Adjust your plan by cutting out two weeks of training that were scheduled to take place later in the season. One way to do this is to make Build 2 three weeks long instead of four and omit Peak 1.

Missing More Than Two Weeks

Missing a significant block of time, such as two weeks or more, requires a return to the Base period, as one or more of the basic abilities—endurance, force, or speed skills—has probably been compromised. If you were already in the Base period when the training time was lost, step back one mesocycle. Let's say you were in Base 3 and had to miss three weeks of training for some reason. Return to Base 2. If you were in Build 2 when it happened, go back to Base 3 and then continue on from this new starting point. You will need to make major revisions to your Annual Training Plan to accommodate this change by omitting some portion of Build 2 and by possibly shortening the Peak period from two weeks to one.

No matter which of these unfortunate situations occurs, you will have less fitness on race day than you had originally hoped. You can't force in the extra workouts, because there is a limit to how much stress your body can handle. You can't force it to become just as fit on less training. This is why it is so important to avoid taking high risks in training; if you become injured, you could miss critical training hours while forced to take time off to recuperate. In any case, remember that missing some training isn't a disaster, it's simply a situation that you need to manage. Adjust your plan and move on.

NEVER COMPROMISE RECOVERY

As mentioned in Chapter 1, consistency is the key to success in athletic training. If you train inconsistently as a result of frequent physical breakdowns or mental burn-out, you will never achieve a high level of race readiness. To maintain consistent training, you must provide adequate recovery days every week. One of those days should be very light. For a triathlete who trains fewer than 10 hours each week, this could mean a day off; for someone who does 15 hours a week, it could mean doing an hour of weight lifting instead of riding; and for a 25-hour-per-week triathlete, it could mean a two-hour, easy ride. The other weekly recovery workouts should be done at a low intensity—in heart rate zone 2

Not everyone respects recovery days. I often see self-coached athletes miss workouts or become frustrated with their progress, then overcompensate by making their recovery days harder. That's exactly the wrong thing to do. You will only create more fatigue and lower your workout quality on the harder days. The solution in this case is to make the hard training days harder and the easy days easier. Making workouts harder means either making them longer, doing them at a higher intensity, or doing more high-intensity volume, such as more intervals. Whatever your approach, never compromise recovery to gain fitness. It doesn't work.

PLANNING A WEEK

All too often, athletes—particularly young ones—equate improvements in performance solely with hard physical training. . . . It's really only part of the picture.
—ROD CEDARO, EXERCISE PHYSIOLOGIST

IF THERE'S ONE THING you're getting out of this book so far, I hope it's that training should be purposeful and precise to meet your unique needs. Training haphazardly brings results initially, but to reach the highest level of racing fitness, carefully planned workouts are necessary. Before starting any training session, from the easiest to the hardest, you must be able to answer one simple question: What is the purpose of this workout? If that question goes unanswered, you are unlikely to make much progress in your swimming, cycling, or running session. The answer to this question relates to your objectives, goals, strengths, and limiters. You are either trying to improve some specific aspect of physical and/or mental fitness, or you are maintaining.

Another possibility, and one that's too often overlooked by athletes, is that the purpose of the planned workout is to promote active recovery. Other purposes involve testing and race simulation. Deciding in advance what benefit the workout will provide, and reviewing its purpose before starting, will help you get the most out of each and every training session, which is critical to peaking at the right moments in the season. Of course, this principle is predicated on first having a well-conceived plan.

The purpose of this chapter is to explain the principles of workout scheduling and show you how to apply them. In Chapter 7 you completed the Annual Training Plan. By the time you finish this chapter you will have determined the key workouts for each week of the season and have a good understanding of how they blend into a weekly schedule. As I suggested before, do all of your work on the Annual Training Plan in pencil or electronically at TrainingPeaks.com, as changes are usually necessary during the year. Review your

Annual Training Plan weekly alongside your training diary as you prepare for the next training week. Later, in Chapter 15, you will learn how to use the diary in conjunction with your Annual Training Plan to produce a comprehensive daily and weekly schedule.

COMPLETING YOUR SEASON DESIGN

STEP 7: SCHEDULE WEEKLY WORKOUTS

In Chapter 7 I led you through the first six steps in designing your season using the Annual Training Plan. By now you should have completed the sections of the plan related to annual hours, season goals, training objectives, races, priorities ("Pri"), periods, and hours. Now you have reached the meat of the plan—the workout categories.

Across the top right side of the Annual Training Plan are the headings "Swim," "Bike," and "Run," and below each are six columns for the abilities discussed in previous chapters (endurance, force, speed skills, muscular endurance, anaerobic endurance, and power) and a column for testing. In this step, you will assign workouts in these categories to each week of the season. Then, when you are ready to start a given week, you will determine the specific workouts that will most benefit each of the abilities. Appendices B, C, D, and E list workouts by each of the abilities, and you can choose the appropriate one for any given day. This listing of workouts is by no means exhaustive. There are many other possibilities, including combining elements of these workouts into a unique session that challenges more than one ability.

WEIGHTS

Before getting started on the swim, bike, and run workout sections, however, notice that there is a column to the left headed "Weights." In this column you can note the phases of weight-room strength training for the season. Some multisport athletes neglect this aspect of training, especially if their limiter is force. Measurable results are initially quite evident from this type of training, however, particularly in cycling. Newcomers to weight training are usually amazed at how strong they feel on hills in the spring after a winter of weights.

The details of the five strength phases are discussed in Chapter 13, but with a little information you can complete the "Weights" column now by penciling in the abbreviations for the various phases. Here's how to determine the duration of each phase. If you're a bit confused, flip ahead to Chapter 9 for examples of completed Annual Training Plans.

Anatomical Adaptation (AA) Phase. If you have not done strength work for at least four weeks, include four to six weeks of AA at the outset of your training year, preferably during the Preparation period at the start of the season. If it has been less than four weeks since you have done weight training, assign two to four weeks of AA during Prep.

Maximum Transition (MT) Phase. Schedule two weeks of MT between AA and MS. The purpose of this phase is to prepare the body for the heavier loads of MS.

Maximum Strength (MS) Phase. If force, especially on the bike, is a limiter for you, schedule MS workouts for the next six weeks; otherwise, schedule just four weeks of MS. This phase usually works best in the Base 1 period of the season.

Strength Maintenance (SM) Phase. Assign SM to the remainder of the Base period. At this point in the year, about the time Build 1 begins, many athletes in their twenties and even into their early thirties stop weight training. Most masters men and all women, however, are well advised to maintain their strength gains from the winter months throughout most of the remaining season. Schedule no weight training during the week of A races.

PERIODIZATION OF WORKOUTS

The following sections will help you complete the swim, bike, and run portions of the Annual Training Plan. As the rest and recovery weeks are usually neglected, but are in some ways the most important parts of the entire plan, I will start with them. If you are at all confused about how to mark the Annual Training Plan, see the examples in Chapter 9. Women, masters, those new to multisport, and elite athletes should read the appropriate parts of Chapter 14 before continuing.

R&R Weeks

Every fourth week during the Base and Build periods is reserved for rest and recovery from the accumulated fatigue of the previous three weeks. Without such regular unloading of fatigue, fitness won't progress for long. You have already partially incorporated R&R by assigning reduced weekly hours during the fourth weeks of Base and Build, based on Table 7.2. Now we'll assign the workouts to those low-volume weeks.

For each of the R&R weeks, place an "X" under the Endurance and Speed Skills columns for each sport. In the Base and Build periods, put an "X" under the Testing column if there is not a race. Except for possibly one strength session, that's all for those weeks. The idea is to recover from the collected stress; feel rested by week's end; maintain endurance, speed skills, and force; and test your progress, once you are rested. In the Build and Peak periods there may be a B or C race at week's end that serves as a test. Chapter 5 and Appendices B, C, and D describe tests you may do during R&R weeks.

An exception to R&R-week scheduling may be made for those who recover quickly after several weeks of heavy training. These are usually younger, highly fit, experienced athletes. Being able to recover quickly is also related to diet, lifestyle stress, and other factors. If you find during R&R weeks that within four to six days you are feeling fully recovered, then return to more stressful training before the week is over. This will mean that your R&R-week weekends are nearly the same as the other weekends in your schedule. The details of this exception are discussed in greater detail in subsequent chapters.

Now you are ready to complete the workout categories for the other, "non-R&R" weeks of the year by indicating which abilities will be targeted. When you are ready to choose exact workouts for a given week, you will consult Appendices B, C, D, and E.

Preparation Period

Place an "X" in the Endurance and Speed Skills columns for each week of the Preparation period for each sport. Endurance training during this period concentrates on improving the endurance characteristics of the heart, blood, and lungs, referred to collectively as the cardiorespiratory system. Crosstraining is an option during this period, especially when poor weather interferes with bike and run sessions, but since multisport already is so diverse, swimming, cycling, and running may otherwise continue normally. Also place an "X" under Testing in the first and last weeks of the Preparation period.

Base 1

Again, mark the Endurance and Speed Skills columns for each week of the Base 1 period. During this period, endurance workouts are longer and speed-skills work increases. Weather is often the determining factor for the bike and run training done now. Mountain-bike rides, cross-country skiing, or snowshoe sessions are excellent alternatives during this period when the weather makes road work difficult. A good indoor bike trainer and a treadmill are also great tools throughout the Base period when you can't train on the roads.

Base 2

Place an "X" in the Endurance, Force, Speed Skills, and Muscular Endurance columns for each non-R&R week of the Base 2 period. As you can see in the suggested workouts for this period in Appendices B, C, and D, muscular endurance is done at moderate intensities, and force training is in the initial stages. You have gained strength in the just-completed MS phase; now your training emphasis will shift from the general to the specific as you begin to build swim-, bike-, and run-specific force. Endurance workouts continue to increase in duration.

Base 3

Mark the Endurance, Force, Speed Skills, and Muscular Endurance columns for each week of the Base 3 period, other than R&R weeks. Training volume reaches a maximum level during this period. Intensity also rises slightly with the addition of more force and, perhaps, higher intensities in muscular endurance work.

Build 1 and Build 2

Schedule workouts for Endurance and Muscular Endurance for each non-R&R week of the Build 1 and Build 2 period. Also select your greatest limiter for each sport and mark that column. If you are not sure which limiter to schedule, choose the Force column for the bike and run and the Anaerobic Endurance column for swimming. With few exceptions, anaerobic endurance training for the other sports is primarily for front-of-the-pack athletes doing sprint- and Olympic-distance races. It is unlikely that Power will be marked for your training, as this relates primarily to elite athletes in sprint-distance events and draft-legal, Olympic-distance races. If Power and Anaerobic Endurance are not selected for a sport, also mark Speed Skills for that sport. In this period, you can train two or more abilities in one workout session to more closely simulate the stresses of racing.

Races count as workouts, too. A sprint-distance race may take the place of an anaerobic endurance workout. Hilly races may act as substitutes for force workouts, and Olympic- and half-Ironman-distance events are both muscular endurance and endurance workouts. Early-season races in the Build 1 period are best as C-priority. The week of B-priority races, schedule training for only one ability in each sport. Remember, you're training through C-priority races, so you won't have extensive rests before them. Schedule each Build 1 and Build 2 period on your Annual Training Plan the same way.

Peak

Place an "X" in the Endurance and Muscular Endurance columns for each sport. If the race you are peaking for is an Olympic-distance race or shorter, also mark your remaining greatest limiter for just one sport for each week of the Peak period. If you are unsure of your next-greatest limiter, and you are a fast athlete, select Anaerobic Endurance in your weakest sport. Select Speed Skills if you are unsure and you are also back of the pack. If you are not marking Anaerobic Endurance or Power, you may also mark Speed Skills for each sport. If the race is a half-Ironman or an Ironman, schedule only Speed Skills in addition to Endurance and Muscular Endurance for each sport.

Races may be substituted for workouts using the same criteria as in the Build period. C races in the Peak period are excellent tune-ups for the approaching A races, as they get you back into a racing mode again. These are best at distances shorter than your targeted A-priority race but no longer than Olympic distance. You should plan to do a race-intensity simulation workout every 72 to 96 hours in Peak. Remember that race-intensity bike and run workouts are combined into one workout on the days of these simulations, along with a quality swim session. Mark all Peak periods in this same way.

Race

During each week of this period, either race or complete a race-effort simulation, such as a "brick"—that is, a combined bike and run session with a race-effort swim on the same day at week's end. Mark all Race periods in the same manner. R&R weeks with a B-priority race at the end may be treated like Race weeks. In Race weeks, the race provides the workout for other abilities.

Transition

Don't mark anything for the Transition week. This is an unstructured period that is meant to recharge your mental and physical batteries. You should, however, stay active, especially in sports that you enjoy other than swimming, cycling, and running. You could play team games such as soccer, basketball, volleyball, or hockey, for example, or take part in endurance activities such as cross-country skiing, power hiking, or in-line skating. Don't become a couch potato, but also don't train seriously. Take several days off from tri-specific sports, and rest as much as you can.

BREAKTHROUGH AND RECOVERY WORKOUTS

The only workouts you have scheduled so far are those meant to challenge or maintain your racing abilities. Those that challenge you are called "Breakthrough"—or "BT"—workouts. The difficulty of any given BT workout will vary by period. For example, a session with lots of zone 3 time challenges your muscular endurance in the Base period. In the Peak period, however, this same workout would probably not be considered very challenging. In the same way, a long endurance session in Base 1 may really tax you, but later on, once your endurance is well established, such a session places little demand on your body.

Recovery workouts that are placed between BT sessions are not listed on the Annual Training Plan, but they are obviously an integral part of any program and should be included frequently. Appendices B, C, and D offer suggestions for such workouts, and the following section on weekly training patterns describes how to incorporate them into your schedule.

WEEKLY TRAINING ROUTINES

Now that your Annual Training Plan is complete, with each week sorted into periods, the only issue left to decide is the weekly routine—on what day to do which workout and for how long. That's no small task. You could have the best possible plan, but if you do not blend workouts in such a way as to allow for recovery and adaptation, then it's all for nothing. The problem is that you must mix in both long- and short-duration workouts with workouts that are of high and low intensity in three sports in addition to scheduling training in other modes such as weights.

Chapter 15 will provide a weekly training journal format on which to record each day's scheduled workouts and results. For now, let's consider ways to determine each day's routine.

PATTERNS

Figures 8.1a through 8.1k illustrate one possible pattern for blending daily volume and intensity for each week of the year's training periods plus the R&R and Race weeks. These are only examples, as there are too many individual variables, such as different combinations of limiters and different amounts of time available for training, to provide patterns that work for every athlete. Use these only as suggestions to help you design your own patterns and not as the ultimate solutions.

On these figures, duration and intensity are categorized as high, medium, low, or recovery. Obviously, what is high volume for one athlete may be low for another, so these levels are meaningful only to you. Recovery days can be active (very light workout) or passive (day off) depending on your experience level. Novices usually benefit from taking the day off entirely.

Scheduling BT workouts is a balancing act. The goal is to create appropriate levels of adaptation-causing stress, on one side, and allow for recovery, on the other. It is during recovery that the adaptation to the stress actually occurs and you make the physiological gains you are seeking. Within a given week there are two commonly accepted ways of structuring this. One is to take the standard hard-day, easy-day approach. In other words, a BT day is followed by a recovery day. Another widely used pattern in triathlon is "block" training, in which two or even three BT workouts are placed back to back, then followed by days of recovery and maintenance. Triathlon favors block training because the three sports can stress different muscle groups on back-to-back workout days. A BT run on one day, for example, can usually be followed by a BT swim the next. Many multisport athletes find that they can even do two BT sessions on the same day in different sports if one, usually the second of the day, is less intense, such as a muscular endurance workout, or if one is a swim. Individual differences in the capacity to recover dictate which method you use and how densely spaced the BT sessions are. Figure 8.1 illustrates the block approach.

The "workout options" in Figure 8.1 are codes based on Appendices B, C, D, and E. You may want to create other workouts to better fit your individual needs. Write these down and assign codes to them. These codes may be used as shorthand notations when scheduling workouts in your training diary at the start of the week.

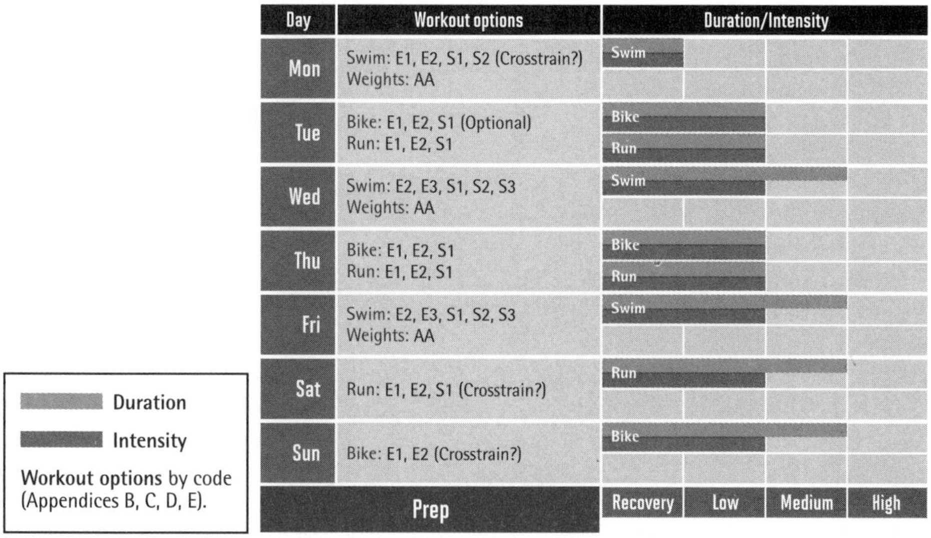

Day	Workout options	Duration/Intensity			
Mon	Swim: E1, E2, S1, S2 (Crosstrain?) Weights: AA	Swim			
Tue	Bike: E1, E2, S1 (Optional) Run: E1, E2, S1	Bike Run			
Wed	Swim: E2, E3, S1, S2, S3 Weights: AA	Swim			
Thu	Bike: E1, E2, S1 Run: E1, E2, S1	Bike Run			
Fri	Swim: E2, E3, S1, S2, S3 Weights: AA	Swim			
Sat	Run: E1, E2, S1 (Crosstrain?)	Run			
Sun	Bike: E1, E2 (Crosstrain?)	Bike			
Prep		Recovery	Low	Medium	High

Duration
Intensity
Workout options by code (Appendices B, C, D, E).

FIGURE 8.1a

Sample Prep Training Week

FIGURE 8.1b

Sample Base 1
Training Week

Day	Workout options	Duration/Intensity			
Mon	Swim: E1, E2, S1, S2 / Weights: MS	Swim			
Tue	Bike: E2, S1, S2 / Run: E3, S1, S2	Bike / Run			
Wed	Swim: E2, E3, S3 / Bike: E1	Swim / Bike			
Thu	Bike: E3, S1, S2 / Run: E2, S1, S2	Bike / Run			
Fri	Swim: E2, E3, S3 / Weights: MS	Swim			
Sat	Run: E2	Run			
Sun	Bike: E2	Bike			
Base 1		Recovery	Low	Medium	High

FIGURE 8.1c

Sample Base 2
Training Week

Day	Workout options	Duration/Intensity			
Mon	Swim: E1, E2, S1, S2 / Weights: PE	Swim			
Tue	Bike: E1, S1, S2 / Run: E3, F1, M1, P3	Bike / Run			
Wed	Swim: F1, F2, F3, M1, M2 / Bike: E1	Swim / Bike			
Thu	Bike: E3, F1, M1 / Run: E3, E2, S1, S2	Bike / Run			
Fri	Swim: E2, E3, S1, S2, S3 / Weights: PE	Swim			
Sat	Run: E2, E3, F1	Run			
Sun	Bike: E2, E3, F1	Bike			
Base 2		Recovery	Low	Medium	High

FIGURE 8.1d

Sample Base 3
Training Week

Day	Workout options	Duration/Intensity			
Mon	Swim: E1, E2, S1, S2 / Weights: ME	Swim			
Tue	Bike: E2, S1, S2 / Run: F1, F2, M1, M2, P3	Bike / Run			
Wed	Swim: F1, F2, F3, M1, M2, M3 / Bike: E1	Swim / Bike			
Thu	Bike: F1, F2, M1, M2 / Run: E2, S1, S2	Bike / Run			
Fri	Swim: E2, E3, S1, S2, S3 / Bike: E2, S1, S2	Swim / Bike			
Sat	Run: E2, E3, F1, F2 / Combined: E1, E2, F1 (Optional)	Run			
Sun	Bike: E1, E2, E3, F1, F2	Bike			
Base 3		Recovery	Low	Medium	High

Duration / Intensity

Workout options by code (Appendices B, C, D, E).

Day	Workout options	Duration/Intensity			
Mon	Weights: Optional				
Tue	Run: E1	Run			
Wed	Swim: T1, T2 Bike: E1	Swim Bike			
Thu	Run: E2	Run			
Fri	Swim: E2, S1, S2 Bike: T1	Swim Bike			
Sat	Bike: E2	Bike			
Sun	Run: T1	Run			
Base R&R		Recovery	Low	Medium	High

FIGURE 8.1e

Sample Base
R&R Week

Day	Workout options	Duration/Intensity			
Mon	Swim: E1, E2, S1, S2 Weights: SM	Swim			
Tue	Bike: E2, S3 Run: F2, F3, M2, M3, M4, A1, A2, A3, P1	Bike Run			
Wed	Swim: F1, F2, F3, M1, M2, M3, A1, P1 Bike: E1	Swim Bike			
Thu	Bike: F1, F2, M2, M3, M4, A1, A2, A3, P1 Run: E2, S1, S2	Bike Run			
Fri	Swim: E2, S1, S2, S3 Bike: E1	Swim Bike			
Sat	Combined: E1, E2, F1, S1	Combined			
Sun	Bike: Alternate weeks E2 Run: Alternate weeks E2	Bike Run			
Build 1		Recovery	Low	Medium	High

FIGURE 8.1f

Sample Build 1
Training Week

Day	Workout options	Duration/Intensity			
Mon	Swim: E1, E2, S1, S2 Weights: SM	Swim			
Tue	Bike: E2, S3 Run: M2, M3, M4, M5, A1, A2, A3, A4, A5, A6, A7, P1, P2	Bike Run			
Wed	Swim: F1, M1, M2, M3, A1, A2, P1 Bike: E1	Swim Bike			
Thu	Bike: F3, M2, M3, M4, M5, A1, A2, A3, A4, A5, A6, A7, P1, P2 Run: E2	Bike Run			
Fri	Swim: E2, S1, S2, S3	Swim			
Sat	Combined: F1, M1, A1, A2, S1	Combined			
Sun	Bike: E2	Bike			
Build 2		Recovery	Low	Medium	High

FIGURE 8.1g

Sample Build 2
Training Week

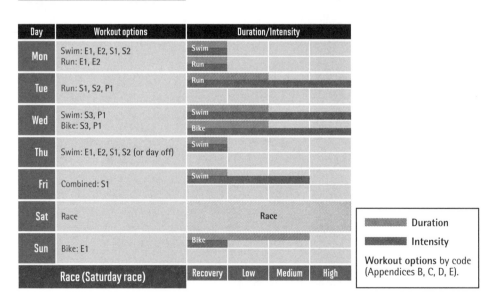

FIGURE 8.1h

Sample Build
R&R Week

Day	Workout options	Duration/Intensity			
Mon	Weights: Optional				
Tue	Run: E2	Run			
Wed	Swim: T1, T2 Bike: E1	Swim Bike			
Thu	Run: E2	Run			
Fri	Swim: E2, S1, S2 Bike: T2	Swim Bike			
Sat	Bike: E2	Bike			
Sun	Run: T2	Run			
Build R&R		Recovery	Low	Medium	High

FIGURE 8.1i

Sample Peak
Training Week

Day	Workout options	Duration/Intensity			
Mon	Swim: E1, E2, S1, S2 Weights: SM	Swim			
Tue	Bike: E2, S3 Run: E2, S1	Bike Run			
Wed	Swim: F1, M1, M2, M3, A1, A2, P1 Combined: M1, A1, A2	Swim Combined			
Thu	Bike: E1	Bike			
Fri	Swim: E2, S1, S2, S3 Run: E1	Swim Run			
Sat	Combined: M1, A1, A2	Combined			
Sun	Bike: E1	Bike			
Peak		Recovery	Low	Medium	High

FIGURE 8.1j

Sample Race
Week with Race
on Saturday

Day	Workout options	Duration/Intensity			
Mon	Swim: E1, E2, S1, S2 Run: E1, E2	Swim Run			
Tue	Run: S1, S2, P1	Run			
Wed	Swim: S3, P1 Bike: S3, P1	Swim Bike			
Thu	Swim: E1, E2, S1, S2 (or day off)	Swim			
Fri	Combined: S1	Swim			
Sat	Race		Race		
Sun	Bike: E1	Bike			
Race (Saturday race)		Recovery	Low	Medium	High

━━━ Duration
━━━ Intensity

Workout options by code
(Appendices B, C, D, E).

Day	Workout options	Duration/Intensity				
Mon	Swim: E1, E2, S1, S2 (or day off)	Swim				
Tue	Bike: E1 Run: S1, S2, P1	Bike				
		Run				
Wed	Swim: S3, P1	Swim				
Thu	Bike: S3, P1 Run: E1	Bike				
		Run				
Fri	Swim: E1, E2, S1, S2 (or day off)	Swim				
Sat	Combined: S1	Combined				
Sun	Race	Race				
Race (Sunday race)		Recovery	Low	Medium	High	

FIGURE 8.1k

Sample Race Week with Race on Sunday

RISK ANALYSIS

As we discussed in Chapter 5, each workout you do has associated risks and rewards. Before you begin fleshing out your daily workouts schedule, it's a good idea to step back and reevaluate the degree of risk you are willing to take on and capable of sustaining. Some workouts are low risk but also produce a low return on your investment of time and energy. Other workouts are risky but can produce dramatic results if you are wise and "invest" in them cautiously. The risks associated with breakthrough workouts are over-training, injury, illness, and burnout. When these setbacks occur, the overly aggressive athlete must return to basic, low-risk, low-reward training in order to reestablish their foundation of fitness. Athletes who experience these conditions frequently are probably addicted to high-risk training and should reexamine their priorities and methods. Figure 8.2 illustrates the workout risk and reward curves.

Risk as associated with training comes from some combination of the frequency, intensity, duration, and mode of training and is unique for each athlete. What is high risk for one athlete may be low risk for another. The difference has to do with experience, fitness levels, susceptibility to injury, previous training adaptations, age, and other factors.

Each athlete has a workout frequency that is optimal. An elite triathlete may work out three times a day for several days in a row and become more fit. But a novice triathlete trying to do three-a-days will soon break down. An athlete who gets "too much too soon" is forced to stop training for several days in order to recover. It's imperative that you find a workout frequency that works for you and then stick to it.

The same holds true for the intensity and duration of workouts. A lot of training done at high intensity, such as intervals on consecutive days in the same sport, is very risky

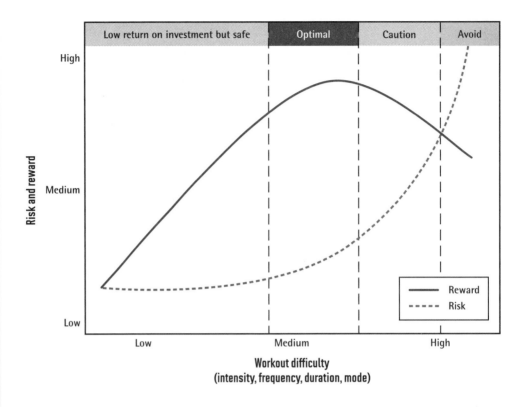

FIGURE 8.2

Risk and Reward
in Training

but potentially rewarding. Extremely long workouts, such as four-hour runs or seven-hour bike rides, are also very risky, but potentially rewarding. Taking these risks before you are ready for them can be a big mistake; in fact, doing workouts that are excessive, particularly in terms of duration, is the most common training mistake that self-coached, long-course athletes make.

Risk associated with "mode" refers to the type of workout you do—swim, bike, run, or crosstraining. Of the three triathlon sports, running is the riskiest because of the stress it places on bone and soft tissues. For some athletes, a lot of running can lead to injury, but with the right precautions, the risk can be reduced. This means strengthening running-related tissues and bone gradually. For most athletes, swimming is the least risky of the three triathlon sports.

The risk of injury due to high frequency, intensity, or duration is also minimized when an athlete includes sufficient recovery time in his or her training program. Whenever you work out in the same sport for two consecutive training sessions, be sure to include recovery time. Frequent recovery is the key to keeping this type of risk at a manageable level.

Strength training also can be a high-risk mode of training. Going to high-load weight lifting before the body is ready can easily cause injury, especially if an athlete becomes too aggressive with the risks they take in the weight room.

Within a weight training regimen, some exercises are riskier than others. Freebar squats, for example, can be troublesome. A heavily loaded bar placed on the shoulders can be especially risky for the athlete who is new to the weight room, has experienced knee or hip injuries, or is older and has degenerating spinal disks. But if you can handle it, the reward reaped from squats is significant. Less risky but also less rewarding are exercises that work similar muscle groups, such as leg presses, step-ups, and lunges.

Plyometric exercises—explosive movements done to build power, especially for running—are also both high risk and high reward. Eccentric-contraction plyometrics are riskier but potentially more rewarding than concentric-contraction plyometrics. An example of an eccentric-contraction plyometric exercise is jumping off of a high box, landing on the floor, and then immediately springing back up to a second high box. A concentric-contraction version of this same exercise eliminates the jump down and landing. There is less potential for reward this way, but also less risk of injury. Chapter 13 considers inclusion of plyometrics in complex training sessions (see Table 13.8).

When selecting a workout, you need to consider the reward that you hope to derive from it as well as the risk involved in performing it. By investing wisely in your training, you can increase your likelihood of building excellent fitness while avoiding the common pitfalls of overly aggressive triathlon training. If you make a mistake in your training, make it on the side of low risk rather than high risk. I guarantee that if you do, you will do better in the long term.

DAILY HOURS

In general, triathlon exaggerates a proficiency for cycling, since that leg of the race typically makes up about half of a triathlon finishing time. Therefore, it seems reasonable to spend about half of your training time on the bike. In the real world of training, that's not always possible, although cycling should usually make up the largest portion of workout time. There are exceptions. For example, triathletes living in the more northern latitudes find it difficult to ride outside in the winter because of the cold weather and snow. In the more equatorial latitudes, summer heat and humidity also favor indoor training. In addition, work responsibilities may force training to early morning or late evening times when there is insufficient light for riding outdoors. For these reasons, a quality indoor bike trainer is of paramount importance for the multisport athlete with high aspirations. Even if you use a stationary trainer regularly, your cycling volume will almost certainly suffer if you cannot get outside on your bike. There are only so many hours you can put in on an indoor trainer. That's just the way it is, and the creative athlete takes it in stride while making training adjustments for these conditions.

Since bike workouts are longer than swim or run workouts, weekly training volume also needs to decrease when weather or other such hurdles force riding indoors. But most athletes know in advance what may interfere with riding on the roads and can plan their annual hours to allow for these factors. If you lived in Minnesota, for example, you would know that in the wintertime nearly all of your cycling would have to be indoors, but in the summertime outdoor riding would be possible. You would therefore schedule your riding time accordingly—for example, you might plan on training on the bike for 350 hours in the winter and 450 hours in the summer.

If you are already a highly proficient cyclist but you have a major limiter in either swimming or running, you may also want to spend less than half of your training time on the bike. To determine whether you fit this category, compare your A-race splits by sport with those of your age-group peers. If, for example, you rank fifteenth on the swim, fourth on the bike, and twentieth on the run, you should focus more on swimming and running and less on biking. In such situations, your workout volume should shift from time on the bike to time training in the limiting sport.

In the Hours column of your Annual Training Plan, you have already indicated the volume for each week of the season. All that remains is to decide how those hours should be allocated during the week. Table 8.1 offers a suggested breakdown. In the left-hand column, find the hours you have scheduled for the first week of the season. By reading across to the right, you'll find the weekly hours broken down into daily amounts. For example, find the "12:00" in the Weekly Hours column. To the right are seven daily hours, one for each day of the week, adding up to twelve hours: 3:00, 2:00, 2:00, 1:30, 1:30, 1:00, and 1:00. This means that the longest workout that week will be three hours. The other daily hours may be divided between two workouts on the same day, especially in the Base period when volume is high. In fact, there are some advantages to working out two times a day, such as an increase in quality for each workout. These daily hours include all the training you do—swimming, biking, running, weights, and any other crosstraining activities.

This table works best for sprint- and Olympic-distance racing. For long-course events, the volume must shift in favor of the longer workout days even though the weekly volume remains the same. For example, the same twelve-hour week described above may have a longer "long" day: 4:00, 2:00, 2:00, 1:30, 1:30, 1:00, and 0:00 (day off).

TIMING WORKOUTS

Figure 8.1 suggests days on which to swim, bike, run, or do combined workouts or weight workouts, but this pattern may not work for your particular lifestyle, job, facility availability, and training groups. How then do you schedule your training sessions? By taking all of the above factors into account and designing your own customized training week, one that you can repeat week after week for the entire season with only minor changes as new circumstances arise. Here's how to do that.

ANCHOR WORKOUTS

These are workouts that must occur on given days each week and over which you have little or no control. For example, if your masters group swims on Tuesdays, Thursdays, and Saturdays, those are the sessions you must plug into your weekly plan. Likewise, if

WEEKLY HOURS	SUGGESTED DAILY HOURS						
3:00	1:30	0:45	0:45	Off	Off	Off	Off
3:30	1:30	1:00	1:00	Off	Off	Off	Off
4:00	1:30	1:00	1:00	0:30	Off	Off	Off
4:30	1:30	1:00	0:45	0:45	0:30	Off	Off
5:00	1:30	1:00	1:00	1:00	0:30	Off	Off
5:30	1:30	1:15	1:00	1:00	0:45	Off	Off
6:00	1:30	1:15	1:00	1:00	0:45	0:30	Off
6:30	1:30	1:15	1:00	1:00	1:00	0:45	Off
7:00	1:30	1:30	1:15	1:00	1:00	0:45	Off
7:30	2:00	1:30	1:15	1:00	1:00	0:45	Off
8:00	2:00	1:30	1:15	1:15	1:00	1:00	Off
8:30	2:00	1:30	1:15	1:15	1:00	1:00	0:30
9:00	2:00	1:30	1:30	1:15	1:00	1:00	0:45
9:30	2:30	1:30	1:30	1:15	1:00	1:00	0:45
10:00	2:30	2:00	1:30	1:15	1:00	1:00	0:45
10:30	2:30	2:00	1:30	1:30	1:00	1:00	1:00
11:00	2:30	2:00	1:30	1:30	1:30	1:00	1:00
11:30	3:00	2:00	1:30	1:30	1:30	1:00	1:00
12:00	3:00	2:00	2:00	1:30	1:30	1:00	1:00
12:30	3:30	2:00	2:00	1:30	1:30	1:00	1:00
13:00	3:30	2:30	2:00	1:30	1:30	1:00	1:00
13:30	3:30	2:30	2:00	2:00	1:30	1:00	1:00
14:00	4:00	2:30	2:00	2:00	1:30	1:00	1:00
14:30	4:00	2:30	2:00	2:00	1:30	1:30	1:00
15:00	4:00	2:30	2:30	2:00	1:30	1:30	1:00
15:30	4:00	2:30	2:30	2:00	2:00	1:30	1:00
16:00	4:00	3:00	2:30	2:00	2:00	1:30	1:00
16:30	4:00	3:00	2:30	2:30	2:00	1:30	1:00
17:00	4:00	3:00	2:30	2:30	2:00	2:00	1:00
17:30	4:30	3:00	2:30	2:30	2:00	2:00	1:00
18:00	4:30	3:00	3:00	2:30	2:30	2:00	1:00
18:30	4:30	3:00	3:00	2:30	2:30	2:00	1:00
19:00	4:30	3:30	3:00	2:30	2:30	2:00	1:00
19:30	4:30	3:30	3:00	3:00	2:30	2:00	1:00
20:00	4:30	3:30	3:00	3:00	2:30	2:30	1:00
20:30	5:00	3:30	3:00	3:00	2:30	2:30	1:00
21:00	5:00	3:30	3:30	3:00	2:30	2:30	1:00
21:30	5:00	3:30	3:30	3:00	3:00	2:30	1:00
22:00	5:00	4:00	3:30	3:00	3:00	2:30	1:00
22:30	5:00	4:00	3:30	3:30	3:00	2:30	1:00
23:00	5:00	4:00	3:30	3:30	3:00	2:30	1:30
23:30	5:30	4:00	3:30	3:30	3:00	2:30	1:30
24:00	5:30	4:00	4:00	3:30	3:00	2:30	1:30
24:30	5:30	4:00	4:00	3:30	3:30	2:30	1:30
25:00	5:30	4:30	4:00	3:30	3:30	2:30	1:30
25:30	5:30	4:30	4:00	4:00	3:30	2:30	1:30
26:00	6:00	4:30	4:00	4:00	3:30	2:30	1:30
26:30	6:00	4:30	4:00	4:00	3:30	3:00	1:30
27:00	6:00	4:30	4:30	4:00	3:30	3:00	1:30
27:30	6:00	4:30	4:30	4:00	4:00	3:00	1:30
28:00	6:00	5:00	4:30	4:00	4:00	3:00	1:30
28:30	6:00	5:00	4:30	4:30	4:00	3:00	1:30
29:00	6:00	5:00	4:30	4:30	4:00	3:30	1:30
29:30	6:00	5:00	4:30	4:30	4:00	3:30	2:00
30:00	6:00	5:00	5:00	4:30	4:00	3:30	2:00
30:30	6:00	5:00	5:00	4:30	4:30	3:30	2:00
31:00	6:00	5:30	5:00	4:30	4:30	3:30	2:00
31:30	6:00	5:30	5:00	5:00	4:30	3:30	2:00
32:00	6:00	5:30	5:00	5:00	4:30	4:00	2:00
32:30	6:00	5:30	5:30	5:00	4:30	4:00	2:00
33:00	6:00	5:30	5:30	5:00	5:00	4:00	2:00
33:30	6:00	6:00	5:30	5:00	5:00	4:00	2:00
34:00	6:00	6:00	5:30	5:00	5:00	4:30	2:00
34:30	6:00	6:00	5:30	5:30	5:00	4:30	2:00
35:00	6:00	6:00	5:30	5:30	5:00	5:00	2:00

Note: May be two-a-day workouts, or three-a-day workouts for elites.

TABLE 8.1

Daily Training Hours

you swim alone but the pool is only available for lap swimming on Mondays, Wednesdays, and Fridays, that is when these anchor workouts must be placed in your weekly plan. Other typical anchor workouts are group bike or run sessions that are scheduled for certain times and days each week. Your longest bike ride and longest run may also be anchor workouts because you typically must do these on the weekend when you have more time available.

TIME-FLEXIBLE WORKOUTS

Next, you'll schedule in the remaining workouts, those that are not anchors and may be done on any day of the week. If you are a high-training-volume athlete and do four or more workouts per sport each week, then putting them on your calendar will be fairly easy—just list two workouts a day and be done with it. But if you do only two or three weekly sessions in a given sport, then how you space them is important. For example, if you run only two times a week, you would not want those sessions to be on Tuesday and Wednesday, as that leaves five consecutive days without running. With that many days off, you would lose any physical gains that you made during the two workouts. In this case, you should separate the two runs with two to three days of no running. This could mean running, for example, on Tuesdays and Fridays.

With three workouts in a given sport, separate each with a day off from that sport. For example, run on Tuesdays, Thursdays, and Saturdays.

DAILY ORDER OF WORKOUTS

Now you'll fine-tune the order of your daily workouts. This is where your appetite for risk and reward will play out. With the anchor workouts, the time of day will probably already be established. But with the flexible workouts there is a primary concern that must be addressed: when you run. It bears repeating that running is the sport in which you are most likely to get injured, due to the extraordinary stress it places on bones, muscles, tendons, and cartilage. If you get a running injury and have to miss several days or even weeks of training, then much, if not all, of your fitness gains will be lost. You need to treat run workouts with caution and do everything you can to prevent injury. One of the most common causes of running injuries is running on tired legs, especially during long or fast runs. You must ensure that your legs are relatively fresh going into these workouts.

Leg fatigue can be a problem any time you are doing a long or fast run within 24 hours of another challenging run or a bike ride. For example, it is best not to do a long bike ride on Saturday and then follow that with a long run on Sunday. Many triathletes attempt this, believing they are preparing themselves for what will happen in a race when they must run on tired legs. The fatigue experienced the day after a big ride, however, is not the same as the fatigue experienced on race day. In reality, there are many causes of fatigue as explained in Chapter 4. Your risk of injury is magnified several times over when you take a long run the day after a long bike ride. The solution is to schedule your long run the day before your long ride. So if these are anchor workouts for the weekend, do your long run on Saturday and your long ride on Sunday.

In the same way, you must be cautious with combination workouts, which are known as "bricks." Although combining a long bike ride with a long run may be similar to what you must do in a race, it is also very risky. If you are prone to getting running-related injuries, this is not a good combination for you, and I'd suggest alternating two other types of brick workouts—bike-emphasis and run-emphasis. In a bike-emphasis brick, you will do a long ride followed by a short run, such as a 15-minute one. Although that is very short, it accomplishes one of the goals of a brick workout—learning to run effectively and efficiently when you have just gotten off of the bike. This combination works well for Ironman-distance triathletes. The run-emphasis brick starts with a short bike ride, which may include a few race-intensity efforts. "Short" means 30 to 90 minutes, depending on your weekly volume. The run may then be a long one.

TIME BETWEEN WORKOUTS

Finally, it's time to schedule some downtime. If you are doing two or more separate workouts—not bricks—in the same day, it is generally best to provide for some rest between them. There may well be some lifestyle circumstances that prevent this, such as when you must fit in a run and swim before going to work in the morning. But generally you will reap greater benefits from your training if you are at least partially recovered from the previous session before starting the next, even though they are in different sports. The time between workouts should include refueling and is best spent sitting down whenever possible.

Given all of the above, you should now be able to design a customized training week that makes the best use of your available time and produces the greatest possible race readiness given your lifestyle.

ONE WORKOUT OR TWO?

Are two workouts as good as one? Is it just as good for you, for example, to do two 45-minute runs as it is to do one 90-minute run? The answer depends on the purpose of the workout. If your objective is to improve your endurance for long events, the answer is no. But if you want to improve any other ability, such as speed skills, force, muscular endurance, or anaerobic endurance, the answer is yes. In fact, for these purposes two runs on the same day are far better than a single long run.

Most triathletes want to improve their endurance, though, so for multisport training, two workouts on the same day are seldom beneficial. Here's why. The physiological benefits of endurance workouts require that you stress not only the many parts of the aerobic system—primarily the heart, lungs, and blood—but also the muscular and nervous systems. In addition, energy, hormone, and enzyme production improvements are necessary for aerobic fitness. Longer workouts are better for stimulating the development of all of the body's aerobic endurance functions. There is also a psychological benefit that comes from completing long workouts.

One reason that one long workout is better than two short ones for improving aerobic endurance has to do with how the body produces energy from fat and carbohydrate during moderate-intensity exercise. As you start a workout, the body relies heavily on carbohydrate stores to provide energy for exercise. But as the duration of the workout increases, there is a steady shift from burning carbohydrate to burning fat. This fat-burning condition is one of the benefits we hope to get from aerobic exercise in order to improve endurance. So if you do two 45-minute runs in the same day rather than one 90-minute run, you will spend less time that day using fat for fuel, and therefore the workouts will produce less of a benefit for the energy-production system. The same example may be applied to the other systems listed above. So when it comes to endurance, one long workout beats two short ones.

COMBINED WORKOUTS

Preparing for races beyond the Olympic distance, or for your maximum performance at any distance, practically requires training twice a day in order to fit everything in. Elite athletes who race for a living and have few demands on their time outside of multisport should seriously consider regular doses of three-a-days, but three workouts a day are seldom, if ever, necessary for the age-group athlete. For most serious recreational athletes who have jobs, families, homes, and other responsibilities, such a frequency of training is likely to lead to overtraining, burnout, illness, or injury. Two good workouts are always better than three mediocre ones.

Besides two-a-days, it's beneficial in the Build periods to combine workouts in two abilities into one session. This practice not only makes better use of your available time but also more closely simulates the stresses of multisport racing. The two ways to accomplish this are with "bricks," as described in Appendix E, and multi-ability sessions, which are detailed in Appendices C and D (called AE Intervals + Threshold).

BRICKS

Once the basic abilities of endurance, force, and speed skills are established, combined bike and run workouts, or bricks, begin to play an important role in training. Bricks come in many forms and can enhance aerobic endurance, race pacing, muscular endurance, and hill strength. They can even streamline the way that you conduct your final equipment check before a race. To select appropriate bricks from Appendix E, understand the demands of your upcoming races and match the workout to your needs.

MULTI-ABILITY WORKOUTS

In the Build and Peak periods, it is often necessary to combine two abilities for a single sport into one session. These multi-ability workouts make better use of your time than single-ability workouts and also produce stress levels that more closely simulate racing. A general rule of thumb is to combine either endurance or muscular endurance work with force, speed-skills, anaerobic endurance, or power work.

In these combinations, the endurance or muscular endurance work, which is less intense than the work in the other categories, should come second within the workout. So, for example, a combined run workout, following a warm-up, could start with intervals on the track that challenge anaerobic endurance and then progress to a steady run at near LT for muscular endurance. Three (or even more) abilities may be combined: for example, speed skills, muscular endurance, and endurance work can all be combined into a single workout. Such a session is excellent for developing the type of fitness necessary for a race.

PLANNING TO RACE

The feeling I get at the starting line is that it's over—all the hard work and training are over. The race is the fun part.
—JULIE MOSS, PROFESSIONAL TRIATHLETE

THE PREVIOUS TWO CHAPTERS provided annual and weekly tools for planning a peak performance. These tools, along with the information presented in Chapters 3 through 6, make up the science of self-coaching for multisport. The less definitive and more difficult part to learn is the art of self-coaching. This side of the process is more intuitive than the scientific side and involves detecting, scrutinizing, and remodeling the many variables that go into designing a season. Sometimes such decisions require careful thought and evaluation; other times they are simply gut-level feelings born of experience. Many successful athletes, especially those who have trained for a long time, operate entirely within this visceral arena. This is not to say that the art of training can't be partly learned.

One way of developing comprehensive self-coaching skills is to study how others have put together their annual and weekly plans. The case studies that follow are all based on real-world athletes with high aspirations, limited time, and great commitment. Their stories may help you see other options for setting up your season. As you read, look especially for ways in which they bent the "rules" described in the previous chapters in order to meet unique sets of circumstances. Their plans as presented here are not necessarily the only possibilities, but they are sound and potentially effective. Regardless of your goal race distance, I suggest that you read all of these case studies because they may offer you new insights into the process of planning.

SPRINT-DISTANCE TRIATHLON

DM is a 42-year-old surgeon from Florida who has competed in triathlon for four years. Prior to this he was a runner, but recurrent injuries eventually led him to swimming and cycling as crosstraining activities, and finally to triathlon. Running injuries continue to plague DM whenever he increases his mileage too quickly or repeatedly runs on back-to-back days.

Because of the summer heat in Florida, most of DM's races are in the spring and fall; fall is the primary race season. As a surgeon, he has a tight daily schedule, and he can seldom train for more than 10 hours per week. Even that is not possible in some weeks. His Annual Training Plan is based on 450 annual hours. But since his maximal weekly volume is more a matter of how many hours he has available, rather than how many he can physically handle, the weekly hours have all been truncated at 10. This means there is no increase in volume during the Base period. If he built to a volume level of 10 weekly hours as a high point in the third week of Base 3, as suggested in Table 7.2, he would end up being considerably undertrained, since he's capable of handling more than 10 hours weekly.

DM has planned for two peaks, with the fall peak being paramount. His season goals are based on the fall sprint-race series and the national championship. By trying to maintain peak race form for four weeks (from week 43 to 46), DM is stretching it, but since the race during week 46 is the last important one of the season, there is no reason to do otherwise.

Weight-room strength is not a problem for DM, but he has been unable to convert this to on-bike force since taking up triathlon. This limiter is evidenced by his inability to turn a high gear at race cadence. So bike muscular endurance is emphasized in his annual plan, and these workouts will include many cruise intervals and threshold bike sessions in which he repeatedly shifts between a "comfortable" gear and the next higher one in 30- to 60-second bouts. In the brief periods that he is in the higher gear, he will attempt to maintain the same cadence that he used in the lower gear. Such training should improve his ability to drive a bigger gear.

Other limiters for DM, besides bike force and time available for training, are swimming and running anaerobic endurance. Since anaerobic endurance comes around rather quickly once aerobic endurance, force, speed skills, and muscular endurance are developed, high-intensity intervals are scheduled only for the Build periods.

Table 9.1 shows how a typical week in the Prep period is organized. Notice that DM has planned only one bike workout in this period. That's because weight training takes the place of riding during this period. The benefit of greater force appears to have a more direct application to cycling than to swimming and running, with swim performance having the second-closest relationship to high force development. Once the Base period

Athlete: *DM*
Annual hours: *450*
Seasonal goals:
1. *Top 5 finish in sprint series.*
2. *Break 1 hour at nationals.*
3. *—*

Training objectives:
1. *Increase bike LT power 15% by wk 40.*
2. *Run 19-min 5k by wk 36.*
3. *Remain injury free.*
4. *Swim 800 m in <8 min by wk 19.*

Sample Training Plan for a Sprint-Distance Triathlete

Wk#	Mon	Race	PRI	Period	Hours	Weights	SWIM							BIKE							RUN						
							Endurance	Force	Speed Skills	Muscular Endurance	Anaerobic Endurance	Power	Testing	Endurance	Force	Speed Skills	Muscular Endurance	Anaerobic Endurance	Power	Testing	Endurance	Force	Speed Skills	Muscular Endurance	Anaerobic Endurance	Power	Testing
01	1/4			Prep	7.5	MT	X		X					X		X					X		X				
02	1/11			▼	7.5	▼	X		X				X	X		X				X	X		X				X
03	1/18			Base 1	9.0	MS	X		X					X		X					X		X				
04	1/25				10.0		X		X					X		X					X		X				
05	2/1				10.0		X		X					X		X					X		X				
06	2/8			▼	6.5	▼	X		X				X	X		X				X	X		X				X
07	2/15			Base 2	9.5	SM	X	X	X	X				X	X	X	X				X	X	X	X			
08	2/22				10.0		X	X	X	X				X	X	X	X				X	X	X	X			
09	3/1				10.0		X	X	X	X				X	X	X	X				X	X	X	X			
10	3/8			▼	6.5		X		X				X	X		X				X	X		X				X
11	3/15			Build 1	10.0		X			X	X			X			X	X			X			X	X		
12	3/22				10.0		X			X	X			X			X	X			X			X	X		
13	3/29			▼	6.5		X		X				X	X		X				X	X		X				X
14	4/5			Build 2	10.0		X			X	X			X			X	X	X		X			X	X		
15	4/12				10.0		X			X	X			X			X	X	X		X			X	X		
16	4/19	5K Road Race	C	▼	6.5		X		X					X		X					X		X				
17	4/26	Oly Distance	B	Peak	9.5		X		X	X				X		X	X				X			X	X		
18	5/3			▼	7.5	▼	X		X	X				X		X	X				X			X	X		
19	5/10	Sprint Distance	A	Race	6.5	o					X								X							X	
20	5/17			Tran	–	o																					
21	5/24			Base 1	9.0	MS	X		X					X		X					X		X				
22	5/31				10.0		X		X					X		X					X		X				
23	6/7				10.0		X		X					X		X					X		X				
24	6/14			▼	6.5	▼	X		X				X	X		X				X	X		X				X
25	6/21			Base 2	9.5	SM	X	X	X	X				X	X	X	X				X	X	X	X			
26	6/28				10.0		X	X	X	X				X	X	X	X				X	X	X	X			
27	7/5				10.0		X	X	X	X				X	X	X	X				X	X	X	X			
28	7/12			▼	6.5		X		X				X	X		X				X	X		X				X
29	7/19			Base 3	10.0		X	X	X	X				X	X	X	X				X	X	X	X			
30	7/26				10.0		X	X	X	X				X	X	X	X				X	X	X	X			
31	8/2				10.0		X	X	X	X				X	X	X	X				X	X	X	X			
32	8/9			▼	6.5		X		X				X	X		X				X	X		X				X
33	8/16			Build 1	10.0		X			X	X			X			X	X			X			X	X		
34	8/23				10.0		X			X	X			X			X	X			X			X	X		
35	8/30	Sprint Distance	C		10.0		X			X	X			X			X	X			X			X	X		
36	9/6	5K Road Race	C	▼	6.5		X		X					X		X					X		X				
37	9/13			Build 2	10.0		X			X	X			X			X	X			X			X	X		
38	9/20	Sprint Distance	C		10.0		X			X	X			X			X	X			X			X	X		
39	9/27				10.0		X			X	X			X			X	X			X			X	X		
40	10/4			▼	6.5		X		X				X	X		X				X	X		X				X
41	10/11	Sprint Distance	B	Peak	9.5		X		X	X				X		X	X				X			X	X		
42	10/18	Sprint Distance	B	▼	7.5	▼	X		X	X				X		X	X				X			X	X		
43	10/25	Sprint Distance	A	Race	6.5	o				X							X		X					X		X	
44	11/1	Sprint Distance	B		7.5	SM				X							X		X					X		X	
45	11/8	Sprint Nats	A		6.5	o				X							X		X					X		X	
46	11/15	Sprint Distance	B	▼	7.5	SM				X							X		X					X		X	
47	11/22			Build 1	10.0		X			X	X			X			X	X			X			X	X		
48	11/29				10.0		X			X	X			X			X	X			X			X	X		
49	12/6				10.0		X		X				X	X		X				X	X		X				X
50	12/13	Sprint Distance	C	▼	6.5	▼	X		X					X		X					X		X				
51	12/20			Tran	–	o																					
52	12/27			▼	–	o																					

begins, DM will cut his weight-room workouts back to two per week and include more time on the bike.

If you look at the workouts in Table 9.1 (see Appendices B, C, and D for descriptions), you'll notice that nearly all of the aerobic workouts are in zone 1. In the early stages of fitness building it's important to become as fast as possible at a low effort before progressing to the next, higher intensity zone. This ensures comprehensive fitness development.

TABLE 9.1

Week 1 for DM

	MON		TUE		WED		THUR		FRI		SAT		SUN	
Workout 1	Wts MT	:45	Run E1	:45	Swim S1, E2	:45	Run S1	:45	Swim S1, E2	:45	Run E1	1:00	Bike E1	1:30
Workout 2					Wts MT	:45			Wts MT	:45				

Table 9.2 (see Appendices B–E for descriptions) illustrates a challenge commonly faced by endurance athletes: a week that includes high-intensity workouts following a week that ended with a race. Attempting to do an anaerobic endurance running workout on Tuesday would greatly increase DM's risk of injury during week 39. Therefore his track session is moved to Thursday, and the higher intensity bike workout is scheduled for Tuesday. The Tuesday bike session is a power workout. DM will start this workout and assess his capacity to finish it as he progresses. If he feels that his body has not recovered enough to perform the powerful movements safely, he will not attempt to complete the repetitions and will simply ride easily in zone 1 for the remainder of the hour.

TABLE 9.2

Week 39 for DM

	MON		TUE		WED		THUR		FRI		SAT		SUN	
Workout 1	Swim S1, E1	:45	Run E1	:45	Swim M1, A1	:45	Run A2	1:00	Swim S1, E2	:45	Cmb M1	1:30	Bike E2	2:00
Workout 2	Wts SM	:30	Bike P1	1:00	Bike E1	1:00								

Note that the hours in both illustrated weeks do not follow the suggestions provided in Table 8.1. This variation from the normal training program was allowed in order to address DM's unique scheduling needs.

OLYMPIC-DISTANCE DUATHLON

EW is a 53-year-old part-time fitness director at a health club. She has competed in duathlons and running for four years, but started cycling competitively seven years ago. Her greater experience on the bike is evident in her race splits.

At 1.74 pounds per inch, EW is quite lean, even for an athlete, and as is sometimes the case when body mass is low, force development is her major limiter. To achieve her aggressive goals as listed at the top of her Annual Training Plan, year-round weight

Athlete: *EW*

Annual hours: *350 (wks 1-12), 450 (wks 13-52)*

Seasonal goals:
1. *Place top 10 at Duathlon Nats.*
2. *Qualify for Duathlon Worlds.*
3. *Run under 25 min for 5k.*

Training objectives:
1. *Finish half-marathon in wk 12.*
2. *Do 6 step-ups with 75+ pounds by wk 6.*
3. *2nd 5k within 1 min of 1st in A, B races.*
4. *Complete 40k TT in <1:11 by wk 45.*

Sample Training Plan for an Olympic-Distance Duathlete

Wk#	Mon	Race	PRI	Period	Hours	Weights	SWIM End	Force	Speed Skills	Musc End	Anaer End	Power	Testing	BIKE End	Force	Speed Skills	Musc End	Anaer End	Power	Testing	RUN End	Force	Speed Skills	Musc End	Anaer End	Power	Testing
01	1/4			Base 1	8.5	MS								X		X					X		X				
02	1/11			↓	9.5	↓								X		X					X		X				
03	1/18			↓	5.0	↓								X		X					X						X
04	1/25			Base 2	9.0	↓								X		X					X	X	X	X			
05	2/1			↓	10.0	↓								X		X					X	X	X	X			
06	2/8			↓	5.0	↓								X		X					X		X				X
07	2/15			Base 3	9.5	SM								X		X					X	X	X	X			
08	2/22			↓	10.5	↓								X		X					X	X	X	X			
09	3/1			↓	5.0	↓								X		X					X		X				X
10	3/8			Peak	7.5	↓								X		X					X			X			
11	3/15			↓	6.0	↓								X		X					X			X			
12	3/22	Half-Marathon	A	Race	5.0	0										X									X		
13	3/29			Tran	-	0																					
14	4/5			Base 2	9.5	MS								X	X	X	X				X	X	X	X			
15	4/12			↓	11.5	↓								X	X	X	X				X	X	X	X			
16	4/19			↓	12.5	↓								X	X	X	X				X	X	X	X			
17	4/26	15k Road Race	C	↓	6.5	↓								X		X					X		X				
18	5/3			Base 3	10.0	SM								X	X	X	X				X	X	X	X			
19	5/10			↓	12.0	↓								X	X	X	X				X	X	X	X			
20	5/17			↓	13.0	↓								X	X	X	X				X	X	X	X			
21	5/24	Oly Du	C	↓	6.5	↓								X		X					X		X				
22	5/31	5k Road Race	C	Build 1	11.5	↓								X	X	X	X				X	X	X	X			
23	6/7			↓	11.5	↓								X	X	X	X				X	X	X	X			
24	6/14	10k Road Race		↓	6.5	↓								X		X					X		X				
25	6/21			Build 2	10.5	↓								X	X	X	X				X		X		X		
26	6/28			↓	10.5	↓								X	X	X	X				X		X		X		
27	7/5	Oly Du	B	↓	6.5	↓								X		X					X		X				
28	7/12			Build 2	10.5	↓								X		X	X				X		X		X		
29	7/19	Oly Du		↓	6.5	↓								X		X					X		X				
30	7/26	Team Tri	C	Peak	9.5	↓								X	X	X	X				X		X				
31	8/2			↓	7.5	↓								X	X	X	X				X		X				
32	8/9	Du Nats	A	Race	6.5	0													X						X		
33	8/16			Tran	-	0																					
34	8/23			Base 3	12.0	SM								X	X	X	X				X	X	X	X			
35	8/30			↓	6.5	↓								X		X				X	X		X				X
36	9/6			Build 1	11.5	↓								X	X	X	X				X	X	X	X			
37	9/13			↓	11.5	↓								X	X	X	X				X		X				
38	9/20	Oly Du	B	↓	6.5	↓								X		X					X		X				
39	9/27			Build 2	10.5	↓								X		X	X				X			X	X		
40	10/4	Oly Du	C	↓	10.5	↓								X	X	X	X				X		X	X	X		
41	10/11			↓	6.5	↓								X		X				X	X		X				X
42	10/18			Build 2	10.5	↓								X	X	X	X				X		X	X	X		
43	10/25			↓	10.5	↓								X	X	X	X				X		X		X		
44	11/1			↓	6.5	↓								X							X		X				X
45	11/8	40k TT	B	Peak	9.5	↓								X	X	X	X				X		X	X			
46	11/15			↓	7.5	↓								X	X	X	X				X		X	X			
47	11/22	Oly Du	A	Race	6.5	0											X								X		
48	11/29	5k Road Race	B	↓	6.5	0											X								X		
49	12/6	5k Road Race	B	↓	6.5	0											X								X		
50	12/13			Tran	-	0																					
51	12/20			↓	-	0																					
52	12/27			↓	-	0																					

training is necessary, but she will put special emphasis on weight training during the Prep and Base periods.

Although EW will not attend the duathlon world championship this year because of a schedule conflict, qualifying is still a strong incentive and would define her ability as a duathlete. In the previous year she made Team USA and participated in the world championship by qualifying at a regional race, but she has never competed in the duathlon nationals. Next year, she will "age up" to the 55–59 age group, and even loftier goals are on the agenda for that season, including aiming for a medal at nationals and a top five at worlds.

It's usually unrealistic to set goals based on performance in relation to others, since you never know who might show at a race and what their fitness might be. In this case, however, EW knows all of the players, as they have been at these races in the past, and she can count on them being in top form for the national and world championships. So in a way EW has fairly well-known quantities; it is not unreasonable for her to compare her performances against theirs because she is well aware of their abilities. And since the championship courses are never the same two years in a row, the competitors are the only variable that remains somewhat constant.

The other limiter, besides force, that EW must tackle is running muscular endurance. A duathlete's muscular endurance for running is suspect when the second 5 km average per-mile pace is more than 20 seconds slower than the first. Improving this vital element of duathlon fitness involves boosting running endurance and force development separately and then combining them in workouts such as cruise intervals and threshold runs. Following these up with tempo bricks allows for more race-specific training. Table 9.3 illustrates how this process is begun in an early week of EW's training season. Notice that on Saturday of week 7 she is doing a two-hour M1 run workout. The first 75 minutes of this workout are done in zones 1 and 2, and the last 45-minute segment is in zone 3. Table 9.4 shows how this ability reaches its final form with a two-hour M1 brick. This "graduate-level" workout starts with a 30-minute run building from zone 1 to zone 3. The 60-minute bike portion includes a 10 km time trial at the goal effort for her next A-priority race, which comes at the end of week 47. The final 30-minute run includes a 15-minute effort at goal race pace. Late in the season, this workout will seem less intimidating than it would have been if attempted prior to development of the prerequisite abilities.

TABLE 9.3

Week 7 for EW

	MON		TUE		WED		THUR		FRI		SAT		SUN	
Workout 1	Run S1	:45	Run E1	1:00	Run F1	1:30	Run E1	:30	Off		Run M1	2:00	Bike E1	2:00
Workout 2	Wts PE	:45					Wts PE	:45						

Week 43 has a lot of intensity built into it, with bike hill repeats on Tuesday, run hill intervals on Thursday, and the brick on Saturday. So on Wednesday, EW may cut the bike ride short, and on Thursday she may replace the bike jumps with an E1 ride. She can make these decisions shortly after starting the workouts when she is able to assess her level of recovery. Typically, recovery is somewhat improved later in the season as fitness reaches its highest levels of the year. Early in the year such a week may not be possible for EW.

TABLE 9.4

Week 43 for EW

	MON		TUE		WED		THUR		FRI		SAT		SUN	
Workout 1	Run E1	:30	Run E2	:45	Bike E1	1:30	Run A4	:45	Off		Cmb M1	2:00	Bike E2	2:30
Workout 2	Wts SM	:30	Bike F3	1:00			Bike S3	1:00						

OLYMPIC-DISTANCE TRIATHLON

LT is a 29-year-old, second-year professional triathlete. Life as a neopro is not easy, so LT works part time to make ends meet financially. Her husband is a coach at the local college and quite supportive of her career. They have no children.

In college, LT was an All-American runner at 800 meters with a 2:06 personal best, so her running speed is excellent. Prior to this season, she had never run for more than about 75 minutes in a workout, and most sessions were far shorter, so her endurance is questionable. Some disproportionate slowing is evident in her other personal best times as the distance gets longer: 35:30 for 10 km, 16:30 for 5 km, and 2:11 for an Olympic-distance triathlon. Excellent speed, however, is a good starting place for a career in endurance sports.

Other limiters that impact her major goal of qualifying for the national team for the world championship as an elite athlete are swim speed skills, bike force, and bike-handling speed skills in a pack (many of her most important races are draft-legal). These limiters are primarily the result of being new to triathlon—she's in her third season—and having no background in swimming or cycling. While experience will correct these deficiencies, given enough time, she would like to speed the process up this year, as she is almost 30 and rapidly approaching her assumed physiological peak as an endurance athlete. In addition, her long-term goal is to contend for a spot on the national team for the Olympics in three years, so the improvement curve must be steep.

Probably because she is new to the sport, lack of confidence is also holding her back. If LT is to make the world's team and continue growing, frequent success is necessary. To build greater confidence, we have sprinkled several C-priority running races and local Olympic-distance triathlons throughout her Annual Training Plan. She is likely to win these, which will boost her confidence while she gains valuable race experience.

Athlete: *LT*

Annual hours: *550*

Seasonal goals:
1. *Qualify for Worlds team.*
2. *Swim sub-23 min for 1500m.*
3. *Run sub-38 min for 10k in A races.*

Training objectives:
1. *Swim 1k in <15:14 by wk 18.*
2. *Leg press 320+ pounds by wk 10.*
3. *Ride in pack 7 times by wk 29, 16 by wk 45.*
4. *Easily run 90+ min by wk 18.*
5. *Complete 3 crash weeks in 6 weeks by 43.*

Sample Training Plan for an Olympic-Distance Professional Triathlete

Legend for discipline columns (each of SWIM, BIKE, RUN): En = Endurance, Fo = Force, SS = Speed Skills, ME = Muscular Endurance, AE = Anaerobic Endurance, Po = Power, Te = Testing

Wk#	Mon	Race	PRI	Period	Hours	Weights	S-En	S-Fo	S-SS	S-ME	S-AE	S-Po	S-Te	B-En	B-Fo	B-SS	B-ME	B-AE	B-Po	B-Te	R-En	R-Fo	R-SS	R-ME	R-AE	R-Po	R-Te
01	1/4			Prep	9.0	AA	X		X				X	X		X				X	X		X				X
02	1/11				9.0		X		X					X		X					X		X				
03	1/18				9.0		X		X					X		X					X		X				
04	1/25				9.0		X		X					X		X					X		X				
05	2/1				9.0	MT	X		X					X		X					X		X				
06	2/8				9.0		X		X				X	X		X			X		X		X				X
07	2/15			Base 1	11.0	MS	X		X					X		X					X		X				
08	2/22				13.0		X		X					X		X					X		X				
09	3/1				14.5		X		X					X		X					X		X				
10	3/8				8.0		X		X				X	X		X			X		X		X				X
11	3/15			Base 2	12.5	SM	X	X	X	X				X	X	X	X				X	X	X	X			
12	3/22				14.0		X	X	X	X				X	X	X	X				X	X	X	X			
13	3/29				15.5		X	X	X	X				X	X	X	X				X	X	X	X			
14	4/5	5K Road Race	C		8.0		X							X							X						
15	4/12			Base 3	12.5		X	X	X	X				X	X	X	X				X	X	X	X			
16	4/19	Oly Du	B		14.5		X	X	X	X				X	X	X	X				X	X	X	X			
17	4/26				16.5		X	X	X	X				X	X	X	X				X	X	X	X			
18	5/3	Oly Tri	B		8.0		X		X					X		X					X						
19	5/10	Sprint Tri	B	Build 1	14.0		X							X	X		X				X			X	X		
20	5/17				14.0		X							X	X		X				X			X	X		
21	5/24	5k Road Race	C		14.0		X		X					X	X		X				X			X	X		
22	5/31	Oly Du	B		8.0									X			X		X							X	
23	6/7			Build 2	13.0		X		X					X			X	X			X			X	X		
24	6/14	10k Road Race	C		13.0		X		X					X			X	X			X			X	X		
25	6/21				13.0		X		X					X			X	X			X			X	X		
26	6/28	Oly Tri	C		8.0		X							X	X						X	X					
27	7/5			Peak	11.5		X		X					X			X				X		X				
28	7/12	Oly Tri	B		9.5		X		X					X			X	X			X		X				
29	7/19	Tri Nats, Oly	A	Race	8.0	o			X									X								X	
30	7/26			Tran	-	o																					
31	8/2			Base 2	15.5	SM	X	X	X	X				X	X	X					X	X	X	X			
32	8/9	Oly Tri	B		8.0									X			X		X							X	
33	8/16			Base 3	12.5		X	X	X					X	X	X					X	X	X				
34	8/23				14.5		X	X	X	X				X	X	X	X				X	X	X	X			
35	8/30	10k Road Race	C		16.5		X	X	X					X	X	X					X	X	X				
36	9/6	Oly Du	B		8.0									X			X		X							X	
37	9/13			Build 1	14.0		X		X					X	X		X	X			X			X	X		
38	9/20			Crash	14.0	o	X	X	X	X				X	X	X	X				X	X	X	X			
39	9/27	5k Road Race	C	R+R	7.0		X	X						X	X						X	X					
40	10/4			Build 2	13.0	SM	X		X					X			X				X		X				
41	10/11	10k Road Race	C	Crash	13.0	o	X		X					X			X				X		X				
42	10/18	6k XC Race	C	R+R	7.0	SM	X	X						X	X						X	X					
43	10/25			Crash	13.0	o	X	X	X					X	X		X	X			X	X					
44	11/1			R+R	7.0	o	X	X						X	X						X	X					
45	11/8	8k Road Race	C	Peak	11.5	o	X		X					X	X		X	X			X		X				
46	11/15	Tri Worlds, Oly	A	Race	8.0	o			X									X								X	
47	11/22			Tran	-	o																					
48	11/29				-	o																					
49	12/6				-	o																					
50	12/13				-	o																					
51	12/20																										
52	12/27																										

A well-established professional triathlete need not race this frequently, especially in low-key events, and may pick and choose competitions. Besides the world championship, she will enter one or two races in foreign countries to gain experience in traveling and competing, plus two or three major national events. Since her finances are tight, LT will need to convince the national governing body that she is a good investment for the future so that they will pay her travel expenses. Success in races is the only way to do this.

Notice on LT's training plan that her season is rather long, starting with an event in early April and going well into late November. The chance of burnout is quite high when a racing season lasts for 32 weeks, as hers does. R&R weeks and Transition periods are critical in this situation. Also, because of the season's length, LT will return to Base training in week 31 to shore up the most fundamental elements of fitness before building to a second peak for the world championship.

Table 9.5 shows how she will blend a typical B-priority, race-week schedule with an R&R week. The week is treated much as a race week, except more caution is evident because she will have just finished a three-week Build 1 period at relatively high volume and intensity. The race at week's end is an Olympic-distance event that she should complete in about 2:15, including warm-up and cool-down time.

TABLE 9.5

Week 22 for LT

	MON		TUE		WED		THUR		FRI		SAT		SUN	
Workout 1	Wts SM	:30	Run P1	:45	Swim P1	:30	Bike P1	1:00	Off		Cmb S1	:45	Race	2:45
Workout 2			Bike E1	:45	Bike E1	1:00								

In order to reach as high a level of fitness as possible for the world championship, LT will incorporate three "crash" weeks into her late-season preparation in weeks 38, 41, and 43. (Crash weeks are described in greater detail in Chapter 14.) If done correctly, a crash week will dramatically boost fitness. If done recklessly, such a schedule is likely to cause injury. The likelihood of overtraining is possible, but not overwhelming, since the increased training intensity lasts for only a week and is followed by a greater-than-usual reduction in volume. Also, there is only a one-week buildup to crash weeks 38 and 41, so that R&R weeks are spaced just three weeks apart. The last crash week (43) is preceded and followed by R&R weeks. One study showed that, with elite athletes, it usually takes more than two weeks of crash-type training to cause overtraining.

Table 9.6 illustrates a crash week. LT is cautious with swim intensity this week, since her swim stroke is still developing and could easily break down if she swims when fatigued. At this stage in swimming, fitness at the expense of form is not a good trade-off. For the same reason, it is a good idea for her to swim first on double workout days. The hours from Table 8.1 have been redistributed to better fit her needs. The week begins with a reduced-intensity workout on Monday because LT will have raced cross-country on the prior Saturday. You don't want to start a crash week tired. Note that Friday is also a recovery day; in this case it's a day off. A little caution is advisable following the run-emphasis brick on Thursday and the hilly run on Saturday. Running injuries are the most common problem faced in a crash week. She will need to carefully evaluate her recovery before taking on the bike-run brick on Sunday. The swim workout should be a good recovery workout regardless.

TABLE 9.6

Week 43 for LT

	MON		TUE		WED		THUR		FRI		SAT		SUN	
Workout 1	Swim S1, S2	1:00	Run M5	:45	Swim F3, M2	1:00	Swim E2	:30	Swim S1, S2	:45	Run F2	1:30	Swim S1, E2	:30
Workout 2			Bike S3	1:00	Bike M3	1:30	Cmb M1	1:30	Bike E1	1:00			Cmb A1	2:00

HALF-IRONMAN-DISTANCE TRIATHLON

HP is a 35-year-old executive director of a small, nonprofit organization and works about 35 hours per week on a flexible schedule. He is married and has a teenage son. His athletic experience includes 20 years of running and 5 years of triathlon. HP's previous best race times include a 2:15 Olympic-distance event and a 5:12 half-Ironman.

Although HP has perhaps 15 to 20 hours available for training each week, the physical stress such levels have caused in the past mean that this kind of volume is not appropriate for him. His Annual Training Plan therefore calls for 500 annual hours. That means his highest weekly volume of the year is about 15 hours, but much of it is in the range of 12 to 13 hours.

HP's mental skills, especially his motivation to excel, are excellent. Sometimes such enthusiasm can lead to obsessive training, but he has a good working knowledge of the science of training from years of reading, which serves as a moderating factor.

To achieve his goals listed at the top of the Annual Training Plan, HP must improve three limiters: running muscular endurance, climbing force on the bike, and swim speed skills. He has determined that there are five objectives he must work toward in order to strengthen his limiters and ultimately achieve his half-Ironman time goals.

Since the half-Ironman scheduled for week 46 is on a hilly course, developing greater bike force is a priority for HP. He will therefore train with weights year-round and do frequent hilly bike rides (indicated by the "Force" workouts under the bike column). He will sometimes combine these hilly workouts with work in other abilities. On Thursday of week 23, for example, he will do a one-hour M3 ride. This is a cruise-interval session done on a hill while remaining seated. That same week, he will complete a three-hour brick. The emphasis of this workout will be on a one-hour ride on a hilly course followed by a two-hour run. This is the last brick before his first peak of the season, so it will be conducted as a "dress rehearsal" for the race. This means that he will try to simulate race

Athlete: *HP*

Annual hours: *500*

Seasonal goals:
1. *Break 5:00 at Gulf Coast (wk 27).*
2. *Break 5:10 at Clermont (wk 46).*
3. —

Sample Training Plan for a Half-Ironman-Distance Triathlete

Training objectives:
1. *Swim 500m under 8 min by wk 31.*
2. *Leg press 6 x 450 pounds by wk 8.*
3. *Faster bike split than last year in wk 38.*
4. *Run 10k under 38:30 in wk 20.*
5. *Faster run split than last year in wk 38.*

Wk#	Mon	Race	PRI	Period	Hours	Weights	SWIM							BIKE							RUN						
							Endurance	Force	Speed Skills	Muscular Endurance	Anaerobic Endurance	Power	Testing	Endurance	Force	Speed Skills	Muscular Endurance	Anaerobic Endurance	Power	Testing	Endurance	Force	Speed Skills	Muscular Endurance	Anaerobic Endurance	Power	Testing
01	1/4			Prep	8.5	AA	X		X				X	X		X				X	X		X				X
02	1/11			↓	8.5	↓	X		X					X		X					X		X				
03	1/18				8.5	MT	X		X					X		X					X		X				
04	1/25			▼	8.5	↓	X		X				X	X		X				X	X		X				X
05	2/1			Base 1	10.0	SM	X		X					X		X					X		X				
06	2/8				12.0		X		X					X		X					X		X				
07	2/15				13.5		X		X					X		X					X		X				
08	2/22			▼	7.0	↓	X		X				X	X		X				X	X		X				X
09	3/1			Base 2	10.5		X	X	X	X				X	X	X	X				X	X	X	X			
10	3/8	(Swim camp)			12.5		X	X	X	X				X	X	X	X				X	X	X	X			
11	3/15				14.0		X	X	X	X				X	X	X	X				X	X	X	X			
12	3/22			▼	7.0		X		X				X	X		X				X	X		X				X
13	3/29			Base 3	11.0		X	X	X					X	X	X					X	X	X				
14	4/5				13.5		X	X	X					X	X	X					X	X	X				
15	4/12				15.0		X	X	X					X	X	X					X	X	X				
16	4/19			▼	7.0		X		X				X	X		X				X	X		X				X
17	4/26			Build 1	12.5		X		X	X	X			X		X					X		X				
18	5/3				12.5		X		X	X	X			X		X					X		X				
19	5/10				12.5		X		X	X	X			X		X					X		X				
20	5/17	10k Road Race	C	▼	7.0		X		X				X	X		X				X	X		X				X
21	5/24			Build 2	12.0		X		X	X	X			X		X	X	X			X		X	X			
22	5/31				12.0		X		X	X	X			X		X	X	X			X		X	X			
23	6/7			▼	12.0		X		X	X				X		X	X				X		X	X			
24	6/14	Sprint Tri	C	▼	7.0	↓	X							X							X						
25	6/21	Oly Tri	B	Peak	10.5	o	X		X	X				X		X	X				X		X				
26	6/28			▼	8.5	SM	X							X		X	X				X		X	X			
27	7/5	Half-Ironman	A	Race	7.0			X											X							X	
28	7/12	Sprint Tri	B	▼	7.0	SM		X		X							X							X			
29	7/19			Tran	-	o																					
30	7/26			Base 3	13.5	SM	X	X	X	X				X	X	X	X				X	X	X	X			
31	8/2				15.0		X	X	X	X				X	X	X	X				X	X	X	X			
32	8/9			▼	7.0		X		X				X	X		X				X	X		X				X
33	8/16			Build 1	12.5		X		X	X	X			X		X	X				X		X				
34	8/23				12.5		X		X	X	X			X		X	X				X		X				
35	8/30	Sprint Tri	B	▼	7.0			X			X								X						X		
36	9/6	Oly Du	B	Peak	8.5	↓	X		X					X		X					X		X				
37	9/13			▼	8.5		X		X					X		X					X		X				
38	9/20	Oly Tri	A	Race	7.0	o		X							X										X		
39	9/27			Base 3	13.5	SM	X	X	X	X				X	X	X	X				X	X	X	X			
40	10/4				15.0		X	X	X	X				X	X	X	X				X	X	X	X			
41	10/11	Oly Du	B	▼	7.0	↓		X							X										X		
42	10/18			Build 1	12.5	o	X		X	X	X			X		X	X				X		X				
43	10/25				12.5		X		X	X	X			X		X	X				X		X				
44	11/1	Sprint Tri	C	▼	7.0		X		X					X		X					X		X				
45	11/8			Peak	8.5		X		X	X				X		X	X				X		X	X			
46	11/15	Half-Ironman	A	Race	7.0			X			X								X						X		
47	11/22			Tran	-																						
48	11/29				-																						
49	12/6				-																						
50	12/13			▼	-	↓																					
51	12/20																										
52	12/27																										

conditions as closely as possible. He should maintain the same workout intensity that he plans to use in the race; have his bike set up in race condition, with the same tires and other components; wear the same running shoes that he plans to wear in the event; take along the same sports nutrition foods and fluids; and follow the same feeding schedule that he plans to follow on the day of the race.

Throughout the season, HP will include frequent swim drills, and he will do an "extra" swim on Saturdays to focus on technique (Table 9.7). If time is tight on any given Saturday, he can move the swim session to Sunday. These weekend workouts will include drills specific to his needs and short, race-effort repetitions in which he applies what he's learning in the drills. Short bouts of swimming—for example, 25 to 50 meters or yards with long recoveries—will allow HP to concentrate on skills at race speed. Frequent swim drilling without applying the skills at anticipated race velocity, however, would be of little value.

TABLE 9.7

Week 23 for HP

	MON		TUE		WED		THUR		FRI		SAT		SUN	
Workout 1	Swim S1, S2	:45	Run M5	:45	Swim S3, M1, A1	1:00	Run S1	:45	Swim S3, E2	:45	Swim S1, E2	:45	Bike E2	2:00
Workout 2	Wts SM	:30	Bike S3, E2	1:00			Bike M3	1:00			Cmb F1	3:00		

Table 9.8 shows how HP will rest while maintaining his fitness the week before his last race of the year. Notice that the annual plan calls for seven hours of training that week, but that his weekly duration actually adds up to five hours. However, he should complete the race at the end of the week in just over five hours, based on his goal of 5:10, and there is a pre-race warm-up. In all, his actual time for the week will total more than ten hours. Weekly hours in race weeks will fluctuate depending on the type of race planned. The volume scheduled for these weeks is simply a rough guideline intended to reflect the reduction in training that will help HP prepare for race day.

TABLE 9.8

Week 46 for HP

	MON		TUE		WED		THUR		FRI		SAT		SUN	
Workout 1	Swim S1, E2	:45	Run P1	:45	Swim P1	:30	Run E1	:30	Off		Cmb S1	:45	Race	5:30
Workout 2			Bike E1	1:00			Bike P1	:45						

Also note that in week 46 HP does a power workout in one sport each on Tuesday, Wednesday, and Thursday. The purpose of these workouts is to maintain the ability to call on and use fast-twitch muscles, keep blood volume high, and feel mentally ready to go fast. Total rest in a race week with only easy distance frequently results in feelings of "flatness" on race day. Along the same line, doing a brief workout with short, high-intensity efforts the day before the race encourages sharpness on race day while relieving nagging concerns about whether enough training has been done in the last few days before the event. Many triathletes find that taking a day off 48 hours prior to the race is effective for ensuring recovery.

IRONMAN-DISTANCE TRIATHLON

JH is a 46-year-old mortgage broker who is married and has two high-school-aged children. He has competed in triathlons for six years, mostly at the Olympic- and half-Ironman distances.

Last year JH completed his first ultra-distance race at Ironman Canada in Penticton, British Columbia. On minimal training, his time was 11:05, primarily the result of a strong swim and good climbing performance on the bike. His run was mostly a jog-walk in that race, as he posted a marathon split of 4:07. At 140 pounds, his strength-to-weight ratio is excellent for climbing, and his good swimming skills stem from his days as a collegiate swimmer.

Running endurance has always been JH's major limiter, although he has good anaerobic endurance and leg speed, as evidenced by his sub-18-minute times in the 5 km run. He attempted a marathon two years ago but did not finish. The following year he ran a 3:20, which, based on his 10 km time of 37:20, is at least 25 minutes slower than his potential, according to prediction tables. To achieve his goals of qualifying for Ironman Hawaii and finishing in 10:30 or better, JH must, first of all, improve his running endurance. He also needs greater bike force for the windy portions of the Hawaii course because, although he's a good climber—largely because of his small size—his ability to drive a high gear into the wind is not as good as it could be.

JH's Olympic-distance race times are around 2:08. Multiplying this by 4.67 to 5.0 yields an estimated range for the Ironman of 9:57 to 10:40, so his sub-10:30 goal seems reasonable. Projected splits for his Ironman are a 1:05 swim time, a 5:40 bike time, a 3:35 run time, and 10-minute transitions. Assuming he will slow down 20 percent on the marathon leg from his best performance in a run-only marathon race, he should be capable of running the 3:35 final split if he can set a 2:55 marathon personal best. His Annual Training Plan has him aiming for a marathon in week 12 with that objective in mind.

In preparing for this early-season marathon, JH will devote most of his training time in weeks 1–12 to running, with swimming and cycling in a maintenance mode. Since marathon training does not take as many hours as Ironman training, his annual volume for weeks 1–12 are based on 450 hours, but starting in week 14 it escalates to 550 hours. Once his running endurance is established, and assuming the marathon goes well, the emphasis of his training will shift toward cycling as running fitness is maintained.

The two biggest challenges facing any runner who is training for a personal-best marathon are injury prevention and overtraining avoidance. JH's training is therefore

Athlete: *JH*

Annual hours: *450 (wks 1-12), 550 (wks 14-50)*

Seasonal goals:

1. *Qualify for Ironman Hawaii*
2. *10:30 or faster at Ironman*
3. —

Training objectives:

1. *Run marathon (wk 12) faster than 2:55.*
2. *Leg press 410+ pounds 6 times by wk 17.*
3. *Wk 25 race bike split faster than 1:04.*
4. *Spend more time with family in R&R wks.*
5. *Complete at least 3, 5+ hour bricks (wks 42-48).*

Sample Training Plan for an Ironman-Distance Triathlete

Column key — each discipline (SWIM, BIKE, RUN) has: Endurance (End), Force (For), Speed Skills (SS), Muscular Endurance (ME), Anaerobic Endurance (AE), Power (Pow), Testing (Test).

Wk#	Mon	Race	PRI	Period	Hours	Weights	S-End	S-For	S-SS	S-ME	S-AE	S-Pow	S-Test	B-End	B-For	B-SS	B-ME	B-AE	B-Pow	B-Test	R-End	R-For	R-SS	R-ME	R-AE	R-Pow	R-Test
01	1/4			Base 1	10.5	MS	X		X					X		X					X		X				
02	1/11				12.0		X		X					X		X					X		X				
03	1/18			↓	6.5		X		X					X		X					X		X				X
04	1/25			Base 2	11.5		X		X					X		X					X	X	X	X			
05	2/1				12.5		X		X					X		X					X	X	X				
06	2/8			↓	6.5		X		X					X		X					X		X				X
07	2/15			Base 3	12.0		X		X					X		X					X	X	X				
08	2/22				13.0	↓	X		X					X		X					X	X	X				
09	3/1			↓	6.5	SM	X		X					X		X					X		X				
10	3/8			Peak	9.5		X		X					X		X					X		X				
11	3/15			↓	7.5	↓	X		X					X		X					X		X	X			
12	3/22	Marathon	A	Race	6.5	o			X					X												X	
13	3/29			Tran	–	o																					
14	4/5			Base 2	12.5	MS	X	X	X	X				X	X	X	X				X	X	X	X			
15	4/12				14.0		X	X	X	X				X	X	X	X				X	X	X	X			
16	4/19				15.5		X	X	X	X				X	X	X	X				X	X	X	X			
17	4/26			↓	8.0	↓	X		X				X	X		X				X	X		X				X
18	5/3			Base 3	12.5	SM	X	X	X	X				X	X	X	X				X	X	X	X			
19	5/10				14.5		X	X	X	X				X	X	X	X				X	X	X	X			
20	5/17				16.5		X	X	X	X				X	X	X	X				X	X	X	X			
21	5/24	Oly Du	C	↓	8.0		X		X				X	X		X				X	X		X				X
22	5/31			Build 1	14.0		X			X	X			X	X		X				X		X				
23	6/7				14.0		X			X	X			X	X		X				X		X				
24	6/14				14.0		X			X	X			X	X		X				X		X				
25	6/21	Oly Tri	B	↓	8.0		X	X						X			X				X		X				
26	6/28			Build 2	13.0		X			X	X			X	X		X				X			X			
27	7/5				13.0		X			X	X			X	X		X				X			X			
28	7/12	Oly Tri	C		13.0		X			X	X			X	X		X				X			X			
29	7/19			↓	8.0		X	X					X	X	X					X	X	X					X
30	7/26			Peak	11.5		X		X	X				X	X	X	X				X		X	X			
31	8/2			↓	9.5	↓	X		X	X				X		X	X				X		X	X			
32	8/9	Half-Ironman (Q)	A	Race	8.0	o				X							X									X	
33	8/16			Tran	–	o																					
34	8/23			Base 1	11.0	MS	X		X					X	X	X					X		X				
35	8/30				13.0		X		X					X	X	X					X		X				
36	9/6				14.5		X		X					X	X	X					X		X				
37	9/13	Oly Tri	C	↓	8.0	↓	X		X					X		X					X		X				
38	9/20			Base 2	12.5	SM	X	X	X	X				X	X	X	X				X	X	X	X			
39	9/27				14.0		X	X	X	X				X	X	X	X				X	X	X	X			
40	10/4	Half-Ironman	B		15.5		X	X	X	X				X	X	X	X				X	X	X	X			
41	10/11			↓	8.0		X		X				X	X		X				X	X		X				X
42	10/18			Base 3	12.5		X	X	X	X				X	X	X	X				X	X	X	X			
43	10/25			↓	14.5		X	X	X	X				X	X	X	X				X	X	X	X			
44	11/1			↓	8.0		X		X				X	X		X				X	X		X				X
45	11/8			Base 3	14.5		X	X	X	X				X	X	X	X				X	X	X	X			
46	11/15				16.5		X	X	X	X				X	X	X	X				X	X	X	X			
47	11/22			↓	8.0		X		X				X	X		X				X	X		X				X
48	11/29			Peak	11.5		X		X	X				X	X	X	X				X		X	X			
49	12/6			↓	9.5	↓	X		X	X				X	X	X	X				X		X	X			
50	12/13	Ironman	A	Race	8.0+	o				X							X									X	
51	12/20			Tran	–	o																					
52	12/27			↓	–	o																					

scheduled in three-week periods instead of the more usual four during the endurance buildup, with the third week set aside for rest and recovery. Weeks 42 through 47 of his final preparation for the Ironman are scheduled in the same manner. There is a four-week Prep period preceding Base 1 that starts in week 1. During this Prep period JH was doing the Anatomical Adaptation (AA) and Maximum Transition (MT) weight training phases.

SIDEBAR 9.1

Ironman
Benchmark
Workouts

How do you know if you are on track for a good Ironman-distance performance? Here are some benchmark workouts that may help you decide, whether your goal is simply to finish the race or to have a fast race time. Once you've refined your pacing and refueling strategies, you will be ready to write a race plan. Be sure to stick to it on race day.

RACE GOAL: **Finish an Ironman**

Swimming Benchmark Workout: Plan two open water swims in the last eight weeks—swim with a partner, a following boat, or a lifeguard on shore. You should be able to swim nonstop for 40 minutes with seven weeks to go and for 60 minutes with three weeks remaining.

Not on Target? If you can't complete these benchmark swims, find a swim instructor to help you with your technique. You're wasting too much energy.

Cycling Benchmark Workout: Starting eleven weeks before the race, do a long ride two out of every three weeks. This means you will get in six such rides before the race. Starting eleven weeks out, you should be able to ride three and a half hours. Add about 30 minutes each time. Do your last long ride three weeks before the race; it should be about six hours. Eat and drink exactly as you will in the race.

Not on Target? If you find it difficult to finish any of these long rides, you are either trying to ride too fast early in the workout, not taking in enough calories, or both. Make adjustments in pacing and refueling until you get it just right. Then follow that pattern *exactly* in the race. Do *not* inflate your goal the week of the race.

Running Benchmark Workout: Your goal is to finish the run—not to see how fast you can go. Combine walking and running just as you will do in the race. Complete a long run two out of every three weeks, so that you get in six of these endurance workouts before the race, just as you did with cycling. It's best to space these long bike and long run workouts so that you have at least 48 hours between them each week. If that's not possible, then do the long run the day before the long ride—not the other

Continued >

< Sidebar 9.1 Continued

way around. The first such run should be at least an hour and a half. Add 15 to 20 minutes each time until you build your run to a three-hour workout with three to four weeks to go before the race. Do not go longer than three hours.

Not on Target? If you find it almost unbearable to finish your long run every time you attempt it, then you are either trying to run too fast, not walking enough, or not taking in enough calories. Gradually refine your run pacing and refueling strategy after each long workout until you have it nailed down tightly. Then stick to your plan on race day.

RACE GOAL: Fast Ironman

Swimming Benchmark Workout: Warm up for 10 minutes in a pool. Then swim 500 meters six times with 30-second recoveries. The pace on each 500 should be your race goal pace. If you expect to go out fast in the first 500 meters of the race to get into position, then swim the first 500 of this set at that effort, and settle into the slower pace on the subsequent sets. Record your split times for each 500. Do this workout twice in your Build period, once on each of the "Big Days" (see Sidebar 9.2, "Ironman Big Day").

Not on Target? Is your 500-meter time remaining constant within a few seconds for the last five intervals? It should be. If not, then you are going too fast early in the set and need to pace yourself. Consider whether your goal pace is realistic.

Cycling Benchmark Workout: After a few weeks of building your longest weekly ride to five or six hours, you will be ready for long aerobic threshold rides. Do four to six of these, with two of them on your "Big Days." These long race simulations will prepare you physically and mentally for the stresses of the race. Warm up for 30 minutes and then ride steadily for two to four hours. Gradually increase the duration over several weeks. Stay in the upper half of heart rate zone 2 for the entire two- to four-hour period of each ride. Or, with a power meter, ride at 65 to 75 percent of your functional threshold power. Cool down for 30 minutes. Be sure to eat and drink exactly as you will do in the race.

Not on Target? These aerobic threshold rides are essentially race-effort simulations done at goal race intensity. If you can't maintain a steady effort for two to four hours, you won't be able to do it in the race for a longer time. So reduce the target heart rate or power until you have it dialed in by the time you ride for four hours. The last such ride should occur three to four weeks before race day.

Running Benchmark Workout: Two out of every three weeks, starting eleven weeks before the race, complete a long run of two and a half to three hours, so that you do six such long runs before the race. In each of them a portion is run at aerobic threshold in the upper half of heart rate zone 2. Three to four weeks before the race, this aerobic threshold portion should be two hours long within the longer run time. Build up to that two-hour portion over the course of the four to six long runs. It's best to separate the long rides and runs by at least 48 hours each week. If that doesn't work with your lifestyle, then do the long run the day before the long ride. This will reduce your risk of injury.

Not on Target? If you are wearing a GPS watch or accelerometer, notice whether your pace is remaining steady. If you are slowing down appreciably even when your heart rate remains constant, then start more conservatively on your next such run. It is also possible that you are not taking in enough calories. By the last long run you should have a good idea of what your Ironman goal pace and heart rate should be.

As anyone who has ever contemplated Ironman Hawaii knows, the biggest challenge is qualifying. JH is aiming for the half-Ironman qualifier in week 32. This is his second peak of the season. There is also a qualifier at the Olympic distance in week 25. He will not be ready for a peak performance by week 25, but this race will serve as a good opportunity for self-assessment and give him a preview of what the competition could be like in week 32. It will also motivate him for the final seven weeks before the qualifier. The week-25 race could also hurt his confidence, however, if his performance is relatively poor and he feels he lacks time to make the necessary improvements. So it is imperative that he exercise great caution when it comes to workout intensity and duration on the weekend before this race. It may be wise for him to reduce his volume during week 24, regardless of what the tables say.

An Ironman hopeful should schedule few, if any, races during the last twelve weeks before an Ironman event. An Ironman event in fact cuts into training on both sides of the schedule because it is necessary to rest up beforehand and also to recover afterward. So the week-40 half-Ironman is tentative, and JH may well decide to skip it if his training is not progressing at the desired level. If his training is progressing as planned, this race can serve as an excellent indicator of progress. Backing off of training in the days preceding this race is probably necessary, so JH's weekly hours at this time are tentative. Since this race is followed by an R&R week, there will be adequate opportunity for him to recover before returning to Ironman-specific training.

TABLE 9.9

Week 39 for JH

	MON		TUE		WED		THUR		FRI		SAT		SUN	
Workout 1	Swim S1, E2	:30	Run S1, M1	:45	Swim S1, M2, F3	1:00	Run E1	45	Swim S1, E1	1:00	Run F1	2:30	Bike M1, E3	3:45
Workout 2	Wts SM	:30	Bike S1, E2	:45	Bike E1	1:00	Bike F1	1:15					Run E3	:15

TABLE 9.10

Week 46 for JH

	MON		TUE		WED		THUR		FRI		SAT		SUN	
Workout 1	Swim S1, E1	:45	Run S1, M2	1:00	Swim F1, E2	1:15	Run E1	1:00	Swim S1, E1	1:00	Cmb F1	5:00	Bike E1	2:30
Workout 2	Wts SM	:30	Bike S1, E2	1:00	Bike E1	1:00	Bike M2	1:30						

TABLE 9.11

Week 49 for JH

	MON		TUE		WED		THUR		FRI		SAT		SUN	
Workout 1	Swim S1, E1	:45	Run S1	:45	Swim F1	1:00	Bike E1	1:00	Swim S1, E2	:30	Cmb M1	1:30	Bike E1	:45
Workout 2	Wts SM	:30	Bike E2	:45	Cmb A1	1:30			Run E1	:30				

JH's weeks 39, 46, and 49 are shown in Tables 9.9, 9.10, and 9.11 to depict how Ironman training should be scheduled in the early weeks of endurance development in Base 2, during the Ironman-specific training of Base 3, and in the penultimate week, when training volume is greatly reduced but fitness is maintained. Remember that JH's strengths are swimming and climbing hills on the bike, and that his greatest limiter is running endurance. In light of those facts, it may seem surprising that his weekly running volume is only about four hours. The reason for this is that once three or four weekly workouts are achieved, the greatest improvement in endurance comes not from doing more workouts, but from extending the length of one of those workouts. Increasing the frequency of JH's runs is likely to cause injury.

Note that in Table 9.10 (week 46), the suggested hours from Table 8.1 are rearranged so that the brick is the longest workout, at five hours instead of the four hours proposed in the table. Remember that Table 8.1 and Figure 8.1 are only suggestions, and it is often necessary to modify them.

Training for an Ironman must include a challenging training event that occurs twice during the season: the "Big Days." As the name implies, a Big Day is intended to significantly simulate the stresses of race day. It tests your preparation in every way. One of your Big Days should occur about eight weeks prior to your Ironman-distance race and the other one about four weeks before the race. It's best to space these stressful days out like this so that you can have several days of recovery after each one. This workout should only be done by triathletes who are competitive within their categories. Ironman "finishers" can do the workout but at a lower intensity than described below.

Start the day just as you plan to do on race day by eating your pre-race breakfast. See Chapter 16 for more details on this. Then, at about race start time, swim for 60 to 75 minutes (in open water, if possible). This swim should include long race-effort sets with short recoveries. My favorite for this day is six 500-meter swims with 30-second recoveries done at goal race pace.

After your swim, rest for 90 minutes and eat a light meal. Follow this with a bike ride of five hours, preferably on a course that simulates the terrain you'll encounter on Iron-race day. Warm up for about 30 minutes, then ride for four hours steady in heart rate zone 2 (see Chapter 4 for zones) or at 65 to 75 percent of your functional threshold power. Set up your bike just as it will be on race day, ride in an aerodynamic position, and use the same clothing, shoes, and equipment you will use on race day. Eat, drink, and supplement with sodium *exactly* as you will do in the race.

After the ride, rest for 90 minutes and eat a light, mostly liquid meal. Then start a two-hour run on a course as similar to the race course as possible. Warm up for 15 to 30 minutes and then start a 90-minute run in heart rate zone 2 or at goal race pace. Eat, drink, and supplement with sodium *exactly* as you intend to do in the race.

This is roughly an eight-hour training day that gives you a taste of what it will be like on race day. But knowing how driven Ironman triathletes are, I probably should emphasize that you should *not* attempt to do the full eight hours nonstop. Be sure to take the two 90-minute breaks, and be sure to refuel and rehydrate during this time. Doing this workout continuously is just too stressful and would require far too long of a recovery.

When you do your two Big Days eight weeks and four weeks before your Ironman event, you'll likely discover some things that need adjusting, such as pacing, equipment, and nutrition. Make the changes and you're that much closer to having a rewarding Ironman.

For more on Big Days and Ironman training refer to *Going Long: Training for Ironman-Distance Triathlons,* 2nd edition (VeloPress, 2009), a book I coauthored with Gordon Byrn, who has taught me a lot about Ironman-distance training and racing.

CASE STUDIES SUMMARY

Notice that each of the athletes included in these case studies adapted the guidelines for designing an Annual Training Plan in order to meet their specific needs. Such modifications are often necessary. Don't be afraid to bend the rules, but have a reason for doing so. That reason could be that it just felt right given your unique circumstances. If the change worked—great! If not, learn from your experience. Success will come not from rigidly following a set of rules, but through a dynamic process of making informed decisions, evaluating your progress, and making adaptations as needed.

PART V

RACING AND RECOVERY

Back in the 1950s and 1960s, there was a television program called *The Ed Sullivan Show.* It was the last of the old vaudeville shows, offering a variety of the short acts that had been so popular in the early twentieth century. One of the show's favorite repeat performers was a juggler who would spin and balance plates on long poles. His act involved keeping several plates spinning at the same time and constantly starting more, while maintaining the spin on those that slowed down, threatening to crash to the floor. Each time he came on the program he tried to keep more plates spinning than in his previous performances. He had nothing on multisport athletes.

We are masters at keeping lots of plates spinning while avoiding calamity. We balance family, career, home upkeep, relationships, and community responsibilities while swimming, biking, running, and lifting weights, all with the intended purpose of producing peak race performance. Few of us get paid for doing all of this training. There is another reward that we seek.

The real reward is the perfect race—the one in which we feel strong and in control, with each leg of the race a personal best. For that elusive goal, we endure workouts that most "normal" people would never even imagine possible. Unfortunately, some of us occasionally get caught up in spinning more and more plates and allow some to crash to the floor. This mistake is most common in the week before a race—or at any time when we are so driven to succeed that we don't consider taking a break to be an option.

Part V looks at the times when less training means more fitness. Chapter 10 shows how to plan your taper during race week and expend your energy during the race. Chapter 11 examines how to avoid the problems that come from not allowing your body to recover. Knowing how to reduce the number of spinning plates at these times can enable you to avoid calamity and achieve triathlon and duathlon success.

RACING

10

Race day is harvest time; that's when you reap the benefits.

—MARK ALLEN

THIS IS IT! The first A-priority race of the year has finally arrived. All of the blood, sweat, and tears of weeks, months, and years of training have brought you to this point. Your fitness is at its highest level of the young season, and you are ready to go.

Wouldn't it be a shame to ruin all of this in the last few days before the race? Many an athlete has done just that by training in inappropriate ways in the final week of the big race. The most common error for serious multisport athletes is continuing to train at a high workload in the mistaken belief that race form is improved only by hard work. It isn't so. Form improves during rest. In fact, it's unlikely that any highly stressful training done in the last week can cause physiological changes along the lines of what was accomplished in the Base and Build periods. There's no doubt about it: It's better to rest.

Rest does have its shortcomings, though, so as odd as it may sound, you need to know how to rest the right way. Several studies have shown that total rest causes a steady loss of fitness (see Table 3.1). It's best to find a balance point between your normal training workload and inactivity during race week. This chapter examines that issue and takes you through final race-day preparation, the race itself, and post-race activities. Let's start with your race plan.

THE RACE PLAN

Having the performance and race results you want in an A-priority race largely depends on having an effective strategy. A race strategy is nothing more than a plan that covers the race-day variables over which you have control. You don't, for example, have control over the weather or how fit your competition is. You can, however, plan how you will deal with various weather conditions and how to pace yourself relative to other athletes. You should plan for all of the variables that are within your control.

Any plan, even a sketchy one, is better than no plan at all. The plan for a sprint-distance race may cover only a few items, whereas an Ironman-distance event plan will be quite lengthy. Sidebar 10.1, "Example of an Ironman Race Plan" (see page 168), shows how detailed a plan can be.

Some athletes just discuss a plan with someone or give it a little thought. But the most effective way to plan is to write out your thoughts and objectives. I like to have the athletes I coach do this about a week before the race. By all means, share your plan with your coach, but don't just go over it verbally—put it in writing first. You could also discuss your written plan with a seasoned veteran who may notice if you have listed something that is unreasonable or if you have overlooked something important.

The race plan is already taking shape twelve weeks before the event. One week before the race you should have a pretty good idea of what you are capable of doing. Start with your season's goal for this A-priority event. Does it still seem reasonable? Has your training gone as expected? If so, it should be easy to prepare the plan. If not, then consider what you are realistically capable of doing in this race—either at a higher or a lower level than you originally thought possible—and create a plan that addresses the revised goal.

Of course, there could be more than one goal for a race, with some more important than others. You may have a goal to complete the race in a certain time, for example, but also have secondary goals. If something happens to prevent you from achieving the primary goal, having secondary goals can allow you to produce a worthy outcome. For example, let's say your primary goal was to finish an A-priority, Olympic-distance race in less than 2:20, but a flat tire on the bike prevented that. If you had a secondary goal of running the 10 km in a career-best 45 minutes, something positive could still be salvaged. There is no limit on secondary goals. Or you can have Plan A and Plan B. If Plan A falls out of the realm of possibility, this gives you another goal to reach for.

What should your race plan include? The following is a list of strategic variables to consider. You may not want all of these in your race plan, or you may have other important items unique to your situation that you would like to include. The variables presented below are suggested to help you get started.

Pacing. How will you control speed, effort, or power in each sport? In the swim, will you focus on going out fast in order to stay with the leaders, or will you swim a steady pace? This decision may also help you determine where to line up at the start—front and center, to the side, or at the back. Will you watch power or heart rate on the bike? What numbers will you try to hold? How will you pace the run? Pacing is generally best based on effort, power, or heart rate—not time. External factors, such as wind, can impact time goals. Pacing is perhaps the most critical part of the plan.

Equipment. What equipment is best for this race? For the swim, consider sleeveless or full-sleeved wetsuits, or no wetsuit at all. How about wheels for the bike? How much air pressure will you put in the tires given this type of course? If the pavement is wet or there are lots of turns, consider using a lower pressure, such as 90 to 100 psi. Will you run in race flats, lightweight trainers, or your standard training shoes? How about the type of helmet, hat, or fuel belt you will use, or any other special equipment needed for the conditions of this race?

Transitions. How will you setup your transition stall, and how do you plan to flow through the transition process?

Nutrition. What will you eat or drink? How many calories will you take in and when? How much fluid? Will you take extra sodium? How much and when? Will you rely on aid stations or special-needs bags, or will you carry everything you expect to need?

Weather. What clothing and equipment changes will you need to make if there is rain, snow, or wind? What if it is unexpectedly cold, hotter than usual for the time of year, or very humid? How will you need to adjust your pacing with these unusual weather conditions?

The Sky Is Falling. Expect the unexpected and be prepared for it. How will you handle a flat tire? What if your stomach becomes upset? If this happens, what changes will you make in your eating and drinking? If this just isn't your day and things aren't going as planned, when will you decide to go to plan B?

In the week leading up to the race, review the plan daily. You will also need a plan for how to train this week, as there is a tendency for athletes to do too much as they get closer to the race. Avoid the all-too-common urge to do one last mega-workout this week. It's too late for a major workout to help you now. If you make any mistakes, make them on the side of doing too little. And beware of goal inflation this week. Yes, you're feeling great, but that doesn't mean you've become a superhero.

Hold yourself accountable to the plan during the race. Realize that following the race you will review how you did relative to the plan. Did you follow it? If not, why not? Frequently ask yourself what you are learning in this race that will help you do a better job of planning for the next one. If the race doesn't go as planned, it's that much more important to ask these questions and to seek constructive answers.

During the race, execute the plan, stay in the present moment, and simply do your best at all times. Take the race in little chunks. Quietly celebrate the completion of each chunk and then focus on the next—as planned. There will be good and bad patches. Stay positive in the bad patches while always moving forward. Keep the plan at the forefront of your thinking at all times. When you must make quick decisions along the way, base your choices on your race plan, not your emotions at the moment. If you've done your homework, you're ready. Bring it on!

Example of
an Ironman
Race Plan

The following is an actual race plan created by Justin Daerr, one of the pro triathletes I coach.

RACE WEEK

I arrive on Tuesday late in the day. Wednesday morning I will swim at the race venue and bike afterward. Then I will head to packet pickup to register. The rest of the day is taking it easy.

Thursday is similar. I will not attend the carbo load. I'll spend this evening with my brother since he will be getting into town that day.

Friday I'll do my workouts in the morning and turn in my bike and bags. I'll keep the bags simple, no need to overpack. I may go to an early afternoon movie, see my folks afterward, and have dinner solo. They will go out that evening and I can go to sleep before they return.

RACE DAY

Saturday (race day) I'll wake up around 3:30 a.m., drink four Ensures, and eat one bagel or a couple pieces of toast. This comes to 1,200 to 1,300 calories. Then I'll sip water until race start, stay relaxed, and head to the race. I'll set my tire pressure to 120 psi and put everything in special-needs bags. I'll double-check the other bags, but avoid being a freak about it, and head to beach around 6:00ish. I'll try to get a short warm-up swim in. Nothing major. Just moving some blood around.

SWIM

I'll line up toward the middle inside along the front. At the gun I'll steadily move into the water and dolphin dive until the water is deep enough. Then I'll focus on long, strong strokes. I won't worry too much about everyone around me until a few hundred meters have gone by. I'm looking for a moderate start that gives me a steady sensation once I find a rhythm. Going out hard does nothing for me. I've tried it in training and I've seen the consequences. Strong and steady, looking for feet the whole time is the key.

TRANSITION TO BIKE

I will get out of T1 smoothly. Bike shoes will be clipped into bike if allowed by the race director. Grab my helmet, sunglasses, two gel flasks, and race belt, get on the bike, and get going.

BIKE

I'll keep it comfortable to start and wait to begin racing until we turn north out of town. That should give me enough time to relax and get comfortable. I'll have two 24-ounce bottles with a combo of Endurathon and Catapult from EAS with additional sodium added. Should be around 150 calories/bottle with 100 mg of caffeine/bottle. I'll have two flasks, each with 500 calories of Hammer gel, on the bike. I'll use a sports drink from the aid stations to keep the fluids and calories up in addition to that. My special-needs bag will include two bottles identical to what I started with, but it's only there for backup.

I will try to take in close to 2,500 calories. It will be lower than that in reality, but if it's over 2,000 I think I will be just fine.

My pacing on the bike will be based on feel and reinforced by power. I will avoid extended time over 240 watts unless I need to make a move for positioning reasons. I never want to do this, but I did do it in Ironman Florida in 2003 and Kona in 2004 to get away from draft packs. I believe that racing ethically is worth the few minutes of higher power. Perhaps this won't be an issue with my improved swimming and cycling.

I will be taking splits every 5 to 10 miles and I'll be watching the average power of each. This will keep me honest. I'll soft pedal when I can and will be a bit more conservative if a tailwind is giving me 42 kph or more with lower watts. I plan to use the north winds to my advantage when they appear. Those will be good opportunities to back off and get calories in while keeping the speed high. I'll stand for 10 to 15 seconds after the aid stations to stretch a little.

TRANSITION TO RUN

I will be wearing the same one-piece suit for the run, so no clothes change needed. I'll put on socks and shoes, grab my water bottle, and go.

RUN

The first 3 miles are easy as I take in 200+ calories from gels in this time period. After that I switch to a sports drink from the aid stations and cola for energy needs. I will take in a couple of extra gels throughout the run as I see fit—probably around miles 10 and 18.

After mile 3 I should find my effort. I'll use pace and feel to guide me and will use heart rate as reinforcement. Easy will become steady, steady will become a challenge in and of itself. Heart rate will likely be in the 155 to 165 range based on heat, fatigue, etc.

One major difference this year is that I'm putting a fuel belt in my special-needs bag. I had issues with crowded aid stations on the second loop last year so I'll be using this as back up so I won't have to completely rely on aid stations for loop 2.

My run is split into various sections. Miles 1 to 3 are easy and will revolve around getting some calories in. Then in miles 4 to 6.5 (first turnaround) I'll settle into my pace and see where I am positioned relative to the rest of the field. Miles 6.5 to 13.1 are steady as she

Continued >

< Sidebar 10.1 Continued

goes. I'll get another good look at the positions of the field at this time. For miles 13.2 to 20 I really have to focus on holding pace as well as I can; if I can do that, I know I can run well relative to the field. The last 6.5 miles is the hardest part of the hardest hour of the year. I've been thinking about this hour for a long time. It's one hour, one hour that can be so rewarding if I take it one step at a time and don't back down.

I've been thinking and focusing on this race for a long time. I feel prepared and I believe in my abilities. I trust my fitness, and I'll make this one count. I know that the day could go wrong, but I will not be set back by making bad personal choices. I believe my "steady effort" is effective and competitive and I don't care where I stand until the entire race is over. The "uber" bikers can have their glory early. I'll catch them later. On the run I will be ready to make every single person work if they finish in front of me. Even if I'm racing for 20th, 19th better be ready to race to the finish line.

Also, I know something could happen to me on the bike—flats, mechanicals, whatever. However, this is my race no matter what. If I am sidelined for an hour, I will continue to race as planned. No matter what, my goal is to run well. If that means after a six-hour bike, so be it.

I know every race has dark moments. As in life, I recognize the situation and I'll focus entirely on the task at hand. There is no such thing as a perfect day or a perfect race. Just keep moving forward. I'm excited and I'm looking forward to next weekend. This is what I love to do.

—Justin Daerr

RACE WEEK

There are two extremes to almost everything, and this is true of multisport when it comes to race week. I've warned against working out too hard during race week, but some athletes take the other extreme. They approach race week as if it were a "slough-off" week in which they can piddle around with little effort, since they believe that nothing of physiological value happens except rest.

Although it's true that rest is the major objective of this week, that doesn't mean that you become a couch potato or ignore race preparation. In fact, what you do in the week of a big race is every bit as important as what you do in any other week of training: It's not less important, it just has different objectives and a different way of meeting them. When done right, a taper week peaks all of the abilities needed for the race, boosts your confidence, and allows for psychological rest so that you are mentally prepared for the big day. Let's examine how to plan for a peak performance by counting down the days leading to an A-priority race.

SIX DAYS BEFORE THE RACE

If the race is on a Sunday, six days before is Monday. This is a good day for a zone 1, active-recovery swim or bike ride, since the day before that (Sunday) you probably did a brief race-effort simulation coming at the end of a Peak-period week. Don't lift weights today, or any day this week. Now is not the time to further tear down muscle tissue or even attempt to maintain strength. If you find yourself exceptionally tired from the previous day's workout, taking this day off altogether may be wise. Regardless, don't do anything that is stressful.

This is a good day to get your bike tuned and set up for the race. All rides this week are best done on your race set-up to ensure that everything is in working order and you're comfortable with your position. The one exception is race tires. These are best saved until the day before the race to protect them from cuts and tiny slivers that could go unnoticed. When installing your race tires this week, check them for potential problems.

From this point on, be cautious about your diet. Don't eat too much. With the decreased workload, you need fewer calories than you do on workout days, but your tendency will be to eat your usual amount. By the end of the week you may have gained an extra pound or so, primarily due to "water weight," but avoid adding body fat.

THREE TO FIVE DAYS BEFORE THE RACE

Several university studies have demonstrated that a moderate and decreasing amount of high intensity during a taper week produces better endurance performances than either total rest or easy, slow training. The reason for this is that high-intensity training maintains or even improves muscle-recruitment patterns. Resting more as you approach race day then improves glycogen stores, increases aerobic enzyme levels and activity, boosts blood volume, and allows for connective-tissue repair. Not doing any high intensity in this week is likely to leave you feeling "flat" and even a little awkward at faster paces on race day. Fitness abilities are lost first when workload is reduced, and race-like intensity is the key to maintaining them.

Brief bursts of race-simulation intensity with long recoveries are effective for these days. This would include intensities like those used in speed-skill workouts and shortened versions of interval sets (see Appendices B, C, D, and E). Within one session each day, include three to five repetitions of about 90 seconds each at the maximum effort anticipated in some portion of the race, with 3-minute recoveries. For example, if there is a hill on the bike course of your race, do 90-second repeats at goal race intensity on a similar hill with 3-minute recoveries. Figures 8.1j and 8.1k and Tables 9.8 and 9.11 provide suggested workouts and patterns for these days. Note that these are just suggestions and not necessarily the workouts that are best for you and the race for which you are preparing.

TWO DAYS BEFORE THE RACE

This is Thursday for a Saturday race or Friday for a Sunday race. Take today off from training or include a short swim. It should be your most restful day of the week other than, perhaps, Monday. If you are traveling to the race, now or the night before this is the time to pack your bike. Traveling can be quite stressful, so anything you can do to lessen its psychological and physical impact will be beneficial. A travel checklist that includes everything you want to take reduces your fear of forgetting something such as your helmet or running shoes. Another stress reliever is traveling with a non-racing friend or spouse who can deal with the inevitable hassles as they arise. In airports and at hotels, use a cart or pay a porter to lug your bike around.

SIDEBAR 10.2

Travel Checklist

To reduce stress and the possibility of forgetting something, use this checklist when packing your bags to travel to a race.

SWIM
___ Swim suit/tri suit
___ Goggles (2 pairs)
___ Defogger
___ Wetsuit
___ No-stick spray/lube
___ Swim cap
___ Stretch cord

BIKE
___ Bike
___ Shoes
___ Special pedals
___ Shorts
___ Gloves
___ Helmet
___ Pump
___ Tools
___ Lubricant
___ Spare tire/tube
___ Handlebar computer
___ Race wheels

___ Water bottles
___ Lock and cable

RUN
___ Race shoes
___ Training shoes
___ Shorts
___ Singlet
___ Visor/hat
___ Orthotics

TRANSITION
___ Towel
___ Marker

MISCELLANEOUS
___ Tights
___ Socks
___ Skin lubricant
___ Sunscreen
___ Jacket
___ Sunglasses

___ Clear lenses
___ Backpack
___ Toiletries kit
___ Raincoat
___ Sports drink mix
___ Food/energy bars/gels
___ First aid kit
___ Safety pins
___ Training log
___ USAT license
___ Race confirmation
___ Race number
___ Parking permit
___ Race info packet
___ Airline tickets
___ Bike passes
___ Duct tape
___ Jog bra
___ Eyeglasses or contacts
___ Heart rate monitor
___ Post-race sandals

Besides staying as calm and relaxed as you can today, eat foods that you're accustomed to (you may need to carry some); drink enough water (not sports drinks) to quench your thirst throughout the day, but don't try to "water-load"; and go to bed at a time that is normal for you.

THE DAY BEFORE THE RACE

This morning is the last time to work out before the race. It's also a good time to check out the swim venue from the shore to see where the sun will be rising on race morning. Keep today's workout short, and include some brief bouts of high intensity. If possible, you could do a bike-run brick on the race course as a final workout. Keep it short, with perhaps a 30-minute bike ride and a 15-minute run. All you want to do is get warmed up, throw in a few accelerations to goal race pace or slightly faster, and then stop and stretch. Following this workout, check the bolts on your bike for tightness.

Following a normal breakfast, check off the required pre-race activities at a comfortable pace. Avoid rushing through the process. Keep everything in perspective by minimizing the significance of the inevitable day-before-the-race hassles. Pick up your race packet and attend the pre-race meeting, if there is one. Drive the bike course (or better yet, have someone drive you, so you can look around), paying special attention to hills and the likely gearing needed, mile marks, pavement surface, turnaround points, corners, and weather nuances such as wind direction and shade. Back in the hotel room, fasten the race numbers onto your belt or singlet and bike. Lay out your race-day clothes and pack your race bag using the checklist.

After you've taken care of all these details, get your mind off of the race. Avoid crowds of nervous athletes, and stay off of your legs and out of the sun. Some possible activities include going to a movie, taking a bus tour of the area, renting a videotape, and reading. Throughout the day, continue to sip from a bottle of water (not a sports drink) when thirsty, and don't allow hunger to set in. But in the same spirit of avoiding extreme changes, don't drink too much or overeat today. Have dinner a bit on the early side, avoiding caffeine, alcohol, and roughage. Don't experiment with the local cuisine. Eat foods that are normal for you the day before the race. If you are doing an Ironman-distance race, however, it may be wise to put a little extra salt on your food today.

Following dinner, get away from other competitors to slow your mind and body down even more as you prepare to sleep. Watch television or read in a quiet room with low light. Don't dwell on the "what-ifs" of tomorrow's race. Whenever apprehensive race thoughts pop into your mind, replace them by recalling recent successes you have had in workouts or races. Place a bottle of water next to the bed and turn in at a normal time. Sleeping pills are likely to leave you groggy, but a melatonin capsule an hour before bedtime may help. Don't do this unless you've experimented with melatonin in training or before a C-priority race. It's a good idea to talk with your medical-care provider before using melatonin.

Should You Hyperhydrate?

The day before a race, it's common to see athletes walking around with bottles of water or sports drink. Is this a good idea? Does taking in a large volume of water prevent dehydration the next day? The answer is no. If you were a camel with a large reservoir designed just for holding excess water as you trudged across the desert, excessive drinking would be beneficial. But since you are reading this you are more than likely a human. We don't have a spare tank to fill. Once our limited storage areas are full, most of the excess is shunted to the bladder and removed as urine. If that's all that happened, hyperhydration would not be much of a problem. But it's not.

Excessive drinking has been shown to dilute the body's electrolyte stores, especially sodium. So excessive water intake is likely to increase your risk of hyponatremia. This is a condition in which sodium stores are too low and the body begins to shut down. In the early stages you may experience nausea, headache, muscle cramps, weakness, and disorientation. In the latter stages, seizures and coma are possible.

Although hyponatremia is unlikely to occur in races that take less than about four hours, it simply isn't a good idea to start any race, regardless of distance, with diluted electrolytes. Pay attention to your thirst mechanism. We've been taught that it is not effective and that we shouldn't trust it, but that's an old wives' tale. Drink when you are thirsty. It's that simple.

RACE DAY

If you've prepared well throughout the week, there's little that can physically go wrong today. At this point it's simply a matter of following a detailed procedure—a ritual—that you have done scores of times before now. An A-priority race is not the time to experiment with new pre-race rituals; stick with what you know works.

Pre-race rituals are important because they allow you to operate without thinking as you mentally and physically steel yourself for the coming race. The successful athlete has a confident, focused, and business-like attitude during the pre-race ritual, from the moment of waking until the starting pistol fires. If you don't have a ritual established, use the C-priority races on your schedule to refine one that exactly fits your needs and personality. The following suggestions may help accomplish that.

WAKING, EATING, TRAVELING, AND PREPARING

In *Psyching for Sports,* sports psychologist Brent Rushall suggests that on race day you should start calmly and confidently, following these guidelines:

- Awake with the gentle sound of a subdued alarm clock, not a startling ring. If you're a heavy sleeper, ask your roommate to handle the wake-up chore.

- Prepare a drink that you like and are accustomed to, such as tea or coffee. This may mean carrying a small hot-water-making device with you, staying in a hotel that provides these in the rooms, or simply walking to the lobby where coffee or tea is already made.
- Starting from the moment you awake, smile and think positive thoughts about the race and how you feel.
- Stretch and breathe deeply.
- As your mood becomes more buoyant, dress while quietly repeating positive self-affirmations about your well-established ability.
- Replace anxiety-producing thoughts about the race with positive thoughts about recent successes. Have a mental list of these prepared and well practiced.

Before leaving your room, use the toilet. If your body isn't accustomed to bowel movements first thing in the morning, train it to do so by going to the bathroom every morning before working out. A warm drink or a little food may help with this. Eventually it will become natural.

Eat a pre-race meal two to three hours before your warm-up will start. The purpose of this feeding is to restock liver glycogen stores that have been depleted during your overnight fast. This should be from predominantly low-fiber, moderate- to low-glycemic-index carbohydrates (see Chapter 16 for the glycemic index) such as applesauce with no added sugar, baby food, or fruit. Some athletes find that as a result of a nervous stomach they are better off using only liquid for meals. Products such as Ensure may work well. Besides choosing foods that you know will agree with you, it's always a good idea to use products that you can bring with you or ones that are widely available in grocery or convenience stores.

How much you eat depends on how long it is until your start, the type of event you're training for, and your experience with your digestive system on race days or hard workout days. The more time you have before the race, the more you can eat. For short-course racing, plan on about 200 calories for every hour prior to race time. When preparing for a half-Ironman- or Ironman-distance race, you need to eat more than for shorter races (see *Going Long*, which I coauthored with Gordo Byrn, for more information). Your food intake, of course, should have been rehearsed in training on the days of long bricks just like any other aspect of training. On race day, you are wise to leave nothing to chance that you can control.

Eat and drink nothing else following this meal except water until your warm-up begins. At that time you can begin using a sports drink. The warm-up, of course, should last until your walk down to the start line. If you end the warm-up more than 10 minutes prior to your start, then take in nothing but water in the remaining time. If you're not warming up, save the sports drink until 10 minutes before the race start.

Slightly overdress for the weather conditions that greet you on race morning. You can always remove extra layers. That's better than being chilled, and it assists with the warm-up. The bottom layer should consist of race clothes that are appropriate for the expected weather, but prepare for sudden changes. If the weather is unstable, you may want to carry contingency clothing in a bag to the race site with you. This could include a light rain jacket, arm covers, tights, lightweight gloves, and a headband that covers the ears. While you are at it, put a roll of toilet paper into your bag just in case the portable toilets run out.

Before leaving, ask the hotel's front desk attendant for a late checkout so that you have time to come back to the room and shower. Most will gladly allow this if the requested time is reasonable.

Depart for the race site early enough to allow for a traffic jam as all of the racers funnel into the parking area. Also allow ample time for standing in line for body marking, finding your rack, pumping up tires, checking out the transition, talking with old acquaintances, visiting the toilets several times, and warming up.

When you arrive at the transition area, rack your bike and position your equipment as you always do. Don't try anything new today. Visit the toilet. Acquaint yourself with landmarks for your rack, such as its position relative to trees, light poles, pavement marking, signs, or other permanent markers. Visit the toilet. Walk to the swim and bike finishes and locate your transition stall from those perspectives. Visit the toilet. Rehearse the best route from each to your rack two or three times. And, of course, visit the toilet.

START-LINE STRESS

If your bladder sphincter is becoming difficult to control while your body attempts to shed water it is a sure sign of the anxiety known as "start-line stress." Adrenaline is pumping through your system in the genetic and ancient "fight or flight" preparation the human body goes through whenever it senses a threat. Only now the threat is not a saber-toothed tiger, but a race.

Depending on the sport, adrenaline can have either a beneficial or a detrimental effect on performance. Extremely high arousal is beneficial for power movements requiring only gross motor skills, such as the kickoff in football or the clean and jerk in Olympic power lifting. Very low arousal is needed by the golfer attempting to putt for par. The multisport athlete will reap rewards by keeping arousal at a more moderate level between these extremes. If the arousal state is too great, energy is wasted and pacing strategies fall apart early in the race. Low arousal results in a lethargic and unmotivated performance. Figure 10.1 illustrates the "inverted-U" relationship between arousal and performance, along with indicators of the extremes of arousal.

Most athletes should be more concerned about high arousal than the other extreme. Being able to reduce your excitement or nervous jitters to optimal levels requires good coping skills, and these skills can be learned. You can practice and refine them by participating in C-priority races, for example, and by implementing the strategies that follow. Those who have been around the sport for years will have already mastered them.

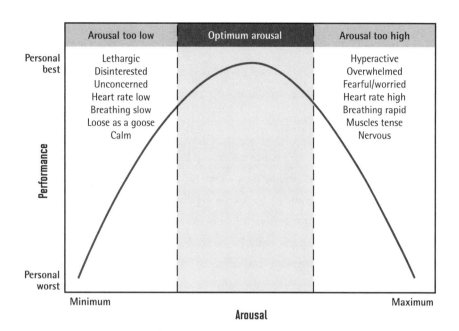

FIGURE 10.1

Balancing Arousal
and Performance

Strategies for Start-Line Stress

*   Physically slow down your movements and relax your muscles by "shaking out" the tension. Breathe slower and use your heart rate monitor as a biofeedback device to slow your pulse.
*   Mentally slow down by replacing negative, fearful thoughts with positive ones that emphasize recent successes.
*   Allow your body to go on "autopilot" throughout the warm-up as your mind dissociates and "plays" with other stimuli such as music, conversation, hobbies, scenery, or anything else that interests you.
*   Learn to trust that your training and racing experience will allow you to perform at near maximal ability without undue effort or pain. Know that when the starting pistol fires, you'll simply flip a switch and race as you always have.
*   Mentally separate yourself from thoughts of winning and losing. Race like a child by simply enjoying the challenge and the event.
*   Don't race against others; you have no control over whether you are better than them or not. You can only control your own effort and skill.
*   Forget about race outcomes. Think only about the here and now.
*   Act as if you were calm. Look at others who appear relaxed and emulate their appearance.
*   Act as if this is merely another workout with friends.
*   Remind yourself that no matter what happens, only good will come from the race. If it's a personal best—great! If not, you'll learn something from the experience that will make you better next time. The difference between winning and losing is that when you lose, you learn something.

WARM UP

Warming up has several benefits for race performance. It starts the flow of fatty acids to the muscles for use as fuel while simultaneously reducing dependence on your limited stores of carbohydrate-based glycogen. It raises the temperature of the working muscles. The capacity of muscles to produce energy rises by 13 percent for every degree Celsius of temperature rise. Heart stroke volume and lung capacity increase with warming up. The production of lactate is reduced following a warm-up, meaning that you are less likely to go anaerobic at the start. Warming up opens the capillaries to allow more oxygen into the muscles. It sensitizes the nervous system for smoother movements so that you waste less energy at the start of the race. And finally, perceived exertion during a workout or race is lower following a warm-up than when no warm-up is done.

Scientific studies have supported the value of warming up when it duplicates the movements of the sport and does not cause undue fatigue. A few studies have shown that a passive warm-up, such as a hot bath or massage, may even have some benefit, but not nearly as much as an active warm-up.

On race day, start warming up early enough that you can take care of minor problems that arise at the last minute, such as your bike not shifting smoothly or your goggles leaking. For Olympic-distance races and shorter, this might mean beginning 45 to 60 minutes before your start time (see Tables 10.1 and 10.2 for suggested warm-ups). For longer races, shorten the warm-up. Most competitors should do little or no warm-up before an Ironman-distance race.

Other factors that influence warm-up duration are your fitness level and the weather. The more endurance base you have built up, the longer your warm-up may be. For example, if your longest workout of any type is two hours and the race will probably take

	TIME (MIN.)	ACTIVITY
	10	**Run.** Slowly increase intensity from zone 1 to 2 or 3.
	5	Run 2–4 x 10–30 seconds at race effort/pace with long, easy recoveries.
	5	Return to transition area. Stretch calves and hamstrings. Walk bike out of transition (or set up trainer).
	10	**Bike.** Slowly increase intensity from zone 1 to 2 or 3.
	5	On bike do 2–4 x 10–30 seconds at race effort/pace with long, easy recoveries.
	5	Return to transition area. Stretch quads and low back. Make sure that everything in transition is in order. Put on wetsuit, if applicable, and walk to swim start.
	10	**Swim.** Slowly increase pace from zone 1 to 2 or 3.
	5	Swim 2–4 x 10–30 seconds at race-start effort/pace with long, easy recoveries.
	5	Report to start area and stretch shoulders.
	60 min. total	

TABLE 10.1

Warm-up for Olympic-Distance Triathlon

TIME (MIN.)	ACTIVITY
10	Bike on road or trainer. Slowly increase intensity from zone 1 to 2 or 3.
5	On bike do 2–4 x 10–30 seconds at race effort/pace with long, easy recoveries.
5	Return to transition area. Stretch quads and low back. Put on running shoes.
10	Run. Slowly increase intensity from zone 1 to 2 or 3.
5	Run 2–4 x 10–30 seconds at race effort/pace with long, easy recoveries.
5	Return to transition area to make sure that everything is in order.
5	Report to start area and stretch calves and hamstrings.
45 min. total	

TABLE 10.2

Warm-up for Olympic-Distance Duathlon

you three hours, a warm-up is not advised. Under such conditions, you are better served by saving your fuel and merely starting slowly on each leg of the race. In cool weather, a longer warm-up is needed, but if the water is cold, stay out of it and use stretch cords or calisthenics to warm up. In hot weather, decrease the length of the bike and run warm-ups. If it's a rainy day, shorten or omit the bike warm-up.

It's usually best to warm up in the reverse order of the event. So for a standard swim-bike-run triathlon, start with the run warm-up, then to the bike, and finally do the swim warm-up. Duathletes should warm up on the bike first and the run last.

Devote 10 to 15 minutes to each sport by beginning at a low effort and heart rate (zone 1), then slowly increased to zone 2 or 3, depending on how you feel. Finish with two to four accelerations to race pace of 10 to 30 seconds each with long recoveries. Stretch briefly after each sport's warm-up is completed.

If possible, end your warm-up no more than 5 minutes before the race is to begin. If this isn't possible and your wait to start time following the warm-up will be much longer, make the race-paced accelerations of the last warm-up portion longer—perhaps 45 to 60 seconds instead of 10 to 30 seconds. These longer efforts will provide a greater "depth" of warm-up, and the long wait for the start will allow for the removal of any lactate created.

Whatever warm-up procedure you use, practice the various portions of the routine weekly before your most intense swim, bike, and run workouts in the Build, Peak, and Race periods of your season. It should become such a natural thing to do that you warm up without even thinking about it.

THE START

In the last 5 minutes or so before the start, review your race strategy. This usually has to do with pacing, target heart rate zones, and maximum allowable efforts. This latter point is of special significance for long races such as half-Ironman- or Ironman-distance races in which going anaerobic may result in a DNF (Did Not Finish). Among elite athletes, race strategy may include position relative to other athletes at various times in the race. For draft-legal bike legs in some professional events, the swim can easily mean the difference between placing well and finishing out of the money. In such cases, a strong commitment to doing whatever it takes in the swim to stay near the front is necessary and should be reviewed before the start.

If swimming is your weakest sport, or if you are new to triathlon, start on the outer edge or at the back of your wave group. Front row and central positions are best left for those who swim strongly. After the initial sprint, settle into your planned effort and look for others to draft behind while frequently checking your preselected navigation landmarks. In the last minutes of the swim, mentally rehearse your upcoming transition by going through the exact steps in your mind: getting to your transition stall; removing the wetsuit; putting on shoes, sunglasses, and helmet; and exiting the transition.

At the start of the bike leg, begin in a lower gear than you plan to race in. Select this gear before the race based on the terrain exiting the transition area, and set it before the start. During the first 3 to 5 minutes, steadily increase the gear size. Pay special attention to hydration and fuel while on the bike. Some athletes even set their wristwatch alarms to sound every 10 to 15 minutes to remind them to drink and eat. Just as at the end of the swim, with a couple of minutes left in the bike portion review the steps of your next transition. With the transition area in sight near the end of the ride, shift to an easier gear and spin more. Unless you are leading and there is a bike prime prize, avoid the temptation to race another athlete to the dismount line. Always make it a habit to remove your helmet only at your transition stall. That will prevent unnecessary penalties.

Start the run by listening to your breathing while ignoring your legs. They will always tell you that you are going too slowly, which is erroneous at this point in the race. Initially, your stride will be shorter than normal, but it will slowly lengthen without the need to force it. During the run, and, indeed, throughout the entire race, forget about outcomes such as finishing in a certain time, placing, or winning. Race only in the here and now. That involves continually checking your form and vital signs, such as breathing and muscle tension, as well as your pace.

Relaxation is a crucial element for success in racing. Too much muscle tension wastes energy. If this is a problem for you, try repeating a personal cue word, such as "relax," whenever you sense tension building. You may even want to tape your cue word to the handlebars as a constant reminder, and, of course, practice using this technique in Breakthrough workouts. Whenever you think the cue word, it should trigger a relaxation response in your nonworking muscles.

POST-RACE

Should you cool down after the race? Unless it was a sprint- or Olympic-distance event, and you have an excellent base of aerobic fitness, there is no reason to cool down by jogging or riding. It further depletes your body of fuel and needlessly increases the stress on damaged muscles, prolonging recovery in the coming days. You are better off walking around for a few minutes while drinking fluids and restocking spent fuel. The usual reason given for a cool-down is the removal of lactic acid, but the lactic acid is gone in a few minutes post-race with or without a cool-down. Besides, lactic acid is not a cause of muscle soreness and does not impact long-term recovery.

The first priority after crossing the finish line is to replace fluid losses, and the second is to replace spent fuel. Water replacement can be enhanced by drinking a sports drink that has sodium in it or eating salty foods. Walking around, drinking, eating, and swapping lies with friends is all that's needed after a race.

RECOVERY

I've learned to back off when I need to.

—MARK ALLEN

THE NEED FOR BALANCE in life is undeniable. For every high there must be a low. For every fast workout, a slow one must soon follow. When at a peak and feeling invincible, you are only one training mistake from losing it all. Failure to maintain balance, especially by shortchanging recovery, will nearly always result in a breakdown that interrupts training consistency and brings a loss of fitness.

Chronic fatigue is not the purpose of training, as some exercise-addicted multisport athletes seem to believe. Increasing fatigue is normal as the volume or intensity of training rises, but it must be unloaded frequently in order for an athlete to maintain fitness growth. Failure to take time for recovery is a training mistake.

Fitness growth results not from the quantity of the exercise, but from the capacity for restoration that your mind and body have. The athlete who recovers the fastest is able to complete the most high-quality workouts. Quick recovery from fatigue is the key. The medals go to those who master this concept, who moderate motivation with patience, and who balance intensity with intelligence.

THE SECRET OF RECOVERY

Athletes like Michael Phelps, who have the genetic gift of recovering quickly from workouts, seem to naturally become the best in their respective racing categories. If you weren't born with this gene, there are ways you can shorten your recovery time, and I'll discuss those later in the chapter. Although there isn't any scientific data to back this up, there does seem to be a strong correlation between one's ability to recover and the rate of one's fitness progression. Recovering quickly really means getting in good shape quickly.

Why? It's during recovery following hard training that the body realizes the changes that we call "form," which is one's potential for performance in a race or in subsequent training. These changes may result in fat-burning enzyme increases, more resilient muscles and tendons, decreases in body fat, greater heart stroke volume, better glycogen storage, and more. Besides overloading your body with the stresses of hard exercise, focusing on recovery is the most powerful thing you can do in training to perform at a higher level. But this is the part of the training process that most self-coached athletes get wrong. They don't allow for enough recovery and overwhelm their bodies with stress.

Recovery may be thought of in many different ways. In terms of periodization, when you insert it in the training plan you created in Chapters 7 and 8, it is important to your eventual success as a triathlete.

YEARLY RECOVERY

In Chapter 7 you inserted Transition periods after Race periods. The purpose of these low-volume, low-intensity Transitions is to allow your body and mind to rejuvenate before you begin another period of hard training. If you have two A-priority races in a season, you should also generally have two Transition periods. The first Transition may only be three to five days, but the one that comes at the end of the season may well last four weeks or even longer depending on how challenging the previous season was, especially the final part.

MONTHLY RECOVERY

Build recovery into your monthly training plan every third or fourth week. This regular period of reduced workload may be three to seven days long depending on what you did in the previous hard training weeks, how fit you're becoming, and other factors.

Figure 11.1 illustrates what happens when you do this. As your fatigue increases over the course of two to three weeks of increasing workloads, your form diminishes. Form is your potential for performance, or how well you may train or race at any given point in time. Notice that fatigue and form follow nearly opposite paths, but form lags behind the changes in fatigue. It takes a few days of reducing fatigue to produce increases in form. A key principle of training is to unload fatigue frequently, which has the effect of improving your readiness to train well again. Without unloading fatigue you become a zombie doing workouts, with low quality and no enthusiasm.

WEEKLY RECOVERY

Within each week there should be hard and easy days. No one, not even elite athletes, can train hard every day with no recovery breaks. Easy days are as necessary for fitness

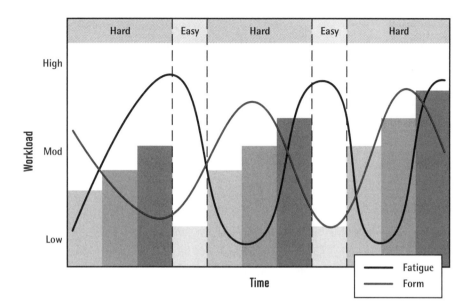

FIGURE 11.1

Impact of
Recovery on
Fatigue and Form

and form as sleeping at night is for health and well-being. Some athletes need a day
completely off from exercise every week. Other athletes, especially those with the quick-
recovery gene who also have a high capacity for work, can exercise seven days a week.
These elite athletes will still need easy days, however. "Easy" days are relative to the individual; there is no universal standard. That said, it is important even for high-capacity
athletes to occasionally have days completely off from exercise.

DAILY RECOVERY

When doing two-a-day workouts, there will be times when both are challenging sessions,
but there will also be days when both are light workouts or one is hard and one is easy.
This is what makes triathlon training so complex and why having a coach is often necessary to achieve high levels of success.

How often you insert recovery into your training program, how long this period of
recovery lasts, and what exactly recovery means to you in terms of workout duration,
intensity, and frequency is an individual matter. The only sure way for you to determine
each of these is through trial and error. Some athletes will find they can recover quite
nicely on short periods of infrequent recovery. Others will discover they need frequent
long periods to recover adequately.

Be aware that the need for recovery is a moving target; it is always changing in response to the total stress in your life and how fit you are. Be conservative when trying
different recovery programs. "Conservative" in this case means erring on the side of too
much recovery.

RECOVERY-RELATED PROBLEMS

With rare exceptions, the setbacks we experience in training are of our own making. Our motivation to excel is exceeded only by our inability to listen to our bodies. The result is often overtraining, illness, or injury.

OVERTRAINING

Athletes often ask me to review their training logs to see what might be behind a recent poor performance. What I usually find is that the athlete has been neglecting recovery and needs a few days of rest. I seldom find athletes who are really overtrained. Fatigue generally prevents athletes from driving themselves into a full-blown overtrained state. But I do find such athletes on occasion. The most common cause is an overwhelming motivation to excel.

A few years ago, a self-coached pro triathlete called me to ask if I could review his log because his race performances were declining. I arranged to meet him to learn more. When we met, I didn't have to read his log to know what the problem was. Sitting in front of me was a lackluster young man with a slumped posture and bags under his eyes who spoke in a monotone. He told me he wasn't sleeping well at night and that he had to drag himself out of bed in the morning to train.

He said he had skipped a couple of Recovery periods, as he was racing so well in the spring that he figured he didn't need them. And with the most important races of the season just around the corner, he decided he could cram in more hard workouts by skipping the rest breaks. This "Superman Syndrome" is common when fitness is high. But when some "Kryptonite" appeared, he tried training harder than before to overcome the downward spiral. That made things even worse. He couldn't reverse the loss of fitness no matter what he did with his workouts. So in frustration, he called me.

I told him exactly what he didn't want to hear but what he suspected deep down was at the heart of the flagging performance—he was overtrained. I had never seen an athlete in such a rundown state. There was only one cure: He had to rest. I advised him to take a complete break from training. I wasn't sure how long it would take—it could be days until he came around, or it could be months—but I suspected it would take a longer time rather than a shorter one for him to recover.

He took a week off and then did a short, easy bike ride. His power was low and his perceived exertion was high. But more telling was that he still experienced deep fatigue, and his enthusiasm for life in general was low. So he took another week off. After a couple of weeks of rest he started to have more energy and desire to train, so I had him gradually return to something approaching normal training. It was still a long way from what he had been doing before all of this started. But at least he was back on the road to racing again.

I was his coach for the next two years until his retirement from professional sport. In that time he won several more big races. He frequently told me that he was never again the same athlete after that overtraining episode. He couldn't train with the volume and intensity he had previously found easy. He believed something about his physiology had changed that spring. He may well have been right. There is still a great deal to be learned about overtraining. It could be that overtraining causes hormonal dysfunction that results in irreversible disturbances in glandular function. We simply don't know.

The bottom line is that you must avoid overtraining at all costs. In just a few weeks you can flood your body with stress hormones that may have a long-lasting and debilitating effect. If you make a mistake in coaching yourself, make it on the side of doing too little rather than too much.

Causes of Overtraining

Overtraining is best described as a decreased work capacity resulting from an imbalance between training and rest. In the real world of multisport, decreasing performance and nagging exhaustion that no longer respond to short-term rest are the best indicators of training gone awry. This condition is also known by coaches and athletes as "staleness." Athletes who experience it usually do not realize the cause, and they are as likely to increase their training as they are to take the needed time off in an effort to get back on track. They are apt to put in more miles, do more intervals, or both. It's a rare multisport athlete who rests more when things aren't going well.

Of course, poor races don't always result from too much training. You could be "overliving" by burning the candle at both ends. A 50-hour-per-week job, two kids to raise, a mortgage, and other responsibilities all take their toll on physical and psychological energy. Training is simply the most easily controlled cause. You sure aren't going to call the boss to ask for the day off when you suspect overtraining. Nor will you tell the kids to get themselves to the Scout meeting. Life goes on. At such times, the smartest option is to train less and rest more.

Figure 11.2 shows what happens when recovery is denied and motivation goes unbridled. Notice that as the training load increases, fitness also increases, up to your personal limit. At that point, fitness declines despite an increasing workload. Training beyond your present capacity causes a loss of fitness.

Increased training loads eventually leading to overtraining can come from one or more of three common training excesses: (1) workouts that are too long (excess duration); (2) exertion that is too high too often (excess intensity); and (3) too many workouts in too little time (excess frequency). Probably the most common cause of overtraining in competitive endurance athletes is excess intensity. Depending on the distance, multisport events are somewhere in the neighborhood of 90 percent aerobic and 10 percent anaerobic. Training should reflect that relationship. Placing excessive emphasis on anaerobic training week after week is a sure way to overtrain. That's why the Build period of training

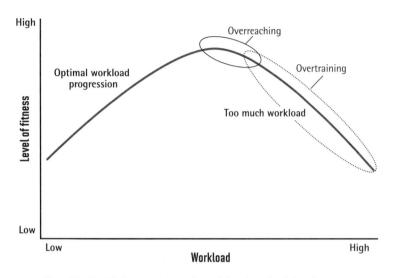

Note: Workload is frequency, intensity, and duration of training plus life's other responsibilities.

FIGURE 11.2

The Overtraining Curve

is limited to six weeks of high intensity plus two recovery weeks.

Many elite athletes have their blood chemistry tested in the Prep or early Base periods of training to establish a healthy baseline for later comparison, should training go awry. When they aren't responding normally to training during other periods of the season, they have their blood drawn and tested again to see if there have been significant changes, such as a decrease in serum iron levels or an increase in allergy indicators. It is not always necessary for most serious age-group athletes to take this precaution. Usually, the only treatment is to get some rest. However, blood testing can be helpful when performance declines, with or without other symptoms. There could be an underlying health problem, particularly anemia, which is a concern especially for women. So check with your physician, but there is little a doctor can do if the problem is overtraining; you must simply rest more and train less.

None of the items listed in the sidebar "Overtraining Indicators," or even those deduced from blood testing, is a sure sign of overtraining. Abnormalities may exist in perfectly healthy athletes who are in top shape. In dealing with overtraining there are no absolutes. You are looking for a preponderance of evidence to confirm what you already suspect.

Stages of Overtraining

There are three stages on the road to becoming overtrained. The first stage is "overload." Training overload is a normal part of the process of increasing the volume or intensity of your training beyond what you are used to in order to cause the body to adapt. If the overload is great enough, but within manageable limits, it results in overcompensation, as described in Chapter 3. During this stage it's typical to experience short-term fatigue, but generally you will feel great and may have outstanding race results. But during this stage it's also common to feel as if your body is invincible—that you can do anything you want. That belief often leads to the next stage.

In the second stage, "overreaching," you begin to train at abnormally high load levels for a period of two weeks or more. Extending the length of the higher-intensity Build period, or even increasing the amount of anaerobic training, may be overreaching. Now, for the first time, your performance noticeably decreases. Usually this happens in workouts before it shows up in races (where high motivation often pulls you through). Your fatigue

Overtraining Indicators

The body responds to the overtrained state by issuing warnings in many forms. In part, these reactions are the body's way of forestalling death by preventing further increases in stress volume. Although many of the problems listed below could have other causes, they could be signs of overtraining.

BEHAVIORAL SYMPTOMS

Apathy
Lethargy
Poor concentration
Changes in sleep patterns
Irritability
Decreased libido
Clumsiness
Increased thirst
Sluggishness
Sugar cravings

PHYSICAL SYMPTOMS

Reduced performance
Weight changes
Morning heart rate changes
Muscle soreness
Swollen lymph glands
Diarrhea
Injury
Infection
Amenorrhea
Decreased exercise heart rate
Slow-healing cuts

seems to last longer than in the overload stage, but with a few days of rest it is still reversible. The problem is that you decide that what you need is still more hard training, which brings on the third stage.

The third and final stage is a full-blown overtraining syndrome. Your fatigue is now chronic—it's with you like a shadow. You're tired when you wake up and throughout the day, whether on the job, in class, or in the pool, on the track, or on the bike, and yet you have trouble sleeping normally at night. Your body is exhausted.

As an athlete, it is your job to manage the overloading process, and the fatigue that comes as a result of it, to reach your peak fitness. At your optimal fitness level you are able to resist or delay fatigue, but there will still be limits to how long you can limit fatigue. If you have ever completed a maximum-effort race on Saturday and tried to race again on Sunday, you are familiar with the way fitness responds to repeatedly high training loads. The second time around, it isn't quite as easy.

Successful triathletes are capable of approaching the edge of overtraining once every four weeks or so, and then backing off before they lose fitness. After three weeks of load increases, it's time to allow for recovery and adaptation. Some athletes, especially masters and novices, may need to recover more frequently, perhaps after only two weeks. To do more is to fall over the edge and start the downward spiral through overreaching to overtraining.

As the body enters a chronically fatigued state, overtraining indicators begin to appear. You may experience poor sleep quality, excessive fatigue, or muscle soreness on a continuing basis. At first, the indicators may be minor in number and severity, but with too great an increase in training load or too prolonged a period of stress, you will find yourself teetering on the edge of overtraining. At this point, if you are wise, you will reduce the amount of training you are doing and rest more. Looking back on Figure 11.1, we can see how every fourth week of training shows a reduction in workload. In this recovery week, fatigue very quickly recovers while form rebounds to a higher level. Fitness follows a similar trajectory to form in this week: Active recovery brings adaptation marked by fitness increasing to a level exceeding the starting level three to four weeks before. By repeating this process several times, you eventually reach your peak fitness.

If you fall over the edge into overtraining, the only option is rest. At the first signs of overtraining, take 48 hours of complete rest, and then try a brief recovery workout. If you're still not feeling peppy, take another 48 hours off and repeat the test workout. It could take five to eight weeks of this routine to fully beat back overtraining, at a great loss of fitness.

The Art of Training

The art of training is knowing where the edge of overtraining is for you. Highly motivated, young, or novice athletes are less likely than seasoned competitors are to recognize when they have crossed the line. That's why many serious athletes are better off training under the guidance of a coach.

Smart training requires constantly assessing your readiness to train. Chapter 15 provides a training diary format with suggested daily indicators to rate. Judiciously tracking these indicators will help you pay closer attention to your body's daily messages. By learning to listen closely to your body, you will become adept at going to the edge safely.

Unfortunately, there is no sure-fire formula for knowing when you have done too much and are starting to overreach. The best prevention is the judicious use of rest and recovery. Just as workouts must vary, with some being hard, some easy, and others somewhere in between, so must weeks and months. It's far better to be undertrained and eager than to be overtrained and unmotivated. When in doubt, leave it out.

ILLNESS

You would think that a lot of training is healthy and might help you avoid illness. Unfortunately, that's not the case. Those who work out frequently are more likely to catch a bug than those who work out occasionally.

A study of runners in the Los Angeles Marathon found that those running more than 60 miles per week were twice as susceptible to respiratory illness as those who ran less than 20 miles weekly. Runners who completed the marathon were six times more likely to be ill in the week following the race as those who trained hard for the race and for some reason did not run it.

Illness and Timing

Getting some rest in the six hours following a high-intensity race or workout (zones 4 or 5) is critical because the immune system is depressed and less capable than usual of fighting off disease. This six-hour period is a good time to avoid people and public places. Wash your hands frequently if you have contact with others during this time. Some objects in public places are more likely than others to collect germs because they are handled by so many people: Doorknobs and telephones are examples. Develop the habit of touching your face only with your left hand and touching objects like these with your right. New Zealand's former world duathlon champion Matt Brick, a physician by training, would wear a surgical mask on airplanes after a race for this reason.

Neck Check

What should you do when a cold or flu bug gets you down? Should you continue to train normally, cut back, or stop altogether? Doing a "neck check" will help you decide. With above-the-neck symptoms such as a runny nose, sneezing, or a scratchy throat, start your workout, but reduce the intensity to zones 1 or 2 and keep the duration shorter than usual. You will probably begin to feel better once you are warmed up, but if you feel worse after the first few minutes, stop and head home. If the symptoms are below the neck, such as chest cold, chills, achy muscles, or a fever, or you are coughing up mucous, don't even start. You've probably got an acute viral infection. Exercising intensely in this condition will increase the severity of the illness and can even cause extreme complications, including death.

Below-the-neck symptoms are sometimes accompanied by the Coxsackie virus, which can invade the heart muscle, causing arrhythmia and other complications. I can speak from experience on this one. In November 1994, following a race, I caught a bad cold and experienced several below-the-neck symptoms, including fever and achy muscles, and I was coughing up mucous. Five months later I had a full-blown Coxsackie virus in my heart. After being inactive for most of the year to recuperate, I was finally able to start training again. I've since run into many others who have had the same experience. No race or any amount of fitness is worth paying such a price. Don't take these symptoms lightly. Suspect Coxsackie virus is present whenever you have a respiratory infection with indicators below the neck.

Recuperating

After an illness has abated, you are likely to be run down for some time. Many people experience a 15 percent reduction in muscle strength for up to a month following a bout of the flu. Your aerobic capacity may be reduced for up to three months, and your muscles may become acidic at lower levels of exercise intensity during this time. This means you will feel weak when working out even though the acute stage of your illness is past. Following a below-the-neck illness, return to the Base period of training for two days for every day you had symptoms. That means putting an emphasis on reestablishing aerobic endurance, force, and speed skills while avoiding intervals or extended anaerobic effort.

Trying to "push" past the flu will likely make your condition worse and cause it to last longer. It's best to get rid of the illness as soon as possible by allowing your limited energy reserves to go into fighting the disease rather than training.

INJURIES

For a serious athlete, there's nothing worse than an injury. As if it's not bad enough that it causes the athlete's fitness to slip away, depression may also set in, especially since so much of an athlete's life is tied to being physical.

Some people seem fragile and especially prone to injuries. Runners call this having "glass legs." Such athletes get hurt doing what others can do without any difficulty. It's more than a nuisance for those so afflicted. One study found that in triathletes, the lower leg and ankle, the knee, the back, the thighs, and the shoulders are the most common sites of injury. Other studies have shown that triathletes have an injury rate of 75 percent over the course of their racing careers, but among those training for an Ironman-distance race, the rate is 91 percent. If you're injury-prone, here are some prevention tips that may help keep you out of the doctor's office.

Equipment Selection

Using equipment that fits correctly and is meant for your needs is paramount to staying injury-free. Riding a bike that is too big or too small for you is an invitation to an injury. This is especially a problem for small women, who often ride bikes designed for men, and for juniors, who often ride bikes they will "grow into." Bike fit is not only important to injury prevention, but also to performance. Shop around when in the market for a new bike, and ask lots of questions. If you are less than 63 inches tall or more than 74 inches tall, or if your arm or leg lengths are disproportionate to your height, a custom bike is the way to go.

Suspect your running shoes at the first sign of discomfort or pain below the waist. A common mistake is trying to get too many miles from shoes. Some triathletes and duathletes get only 200 miles from their favorite model, while others may run for 500 before needing replacements. Most runners examine the outer soles of their shoes for wear, but it's really the midsole and heel cup that should be closely monitored. If injury resulting from shoe breakdown is a common problem for you, learn what the limits of your favorite style are and keep a cumulative record of miles in your diary for each pair. When your shoes are halfway through their anticipated life span, buy a second pair—regardless of how worn the current pair looks—and start breaking them in.

Another common error is buying shoes that are wrong for your foot type or running style. Running shoe design has become quite technical, and a pair of specially designed shoes is likely to cause injuries if they are not right for you. For example, shoes designed to control excessive pronation are excellent for those with such a foot type, but if you underpronate, these shoes may set you up for Achilles' tendinitis, iliotibial band syndrome, stress fracture, or any number of other serious injuries. The best way to avoid such problems is to buy shoes that have worked for you in the past, or to shop at a store where knowledgeable runners can help you make the right choice. If you take your old running shoes to the store with you when you go shopping, the salesperson may be able to recommend a good choice based on the pattern of wear.

Technique

The best way to avoid injury in running, swimming, or cycling is to have good technique. Repeating the same improper movement pattern hundreds of thousands of times under a load can cause leg injury in running, for example, or shoulder problems in swimming. To prevent such injuries, or to pinpoint the cause of any problems you may already be experiencing, have an experienced coach or expert observe your form, either in person or via video analysis, and follow his or her recommendations. Take the time to practice technique so that you can correct your mistakes. Realize, however, that we are not all built exactly the same way, and that some individual variance is to be expected.

Poor biomechanics on the bike can easily injure a joint, especially the knee. Once you have the right equipment for cycling, ask an experienced multisport athlete, bike shop employee, coach, or bike-fit specialist to take a look at your position and offer suggestions for improvement. Be especially concerned with saddle fore-aft position and height. See Chapter 12 for more details on technique.

Training

Be especially careful during the two or three days after very long or intense workouts or races. That is the time when multisport athletes are most likely to be injured. Running at these times is especially risky and is best done slowly and on a softer surface such as grass, if at all. Swimming and cycling are often better choices at such times for the injury-prone. But just after a race, your training should be brief and easy; it is also a good time to take a couple of days off. In the same manner, two or three weeks of high-workload training are best followed by several days of reduced volume and intensity. It may be difficult for you to back off of training like this when your cardiovascular and energy-production systems seem well able to handle more, but keep in mind that your musculoskeletal system is fragile at this time. To stay injury-free, practice restraint.

Strength and Stretching

For most athletes, the muscle-tendon junction is a vulnerable spot where tears and strains are likely to occur. Many muscle-tendon problems can be prevented by improving the strength and range of muscle motion early in the season. One study estimated that up to 80 percent of all running injuries resulted from muscle weakness, muscular imbalance, or lack of flexibility. Proper strength training and stretching can prevent these problems.

Many endurance athletes, however, neglect strength training and stretching. Going for a swim, bike ride, or run is fun, but grunting through a combined strength and stretching session in the gym seems like drudgery. Hang in there, and you will reap the benefits. But don't take these disciplines too far: Excessive strength development or stretching is sometimes the *cause* of injury. Maintain a moderate approach, and you will be safer when you are training and racing. See Chapter 13 for more details on strength and stretching.

Listening

Learn to tell the difference between sore muscles that come from a high-quality effort, on the one hand, and sore joints or tendons that come from improper form, overtraining, or some other problem, on the other. If you are experiencing sore joints or tendons, check your shoes, bike set-up, and running surfaces to see if you can locate the cause of the problem. Examine any training or technique changes you have made. Such probing may lead you to the cause of the injury and its treatment.

If the pain isn't gone within five days of reduced activity, it's time to see a health-care provider. Don't put it off. Injuries are easier to turn around in the early stages than later on, when they may have become chronic. When you talk to your physician, try to describe exactly what you are feeling. Don't just say "My knee hurts." Is it above or below the knee-cap? Is it at the front or the back of the knee? Is it a sharp pain or a dull ache? Does it hurt only while you are swimming, cycling, or running, or all the time? Is the pain worse when you are going upstairs, or down?

If you must take time off from a sport to allow for healing, ask your doctor if you can increase your volume in the sports that are unaffected by the injury. Healing is often speeded up by exercise.

RECOVERY TIMING AND TECHNIQUE

What happens inside the muscles during an intense exercise session, such as anaerobic endurance intervals, is not a pretty sight. If you could look into your leg muscles with a microscope after a race, what you would see would look like a battleground. It would look like a miniature bomb had exploded in your muscles. The torn and jagged cell membranes would be evident, and you would see leaking fluids. The damage might vary from slight to extreme depending on how great the stress was. Under extreme conditions, the muscles and nervous system would be so taxed, and your energy so depleted, that it would be unlikely that you would be ready for such an effort again soon. Another all-out effort would not be possible until the cells were repaired, the energy stores rebuilt, and the cellular chemistry back to normal. Your fitness depends on how long that process takes.

Much of the time needed for recovery has to do with your body creating new muscle protein to repair the damage. Research conducted at McMaster University in Hamilton, Ontario, and at the Washington University School of Medicine in St. Louis found that this protein resynthesis process takes several hours. The study used young, experienced weightlifters and maximal efforts followed by observation of the muscles' repair process. Reconstruction work started almost immediately following the workout. Four hours after the damaging weight session, protein activity had increased by about 50 percent. This was an indication that tissues were already being rebuilt. Twenty-four hours post-workout, protein activity reached a peak of 109 percent of normal. Protein resynthesis was back to normal, indicating that repairs were complete, 36 hours after the hard workout.

While this study used exhaustive strength training to measure recovery time, the results are probably similar to what could be expected following a race or intense workout.

RECOVERY PHASES

The recovery process can be divided into three distinct phases in relation to a workout—before and during, immediately following, and long term. An athlete who follows good recovery procedures in each phase can minimize damage, accelerate repair, and go on to the next quality session sooner than the athlete who neglects recovery principles.

Before and During the Workout or Race

Recovery actually starts with a warm-up before the workout or race, not afterward. Taking the time for a good warm-up before starting to train helps to limit damage by:

- Thinning body fluids to allow for easier muscle contractions;
- Opening capillaries to bring more oxygen to muscles;
- Raising muscle temperature so that contractions take less effort; and
- Conserving carbohydrate and releasing fat for fuel.

During the workout, you can continue to get a head start on the recovery process by replacing your fluids and carbohydrate-based energy stores throughout the session. It is a good idea to drink 18 to 24 ounces of a sports drink every hour that you work out depending on your level of thirst as a guide. If you follow these recommendations, the training session will be less stressful for your body and your energy-production system will recover faster later on.

There are individual differences in how well athletes tolerate carbohydrate drinks and how well they are emptied from the stomach. Find a sports drink that tastes good to you and doesn't upset your stomach when you are working intensely. Before a race, make sure you have plenty of whatever works best for you on your bike. If possible, make sure you have prepared for whatever is offered at the aid stations by using it in training. When mixing your sports drink, follow the directions on the label or make the drink less concentrated. Making a sports drink more concentrated than is recommended on the label may cause you to dehydrate during a race as body fluids are shunted to the gut to digest the carbohydrates. You are most likely to benefit from a sports drink during races and workouts that last more than one hour. In races lasting longer than four or five hours, solid food may be beneficial for some athletes.

Your recovery continues with a brief cool-down. The cool-down should be a mirror image of the warm-up, ending with easy effort in zone 1 for several minutes.

Immediately Following the Workout or Race

As soon as you finish your workout or race, the most important thing you can do to speed recovery is to replace the carbohydrates and protein that you just used for fuel. A long and difficult workout or race can deplete nearly all of your stored glycogen, a carbohydrate-based energy source, and use several grams of muscle-bound protein. In the first 30 minutes after a workout or event, your body is several times more capable of absorbing and replenishing those fuels than at any other time.

At this time, you probably don't want to use the same sports drink you used during the workout or race. It's not potent enough and doesn't include protein. You need something designed for recovery. There are several such products now on the market. As long as you like the taste and can get about 15 to 20 grams of protein and 80 grams or so of carbohydrate from one of them, it will meet your recovery needs. The classic triathlete recovery drink is chocolate milk. Dr. Owen Anderson in *Running Research News* suggests making a recovery "homebrew" by adding 5 tablespoons of table sugar to 16 ounces of skim milk. It's probably best not to use a high-glycemic-index carbohydrate, such as a sugary drink without protein (see Chapter 16 for the glycemic index), as some scientists believe that this may reduce the body's release of growth hormone, further slowing the recovery process. Whatever you use, drink all of it within the first 30 minutes after finishing your exercise session.

Short-term recovery continues for as long as the workout lasted. So if your intense workout lasted two hours, your short-term recovery also lasts two hours. During this time you should focus on getting enough carbohydrates. Include foods that are moderate on the glycemic index scale, such as fruits, along with higher-glycemic-index foods, such as starches. Starch, especially from potatoes, is an excellent choice during this time. Vegetables have been shown to decrease the acidity of the blood, so a potato, being a starchy vegetable, is nearly a perfect recovery food.

Long-Term Recovery

For six to nine hours after a Breakthrough (BT) workout, you must actively seek recovery by using one or more specific techniques. The most basic method is sleep. Nothing beats a nap for rejuvenation, as growth hormone is released in pulses starting about 30 minutes into slumber. In addition to a 30- to 60-minute post-workout nap, be sure to get a good night's sleep. That means seven to nine hours, which is a good rule of thumb every night. Other recovery methods are unique to each individual, so you will need to experiment with several of these to find the ones that work best for you. Sidebar 11.1, "Recovery Techniques," offers several suggestions. By employing some of the specific techniques described here, you can accelerate the recovery process and return to action as quickly as possible. Figure 11.3 illustrates how this happens.

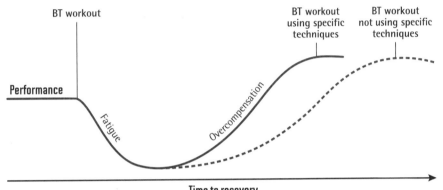

FIGURE 11.3

Effect of Recovery Techniques on Performance

INDIVIDUALIZATION OF RECOVERY

You will find that some recovery techniques work better for you than others do. You may also discover that a training partner doing the same workouts as you and following the same recovery protocol springs back at a different rate. Everyone is different: Some athletes recover faster than others. There are many physiological similarities between athletes, but there are many differences as well, and every athlete responds in his or her own way to any given set of circumstances. You must experiment to discover the best recovery techniques for you.

There are several individual factors affecting recovery. Younger multisport athletes, especially those 18 to 22 years old, recover faster than older athletes. The more race-experienced an athlete is, the quicker he or she recovers. If fitness is high, recovery is accelerated. Females were shown in one study to recover faster than males. Other factors influencing the rate of recovery are climate, diet, and psychological stress.

How do you know if you are recovering? The best indicator is performance in races and BT workouts, but these are the worst times to find out that you are not ready. Typical signs that recovery is fully complete include a positive attitude, feelings of health, a desire to train intensely again, high-quality sleep, normal resting and exercise heart rates, and balanced emotions. If any of these are lacking, continue the recovery process. By closely monitoring such signs, you will soon know just what you need to recover from your workouts quickly.

Recovery
Techniques

Most of these techniques speed recovery by slightly increasing the heart rate, increasing blood flow to the muscles, accelerating the inflow of nutrients, reducing soreness, lowering blood pressure, and relaxing the nervous system.

HOT SHOWER OR BATH: Immediately following the cool-down and recovery drink, take a hot shower or bath for 10 to 15 minutes. Do not linger, especially in the bathtub, as you will dehydrate even more.

ACTIVE RECOVERY: For the experienced triathlete, one of the best recovery methods is to pedal or swim easily for 15 to 30 minutes several hours after the workout and before going to bed. The intensity should be extremely light with heart rate below Zone 1.

MASSAGE: Other than sleep, most triathletes find a massage by a professional massage therapist is the most effective recovery technique. A post-race massage should employ long, flushing strokes to speed the removal of the waste products of exercise. Deep massage at this time may actually increase muscle trauma. After 36 hours, the therapist may apply greater point pressure, working more deeply.

Due to the expense of massage, some athletes prefer self-massage. Following a hot bath or shower, stroke the muscles for 20 to 30 minutes, working away from the extremities and toward the heart.

SAUNA: Several hours following a workout or race you may find that a dry sauna speeds recovery. Do not use a steam room for recovery as it will have the opposite effect. Stay in the sauna for no more than 10 minutes and begin drinking fluids as soon as you are done.

RELAX AND STRETCH: Be lazy for several hours. Your body wants quality rest. Provide it by staying off your feet whenever possible. Never stand when you can lean against something. Sit down whenever possible. Better yet, lie on the floor with your feet elevated against a wall or furniture. Sit on the floor and stretch gently. Overused muscles tighten and can't seem to relax on their own. This is best right after a hot bath or sauna and just before going to bed.

WALK IN A PARK OR FOREST: A few hours after finishing the workout or race, a short, slow walk in a heavily vegetated area, such as a park or forest, seems to speed recovery for some. Abundant oxygen and the aroma of grass, trees, and other plants are soothing.

OTHER METHODS: The sports program of the former Soviet Union made a science of recovery and employed several techniques with their athletes that may or may not be available to you. Many are also unproved in the scientific literature. They included electromuscular stimulation, ultrasound, barometric chambers, sport psychology, and pharmacological supplements, including vitamins, minerals, and adaptogens such as ginseng. These require expert guidance.

RECOVERY IN THE REAL WORLD

If you are following the periodization program suggested in Part Four, you will occasionally experience increasing fatigue. Despite your best recovery efforts, you will not unload all of the fatigue between planned workouts, and go into some BT workouts a bit heavy legged and lacking power. Don't expect full recovery for every type of workout all the time. In fact, a little fatigue at the right times in workouts can bring fitness benefits in the form of "supercompensation"—an increased level of overcompensation. This state can help to prepare you for peak performances. However, you should not let this happen more than about once every third or fourth week. A recovery week should immediately follow a period in which fatigue played a major role in the training load.

The recovery "week" is not necessarily seven days long. Many athletes are fully recovered with only five days of reduced training. For them, taking another two days of reduced training may actually have negative consequences for fitness. Your experience is the best determiner of how long your recovery weeks should be.

PART VI

THE COMPETITIVE EDGE

Up to this point, the focus has been on the more obvious contributors to fitness: training principles; intensity; limiters; planning and periodization; swimming, cycling, and running workouts; tapering; and recovery. While these factors certainly play a role in the attainment of peak fitness, there are many others. In fact, it would be unrealistic to segment your life and say that only these particular things have a bearing on race performance. When you go to the starting line, all of the physical and psychological components of your recent lifestyle have shaped your readiness for that moment.

This part examines a few of those frequently overlooked components that play an important role in your race readiness, including physical skills, muscle strength, flexibility, the needs of unique subgroups, the training diary, and diet. The goal is to refine these aspects of your training and lifestyle so you gain a competitive edge.

SKILLS

Fitness is something that happens to you while you're practicing good technique.
—TERRY LAUGHLIN, SWIM COACH

THERE ARE THREE GOALS multisport athletes typically seek: the capacity to go farther, the ability to go faster, and the stamina to go farther and faster without breaking down. Of these, the most common single goal is to swim, bike, and run faster for a given distance. In fact, faster race times are the reason most of us train.

What can you do to get faster? The answer is simple: Increase how quickly you can move your arms and legs, or how much distance you can cover in each stroke or stride, or some combination of both. In other words, velocity is a product of cadence and stroke/stride length. In running, for example, if you develop the ability to take more strides per minute while the length of each stride stays the same, you will run faster. Or if you build the strength to take a longer stride with the same cadence, running times will improve.

Let's examine this relationship more closely, again using running as the example. If you run a 5 km race with an average step length of 1.5 meters and an average cadence of 170 steps per minute, your finish time will be 19 minutes and 36 seconds. But if you take three more steps per minute and your step length stays the same, you finish 20 seconds faster. Or, if you increase the length of each step by 0.025 meters (about 1 inch) and your stride rate remains 170 per minute, your time is improved by 19 seconds. If you are able to accomplish both the faster stride rate and the longer stride, you lop 39 seconds off of your time and have a new personal best of 18:57. Small changes in technique can produce significant results.

Of course, running with a stride that is both longer and faster means that you must develop the fitness to maintain such an effort. As described in previous chapters, improving the basic abilities of endurance, force, and speed skills, and the more advanced abilities of muscular endurance, anaerobic endurance, and power, will lead you to this goal of greater race velocity. Another way of looking at the necessary fitness components uses the terms of science: Great race fitness results from a large aerobic capacity (VO_2max), a high lactate threshold (LT) as a percentage of aerobic capacity, and an excellent economy of movement.

Aerobic capacity (how much oxygen the body processes at maximal work) and LT (the level of submaximal work at which lactate begins to accumulate in the blood) are generally well understood by endurance athletes. Although you may not be as familiar with economy as you are with those other concepts, it is critical for you to understand how improving economy can help you achieve greater gains. You can reap greater rewards by working on all three than you can by working strictly on aerobic capacity and LT. In fact, your performance in multisport may be limited more by flaws in your economy of movement than by underdeveloped fitness.

ECONOMY

In 1969, in a world record that was not broken until 1981, Australian Derek Clayton ran the marathon in 2 hours, 8 minutes, and 34 seconds. What is surprising about Clayton's feat is that he had a VO_2max of only 69.7 ml/min/kg (milliliters of oxygen used per minute per kilogram of body weight). That is a rather pedestrian VO_2max for a world-class athlete and paled in comparison to the aerobic capacities of many of his running contemporaries, such as Craig Virgin (81.1), Gary Tuttle (82.7), Don Kardong (77.4), and Bill Rodgers (78.5). None of these runners came close to Clayton's time, despite having remarkably "big engines." The reason for Clayton's success was his economy of movement. He simply wasted less energy when he ran than the other athletes did.

The concept of economy is important—all the more so if your parents didn't bless you with genes for a large aerobic capacity. Following Derek Clayton's example, you can enhance your performance by learning to swim, bike, and run in an efficient manner.

UNDERSTANDING ECONOMY

Economy, on one level, refers to the efficiency of your movements: Athletes who carry out a given exercise without extraneous movements will be efficient, or economical. It only makes sense that an athlete who moves efficiently will be faster than one who does not. But it's more than that: Because the economical athlete has fewer muscle contractions per stride or stroke, he will use less oxygen to go a given distance than the uneconomical athlete. Thus, we can state the definition of economy for multisport in this way: Economy refers to how much oxygen you use while swimming, biking, and running.

Since oxygen usage is an indirect indicator of the amount of fuel burned, and economy is a measure of fuel expenditure in relation to work (like miles per gallon in a car), knowing how much oxygen an athlete uses at various velocities reveals how economical he or she is. Fuel efficiency in one sport, however, does not necessarily mean fuel efficiency in others. You may use fuel like a small economy car while running, but be a "gas guzzler" on the bike.

The more economical you are, the faster you can travel at any given effort level. For example, let's say you currently run an 8-minute pace at an oxygen cost of 50 ml/min/kg, but through training you improve your economy by 2 percent. That means you can now run an 8-minute pace at 49 ml/min/kg, so it would feel easier. Or you could run at the same 50 ml/min/kg, but your pace would have improved to 7:50—a ten-second increase in velocity for every mile run. Over the course of a 10 km run, that would result in more than a 1-minute improvement in time. So small changes in economy can produce rather dramatic changes in performance.

It's also important to note that the longer the race is, the more important economy becomes. In a sprint-distance race you may be able to get away with squandering fuel because the event is so short; you may be able to simply "muscle" your way through it. That's not possible in an Ironman-distance event, where the fuel-consumption rate often means the difference between a personal best and not finishing.

It's sometimes easy to spot economical athletes, as they make swimming, biking, and running look effortless. This is especially true in swimming, since water is denser than air and severely penalizes extraneous, wasteful movements. An accomplished swimmer seems to glide through the water. Such a swimmer makes it look so easy that when you check lap splits, you may be surprised at how fast he or she is moving. In the same way, an uneconomical swimmer's thrashing and struggling technique is obvious.

Economy isn't just about mechanics, though. It is also affected by more subtle factors. For example, science has shown that endurance athletes endowed with lots of slow-twitch muscle fibers are somewhat more economical than those who have an abundance of fast-twitch fibers. Body size may also affect economy. Small athletes are generally found to have better economies than bigger athletes. These are factors outside of your control, but there are other variables affecting economy that you can mitigate to improve energy consumption, such as:

- Excess body weight
- Psychological stress
- Equipment (for example, bike and running shoes) weight and shape
- The amount of frontal area exposed to water or wind
- Subtle variances in technique

IMPROVING ECONOMY

This last point, subtle variances in technique, is worth further discussion. By consciously modifying your movement patterns to resemble those of elite swimmers, cyclists, and runners who typically have excellent economy, it may be possible for you to improve your fuel usage. Unfortunately, scientific studies nearly always find that changing technique has little or no positive effect on economy. It's important to understand, however, that testing in economy research is usually limited in ways that could produce misleading findings. Most of the research subjects are college students, for example. This means the study must coincide with the length of a school semester. The motivation of the subjects to carry out the required training may also be a factor. The body's adjustment to changes that could affect economy may take months to fully realize, since many slowly occurring adaptations are required of the nervous system and muscles before the gains are appreciable enough to even be measurable. At first, during that period of adaptation, economy may even worsen.

Experience tells us that it is possible to boost economy, even in elite athletes. A case in point is the experience of American miler Steve Scott, who in the early 1980s, at the height of his running career, broke the American record for the mile after improving his economy by a whopping 5 percent.

There are three principles you must adhere to in training if your economy is to steadily and rapidly improve. The first is to practice the new technique frequently. If your swimming skill needs correction, getting in the pool only once a week is not enough. Three swims spaced evenly throughout the week are probably a minimum, and more is better. The second principle is that once you've mastered the new skill at slower velocities, you must regularly practice it at goal race pace. These race-pace repetitions are kept quite short—on the order of 20 to 30 seconds—to allow you to focus all your concentration on the new skill and to prevent fatigue from interfering as you practice the new movements.

The last principle is perhaps the most important: Complex skills are best learned when the desired movement pattern is broken down into manageable units that are mastered individually before being gradually combined into more complex movements. This means that technique drills are best for helping you learn new skills. You are essentially training the nervous system to choose the best pathways to the exact muscles that need activating. The more often you employ the new technique, the better your nervous system becomes at producing the desired movement pattern. This can be compared to making a path across open land. If enough people take the same shortcut often enough, a path results. This principle is obvious on most college campuses, where students have produced "economical" pathways across the spacious lawns regardless of where the sidewalks are. They walk on the improvised pathways in order to reduce the distance between destinations. In the same way, when you learn a more economical technique, you are forging shorter pathways between your brain and your muscles.

Frequent repetition of inappropriate movement patterns builds bad habits by destroying the fragile pathways you try to build with drills. To fully develop new skills, it's important to let go of old patterns and fully commit to the new. At first this will inevitably result in poorer performance and frustration. You must realize that this is merely a stage of learning that you go through in order to ultimately improve. The best time in the training year to develop new skills is during the Prep and early Base periods, but there is no time like the present for getting started.

SWIMMING SKILLS

The energy cost of a 150-pound triathlete running a kilometer is about 70 kilocalories. But when swimming that same kilometer, assuming the athlete's economy is about the same, 280 kilocalories are expended. Why does swimming require so much more energy? The answer is that water is nearly a thousand times denser than air. Water is a formidable barrier for the human shape to move through. Unfortunately for triathletes, we weren't given the shape and instincts of fish; we're land-based animals and try to apply what works in that world whenever we enter the world of fish. Those land-based skills are seldom effective in water. To become an effective and economical swimmer, you must change the way you think about movement in the watery world.

Essentially, there are two ways to swim faster. The first is to decrease drag by streamlining your body position. The second is to increase propulsion by improving your aerobic and anaerobic fitness. Of these two, studies have found that reducing drag has the potential to produce the greatest gains. Drag is the retarding force created by turbulence around the body as it moves through water. The more streamlined the body is, the lower the resulting drag force.

One swimming authority estimates that the opportunity for improving triathlon performance by reducing drag is more than twice as great as focusing on propulsive effort. Our land-based instincts tell us the opposite, so we spend countless hours in the pool struggling to become more fit to fight drag while paying only lip service to the skills of swimming.

On land, humans discover that running with an increased cadence leads to faster times, so we take that knowledge with us into the water. The problem is, this solution doesn't work in the water. The faster we try to move our arms, the more the water pushes back against us. The solution is to increase stroke length, and, for some triathletes, to decrease stroke rate. Again, research has shown that the swimmers with the longest strokes are the most economical and produce the best results. A good indicator of improving economy in swimming is how many strokes are taken in a given length. For most triathletes, reducing stroke count is the surest way to a new swimming personal-best time.

To improve swimming economy, try counting your strokes for a length of the pool, and set a goal of taking 10 percent fewer. Once you've achieved that lower stroke-count goal—and you will if you concentrate on form rather than fitness—extend the amount of time that you can maintain it. When you can keep it up for more than 2 minutes, it's time to set a new stroke-count goal and start over again.

The best pathway to faster swim times comes from improving drag-reducing skills so that you are more "fishlike" and "slippery"—not from high yardage and propulsion-increasing battles with the water. Instead of trying to overpower the water, develop the skills to slice through it with the least possible amount of energy expended. The best way to achieve these skills is by having a smart coach on deck. That's not always feasible, so let's look at what you can do on your own to improve economy in the water.

REDUCING DRAG

Terry Laughlin is perhaps the leading authority in the United States on swimming drag reduction for triathletes. Through his Total Immersion swim camps, video, workbook, drill guide, magazine articles, and book, he has consistently promoted the concept that better swimming results from mastering three simple techniques. The successes of his students prove that his methods work. Here are his three techniques and one basic drill for each. There are many more drills Laughlin recommends. (For more information on Total Immersion products visit www.totalimmersion.net.)

Swimming "Downhill"

The most common swimming complaint heard from rock-hard triathletes is that they sink in the water. Actually, what sinks are the hips and legs, as the upper body has natural buoyancy due to the lungs. When the lower body sinks, drag forces increase, since more of the body is exposed to the approaching water. Just as improving aerodynamics on the bike requires greatly reducing frontal area, economical hydrodynamics depends on having a small frontal area (see Figure 12.1a). You can see the challenge caused by a large frontal area, as shown in Figure 12.1b.

FIGURE 12.1a

Efficient Hydrodynamics

FIGURE 12.1b

Inefficient Hydrodynamics

Your head controls your hip and leg position relative to the surface of the water. When the head comes up, the legs go down. So if you swim with your face lifted, looking at the far end of the pool, your hips and legs sink and are no longer following your torso through the larger "tube" it has created in the water. This is like dragging an anchor around behind you. Your only option is to work harder to increase the propulsive force, thus wasting a lot of energy—not very economical.

If, however, you look slightly downward while "leaning" on your chest, the hips and legs come up and follow your torso through the tube. When this is done correctly, only a small portion of the back of the head will show above the water line, as will your butt. These are sure signs that you are swimming downhill, and they can be readily confirmed by an observer on the deck. A videotape of athletes swimming with and without the downhill position will clearly show you these economy traits. To see if you are doing it correctly, watch a video of someone doing the proper form, and then have someone take a video of your attempts.

Learning to lean on the chest—"pressing the buoy" as Laughlin calls it—is the most basic skill for you to master in swimming. Until you have this down pat, there is no reason to practice other skills. One drill for developing this skill involves kicking a length of the pool without a board and with your arms at your sides. While kicking in this position, keep your face looking slightly toward the pool bottom as you lean on your chest (your "buoy"), pushing it down into the water. When you look up to breathe, notice that the hips and legs drop immediately, but that you can bring them back up by looking down and leaning more. Figure 12.2 illustrates this drill.

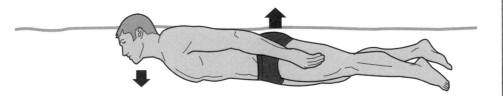

Adapted with permission from Laughlin and Delves 1996.

FIGURE 12.2

"Pressing the Buoy"

Swimming Like a Knife

On land, we mammals move forward by keeping the line of our shoulders perpendicular to the direction of movement. This works fine in the less-dense world of air, but in water it presents a bigger frontal area and increases drag. By swimming on your side, as fish do, you waste less energy and go faster. This position also allows you to make better use of the powerful latissimus dorsi (lats) muscles on both sides of your upper back. So swimming in this position has a double benefit by reducing drag and increasing propulsive force.

Swimming on your side requires you to roll the hips and shoulders, with all rotation happening around the spine. When first attempting such a maneuver you might feel as if you will flop over onto your back; it takes some getting used to. One drill that can improve your comfort level in this position is called "belly-to-the-wall." Swim a length of the pool lying on your left side, with your left arm extended and the right arm lying on your hips, as shown in Figure 12.3. The back of your head is pressed against the biceps of your outstretched arm, and your face is looking up. This is a good drill to do with fins to keep the kick compact and minimize the "risk" of rolling completely onto your back. Change to your right side and kick back down the pool. Remember to keep the side of your chest (your buoy) pressed down into the water.

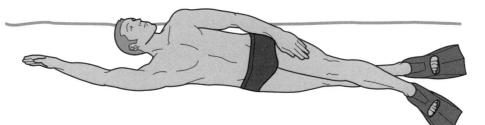

Adapted with permission from Laughlin and Delves 1996.

FIGURE 12.3

"Belly to the Wall"

Once you have become comfortable with this position, practice rolling from one side to the other after a three-count pause on your side. As you roll, bring the top arm and hand slowly up your side as if you were taking your hand out of a pocket. Notice that if you swing this arm out in front of your center of gravity, you immediately flop over onto your chest and belly. As your hand reaches your shoulder, initiate a roll to the prone position (face down) with your hips, and then bring your hands together with the arms outstretched. Hold this position for a count of three while pressing the buoy, just as in the first drill. Then, again using the hips to initiate movement, roll to the other side for a count of three.

Swimming Taller

If you watch elite swimmers, one thing stands out clearly: They fully extend their hands and arms in the reach phase, which allows them to swim quite fast with strokes that seem long and unhurried. This results in a lower stroke rate but a longer stroke, which, as we've seen, is associated with reduced drag and improved economy. They also kick from the hip with minimal bending of the knee, further lengthening their position in the water. This also reduces drag by keeping the legs within the tube described above.

Swimming with a long stroke, including a reach and glide, while staying on your side requires constant practice to make it a habit. Stroke counting to ensure a low number of strokes per length is one way of checking how you are doing. A drill to refine this skill involves swimming a length of the pool while using only one arm, as the other one is fully extended in the reach position, as shown in Figure 12.4. As the "propulsive" arm starts its stroke, you roll onto your side, as in the drill described above, and stretch as far as you can with the reaching arm. At the conclusion of the stroke, the recovery hand returns to touch the "reach" hand as you roll back to your chest. Be sure to continue pressing your chest and face into the water throughout the drill, even when on your side. You may use fins to help keep your legs up as you develop these upper-body skills.

Adapted with permission from Laughlin and Delves 1996.

FIGURE 12.4

One-Arm-Only Drill

SWIM TRAINING

Your swimming is more likely to improve if you think of your pool sessions as "practices" rather than "workouts." Just as golfers spend hours on the practice tee and tennis players endlessly practice their serve, triathletes must devote considerable time and attention to refining their technique, with drills to instill new movement patterns. There are two ways to look at this allocation of valuable pool time for drill work. One is seasonal and has to do with the incorporation of drill work into your periodization plan. The other is within a given practice session. Here are some general guidelines for both areas to help you plan the timing of your drill work.

Annual Periodization

The Prep period is the time in each season to work exclusively on technique. One objective for this period is to correct any stroke flaws that may have found their way into your swimming mechanics by returning to the most basic drills, such as those described above, and gradually making them more complex. This is also a good time to regularly meet with a knowledgeable swim coach, attend a swim camp, read a book on swimming, or have someone videotape your swimming for analysis.

In the Base period, while aerobic and muscular endurance, along with force, are developing, continue to include a good deal of stroke work. The novice triathlete may devote nearly half of each swim practice just to refining technique.

As intensity increases in the Build and Peak periods, great care must be taken not to allow the good stroke mechanics you established in previous periods to erode. In an attempt to push velocity to a higher level, it is common to revert to a higher stroke rate,

Case Study:
Marlene's Swim

I began working with Marlene when she was 43 years old and a strong cyclist. My plan was to help her maintain her bike fitness while emphasizing swimming and running. I thought her running would come along well, as she had a big aerobic engine. But swimming was a different story. She did not have any experience with competitive swimming. She was, however, a golfer and so could relate to a sport primarily based on skill rather than fitness, at least in the initial stages of development.

The first week I coached Marlene I had her do the "T1" workout described in Appendix B. This is an interval test set in which she completed ten 100-meter swims as fast as she could go, with 10-second recovery breaks between efforts. Her average pace for the 100s was 1:57. She wanted to markedly increase her time.

Over the next ten months, Marlene swam by herself with an emphasis on technique, and her average 100-meter time for T1 steadily came down until it reached 1:45— a 10 percent improvement, or about 1 percent per month. Not bad. At about this time she found a masters swim group that had a coach on deck. She also began meeting with the swim coach for underwater video recording and technique instruction. Over the next three months, her T1 test time dropped to 1:34. That was an 11 percent gain, or nearly 4 percent per month.

I've had this same experience with every swimming-challenged triathlete I've ever coached. I don't usually recommend group workouts for cycling or running, but with swimming I've found that they can be beneficial. There is little change in performance when an athlete swims alone, or in the absence of instruction on proper technique. But test and race times start dropping once either group swims or an instructor is added into the mix. If you want to become a faster swimmer, having other swimmers in the pool with you doing the same workouts makes a big difference. So does having an experienced coach on deck giving you feedback on technique. Finally, seeing your stroke on video and learning how to change it makes you more aware of proper technique and hastens the learning process. This is a sure way to become a better swimmer.

since that's what living on land tells us to do. Constantly review and refresh your muscle memory by including drills in every practice session throughout the year.

Daily Practices

The best time to work on skills is when you are fresh, at the start of a swim practice session. Developing new patterns of muscle recruitment means firing scores of small muscles in exquisite harmony for the desired movements to occur. If any of the muscles are fatigued, they will refuse to fire, or fire or relax at the wrong times, frustrating your efforts to improve technique. Early in the practice, following a warm-up, the muscles and nervous system are most receptive to learning new skills.

Near the end of a practice session, as general body fatigue and muscle fatigue begin to set in, concentration on proper technique is paramount to improvement. There is no value to practicing skills by drilling if you then abandon all that you have worked on when the "fitness" portion of a swim session begins.

Total devotion to change is necessary if you are to get better. You must be prepared for a setback at first, as new and yet unrefined skills will slow you down. As you concentrate on stroke mechanics, other swimmers whom you usually "beat" in interval sets will wonder why you are suddenly so slow. Try moving over a lane to avoid the competition. At these times it's important that you stay focused on your ultimate goal—swimming faster in races by wasting less energy. Attempting to "win" workouts will cost you dearly when it really counts in races.

EQUIPMENT TO IMPROVE SWIM ECONOMY

Swimming has many more tools and toys than the other two triathlon sports do. And they really can help you become a better swimmer. But you've got to be a bit cautious with swim aids—they can be addictive. Use them only when you are working on refining technique, not for every set in every swim session.

Fins

The slower you go while swimming, the more likely you are to sink. Your hips and legs are especially prone to sinking, which increases drag, as mentioned above. Using fins eliminates this problem because they promote greater propulsion, allowing you to focus on form while staying high in the water. Look for the short, stubby fins rather than the long type used by divers.

Snorkel

Poor technique, not aerobic fitness, is the primary limiter for most triathletes when it comes to swimming. And the number one contributor to poor technique is inefficient breathing. The need to breathe frequently gets in the way for athletes trying to perfect body position and arm and leg synchronization. One of the best tools to help with this challenge is a snorkel. It allows you to concentrate on getting body mechanics right without constantly turning to get air. Once you've learned correct arm and body technique, the breathing technique is easily incorporated.

Paddles

There are two basic types of hand paddles. The large, flat, squarish-shaped ones are designed primarily to help you improve upper-body strength. They increase the resistance that your hand, arm, and upper body must overcome to move you through the water. As your strength improves, your economy also improves. The other type of paddle is more sleek looking and may have a small "keel" sticking out on the bottom. These are intended to help refine your hand and arm position at water entry by encouraging a high elbow during the catch-and-pull phase of your stroke. But you do not have to purchase both types. If you wear the square type by only using the finger loop and not the wrist strap, it will have the same effect of encouraging correct hand placement.

Cadence Meter

Once you have learned proper technique, you will want to focus on improving your stroke rate (cadence) and your stroke distance. Good freestyle endurance swimmers typically have a stroke rate of about 40 to 55 cycles per minute. One cycle is the time it takes from one right-hand entry to the next right-hand entry. Getting closer to this cadence will help you become more efficient. Using a small cadence meter worn in your swimcap or clipped onto your goggle strap will make you more aware of stroke rate and distance per stroke. It emits an audible beep that can be adjusted to various rates.

CYCLING SKILLS

In cycling, your ability to race well comes down to two variables—how you and the bike fit together, and how effectively you apply force to the pedals. If you ride a bike that doesn't fit, or if the bike set-up is incorrect, you will needlessly waste energy. Once the bike is correctly adjusted to your unique biomechanical needs, most of the force application issues are resolved and all that's needed is some minor tweaking of pedaling skills.

BIKE SET-UP

In setting up a bike for multisport racing, there are four concerns. In relative order from most to least important, they are: (1) safety, (2) comfort, (3) aerodynamics, and (4) power. The following guidelines are concerned mostly with safety, aerodynamics, and power. I can't tell you how to adjust your bike for your own personal comfort, but I suggest making small adjustments as you tweak the fit.

There are three parts of the bicycle that come in contact with the rider that can be adjusted for fit—the seat, the handlebars, and the pedal/cleat. There is no single relationship between these three that works for everyone. Correct position can vary considerably from one person to the next, even when two riders appear to be the same size. Your body proportions, the duration of goal races, personal style, and cycling experience can affect positioning. Consider the methods described here as starting points for your eventual set-up. You will probably want to experiment with adjustments. Bear in mind that it's best to make changes incrementally, especially if you have ridden in one position for a long time. Although a half-inch change of your saddle height may eventually improve your position, it will feel strange at first and may even cause discomfort. Making a

one-quarter-inch adjustment first is probably best, followed by another quar
adjustment a week or so later.

Getting a good bike fit begins with the cleats, proceeds to the saddle, and
the handlebars. Once these three components are correctly positioned, you will ride mo.
economically, which translates into faster bike splits.

Cleat Position

Before setting your cleat position, it's important that you check the length of your
crank arm. Time trialing is generally improved by a slightly longer crank than is typically used for touring or commuting. One way to gauge this length is by basing it on
your leg-inseam length. To determine this, stand in your bare feet with a book between your legs firmly up in the crotch just as when sitting on a bike seat. While facing a wall, mark the top edge of the book on the wall, and then measure the distance
from the mark to the floor. This is your inseam length. Use your inseam measurement
to find your recommended crank length in Table 12.1. If you are nearer the upper end
of the inseam range, select the longer crank. Riders who have a limiter in force generation or climbing may find improvement with a longer crank. But bear in mind that as
the crank gets longer, stress on the knee also increases. An overly long crank may result
in injury.

The starting point for cleat position is placement of the pedal axle directly beneath
the ball of the foot, as shown in Figure 12.5. This "neutral" position works best for most
riders, but some, especially those whose limiter is force or who have difficulty with climbing hills, may benefit from moving
the cleat toward the heel. As the cleat
is moved aft, more force is transferred to the pedal, but the trade-off
is that cadence is slowed. This can
result in an ultimate loss of power
when sudden changes in velocity are
necessary, such as when you are passing another rider, accelerating out of
a turn, or climbing a short, steep hill.
Start by making a quarter-inch adjustment from neutral and see how it
feels after several rides before going
any further.

Find the ball of your foot with
your cycling shoes on, and mark it on
the lateral side of each shoe. Your left
and right foot lengths may be slightly

INSEAM (IN.)	CRANK LENGTH (MM)
<31 (79 cm)	170.0–172.5
31–33 (79–84 cm)	172.5–175.0
33–35 (84–89 cm)	175.0–177.5
>35 (89 cm)	177.5–180.0

TABLE 12.1

Recommended
Crank Lengths

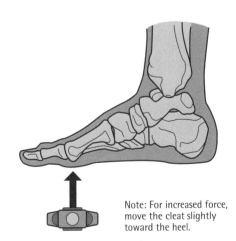

Note: For increased force,
move the cleat slightly
toward the heel.

FIGURE 12.5

Cleat Position

different, so adjust each cleat individually. On an indoor trainer, clip into your pedals while someone checks to see if the marks are over the center of the spindles. Aligning the marks with the axles puts you in the neutral position.

Saddle Fore-Aft Position

For the aero position, your saddle adjustment depends on the length of your thigh and the flexibility of your hips and lower back. To establish the neutral saddle position, put your bike on an indoor trainer and then level it using a carpenter's level on the top tube or spanning the wheel axles. Spin for a few minutes to warm up. Then, with the pedal in the 90-degree (3 or 9 o'clock) position, have a friend drop a plumb line from the knob on the outside of your leg just below the knee (head of the fibula). When the line intersects the pedal axle, the saddle is neutral. Note that this will place your knee and body in a slightly more forward position than if the plumb line were dropped from the front of the knee, as is generally done for cyclists. The more forward position is more economical for the fully aerodynamic body position of triathlon. Figure 12.6 shows how this adjustment is done.

Moving the saddle forward of neutral by up to a half-inch may improve your comfort as well as your power and aerodynamics. One way to tell if you need such an adjustment is to check your flexibility. To do this, sit on the front of a desk with the backs of your knees against the edge. Hold onto a chair in front of you for balance, and then lean over until your chest touches your thighs. If your feet move backward in this position, you would probably benefit from moving the saddle slightly forward. The saddle should be parallel to the floor or slightly tipped down at the nose for comfort.

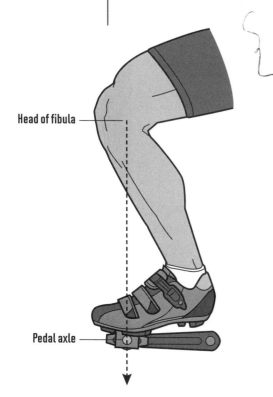

Head of fibula

Pedal axle

FIGURE 12.6

Neutral Knee
Position

Saddle Height

Saddle height, because of its effect on power output, is the most studied aspect of bike fit, and there are scores of formulas for determining it. Perhaps the easiest way to make this adjustment is to sit on your bike, with your shoes off, in the aero position. Place your heel on the pedal at the bottom of the stroke (crank arm lined up with the seat tube). To set the neutral position, adjust the saddle height until your knee is straight. Notice that as the saddle goes up, it also moves aft, and as it is lowered, it shifts forward slightly. So you may need to make some small, correcting changes in the fore-aft setting. For every 2 centimeters (cm) it goes up, it must also move forward about 1 cm; if you lower it 2 cm, move it aft by about 1 cm. Figure 12.7 shows how neutral saddle height is determined.

Handlebar Height, Reach, and Angle

One of the best investments in equipment that you can make is to purchase an adjustable stem such as the Look Ergostem. This kind of stem allows you to make a wide range of small adjustments in position to produce the best possible aerodynamics and maximize your comfort. It also allows for quick and easy changes throughout the season. Early in the Base period, as you are just getting back on the bike again, you will probably want the handlebars higher than they were at the end of the previous season. Then again, you may want to change your position for a

FIGURE 12.7

Neutral Saddle Height Set with Shoeless Heel on Pedal

sprint race in which aerodynamics is more important than comfort, or for an Ironman-distance race, which demands the comfort associated with a slightly higher position.

In the neutral position, the top of the handlebars is about 1 inch (2.5 cm) below the high point of the saddle. To determine this measurement, extend a yardstick from the saddle top out to the handlebars and level it with a carpenter's level. By measuring the distance between the yardstick and the handlebars, you can set the stem height. Very flexible athletes, or those doing short races, may lower the handlebars by as much as an inch. Those who are less flexible, or racing in longer events, may raise it by an inch. As the handlebars are lowered, you must move the saddle slightly forward, opening the angle between the thigh and the trunk. If this is not done, the effort is magnified.

Correct handlebar reach, or stem length, places your ear over your elbow in the aero position. A rough gauge of this is that the distance from the nose of the saddle to the back of the handlebars should be about 1 to 1.5 inches longer than the distance from the back of your elbow to the end of your extended fingers.

When the up-and-down angle of the aero bars is neutral, the bottom of your hand is below the bend in the elbow, and the top of your hand is above it. Handlebar reach and angle are illustrated in Figure 12.8. As always, small adjustments from neutral may improve your comfort.

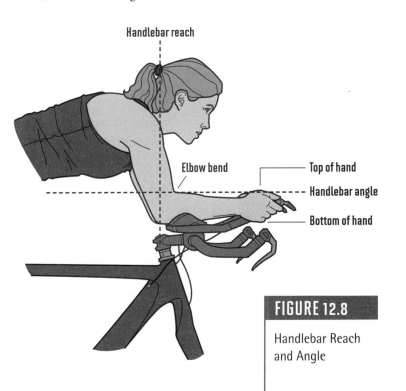

FIGURE 12.8

Handlebar Reach and Angle

PEDALING CADENCE

Economy in riding a bike is based on an interaction between a human and a machine. How well they fit together is a significant determining factor in cadence economy. For example, short crank arms favor pedaling at a high cadence, and a high saddle position slows the cadence.

In triathlon, the cadence you use determines not only how you feel on the bike but also how your legs will feel in the ensuing run. Low cadences put stress on the knees and muscles and require greater muscular force generation than high cadences. High cadences require great metabolic effort, which cause heavy breathing, for example. This means that a high cadence minimizes muscle fatigue but may cause you to use more energy, at least until you are adapted to it.

Observations of elite riders in triathlons reveal a common cadence range of about 80 to 100 rpm. This range is also supported by research. Studies dating back to 1913 have shown the most economical cadence to vary from 33 to 110 rpm. More sophisticated recent studies, however, have tended to favor higher cadences, at least when they are self-selected by accomplished riders.

It is also interesting to compare the cadences used by elite triathletes in races of different lengths. Cadence tends to be low in Ironman-distance races—often around 80 rpm—while in sprint-distance races it is more likely to be in the high 90s.

The bottom line is that it appears that once your bike is set up correctly, pedaling at a cadence in the range of 80 to 100 rpm on a flat course is probably best. Increasing the range of your comfortable cadences ultimately produces a broader range of efficiency. That will give you greater economy even if you race in long events at low cadences such as 80 rpm.

CYCLING-SPEED DRILLS

The pedaling motion appears simple, yet applying force to the pedals is a complex interaction of many muscle groups that takes years to refine. During the learning process, muscles become accomplished at contracting and relaxing at exactly the right times. Once a rider has mastered these movements, economy improves.

Even among the best cyclists, the pedaling motion involves the application of force, mostly in a downward direction throughout the stroke. Contrary to popular belief, good pedaling mechanics do not result from pulling the pedal up on the upstroke. What probably happens is that the economical rider attempts to "unweight" the upstroke pedal, but even for the best riders the weight of the foot and leg, and centrifugal force, still cause a resultant downward pressure on that pedal. Figure 12.9 shows the relative positions of the foot at various points in the stroke and the resultant forces.

The challenge for improving pedaling mechanics is smoothing out the direction changes in the application of force at the top and bottom of the stroke. At the bottom of the stroke (positions "d" and "e" in Figure 12.9), the perceived force direction is backward, although this is only a small component of the total force applied. This movement has been described as "scraping mud from the shoes." You can get a feel for it off the bike by standing on a carpet while leaning forward on a table and sliding your foot backward as an animal would do in "pawing" the ground. As the foot scrapes, the heel comes up before the toes do.

As the foot approaches the top of the stroke (positions "f," "g," and "h" in Figure 12.9), the raised heel is lowered. At the top (position "h"), the foot feels as if it's moving forward in the shoe when the proper technique is exaggerated. That returns the foot to the front side of the stroke, and the heel once again drops slightly as the greatest force of the entire circular movement is applied (positions "a," "b," and "c").

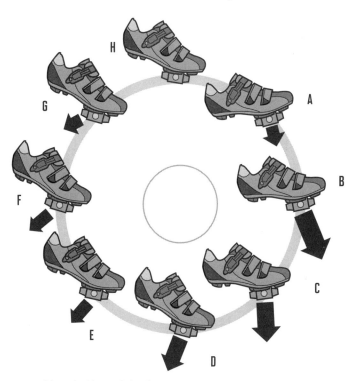

Adapted with permission from Cavanagh and Sanderson 1986.

FIGURE 12.9

Pedaling Biomechanics— Foot Position and Resultant Force

The purpose of pedaling drills is, first of all, to become aware of these three phases of the pedaling motion while practicing them, and second, to make the transition from each phase to the next as smooth and seamless as possible. Here are four ways of accomplishing these objectives. While these may be done year-round, the best times to refine pedaling skills on the bike are in the Prep and Base periods.

Fixed-Gear Riding

For decades, road cyclists have trained on single-gear bikes without freewheels—called "fixed-gear" bikes—to improve pedaling mechanics. Because you can't coast on such a bike, it forces your legs into a constant circular motion at a high cadence (greater than 100 rpm) and teaches your muscles where the transitions are from one phase to the next. After several weeks of fixed-gear riding, the phase transitions smooth out as you learn to quit fighting the bike.

Be forewarned that a fixed-gear bike is dangerous to ride at first as it forces you to break old habits, such as briefly stopping the pedaling motion as you stand up or sit down. You also must learn how to pedal through turns and how to stop while your legs are still going around. The first few rides on a fixed-gear bike may best be done on an indoor trainer so you can get a feel for how it works before venturing out onto the roads for short rides. Approach all fixed-gear rides with caution, riding slowly on flat terrain.

If you have an extra bike frame, a bike shop can set it up for you as a fixed-gear. Or they can order a track bike for you and install a brake on it for use on the road.

Another, and somewhat safer, option is to ride the stationary bikes used by health clubs in spinning classes. The large flywheels on these bikes produce an effect similar to that of riding on a fixed-gear bike.

Indoor Spinning

Ride your bike on an indoor trainer or rollers at a comfortably high cadence in a low gear. Pay particular attention to the sound your rear wheel makes. An oscillating "whir—whir—whir," like a fan that is constantly changing speed means you have a choppy, uneven stroke that exaggerates the downstroke. You may be shifting your body weight from side to side to accentuate the downward force. Concentrate on pedaling smoothly with no rocking of the upper body so that the sound of the rear wheel is a continuous "whirrrrr." If you are having trouble getting it, reduce the resistance until your pedal stroke smoothes out. As you pick up the resistance try to keep your pedal stroke relaxed.

Isolated-Leg Training

On an indoor trainer, pedal with one leg only while the other foot rests on the frame or a chair. Alternate legs, doing 20 to 60 seconds on each side. The "dead" spots in your stroke phase transitions are immediately obvious when you do this exercise, as you are not allowing your legs to compensate for each other. This helps you learn how to pedal smoothly. Use a low gear and a comfortably high cadence. Again, allow your body to relax.

SpinScan

If you are fortunate enough to own a CompuTrainer, pedaling in the "SpinScan" mode provides you with a graphic representation of your stroke on the monitor. This serves as a biofeedback device, allowing you to correct obvious right-left imbalances and make minute adjustments in technique at all workloads.

CORNERING SKILLS

The other major biking skill besides pedaling is cornering, which is a safety and a performance issue. The most common cause of bicycle crashes is poor cornering skills. Improving your cornering skills can also save you a significant amount of time on a course with lots of turns.

As you can see in Figure 12.10, there are three ways to handle your bike when cornering: leaning, countersteering, and steering.

Leaning Method

The leaning method is the most common cornering technique in triathlon regardless of the cornering situation. But it is really best when it is necessary to make a wide, sweeping turn on dry, clean pavement. In the United States and other countries where drivers

| **LEANING** | **COUNTERSTEERING** | **STEERING** |
| Wide sweeping turns, esp. left | Short fast turns, esp. right | Wet pavement or gravel, sand |

FIGURE 12.10

Bicycle Cornering Techniques

and cyclists ride on the right side of the road, it is most effective when turning left. For those countries where drivers and cyclists stay on the left, this is the preferred right-turn method. To use the method, simply lean both the bike and your body into the turn with your weight on the outside pedal. If it is truly a wide, sweeping turn, you may be able to remain in the aero position and continue pedaling.

Countersteering Method

Few triathletes use the countersteering technique, but it is quite effective for tight turns, such as right-hand turns in ride-on-the-right countries and left-hand turns in ride-on-the-left countries. Countersteering will get you around the corner with a much tighter radius than the leaning method will, saving you time.

If you've learned countersteering on a motorcycle, the technique is the same. You must stop pedaling as you enter the turn because the bike tilt will be greater than with the leaning method. The inside pedal is up and your body weight is fully on the outside pedal. Here's where it feels counterintuitive: Straighten your arm on the inside of the turn and bend the elbow on the outside of the turn. It seems backwards, as you're pushing on the opposite handlebar you would use for a sweeping turn. This motion breaks the gyroscopic effect of the turning wheels and causes you to lean the bike sharply into the turn as your body stays upright. You will go around the corner on a tight radius. In order for this technique to be effective, your speed must be at least 15 mph (24 kph) or so. It takes practice to make it habitual.

Steering Method

Use this method when cornering on wet pavement or when there is sand or gravel on the road surface. Regardless of whether this is a right or left turn, you will need to slow down.

If it is a tight-radius turn, such as a right turn in the United States, you must also stop pedaling. The purpose is to safely get around the corner without falling. The proper method involves keeping the bike upright while leaning only your body into the turn. Keep both knees near the top tube of the bike—do not point your knee at the corner.

Other Cornering Considerations

When riding on wet pavement, reduce your tire pressure by about 25 percent. This will give you better traction on the corners and help prevent a crash while having minimal effect on overall speed. The type of tire you use also plays a role when cornering. Tubular tires, also called "sew-ups," corner better than clinchers, as they have round sidewalls, whereas clinchers have straighter sidewalls. Be especially careful when cornering on wet pavement if there is a painted stripe on the road. When wet, these are like ice. Use extreme caution when cornering on wet pavement in steep descents. Apply your brakes well before you get to the corner to reduce speed. Do not use the brakes when cornering.

EQUIPMENT TO IMPROVE CYCLING ECONOMY

The bike portion of a triathlon usually accounts for about half of your race finish time. So improving economy on the bike has the most potential of the three sports to reduce your race times. You can use a variety of equipment to increase your economy.

Rollers

Most triathletes, especially those in northern states, have an indoor trainer of some sort for those winter days when it's too dark and nasty to ride outside. Indoor trainers usually lock the rear wheel of your bike in place against a resistance-generating device. Another type of trainer, less commonly used, consists of freely turning rollers in both front and back that you set your bike on. Since the bike is not locked in place, you balance it while riding just as you do outdoors.

The disadvantage of rollers is that it is more challenging to do certain techniques, like single-leg drills. The advantage is that you can work on pedaling skills in a more realistic condition with the bike moving beneath you, just as it does on the road. This makes working on pedaling skills more effective. But rollers take some getting used to. The first few times you ride on rollers, put the device in a doorway to keep from coming off the side and slamming into a wall.

Power Cranks

The single-leg training described earlier is one of the best drills for improving bike-pedaling skills. With "Power Cranks"™—unconnected crank arms that move independently of each other—you can work on individual leg skills without having to unclip from the pedals. This allows you to pedal with one leg while the other is not moving, as in single-leg drills.

When you are pedaling normally with Power Cranks, each leg is working in isolation from the other leg. This allows you to discover your pedaling weaknesses and focus on them. What too often happens with standard cranks is that the recovery leg on the upstroke side rests on the pedal, forcing the leg on the downstroke side to work harder to lift the lazy recovery leg. This wastes a tremendous amount of energy, which reduces your economy. But your legs cannot get lazy when using Power Cranks.

I'd recommend putting Power Cranks on a second bicycle rather than your primary bike so you don't have to change cranks every time you want to use them. Riding with them two to four times each week in the Base period will do wonders for your pedaling skills. Then ride them once or twice weekly year round to maintain skills. You'll probably find when first starting to use Power Cranks that short rides are best. To find out more, go to Powercranks.com.

Fixed-Gear Bike

As mentioned above, a fixed-gear bike is a bike that has only one gear. It has no derailleurs and won't allow you to coast without pedaling. Whenever the wheels are turning, the cranks are also turning. The typical fixed-gear bike is also usually set up with a low gearing combination that keeps the rider at a fairly high cadence, such as 110 to 120 rpm. And since high cadences encourage the improvement of pedaling skills, the fixed-gear bike is a great tool.

As with Power Cranks, it's best to set up a second bike with a fixed gear. For more information on fixed-gear bikes and to learn how to convert one of your old bikes, go to Sheldonbrown.com/fixed.html.

Q-Rings

Q-Rings are another worthwhile product. These oval-shaped chainrings that replace the standard chainrings on your bike are especially good for triathletes who tend to "mash" the pedals rather than spin the cranks smoothly. When your pedal is at the top and bottom of the stroke, the Q-Ring is in the smallest-radius position (the pointy ends of the oval are parallel to the crank), which means your foot can more easily make the transition. When in the power position at 3 o'clock, the radius is at its greatest length, which gives you more leverage and therefore more power. For example, a 53-tooth Q-Ring is the equivalent of pedaling with a 51 tooth at the top and bottom and a 56 tooth at 3 o'clock. You can find out more about Q-Rings at Rotorcranksusa.com.

Midsole Cleat

Most of the triathletes I coach have found that moving their cleats from the traditional ball-of-the-foot position to the arch of their shoes has improved their economy. And even better, when the cleat is in this position the amount of work done by the calf muscles while pedaling is significantly reduced. That means that the calf muscles, the primary running muscles, are fresher coming off the bike. Such double benefits are hard to come by.

It's not easy to find shoes with midsole cleats. You can have them custom made or you can convert existing shoes. Your local bike shop should be able to help. Not all cycling shoes will accommodate an arch-mounted cleat. If yours will, use an old pair of shoes initially to see whether or not you like this cleat position. You may also have to change your pedal system because slightly cupped cleats won't fit on flat arch areas. You could try a mountain-bike cleat, which generally has only two bolts and will fit snugly on a flat shoe arch area.

If you are unwilling to make such a radical change, try simply moving your cleats as far back toward the heel as your shoe and cleat will allow. This may only be a quarter of an inch, but that will still reduce some of the work your calf muscles must do.

RUNNING SKILLS

Are we born with a natural running form that is set for the rest of our lives, or can it be changed for the better? The inclination among runners is to stick with what comes naturally. Few will ever tinker with their pre-ordained running form beyond tweaking the smallest and least significant of points, such as a cupped hand position or relaxed facial expression. Must we conclude that the aerobic aspects of fitness are the only elements of running performance worth spending time on? This seems a rather self-defeating position to take.

Indeed, the experiences of many formerly awkward lopers would testify that it is in fact possible to effectively modify running technique. It is true that making such changes requires a strong desire to improve, an indomitable dedication, and months of constant practice in every workout. But with good mental skills in place, it is possible to fully realize the benefits of running in a more gazelle-like manner. If you have spent countless hours running over distance, hills, tempo, and intervals with precious little to show for it in terms of faster times, it may be time for you to take a long look at your technique.

Just as with swimming and cycling, in running improved skills can lead to economy of movement, with an accompanying savings in energy expended. This results in faster times in long races. Refined running skills also pay off with a lowered risk of injury. Even though this is also true of swimming and cycling, running injuries are far more pervasive, so the potential gain is much greater. In fact, if you have a history of running-related injuries, this is a signal that something may be wrong with your technique.

RUNNING SKILL FUNDAMENTALS

There are many complex actions involved in running—far too many to address in this chapter—so this section will examine in some detail only four that are critical to performance in multisport. Later on I will describe drills that will help you to develop the skills. All of them are dependent on an overall body posture that provides vertical alignment of the jaw, shoulder, and hip joints; a "proud" carriage, with the head up and back straight; straight-ahead movement at the hip, shoulder, knee, and ankle joints; an uplifted frontal waist area (butt not sticking out); and relaxation of the face and hands. Before you attempt to address any other running skill, make sure you incorporate these elements of good posture.

Posture

Chin on chest; shoulders slumped and sagging; back humped and bent at the waist; arms nearly straight or held high in front of the chest crossing the body midline with every step—these are some of the postural energy wasters seen all too often in age-group runners. Poor posture contributes to slow running times because it forces the body to rely strictly on the legs for propulsion. Running is a total-body activity that demands good form and core strength for efficiency and effectiveness.

Improving your running posture is the first step to improving your performance. One way to check your posture is to have someone shoot a video of you from both the front and side as you run. Then take your camera to a race and record some of the top runners during their warm-ups, or in the race itself, if you're there as a spectator. Watch the movies and compare your technique with theirs. It's likely you will see significant postural differences along the lines of the flaws listed above.

Decide what needs to be changed and go to work on it. It will take several weeks of frequently checking your posture during runs to see if your flaws are under control before the new positioning finally becomes a good habit. You can use video or ask a friend to check your form as you continue to develop positional awareness. Bad form is most likely to appear when you are tired or under mental stress.

Running Cadence

Many triathletes try to get faster by maximizing stride length with a slow cadence. To get this long stride they have to raise their center of gravity by a few inches with every step, bouncing as they run. This "loping" stride has several implications.

The first is that the runner needlessly expends a lot of extra energy. Remember, in a race, the finish line is in a horizontal direction, not a vertical one. The second implication is that once he or she is up in the air, the loping runner is dependent on gravity for a return to earth. On this planet, all objects, including human bodies, fall at the same increasing velocity—32 feet per second per second. Vertical displacement means slower running due to the time spent falling back to the ground. The third implication of loping is that when the runner does come back to terra firma, there is a considerable impact force. Repeating this a few hundred times each mile, mile after mile, year after year, often results in the overuse injuries that plague runners.

So the way to run faster is not with a longer stride, at least not when you are initially trying to improve your running, but rather, with a quicker cadence. Increasing your cadence will minimize your vertical displacement, allowing you more frequent contacts with the ground, which is when horizontal power is applied, and will decrease your risk of injury because you will experience a lighter landing.

The next time you watch a race with world-class runners, count their right-foot steps for 20 seconds. Even toward the end of a marathon you'll almost always find that they take 30 or more right-foot steps—that's a cadence of at least 90 rpm. Even when they are running slowly, you'll find their cadence is relatively high. They aren't loping along at 80 rpm. That makes them very economical.

The Kenyan runners set a great example. Their cadence is typically 96, plus or minus 2, and in any given triathlon or marathon, the Kenyans are usually the ones with the highest cadences in the lead group. They are also among the most economical runners in the world, owing in large part to their high cadences. We could learn a lot from them when it comes to improving our own running economy.

Vertical Foot Movement

Nicholas Romanov—formerly a Russian university professor of physical education who now lives and works in the United States—has spent two decades studying the biomechanics of running. Out of his studies came what he calls the "Pose" method of teaching running technique. One of the basic tenets of Romanov's work is that the sensation the runner experiences when running correctly is that his or her feet are simply moving up and down—not swinging forward and backward. With his technique, the recovery foot is lifted toward the butt, creating a small, acute angle at the knee, and thus a shorter "pendulum" of the recovery leg. (In contrast, when the recovery leg is nearly straight at the knee, a long pendulum results.) The significance is that for the same amount of applied energy, a short pendulum moves through its arc faster than a long pendulum. So the shorter pendulum, resulting from the high foot carriage, helps to produce a high stride rate. In an attempt to increase running velocity, the foot must be raised higher to keep stride rate constant or increasing. Figure 12.11 illustrates the smaller angle that results from a high foot, which makes the stride (pendulum) more efficient.

After the foot has been pulled up, the recovery leg begins to open at the knee as the foot is allowed to drop back down to the road, making contact below or only a

Note small angle of left knee in recovery phase created by right foot moving toward butt.
Adapted with permission from Romanov 2002.

FIGURE 12.11

Efficient Running Form

couple of inches in front of the body's center of gravity. From the runner's perspective, all that has happened is that the recovery foot has been pulled vertically up toward the butt and allowed to drop straight back down to the running surface.

According to Romanov, this movement is similar to the action of a rolling ball in which the point of support is always directly beneath the center of gravity. Such movement is very economical; it also diminishes impact forces, thus reducing the risk of injury. (For more information see www.posetech.com.)

Minimal Support Time

The main limiter for velocity in running has to do with how much force is applied to the ground in a brief instant. As the foot strikes the pavement, it applies a force, and since, according to Isaac Newton, for every applied force there is an equal and opposite reactive force, your body moves up and forward. The distance you move forward (stride length) is partly determined by how quickly the force was applied. Time is a major component of power. As time in contact with the ground decreases, power increases. If, when your running shoe comes in contact with the road, you linger for just a split second too long, the applied power drops, which shortens your stride. You run slower, even though you have now increased your cadence. The idea is to spend very little time with your feet planted on the ground.

It really doesn't take much of a change to speed up your running pace considerably. For example, one study found that runners who learned to keep their feet on the ground only 15 milliseconds (0.015 seconds) less than their previous average—that is, decreasing the time about the length of an eye blink—ran 3 percent faster. By making the same small improvement, a runner doing a 10 km in 40 minutes could shave off more than a minute, and a 4-hour marathon would speed up by 7 minutes. Those are pretty significant time savings, and they are achieved without months of suffering through intervals, hill work, and high mileage.

To decrease ground contact time, you have to change the way your foot initially lands with each stride. There are three ways your foot can strike the ground. You can land on your heel, the ball of your foot, or midfoot with a simultaneous heel and ball landing. Let's examine each.

Heel Landing. Most slow runners use a heel landing. Just before the foot strikes the ground, the knee is extended with the foot leading and the toes pointing up. It's exactly the same thing you would do if you were trying to stop. Once the heel comes in contact with the ground with the toes in the air, the only way to get off of the foot again is to roll forward from heel to toe like a rocking chair. That takes a lot of time, and it requires a considerable amount of power to re-accelerate from braking.

To make matters worse, this kind of landing transmits a lot of shock up the leg, since the heel bone is not designed to absorb such impact forces. The risk of injury to the leg bones, ankle, knee, hip, and lower back is increased.

This is not an effective way to run, and yet it is by far the most prevalent landing style among age-group triathletes, primarily because of shoes. We were not meant to run in them—hunter-gatherers certainly didn't—but we are forced to by the hard surfaces we typically run on. The thick heel pad of your shoe encourages you to land on it. Pay attention the next time you run barefoot. Notice that you don't land on your heels.

Forefoot Landing. Most elite runners land on the forefoot. When they do this, the foot that looks to be almost flat to the ground, but their heels are unweighted. The runner bends the knee an instant before landing with the foot directly below it and parallel to the horizon. The foot "paws back" just a bit before contacting the ground. Actually, it doesn't move backward, it decelerates. Relative to the knee the foot is moving backward. Relative to a camera looking up from the road surface the foot is moving forward but slowing down slightly just before landing. At landing, the fast runner's body weight goes immediately to the forefoot and starts to toe-off. It is more like a rocking chair than a pogo stick—the foot quickly comes off the road without braking.

The forefoot is designed to absorb shock. There are 26 bones in the foot held together by various sinews. When you land on the forefoot, most of these bones spread out laterally, absorbing shock much the same way the shock absorbers on your car do. Your risk of injury to bone and joints is decreased.

I would not recommend, however, that you try this if you are currently a heel striker, for although the risk of injury to bones and joints decreases, the potential for injury to the plantar fascia, Achilles' tendon, and calf increases. Elite runners who do this have adapted to it over many years, usually decades. But as a long-time heel striker, you may find that your legs aren't ready for a sudden change. Instead, make the change to a midfoot landing.

Midfoot Landing. With a midfoot landing, both the heel and the ball of the foot come in contact with the ground at the same time, with body weight fairly evenly distributed between the forefoot and the heel. Just before foot strike the knee is slightly bent, with the foot directly below it, and the foot paws back as in the forefoot landing. Again, be aware that the foot is not actually moving backward from the perspective of the road. But viewed from the knee it is moving backward.

At first you may find that you must breathe more heavily, that you feel like you are working harder, and that you are slower with a midfoot landing than with a heel landing. That's because your body is being forced to adapt to something it isn't used to. Start by doing only six to eight 20-second intervals on grass two or three times each week for a month while concentrating on the paw-back technique. After a month you should be starting to get the hang of it. Then start incorporating the technique into your shortest runs. After a month of this you should be ready to do all of your running with a midfoot landing. Be patient and stick with it. You'll soon run faster than ever.

Figure 12.12 shows how a midfoot strike looks. Essentially, it minimizes the time your foot spends on the ground and enhances the rebound effect while keeping the brakes off. If you are now a well-established heel striker, try to make slow and steady progress toward changing your landing form. Don't try to go too quickly, as landing farther forward on the foot places new stresses on the feet and lower legs that could result in an injury. Save this change for the next Prep period of the training year when run durations are short, and at first run only on soft surfaces, such as grass, dirt, or a track, allowing for plenty of time for recovery between runs.

Minimal Vertical Oscillation

Another big energy waster is bouncing up and down with each step. The energy stored by landing forward on the foot must be converted as much as possible to horizontal, not vertical, movement. Fortunately, reduced bobbing is a normal outcome of taking quicker strides. So if you get your leg speed up to around 90 cycles per minute (180 steps per minute), the conversion of power is more likely to push you closer to the finish line than closer to the clouds. Figure 12.13 shows a runner with excessive vertical oscillation—and other energy wasters.

Another element of running technique that promotes horizontal rather than vertical movement is leaning from the ankle, as can be seen in Figure 12.11. Note that a straight line can be drawn from the ear through the hips to the right ankle. In other words, there is no bending at the waist to achieve a forward lean. It's a bit like pressing the buoy while swimming in that the chest is slightly in front of the hips. This position allows your more powerful forward foot strike to convert the resultant movement into a more horizontal direction. In other words, you'll bounce up and down less.

Note midfoot strike with left foot slightly ahead of center of gravity.

FIGURE 12.12

Efficient Running Form

Note long recovery pendulum of right leg, left foot heel strike well in advance of center of gravity, and excessive vertical oscillation.

FIGURE 12.13

Inefficient Running Form

Why is eliminating vertical oscillation so important? Let's look at an example. In a 10 km race, if you weigh about 150 pounds and your center of gravity rises and falls 2 inches with every stride as you lope along, over the course of the race you will have done an amount of work equivalent to raising about 84 tons 1 foot high. If you can reduce that excess vertical oscillation of your center of gravity to 1 inch per step, you cut the vertical component of your workload by half, to something like 42 tons raised a foot high. That's a tremendous savings in energy that can be converted into forward velocity and faster running times. In fact, the cost of excessive vertical oscillation is even greater than the example indicates, since more energy is also required to decelerate the 2-inch fall when contact with the ground is once again made.

When you reduce the bouncing associated with a long, loping stride, you not only save energy but also ameliorate the impact forces upon landing, thus reducing the risk of running-related injuries.

RUNNING SPEED DRILLS

Drills can help you develop the skills necessary for effective and economical running just as they can help you in swimming and cycling. Here are five running drills to try.

Step Counting

Early in a run, count your right foot strikes for a minute. Then try to raise the count by incorporating one of the skills described above, such as bending the recovery leg slightly, shortening your stride, landing more forward on your foot to decrease the support time, or reducing vertical oscillation. Don't simply shuffle your feet faster. This is a good exercise to do in the Prep and Base periods of the season when the focus is on refining your technique.

Hopping

On a soft surface such as a carpet or mat, place the toes of your left foot on a 12- to 18-inch support behind you with the leg outstretched. Assume the running posture, with your right knee slightly flexed and your arms bent. Figure 12.14 illustrates this position. Quickly lift your right foot toward your

FIGURE 12.14

Hopping Drill

Adapted with permission from Romanov 2002.

butt and allow it to immediately return to the floor. Keep the vertical oscillation of your center of gravity to a minimum, and concentrate on merely lifting and lowering the foot. Don't bounce. Repeat with the other leg. Complete three sets of ten hops on each leg the first time you try the exercise. Allow 48 hours between these exercises. Over the course of a few weeks, gradually increase the number of hops within a set to 30.

Besides teaching you the up and down movement of the leg described under "Running Skill Fundamentals" above, this drill also teaches you proper form for the forefoot landing while building resiliency in the feet and lower legs. It should be done only in the Prep and Base periods of the season.

Rope Jumping

On a mat or other soft surface, jump rope just like you did as a kid. Just as in the hopping drill, minimize the vertical oscillation and concentrate on raising and lowering your feet and legs. This drill is especially good for strengthening the feet and lower legs as it teaches forefoot landing. Rope jumping is also an excellent warm-up to do before a weight workout in the Prep and Base periods.

Skipping

On a soft surface, such as a track or grassy field, skip for 10 to 20 seconds. Complete three to eight sets with 2 to 3 minutes of running in between each set. This drill is a good combination of skills, incorporating the vertical foot lift, minimal support time, and minimal oscillation. It also strengthens the feet and lower legs while teaching proper form for forefoot landing. Figure 12.15 shows how to skip, in case you've forgotten. Left leg skips as right foot remains near buttocks. Skipping is especially effective during the Prep and Base periods when technique refinement is under way, but can be done year round as a part of your warm-up before intervals and races.

FIGURE 12.15

Skipping Drill

Strides

Warm up well. Then, on grass, dirt, or another soft surface, run for 20 seconds down a very slight decline while concentrating on the fundamental skill most in need of improvement for you (high stride rate, vertical foot movement, short support time, or minimal oscillation). These are not sprints, but are run at a velocity a little faster than your 5 km race pace. After each effort, walk back to the starting point, taking 60 to 90 seconds to do so. Repeat five to eight times in a workout.

A variation includes barefoot strides on grass in order to exaggerate leg speed. Be sure the grassy area is free of impediments such as glass, thorns, or uneven spots, and that there are no breaks in the skin on your feet. Another alternative is to count your right-foot strikes for 20 seconds, aiming for a goal of 30. As your stride length improves, you will cover more ground in 30 foot strikes. For a third variation, include 20 seconds of skipping instead of walking as you return to the start point.

You may do this exercise year-round to maintain the techniques. You may also wish to incorporate it into the warm-up you do before intervals and races.

EQUIPMENT TO IMPROVE RUNNING ECONOMY

Breaking old habits can be difficult, and nowhere is this more true than in running. If you have been running for a number of years, adopting the quick cadence and midfoot landing described earlier will be a challenge. The following equipment can help you.

Shoes

The shoes you run in have a lot to do with how economical you are. When buying shoes, always shop at a store that specializes in running equipment, especially if you tend to experience frequent running injuries or need to make changes in your running form. Running shoes are very individualized. The wrong ones can interfere with running mechanics and cause injury. Shoe selection is made all the more challenging by the overwhelming number of constantly changing options on the market.

Be wary of running shoes with thick heels. These will make it hard for you to learn to run with a proper foot landing. The higher your heel, the more side-to-side movements your foot will make while running, which is likely to set you up for an injury. Those who may need higher heels are people prone to plantar fascia, Achilles' tendon, or calf injuries.

You will find many shoes designed to help control excessive pronation. This is because many runners find that their feet flatten out and roll too much to the inside on contact with the road. Interestingly, the higher the heel of the shoe is, the more likely you are to need some sort of pronation-reducing device built into the shoe. Refer to an experienced running-shoe salesperson to help decide whether or not you need pronation-controlling shoes. Bring your worn-out shoes with you so that the salesperson can examine the pattern of wear; this can provide important clues about the style of shoes that will work best for you.

As a general rule, look for the "least shoe" possible. On one hand, if you are small and lean, have a perfect footstrike and high cadence, are light on your feet, run only on soft surfaces, and have no history of injuries, you can use a lightweight trainer or perhaps even a racing shoe. On the other hand, if you are a 200-pounder, land on your heels, run on concrete, excessively pronate, and have experienced several running injuries, you will need a much more substantial shoe. You will probably find that you land somewhere between these two extremes. But don't make a drastic change to a minimalist shoe even if you're convinced they are right for you. Buy a slightly different design and alternate the new shoe with your old ones to allow your body time to adapt over a few weeks. After six weeks or so, consider purchasing an even less restrictive shoe and alternating that with the other pair you most recently bought. Getting into the right shoes could take you several months and costs money. Be patient.

Cadence Meter

Having a device with an audible tone that you can set for various cadences can help you increase your cadence in running just as in swimming with counting strokes. In fact, you can use the same device you use for swimming by fastening it to a running cap. Some watches also have a metronome feature. Or you can buy a small, electronic metronome at a music store and carry it in a pocket. Again, don't try to make the change from a low cadence to a high cadence overnight. This will take several weeks, if not several months, of slight increases that gradually build up to a significant change.

Movie Camera

There is no better way to improve your form than to see visual evidence of exactly how you run. In this regard, a movie camera is one of the best tools available for monitoring your progression.

Have someone record you running both in side view and as you run toward the camera. In the side view, look to see how you are doing in regards to the key features of economical running—you should be leaning slightly forward from the ankle, with your foot below the knee just before footstrike, and you should land with the entire foot coming in contact with the road at the same instant rather than heel first. You should be able to draw an imaginary straight line from your ear through the hip and to the support foot. When examining the front view, check whether or not you can see the black bottom of the shoe before landing. If so, you are landing on the heel. Also check that you aren't swaying from side to side.

Take new videos weekly and compare them with the previous ones to gauge your progression and to see what areas you still need to focus on. Doing this will speed up the learning process and make you a more economical runner sooner than if you just went by the observations of others or by how you felt you were doing. You will be amazed at the continual improvement.

MUSCLES

13

I don't feel like dancin'.

—TOM WARREN,
AFTER WINNING THE 1979 IRONMAN

THERE ARE MORE THAN 660 muscles in the human body, making up some 35 to 40 percent of the total mass. In multisport, the muscles that provide movement for swimming, cycling, and running are critical to performance, and what matters most is how well they contract and relax: Conditioning the muscles to generate great forces while maintaining a wide range of motion leads to improved velocity and a reduced risk of injury. Weak, inflexible muscles produce little power and are likely to experience pulls and strains. Strengthening and stretching the muscles therefore can also significantly improve racing.

Multisport training is a complex undertaking that takes a considerable investment of time. If you are like most triathletes and duathletes, you just don't have the luxury of training as much as you would like. There aren't enough hours in the day to do everything, and so you are often forced to decide what is most important. On any given day, what should you do—swim, bike, run, lift weights, stretch, or combine these in some way? The answer depends on your limiters. If force, power, or susceptibility to injury is holding you back from attaining your race goals, incorporating some form of supplemental muscular training, such as weightlifting and stretching, may prove beneficial. Some athletes have an abundance of strength and flexibility. For these fortunate few, additional time spent lifting weights and stretching will produce few, if any, gains.

If you determine that greater strength and flexibility will help, it's still important for you to periodize and spend an appropriate amount of time in these supplemental activities. This chapter will provide you with the necessary tools so that the time you devote

235

to weights and stretching can be purposeful and effective. You may decide to create your own strength and flexibility program using the concepts presented here, but you can also simply follow the plans offered.

SUPPLEMENTAL FUNCTIONAL EXERCISE

This chapter is primarily about sport-specific strength and flexibility. Becoming stronger while maintaining or improving the range of motion of your joints will help you perform more efficiently and powerfully while preventing injury. But stability, muscular coordination, and muscular balance are also important for muscular performance. Exercises that supplement your primary sports training can do a great deal to improve your triathlon efficiency and power while also preventing many of the problems that develop when muscles are subject to repetitive motions and overuse. You will be doing most of these supplemental exercises in a gym, but you can build some of them into your swim, bike, and run workouts, especially during the warm-ups or cool-downs. They will complement the movements of the three sports.

STABILITY ON THE BIKE

Stability means that you can maintain a position or posture, especially when on an unstable surface. You're certainly familiar with learning to balance a bike as a child. Becoming skilled at this was no small feat, as the surface you were on, two tires with minimal road contact, is really unstable. Many triathletes still have poor balance skills when cornering or avoiding obstacles in the road, especially when riding slowly, as is often required by poor road conditions.

The slalom and bottle-pick-up drills are great for triathletes with poor bike-balance skills. To do the slalom drill, set up a half-dozen water bottles or other soft place-holders in a parking lot. Put them in a straight line about 15 feet apart. As you ride the slalom course, weave around the bottles on alternate sides—go left of the first one, right of the second, left of the third, and so on. Ride with your hands on the bars, not in the aero position. Practice good cornering skills by placing the outside pedal (left pedal when making a right turn) down with your weight on it. Lean the bike into the turn by countersteering with your inside arm straight and the outside arm bent (see Figure 12.10). The faster you go, the more you will lean the bike into the turn. As you get better, move the bottles closer together. Make it a game by timing yourself and doing it with a training partner to see who can negotiate the course faster.

The bottle-pick-up drill is just as it sounds. Place a water bottle upright in a parking lot and ride past it while reaching down to pick it up. Try it on both sides. When you have mastered this drill, repeat it with the bottle on its side, so you have to reach down farther to pick it up. Such drills will improve your ability to balance your bike and make you a more accomplished cyclist.

STABILITY ON THE RUN

Running requires excellent balance, but we usually don't think about it because it seems to come naturally.

Your foot provides little real stability; it is posture and balance that keep you vertical. When you are in midstride with one foot on the ground, you are essentially balancing on a small tripod. The inner and outer edges of the ball of your foot make up two of the support points; the third support point is your heel. In midfoot strike distance running, all three of the support points are very briefly in contact with the ground at the same time. In order to maintain balance for that split second, hundreds of muscles are activated in a coordinated effort throughout your entire body. The better the nervous system is at firing these muscles in the most efficient way, the less effort it takes to run. If balance is poor, you will waste a lot of energy without even being aware of it. The less energy you waste, the faster and farther you run.

The best way to improve balance is to repeatedly challenge yourself with balancing drills. For example, stand on one foot with a bent-knee running posture and play catch with a friend. Try not to touch your raised foot to the ground for as many catches and throws as possible. To make it even more challenging, stand on an unstable surface such as a soft rubber pad, wobble board, or BOSU ball. You may even do some light weight lifting while standing on one leg or on an unstable surface. Challenge your balance frequently in the early Base period and then less frequently, but regularly, in the Build period.

One word of caution is necessary here. Do not attempt the heavy weight training suggested in this chapter while standing on unstable surfaces. Not only is it dangerous, it is also not an effective way to develop maximal, sport-specific strength. When attempting the exercises described later in this chapter, always do them on stable floors and equipment.

MUSCULAR COORDINATION

When we say someone has "good coordination," we mean that his or her movements have a certain smoothness and grace. "Muscular coordination" simply refers to the ability to time the contractions and relaxations of all the muscles involved in a smooth movement. For swimming, biking, and running, most of the body's muscles must be innervated and relaxed in an intricate pattern.

You'll notice in this chapter that most of the strength exercises involve two or more joints bending and straightening in a coordinated way. That is because single-joint exercises, such as a knee extension, do little to improve the intricate muscle-firing patterns necessary for sport performance. Multijoint exercises, such as a squat, involve muscle-firing patterns that more closely approximate the movements of running and pedaling. The role of single-joint exercises for the triathlete is to improve the strength of a muscle group that is unusually weak and susceptible to injury.

Age-group triathletes, especially masters, tend to have poor coordination because, like most people, they initially learned to swim, bike, and run with poor skills and inappropriate muscle-firing patterns. These patterns were thoroughly ingrained over several years of training. Breaking longtime patterns can be a difficult challenge.

The starting point for changing poor skills and bad habits is awareness. Until you are aware of where your hand enters the water, where your knee is at the top of the pedal stroke, or where your recovery foot is when running, you will never be able to improve them. Pay close attention to body positions when working out, using video or even mirrors to observe your movements, when possible.

The drills mentioned in Chapter 12 will train your muscles to fire and relax at the right times, but only if you pay attention to where your head, shoulders, arms, knees, feet, and various other body parts are throughout the drills. Doing them without paying close attention and making small, almost imperceptible, corrections is a waste of time.

MUSCULAR BALANCE

Because swimming, biking, and running all involve straightforward, repetitive movements, it is possible for the human body to make exceptional muscular and nervous system adaptations to perform them economically and efficiently. Through several years of training, the serious triathlete becomes very good at them. But for the same reason, they can also be detrimental as a result of the imbalances and postural changes that can occur. The most likely downside is injury when the forward-moving muscles are overdeveloped and the lateral ones all but ignored.

To improve muscular balance for swimming, include other strokes in workouts, especially in the warm-up and cool-down. The back stroke, fly stroke, and breast stroke will help correct muscular imbalances caused by doing only freestyle swimming.

Overcoming muscular imbalances due to cycling is difficult since you can't change your position on your bike very much, or the single-plane movements of your feet while attached to the pedals. But in the weight room you may include some lateral strength building exercises, such as side lunges, side step-ups onto a box, and leg abduction and adduction exercises, to help balance out your muscular development.

One exercise I often have runners do is called "carioca." This is great for improving the strength of the lateral muscles of the hip, especially the gluteus medius. This is a small muscle in your hip that is about where the outer seam of the rear pocket of your jeans is located. I've yet to find a serious runner with strong glute meds. Weakness in this muscle causes the athlete to rely more heavily on the tensor fascia latae (TFL) muscles on the sides of the hip. As the TFLs become overdeveloped, excess tension is placed on the iliotibial band running down the outside of the thigh, which often results in lateral knee pain. This is one of the most prevalent injuries in runners and also one of the slowest to heal.

To do the carioca, simply run sideways to the right by crossing the left leg behind the right on step 1, then the left leg in front of the right leg on step 2, left behind right for step 3 and so on. Run for 20 seconds or so like this and then run to the left, reversing the leg-crossover pattern. This is a great exercise to include in your warm-up and will give you much greater lateral hip strength and hip mobility.

STRENGTH

There was a time when endurance athletes avoided strength training like the plague. Today there are still reasons why some don't strength train. Many have a great fear of gaining weight. While there are those who have a tendency to increase their muscle mass, few multisport athletes are genetically inclined to great muscle gain, especially on an endurance-based program. If a couple of extra pounds result from weight training, the increased power typically more than offsets the mass to be carried, if the appropriate muscle groups are developed. For most triathletes, strength training does not cause any appreciable weight change.

Triathletes and duathletes, more than most other endurance athletes, are aware of what weight training can do for racing performance, perhaps because so many of them are interested in extending the boundaries of training in innovative ways. But I'm not touting the benefits of weight lifting for multisport based solely on a few success stories about high-profile athletes; several recent studies have also supported the value of weight training for endurance events.

I should point out that there is also research indicating that no performance gains result from weight training for endurance athletes. What this contradiction tells us is that under certain circumstances, some athletes, particularly those with muscle imbalances, will benefit from lifting weights, but not all will. This brings us back to the principle of individuality discussed in Chapter 2. Your unique physical make-up will determine whether you experience benefits, and trying it out may be the only way for you to find out.

STRENGTH TRAINING BENEFITS

In the studies finding that weight lifting benefits endurance athletes, the athletes' time to exhaustion increased, meaning that subjects could ride farther at a given intensity level after following a leg-strength program for a few weeks. The endurance improvements have usually ranged from 10 to 33 percent, depending on the intensity.

The studies do not generally find any improvement in aerobic capacity (VO_2max) following a strength program. What may be happening is that the slow-twitch, endurance muscles are stronger from weight training and are therefore able to carry more of the workload, so that fewer fast-twitch, power muscles are required at higher efforts. Since fast-twitch muscles burn glycogen, a precious fuel in short supply in the body, and produce lactic acid, endurance improves when the strength of the slow-twitch muscles increases. In effect, the lactate threshold (LT) has been raised. This finding was confirmed by a study conducted at the University of Maryland; there, strength trained cyclists increased their LT by an average of 12 percent. Strength training has also been demonstrated to improve athletes' economy—that is, the amount of oxygen needed at submaximal efforts.

Most multisport athletes discover that weight training, especially with relatively heavy loads, seems to benefit cycling and swimming more than running, even though all are endurance sports. This apparent dichotomy is explained by Pennsylvania State University's Dr. Vladimir Zatsiorsky, a renowned authority on sport biomechanics and the training of elite athletes. His work supports the notion that if the force required to produce a given movement, such as the force applied to the ground in a running stride at race effort, demands less than 20 to 25 percent of the athlete's maximum strength, then heavy weight training is of little or no value. It appears that riding a bike, especially uphill, and swimming in the dense medium of water both require the application of relatively greater forces than running does. This principle may help us to understand why weight lifting benefits the cycling and swimming legs of triathlon more than the running leg. The greatest benefit of strength training to running is the prevention of injuries.

Whatever the mechanism of improvement, there's little doubt that greater strength will help those who have low levels of force development, especially while climbing hills on the bike and swimming in open water.

GETTING STARTED

There are two challenges for the athlete determined to improve his or her racing by lifting weights. The first is that there are many strength programs in the popular literature, each usually associated with glowing reports of improvement from elite athletes. The average triathlete or duathlete doesn't know which program to follow. The second obstacle is time. Given jobs, family, and life in general, most age-group athletes just can't afford the great blocks of time in the gym that many pros can. The program described here has been pared down to fit into the "normal" athlete's busy lifestyle, focusing on the exercises and routine that will produce the greatest gains in the least time. Even if you could find more gym time, the benefits would not be much greater.

Strength training in the United States has been heavily influenced by bodybuilding. However, using resistance exercise the same way bodybuilders do is likely to decrease, rather than increase, endurance performance. Bodybuilders organize their training to maximize and balance muscle mass while shaping their physiques. Function is not a concern for them. Endurance athletes' goals are far different, but all too often, for lack of a better way, they learn the bodybuilders' methods at their gyms and employ them.

The purpose of strength training for multisport is strictly functional—the application of force to the pedals or water. To accomplish this, the triathlete or duathlete needs to improve the synchronization and recruitment patterns of muscle groups—not their size and shape. This means that the resistance work must not only develop the muscles, but also the central nervous system, which controls muscle use.

WEIGHT TRAINING GUIDELINES

How can you ensure that your weight training program develops function and not simply form? The following guidelines will help, regardless of what else you may do.

Focus on Prime Movers

Prime movers are the big muscle groups that do most of the work. For example, a prime mover for cycling is the quadriceps muscle group on the front of the thigh. Other prime movers for cycling are the hamstrings and gluteus (butt). In swimming, the prime movers are the latissimus dorsi (lats) and pectoralis (chest).

Prevent Muscle Imbalances

Some of the injuries common to multisport athletes result from an imbalance between muscles that must work in harmony to produce a movement. For example, if the quadriceps muscle on the outside of the thigh—the vastus lateralis—is overly developed relative to the vastus medialis—the muscle above and inside the knee—a knee injury known as chondromalacia patella is likely.

Use Multijoint Exercises Whenever Possible

Biceps curls are a single-joint exercise, as only the elbow joint is involved. This is the type of muscle-isolation exercise bodybuilders do. Squats, a basic cycling exercise, in contrast, involve three joints—the hip, knee, and ankle. Such exercises more closely simulate the dynamic movement patterns of the sport and also enable you to make the most of your time in the gym. The exceptions to this rule are the single-joint exercises done for muscular balance. For example, the knee-extension exercise—a knee-only movement—helps to maintain vastus lateralis–vastus medialis balance and therefore healthy knees.

Mimic the Positions and Movements of the Sport

Position your hands and feet such that they are similar to their position in the associated sport. When doing leg presses on a leg-press sled, for example, keep your feet about pedal-width apart. You don't ride with your feet spread 18 inches apart and your toes turned out at 45 degrees. Another example: When initiating the swim pull, your hand should be in line with your shoulder, not 12 inches or so outside of the shoulder. Remember this when doing lat pull-downs.

Include the Core

When you are swimming or cycling, the forces applied by your arms and legs must pass through the abdominals and lower back. If these areas are weak, much of the force is dissipated and lost. A strong core means, for example, that when you are climbing out of the saddle, more of the force that you generate by pulling against the handlebars is transferred to the pedals. In swimming, a weak lower back causes the legs and hips to sink while confounding the harmony of the upper- and lower-body movements. In running, a strong core keeps the pelvis in a neutral position. If the abdominal fatigues late in the race, the front of the pelvis sags and the butt protrudes, thus shortening the stride.

Keep the Number of Exercises Low

To concentrate on improving specific movements, focus more on the number of sets you do than on the number of exercises. This essentially means that your weight workouts will have greater depth than breadth and will therefore be more likely to produce a significant improvement. Following the initial Anatomical Adaptation (AA) phase, reduce the number of exercises to those that will provide the greatest gain for the least time invested. The idea is to spend as little time in the weight room as possible and yet still boost race performance.

Periodize Strength Training

The Maximum Strength (MS) phase of weight training, usually done during the early winter, can be crucial for developing force. Later, the strength gained will be converted to power endurance and muscular endurance on the road and in the pool. These are forms of strength directly applicable to triathlon and duathlon racing. Once the season is in full swing and you are putting greater effort into swimming, cycling, and running, generally in Base 2, you will deemphasize strength training and relegate it to a maintenance role.

The following suggested strength program uses the above guidelines and was designed specifically for multisport athletes. If you have been training like a bodybuilder, you may feel guilty at times using light weights, high repetitions, and only a few exercises. Stay with the program and you will likely see improvements in race performance, though you won't look much different in the mirror or on the scales.

PHASES AND PERIODIZATION

The triathlete and duathlete should progress through four phases in weight training during the year. Those phases and their periodization are as follows.

ANATOMICAL ADAPTATION (AA)

AA is the initial phase of strength training and usually occurs in the late fall or early winter during the Prep period. Its purpose is to prepare the muscles and tendons for the greater loads of the Maximum Strength phase. More strength training exercises are done at this time of year than at any other, since improved general body strength is a goal and other forms of training are minimal. Machines can be used in this period, but some free-weight training is beneficial. If desired, do some circuit training, as this can add an aerobic component to this phase.

In the AA phase, as in most others, the athlete should increase the loads gradually; many multisport athletes find that increasing the loads by about 5 percent every four or five workouts is about right. Sidebar 13.1 provides the details.

Anatomical Adaptation (AA) Phase

		AA
Total sessions/phase	8–12	
Sessions/week	2–3	
Load (% 1RM)	40–60	
Sets/session	3–5	
Reps/set	20–30	
Speed of lift	Slow	
Recovery (in minutes)	1–1.5	

TRIATHLON EXERCISES

(in order of completion):

1. Hip extension (squat, leg press, or step-up)
2. Standing, bent-arm lat pull-down
3. Hip extension (different from #1)
4. Chest press or push-ups
5. Seated row
6. Personal weakness (hamstring curl, knee extension, or heel raise)
7. Abdominal with twist

DUATHLON EXERCISES

(in order of completion):

1. Hip extension (squat, leg press, or step-up)
2. Seated row
3. Hip extension (different from #1)
4. Chest press or push-ups
5. Personal weakness (hamstring curl, knee extension, or heel raise)
6. Upper-body choice (lat pull-down or standing row)
7. Abdominal with twist

MAXIMUM TRANSITION (MT)

MT is a brief phase at the end of the Prep period that occurs between the AA and MS phases. Its purpose is to prepare the body for the greater loads to follow. You should be ready to begin MS after only a few MT workouts. You will increase the loads during this phase, but in order to avoid injury, be cautious and don't increase them too rapidly. Sidebar 13.2 provides details for the MT phase.

SIDEBAR 13.2

Maximum
Transition (MT)
Phase

Total sessions/phase	3–5	**MT**
Sessions/week	2–3	
Load	Select loads that allow only 10–15 reps*	
Reps/set	10–15*	
Speed of lift	Slow to moderate, emphasizing form	
Recovery (in minutes)	1.5–3*	

*Note: Only boldfaced exercises below follow this guideline. All others continue AA guidelines.

TRIATHLON EXERCISES

(in order of completion):

1. **Hip extension (squat, leg press, or step-up)**
2. **Seated row**
3. Abdominal with twist
4. Personal weakness (hamstring curl, knee extension, or heel raise)
5. **Standing, bent-arm lat pull-down**

DUATHLON EXERCISES

(in order of completion):

1. **Hip extension (squat, leg press, or step-up)**
2. **Seated row**
3. Abdominal with twist
4. Personal weakness (hamstring curl, knee extension, or heel raise)
5. Upper-body choice (lat pull-down, standing row, chest press, push-ups)

LOAD GOALS BASED ON BODY WEIGHT (BW)

Squat	1.3–1.7 x BW
Leg press (sled)	2.5–2.9 x BW
Step-up	0.7–0.9 x BW
Seated row	0.5–0.8 x BW
Standing, bent-arm lat pull-down	0.3–0.5 x BW

MAXIMUM STRENGTH (MS)

The purpose of the MS phase is to improve force generation. As resistance gradually increases and repetitions decrease, more force is generated. This phase, usually included during the Base 1 period, is necessary to teach the central nervous system to recruit high numbers of muscle fibers. With practice, your nervous system will be able to do this easily. Care must be taken not to cause injury in this phase, especially with free-weight exercises such as the squat. Select loads conservatively at the start of the phase and in the first set of each workout. However, you may gradually increase the loads throughout this phase up to the goal levels based on body weight (BW) detailed in Sidebar 13.2. Generally, women and those new to weight training will aim for the lower ends of the ranges, whereas men and those used to weight training will go for the upper ends.

Only the exercises with specified load goals in Sidebar 13.3 are done following the low-rep, high-load routine in the MS phase. All other exercises, such as abdominal and personal weakness areas, continue with the AA-phase routine of light weights and 20 to 30 repetitions per set.

Once you've achieved the aforementioned goals, you may increase your repetitions, but the loads should remain constant. For example, a 150-pound male triathlete doing the leg press has a goal of 435 pounds (150 x 2.9). Once he can lift this weight six times, he will increase the repetitions beyond six while keeping the load at 435 pounds. There is no reason to go beyond eight MS workouts once the goal weights are achieved. But if you have not reached the goal loads after twelve MS workouts have been completed, end the phase and go on to the next.

Some athletes will be tempted to do more than one hip-extension exercise, or to increase the loads beyond the goals listed above. Others will want to extend this phase beyond the recommended number of workouts in Sidebar 13.3. Doing so is likely to result in muscle imbalances, especially in the upper leg, which may contribute to hip or knee injuries. During the MS phase, your endurance performance may suffer and your legs and arms may feel "heavy." As a result, your pace for any given effort will be slow.

STRENGTH MAINTENANCE (SM)

This phase maintains the basic strength you have established in the previous phases, while the hills, intervals, open-water swims, and steady-state efforts you are doing will maintain your power and muscular endurance. Stopping all resistance training at this point may cause a gradual loss of strength throughout the season. It is particularly important for women and masters athletes to maintain their strength during race season. Some athletes, particularly males in their twenties, seem capable of maintaining adequate levels of strength without continuing a weight training program throughout the late Base, Build, and Peak periods.

Maximum
Strength (MS)
Phase

		MS
Total sessions/phase	8–12	
Sessions/week	2	
Load	BW Goal*	
Sets/session	3–6	
Reps/set	3–6+*	
Speed of lift	Slow to moderate*	
Recovery (in minutes)	2–4	

*Note: Only boldfaced exercises below follow this guideline. All others continue
   AA guidelines.

TRIATHLON EXERCISES

(in order of completion):

1. **Hip extension (squat, leg press, or step-up)**
2. **Seated row**
3. Abdominal with twist
4. Personal weakness (hamstring curl, knee extension, or heel raise)
5. **Standing, bent-arm lat pull-down**

DUATHLON EXERCISES

(in order of completion):

1. **Hip extension (squat, leg press, or step-up)**
2. **Seated row**
3. Abdominal with twist
4. Personal weakness (hamstring curl, knee extension, or heel raise)
5. Upper-body choice (lat pull-down, standing row, chest press, push-ups)

LOAD GOALS BASED ON BODY WEIGHT (BW)

Squat	1.3–1.7 x BW
Leg press (sled)	2.5–2.9 x BW
Step-up	0.7–0.9 x BW
Seated row	0.5–0.8 x BW
Standing, bent-arm lat pull-down	0.3–0.5 x BW

In the SM phase, only the last set is meant to stress the muscles. This set is done at about 80 percent of your one-repetition maximum (that is, the maximum load that a muscle group can lift in a single repetition). The one or two sets that provide the warm-up for this last set are accomplished at about 60 percent of one-repetition maximum. The details of the SM phase are listed in Sidebar 13.4.

Total sessions/phase	Indefinite	
Sessions/week	1	**SM**
Load (% 1RM)	60, 80 (last set)*	
Sets/session	2–3*	
Reps/set	6–12*	
Speed of lift	Moderate*	
Recovery (in minutes)	1–2*	

Note: Only boldfaced exercises below follow this guideline. All others continue AA guidelines.

SIDEBAR 13.4

Strength Maintenance (SM) Phase

TRIATHLON EXERCISES

(in order of completion):

1. **Hip extension (squat, leg press, or step-up)**
2. **Seated row**
3. Abdominal with twist
4. Personal weakness (hamstring curl, knee extension, or heel raise)
5. Standing, bent-arm lat pull-down

DUATHLON EXERCISES

(in order of completion):

1. **Hip extension (squat, leg press, or step-up)**
2. **Seated row**
3. Abdominal with twist
4. Personal weakness (hamstring curl, knee extension, or heel raise)
5. Upper-body choice (lat pull-down, standing row, chest press, push-ups)

Hip-extension training (squats, step-ups, and leg presses) is optional during the maintenance phase. If you find that hip-extension exercises help your racing, continue doing them. If, however, working the legs only deepens your fatigue level, eliminate them. You can continue to work on your core muscles and personal weakness areas to maintain your strength needs. Starting seven days before A-priority races, eliminate all strength training to allow for peaking.

DETERMINING LOAD

Perhaps the most critical aspect of sidebars 13.1 through 13.4 is the load selected for each phase. While they suggest loads as a percentage of the maximum weight you can lift for a single repetition (1RM), it's not typically advised that you determine your 1RM through trial and error—literally lifting heavy weights until you can only do a single repetition. You could encounter prolonged soreness as a result of such an effort, eliminating most, if not all, training for two or three days. The possibility for injury, especially to the back, also presents a great risk.

Another way to decide how much weight to use is to estimate the load based on experience, and then make adjustments as the phase progresses. Always start with less weight than you think you can lift for the goal number of repetitions, and cautiously add more later.

One-repetition maximums may also be estimated from a higher number of reps done to failure. Start by doing a warm-up set of 10 repetitions with a light weight. Then select a resistance you can lift at least 4 times, but no more than 10. You may need to experiment for a couple of sets. If you do, rest for at least 5 minutes between attempts. To find your predicted 1RM, divide the weight lifted by the factor in Table 13.1 that corresponds with the number of repetitions completed.

Either exercise machines or free weights may be used in all phases. Most athletes employ both, with their choice depending on the exercise and the availability of equipment. During the MT and MS phases, free weights are likely to bring greater results than machines, since barbells and dumbbells are better for developing the small muscles that aid balance. If you use free weights in these phases, also include them in the latter sessions of the AA phase. Again, be cautious whenever using barbells and dumbbells. To avoid injury, never "throw" the weight, but always keep it under control, and avoid rapid movements. If you're taller than 72 inches or shorter than 63 inches, you may find it difficult to use some exercise machines; in this case, free weights, again, are preferable.

TABLE 13.1

Predicting Your
One-Repetition
Maximum

REPETITIONS	FACTOR
4	0.917
5	0.889
6	0.861
7	0.833
8	0.805
9	0.778
10	0.750

UNDULATING PERIODIZATION OF STRENGTH TRAINING

The linear strength training periodization model explained above corresponds to the training model described in Chapter 3. That chapter also mentioned another model, "daily undulating" periodization, that can also be beneficial.

Undulating periodization is a simple scheme to follow daily. During the six weeks or so devoted to the MT and MS phases in the linear model, you do both MT and MS in a combined workout for each weight lifting exercise in each workout. If, for example, you are doing three sets, you would do the first set with a load that you could lift only about 15 times. You would do the second set with a load you could lift 10 times, and the third set with a load you could lift only 5 times.

During the six weeks that you are using this daily undulating model, you should feel comfortable with the increasing loads for each set. The AA and SM phases are unchanged.

Total sessions/phase	12–18
Sessions/week	2–3
Load (% 1RM)	Build with each set
Sets/session	2–3
Reps/set*	Set 1: 15
	Set 2: 10
	Set 3: 5
Speed of lift	Slow to moderate*
Recovery (in minutes)*	2–4

*Note: Only boldfaced exercises below follow this guideline. All others continue AA guidelines.

EXERCISES

(in order of completion):

1. **Hip extension (squat, leg press, or step-up)**
2. **Seated row**
3. Abdominal with twist
4. Upper-body choice (chest press or lat pull-down)
5. Personal weakness (hamstring curl, knee extension, or heel raise)
6. Standing row

LOAD GOALS BASED ON BODY WEIGHT (BW)

Freebar squat	1.3–1.7 x BW
Leg press (sled)	2.5–2.9 x BW
Step-up	0.7–0.9 x BW
Seated row	0.5–0.8 x BW
Standing row	0.4–0.7 x BW

SEASONAL PERIODIZATION OF STRENGTH TRAINING

Strength training with weights needs to dovetail with your triathlon-specific training so that the two modes are complementary. If they don't mesh well, then you may find that you are tired frequently and that your swim, bike, and run training isn't progressing. Table 13.2 shows you when to do each phase of strength training during your annual season.

TABLE 13.2

Periodization of
Strength Training

PERIOD	STRENGTH PHASE
Prep	AA-MT
Base 1	MS
Base 2	SM
Base 3	SM
Build 1	SM
Build 2	SM
Peak	SM
Race	(None)

If you have two or more Race periods in a season, it is recommended that you return to the MS phase whenever you repeat the Base period, even if it is just for 4 to 6 sessions before you return to SM. Should you have a periodization plan with only one Race period, which generally is not a good idea but sometimes done, return to MS (or daily undulating workouts) for 4 to 6 sessions about every 16 weeks. The challenge when doing this is that your swim, bike, and run training may decline when you are lifting heavy loads. You will need to allow for this by reducing the intensity of triathlon-specific workouts, especially the day after a strength session. In essence, you would be inserting mini–Base periods every 16 weeks and emphasizing duration at these times.

OTHER CONSIDERATIONS

In carrying out a strength development program, there are several other considerations to keep in mind.

EXPERIENCE LEVEL

If you are in the first two years of strength training, emphasize perfecting the movement patterns with light loads. It will take time for you to strengthen your connective tissue to prepare your muscles for greater gains. Veteran athletes are less likely than novices to sustain injuries during the high-risk Maximum Transition and Maximum Strength phases. Still, caution must guide all weight workouts, even for the seasoned athlete.

WARM-UP AND COOL-DOWN

Before an individual strength workout, warm up with 5 to 10 minutes of easy aerobic activity. Running, rowing, stair climbing, or cycling are good choices. Following a weight session, spin on a stationary bike with a light resistance at a comfortably high cadence, such as 90 rpm, for 5 to 10 minutes. Use little effort and allow your body to relax. Do not run immediately following a strength workout as this raises your risk of injury.

RECOVERY INTERVALS

Notice that the time between sets is specified in the tables. These recovery periods are important for deriving a benefit from strength work. During this time, your heart rate drops as your short-term energy supply is rebuilt in preparation for the next set. Some phases require longer recovery intervals than others due to the nature of the work. During the recovery time, relax for the recommended time, gently stretching the muscles just exercised. Later in this chapter, illustrations of stretches are provided.

EXERCISE ORDER

Exercises are listed in the tables in a particular order to allow for a progression from large to small muscle groups and for muscle-group recovery. In the AA phase, you may incorporate the exercises into a circuit training workout by completing the first sets before starting the second sets. For example, in AA you might do the first set of hip extensions followed by the first set of the next exercise, and then go on to the third station for one set.

If the weight room is crowded, of course, this approach won't work; you would be unable to go quickly from one exercise to the next because of the waiting time involved. In that case, simply complete all the sets of one exercise before going on. In the other phases, all sets of each exercise are done to completion before progressing to the next exercise. If time is tight, you may do two exercises as a "superset," alternating sets between the two exercises to completion. Supersetting makes better use of your time in the gym because you spend less time waiting for recovery of a specific neuromuscular group.

RECOVERY WEEKS

Every third or fourth week, you should reduce your training volume in the gym to coincide with a recovery week on your Annual Training Plan. This means reducing the number of strength workouts that week or reducing the number of sets within workouts.

STRENGTH EXERCISES

If you are at all confused about how to perform the following exercises, meet with a certified personal trainer, coach, or experienced athlete who can answer your questions.

HIP EXTENSION: SQUAT

QUADRICEPS, GLUTEUS, HAMSTRINGS

Improves force delivery to the pedals in cycling. For the novice, the squat is one of the most dangerous exercises in this routine. Great care is necessary to protect the back and knees. If you are concerned about injury, use a machine to perform an assisted squat. Wear a weight belt during the MT and MS phases.

1. Stand with the feet pedal-width apart, about 10 inches (25 cm), center to center, with toes pointed straight ahead.
2. Keep the head up and the back straight.

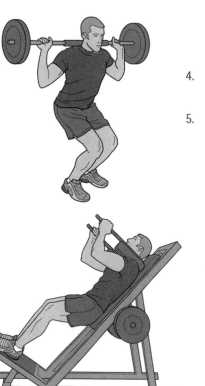

3. Squat until the upper thighs are just short of parallel to floor—about the same knee bend as at the top of the pedal stroke.
4. The knees point straight ahead, staying over your feet at all times.
5. Return to the starting position.
   Stretches: Stork Stand and Triangle.

FIGURE 13.1a

Squat

FIGURE 13.1b

Squat with
Machine

HIP EXTENSION: STEP-UP

QUADRICEPS, GLUTEUS, HAMSTRINGS

Improves force delivery to the pedals in cycling. The step-up mimics the movement of pedaling quite closely, but takes more time because each leg is worked individually. Caution is necessary to assure a stable platform and overhead clearance. The platform height should be about twice the length of your bike's crank arm—approximately 14 inches (35 cm). Do not use a knee-height platform, as this is likely to cause knee discomfort and raises the possibility of injury.

1. Place the left foot on the platform with the toes pointing straight ahead.
2. Step up with the right foot touching the platform, then immediately return that foot to the starting position.
3. Complete all right-leg reps before repeating the exercise with the left leg.
   Stretches: Stork Stand and Triangle.

FIGURE 13.2a

Step-up

FIGURE 13.2b

Step-up with
Dumbbells

HIP EXTENSION: LEG PRESS

QUADRICEPS, GLUTEUS, HAMSTRINGS

Improves force delivery to the pedals in cycling. This is probably the safest of the hip-extension exercises, and it generally takes the least time.

1. Center the feet on the middle portion of the platform about 10 inches (25 cm) apart, center to center. Feet are parallel, not angled out. The higher the feet are placed on the platform, the more the gluteus and hamstrings are involved. The lower the foot position, the less the gluteus-hamstring use.
2. Press the platform up until the legs are almost straight, but with the knees short of locking.
3. Lower the platform until the knees are about 8 inches from your chest, but no lower.
4. The knees remain in line with the feet throughout the movement.
5. Return to the starting position.
    Stretches: Stork Stand and Triangle.

FIGURE 13.3

Leg Press

SEATED ROW

UPPER AND LOWER BACK, LOWER LATS, BICEPS

Simulates the movement of pulling on the handlebars while climbing a hill in a seated position in cycling. Strengthens the core and lower back.

1. Grasp the bar with arms fully extended and hands about the same width as when gripping the handlebar.
2. Pull the bar toward the lower chest, keeping the elbows close to the body.
3. Minimize movement at the waist, using the back muscles to stabilize position.
4. Return to the starting position.

    Stretch: Pull-down.

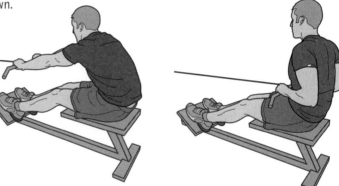

FIGURE 13.4

Seated Row

CHEST PRESS

PECTORALS, TRICEPS

Stabilizes the shoulder for swimming and increases force of the push phase of the stroke. With free weights, a spotter is necessary in the MS phase.

1. Grasp the bar with hands above the shoulders, hands placed about as wide as they would be on the handlebars.
2. Lower the bar to the chest.
3. Keep the elbows close to the body.
4. Return to the starting position.

    Stretch: Pull-down.

FIGURE 13.5

Chest Press

PUSH-UP

PECTORALS, TRICEPS

Stabilizes the shoulder for swimming and increases force of the push phase of the stroke.

1. Keep hands directly below or slightly wider than the shoulders.
2. Keep the back straight and the head up.
3. Keeping body rigid, lower the body until the chest almost touches the floor. This may be done with the knees on the floor while strength is developing.
4. Keep the elbows close to the body.
5. Return to the starting position.
   Stretch: Pull-down.

FIGURE 13.6

Push-up

HEEL RAISE

GASTROCNEMIUS

May reduce susceptibility to calf and Achilles' tendon injuries.

1. Stand with the balls of the feet on a 1- to 2-inch (2.5 to 5 cm) riser, with the heels on the floor.
2. The feet should be parallel and 6 to 8 inches apart, inside edge to inside edge.
3. Rise onto the toes.
4. Return to the starting position.
   Stretch: Wall Lean.

FIGURE 13.7

Heel Raise

KNEE EXTENSION

MEDIAL QUADRICEPS

May help by improving balance between the lateral and medial quadriceps.

1.   Start with the knee fully extended and the toes pointing slightly to the outside.
2.   Lower the ankle pad about 8 inches (20 cm)—do not go all the way down, as this may increase internal knee pressure, making the underside of the kneecap sore.
3.   Return to the starting position.
     Stretch: Stork Stand.

FIGURE 13.8

Knee Extension

LEG CURL

HAMSTRINGS

Improves the strength ratio between two major movers, the hamstrings and the quads. Leg curls may be done on either prone or standing machines.

1.   Curl leg to about a right angle at the knee.
2.   Return to the starting position.
     Stretch: Triangle.

FIGURE 13.9

Leg Curl

ABDOMINAL WITH TWIST

RECTUS ABDOMINUS, EXTERNAL OBLIQUES

Improves the transfer of energy from the upper to the lower body. Also important for maintaining body position in rough, open-water swims.

1. Sit on decline board with the knees bent at about 90 degrees.
2. Arms are crossed over the chest (do *not* pull on the head). Holding a weight plate is optional.
3. Lower the upper body to about a 45-degree angle, roughly halfway toward being parallel with the floor.
4. Return to the starting position with a twist. With each repetition, alternate looking over the right and left shoulders as the torso twists to the right and left.
    Stretch: Arch the back and extend the arms and legs.

FIGURE 13.10

Abdominal with Twist

LAT PULL-DOWN

LATISSIMUS DORSI, BICEPS

Stabilizes the shoulders.

1. Grasp the bar with the arms fully extended and the hands placed about as wide as they would be on the handlebars.
2. Pull the bar toward the upper chest, keeping the elbows close to the body.
3. Minimize both movement at the waist and rocking back and forth, using the back muscles to stabilize this position.
4. Return to the starting position.
    Stretch: Pull-down.

FIGURE 13.11

Lat Pull-down

STANDING, BENT-ARM LAT PULL-DOWN

LATISSIMUS DORSI, ROTATORS

Mimics the movement of the swim pull and stabilizes the shoulders.

1. Standing (or on knees) at the lat pull-down station, position the bar so it is a few inches above the head.
2. Place the hands on top of the bar, about as wide as they would be on the handlebars, with the arms slightly bent at the elbow.
3. While maintaining a high elbow position, push the bar down by rotating the shoulders until the bar is a few inches below the head.
4. Return to the starting position. *Stretches:* Shoulder Reach, Pull-down.

FIGURE 13.12

Standing,
Bent-Arm Lat
Pull-down

STANDING ROW

DELTOIDS, BICEPS

Stabilizes shoulders.

1. At the low-pulley station (or with free weights), grasp the bar at thigh height with the hands handlebar grip-width apart.
2. Pull the bar to the chest.
3. Return to the starting position. *Stretch:* Shoulder Reach.

FIGURE 13.13

Standing Row

COMPLEX TRAINING

One of the most effective ways to build muscular power, especially for running and cycling, is with plyometrics, a form of exercise involving explosive movements, such as jumping over or onto a high box (Figure 13.14). Including such exercises in your weekly training routine can be quite effective, although fitting in one more workout may seem impossible. The answer is to combine plyometrics and weights into one session. This is known as "complex training."

Complex training not only saves time but also magnifies the benefit of the plyometrics. This is because lifting weights stimulates the nervous system to activate more muscle fibers for a couple of minutes following an exercise. And activating large numbers of muscle fibers during a plyometrics exercise means greater power generation. Combining the two disciplines into one workout radically improves power.

To do a complex training workout, you simply alternate strength training and plyometrics: After a set of weight lifting, rest for 1 minute and then do one set of 10 to 15 repetitions of a plyometric exercise that involves the same muscle groups in essentially the same movement patterns as the preceding weight exercise. For example, following a set of step-ups, squats, or leg presses, do a set of explosive jump-ups onto a box. Table 13.3 offers examples of plyometric workouts to pair with weight lifting exercises.

The quality of training is the key to gaining both strength and power. This means gradually increasing your effort—lifting heavier weights, jumping higher, throwing farther, using heavier implements, and moving with increased speed. By combining weights and plyometrics into a single workout and limiting exercises to only the multijoint movements that most closely simulate the movements of swimming, cycling, and running, you can dramatically improve both strength and power.

Training for both strength and power should be considered a long-term process. Generally it takes six weeks to build muscle, so if you decide to do complex training, make the commitment to incorporate it throughout the season. Doing only a couple of weeks of this type of training will do more harm than good. Early on in the season, during the Anatomical Adaptation period, the exercises involve low weight loads and low-intensity plyometrics movements. This is when you are getting the hang of doing the movements that are involved in both types of training and refining them.

FIGURE 13.14

Jump-up

TABLE 13.3

Complex Training
Exercise Pairings

STRENGTH EXERCISE	PAIRED PLYOMETRIC EXERCISE
Step-up, Squat, Leg Press	Rope skipping, jumps onto low box, jumps onto high box
Lat Pull-down	Overhead medicine ball throw (increase ball weight or throw distance)
Bench Press, Push-up	Clap push-up (increase reps)
Abdominal	Medicine ball "catch and throw" on decline bench (increase ball weight or throw distance)
Heel Raise	Vertical jump for height

Following AA, as you move into the MT and MS periods, gradually increase both the weight loads and the plyometric intensities. For example, move from rope skipping to low-box jumping to high-box jumping.

The MS period is when you will take on the most challenging exercises and should last about four weeks, with eight to twelve total sessions. The development of strength and power is the primary focus of your training during this period, which coincides with Base 1. After Base 1 you should begin to cut back on both weight training and plyometrics in order to shift the emphasis to swimming, cycling, and running.

Complex training is called "complex" because it involves the combination of two disciplines, but it is also "complicated." There is no simple way of laying out a program that fits everyone. The serious athlete who decides to try complex training will need to experiment—cautiously. Be conservative with the increases you undertake, not only in terms of loads and repetitions with weights, but also in regard to the height, weight, distance, and repetitions of the plyometrics exercises.

STRETCHING

When it comes to the muscles, swimming, cycling, and running are not perfect. No sport is. One of the "problems" resulting from vigorous exercise is a shortening and tightening of connective tissue. Arm and leg muscles lose elasticity because they must contract repeatedly and seldom go through a full range of motion. On every stroke or stride, they stop short of full extension and complete flexion.

Of the three sports, swimming requires the greatest flexibility, especially in the shoulders and ankles. A flexible shoulder allows the hand to recover close to the body, thus permitting a full roll and a long stroke. An ankle capable of completely flattening out (plantar flexion) produces little drag. Try swimming with your ankles at a 90-degree angle sometime and see how much it slows you down.

During cycling, banjo-tight hamstrings limit your performance. Rigid hamstrings restrain the leg during the downstroke. They try to prevent the leg from straightening, and in so doing reduce the force produced in hip and knee extension. In an attempt to alleviate the tension felt in the back of the leg, the athlete will often lower his or her saddle. A saddle that is set too low further reduces force generation, dropping the power output even more.

In the same manner, flexible quadriceps and hip flexors aid running by allowing the recovery leg to swing through a wider arc. Tightness in these muscle groups reduces the range of motion in the hip, giving the athlete a constricted look while possibly increasing the energy cost of running.

Tight hamstrings can also contribute to a tight lower back, which haunts some athletes regardless of the sport and can result in a race "DNF" (did not finish). This low-back tightness may become chronic low-back pain requiring medical attention. A consistent and effective program of stretching may prevent such problems from occurring. Prevention is always more comfortable, less time consuming, and cheaper than treatment.

STRETCHING BENEFITS

Besides improving performance, stretching following workouts also appears to aid the recovery process by improving the uptake of amino acids by the muscle cells, promoting protein synthesis within the muscle cells, and maintaining the integrity of the muscle cells.

In addition, the injury-reducing reputation that stretching has earned among multi-sport athletes is well established and has garnered some support in the scientific literature, although it's not universally acclaimed by research. For example, a study of 1,543 runners in the Honolulu Marathon found that those who stretched regularly following workouts had fewer injuries than those who did not. It's interesting to note that in this same study, those who stretched only *before* workouts had the highest rate of injuries.

Another study, conducted by the New Jersey Medical School, also revealed that flexibility might reduce injury risk, especially for men. More than 200 college athletes, at their preseason physical examinations, were graded on a 10-point scale for flexibility of the hip and leg muscles and ligaments. They were then followed over the course of the season. As the muscle tightness of the males increased by 1 point on the 10-point flexibility scale, their risk of injury increased by 23 percent. There was no relationship between the flexibility scale and the risk of injury for the females.

Don't get the idea, however, that stretching is a panacea for injury. Muscle and tendon trauma in endurance sports is seldom the result of failure to stretch enough, as some athletes believe. At best, stretching may play a minor role in injury prevention, and at worst it may actually contribute to injury by making tendons and ligaments overly slack. Moderation in stretching, as in most other aspects of life, is best.

Stretching after a workout takes less than 15 minutes and can be done while you are downing a recovery drink and chatting with your training partners. This is the best time to work on flexibility, as the muscles are warm and supple.

Another important time to stretch is during strength workouts. The act of forcefully contracting muscles against resistance creates extreme tightness. As described in the previous section, following each strength set, you should gently stretch the exercised muscles. In fact, correctly doing a strength workout means spending more time in the gym stretching than lifting weights.

Stretching a little bit throughout the day may also benefit long-term flexibility and performance. While sitting at a desk, working, or reading, you can gently stretch major muscle groups such as the lower back, hamstrings, and calves. Stretch gently while watching television, standing in line, talking with friends, and first thing in the morning when you are still in bed.

STRETCHING GUIDELINES

Stretching didn't become an accepted aspect of fitness training until after World War II. Over the past 40 years, however, it has gained in popularity, and four major stretching methods have been popular at one time or another.

Ballistic

In the 1960s, ballistic stretching was common. Bouncing movements were thought to be the best way to make muscles limber. Later we learned that this technique had just the opposite effect: Muscles resisted lengthening and could even be damaged by overly motivated stretchers. Today almost no one stretches this way.

Static

In the 1970s, a Californian named Bob Anderson developed a new stretching method, and in 1980 he released a book called *Stretching*. Anderson's approach involved static stretching with little or no movement. He instructed people to stretch the muscle to a level of slight discomfort, and then hold it in that position for several seconds. Static stretching probably remains the most popular style today.

PNF

Another method surfaced at about the same time as static stretching but did not receive much exposure or support until the 1990s. Several university studies going back to the early 1970s found it to be 10 to 15 percent more effective than static stretching. This method, called proprioceptive neuromuscular facilitation, or PNF, has many variations, some of which are quite complex. Here are the steps in one easy-to-follow version:

1. Static stretch the muscle for about eight seconds.
2. Contract the same muscle for about eight seconds.
3. Static stretch the muscle again for about eight seconds.
4. Continue alternating contractions with stretches until you have done four to eight static stretches. Always finish with a static stretch.

You should find that the static stretches become deeper with each repeat as the muscles seem to loosen up. Using this PNF method, a stretch would take 1 to 2 minutes to complete.

Active Isolated

A relatively new arrival on the fitness scene, active-isolated stretching involves brief, assisted stretches that are repeated several times. Here is a typical routine:

1. Contract the opposing muscle group as you move into position.
2. Use your hands, a rope, or a towel to enhance the stretch.
3. Stretch to the point of light tension.
4. Hold for two seconds and then release.
5. Return to the starting position and relax for two seconds.
6. Do one or two sets of eight to twelve repetitions of each stretch.

STRETCHING EXERCISES

The following are selected stretches for each sport. You may find that some are more important for you than others, or that you need to include stretches not illustrated here. Many of these stretches followed the strength exercises that were illustrated earlier in the chapter. You'll find those exercises cross-referenced here as well.

SHOULDER REACH

LATISSIMUS DORSI

Swimming/Weights: Standing, bent-arm lat pull-down

1. Extend the arms overhead and cross one wrist over the other while interlocking hands.
2. With elbows behind the ears, straighten the arms and reach up.

FIGURE 13.15

Shoulder Reach

ANKLE SIT

TIBIALIS

Swimming

Don't do this stretch if you have knee problems.

1. Sit on your shins on a padded surface or towel with toes pointed (not flailed to the sides).
2. Do not sit with your butt between your heels.
3. With your butt on your heels, lean backward slightly until you feel an easy stretch.

FIGURE 13.16

Ankle Sit

TWISTER

PECTORALIS

Swimming/Weights: Chest press

1. With your back facing a wall, grasp a stationary object at shoulder height.
2. Look away from the arm being stretched and twist your body away from it.

FIGURE 13.17

Twister

STORK STAND

QUADRICEPS

Cycling and Running/Weights: Hip extension and seated knee extension

1. While balancing against your bike or a wall, grasp your right foot behind your back with your left hand.
2. Gently pull up and away from your butt with your hand.
3. Keep your head up and stand erect—do not bend at the waist.

FIGURE 13.18

Stork Stand

TRIANGLE

HAMSTRING

Cycling and Running/Weights: Hip extension and leg curl

1. Bend forward at the waist while leaning on your bike or a wall.
2. Place the leg to be stretched forward with the foot about 18 inches from the support.
3. The other leg is directly behind the first. The farther back this leg is placed, the greater the stretch.
4. With your weight on the front foot, sag your upper body toward the floor. You should feel the stretch in the hamstring of your forward leg.

FIGURE 13.19

Triangle

PULL-DOWN

LATISSIMUS DORSI, TRAPEZIUS, PECTORALIS, TRICEPS

Swimming and Cycling/Weights: Standing bent-arm lat pull-down, chest press, and seated row

1. Hold onto your bike or a railing for balance with your weight resting on your arms.
2. Allow your head to sag deeply between outstretched arms to create a stretch in your lats.

FIGURE 13.20

Pull-down

SQUAT

LOWER BACK, SOLEUS, QUADRICEPS, GLUTEUS

Cycling and Running/Weights: Seated row

1. Holding onto something for balance, squat down while keeping your heels on the floor (this is easier to do without shoes).
2. Allow your butt to sag close to your heels as you rock forward. Hold this position for about 30 seconds.

FIGURE 13.21

Squat

WALL LEAN

GASTROCNEMIUS, SOLEUS

Running/Weights: Heel raise

1. Lean against a wall with the leg to be extended straight behind you, and the forward leg holding most of your weight.
2. Keep the heel of the rear foot on the floor with the toe pointed forward.
3. The farther forward your hips move, the greater the stretch in the calf.
4. To stretch the gastrocnemius, straighten the rear knee. Stretch the soleus by bending the rear knee.

FIGURE 13.22

Wall Lean

UNIQUE NEEDS

*If you want to be competitive with the best
as a pro or even in the hotly contested age
divisions, every minute counts, and you had
better be prepared to race the entire day.*
—BRAD KEARNS, PROFESSIONAL TRIATHLETE

CAN EVERYONE TRAIN in the same manner using the guidelines presented so far in this book? Most certainly not. As discussed in Chapter 3, the principle of individualization demands that in order to achieve athletic success, the various training components (volume, workload, intensity, frequency, duration) must match the unique needs and capabilities of the athlete. Although it is not possible to provide specific details for every individual in a book such as this, it is possible to provide general direction for rather homogeneous groups. Five clusters of athletes are examined in this chapter—women, masters, juniors, novices, and elite athletes.

There is limited scientific information relating to these groups because they are relatively small; it is difficult for researchers to recruit them in great enough numbers to draw significant conclusions from testing. University studies are usually based on male college students, since they are willing to participate and obviously handy for university-based research. Because multisport research is a relatively new field, studies using even male multisport athletes as subjects are rare. Consequently, "how-to" questions concerning females, old and young athletes, and those at either end of the multisport experience curve are largely left open to conjecture. Nevertheless, in this chapter I attempt to provide some guidelines for those groups of athletes, using science wherever possible, but more often using the observations of athletes and coaches.

WOMEN

Throughout much of the past century, the only sports considered ladylike, and in which competition was on a nearly equal level with men's, were equestrian sports, tennis, golf, gymnastics, and figure skating. But despite a lot of male bias and foot-dragging, especially in terms of endurance events, women have made great progress toward full acceptance. For example, in the 1928 Olympic Games in Amsterdam, the longest race in which women were allowed to compete was the 800-meter run. In that Olympiad three runners broke the world record for the distance, but they finished in "such a distressed condition" that horrified officials dropped the event from future competition. "Women just weren't meant to run that far," was the position of many men, including scientists. It wasn't until the 1964 Tokyo Games that the women's 800-meter run was resurrected.

The 1984 Los Angeles Olympics finally included the women's marathon in competition—nearly two decades after women began competing at the distance. To this day, some endurance sports, such as road cycling, continue to discriminate by restricting competitive distances for women.

Multisport reflects the more recent attitudes of our society about women in sport. Race distances are the same regardless of gender. Men and women duathletes and triathletes train and compete together as equals, a situation unheard of in most sports just twenty years ago. Many, but not all, races have equal prize money for females and males.

UNIQUE CONSIDERATIONS

The changes in attitudes toward women over the years reflect the now-dominant view that there is really little difference between male and female athletes. There are, of course, a few obvious physical distinctions. Women tend to have wider hips, a shorter torso relative to leg length, a lower center of gravity, and a more "knock-kneed" stance. All of these differences affect the bicycling equipment women use and, to some extent, the swimming and running techniques they use. There are also a few significant performance-related differences between the sexes. Women, on average, have a smaller aerobic capacity than men, for example, with smaller hearts and a lower oxygen-carrying capacity. Also, women have a higher percentage of body weight as fat than men and can generate less absolute muscular force as a result of their smaller muscle mass. These differences contribute to about a 10 percent variance in the world records of males and females in events ranging from weight lifting to sprinting to endurance sports.

Despite these differences, men and women athletes are really more alike than they are different. Women can and do train at the same volumes and intensities as their male counterparts. They are fully capable of doing the same workouts as men. And they respond to a relative training load in the same way. There is no reason women athletes shouldn't train just as men do, with a few exceptions.

Of course, in multisport, women don't train to compete with men—they train to compete with other women. So making training comparisons to men is of little value to the female athlete. What a female multisport athlete wants to know is how to improve relative to her female competition. Generally, there are three areas that every woman competing in triathlons and duathlons should consider in order to train better and race more competitively: strength, psychology, and diet.

Strength

Although I advise many athletes to stop strength training during the racing season, women in particular benefit from year-round strength training. Unlike men, women tend to lose muscle mass more quickly once they stop working in the weight room. There are also specific target areas that women should address.

Most women duathletes and triathletes are relatively stronger in their legs than in their upper bodies. Especially in need of strength are the abdominal muscles and arms. This weakness impacts climbing hills when on the bike. While standing on the pedal, the leg force generated in powering the bike uphill must be counterbalanced by the arm pulling against the handlebars on the same side, with stability provided by the abdominal muscles and back. If that arm is a wimpy noodle, and the midsection is like an accordion, the unbalanced force will tip the bike over. Upper-body strength, therefore, is required for powerful climbing.

Female triathletes who develop their upper-body strength have a definite advantage not only in cycling but also in rough, open-water swims. Maintaining an effective body position when the chop is great enough to otherwise disrupt the stroke is crucial to success.

Strength work for the upper body involves doing pushing and pulling exercises that use all of the arm joints plus the back muscles and abdominal muscles. Whenever possible, women triathletes should work these three components of upper-body strength together rather than working each one in isolation. The seated-row exercise described in Chapter 13 is a good example of a multijoint exercise that benefits cycling. This station builds the arms and back in a way that targets the muscles necessary for climbing hills on a bike. Another exercise to emphasize is the standing bent-arm lat pull-down. This one is useful for building up muscles used in swimming. The chest press is also good because it will provide muscular balance. Finally, abdominal strength should be emphasized because of the larger and wider shape of the female pelvis.

Psychology

Men and women are not just different physically; they also have different tendencies psychologically. Women are usually better than men at dealing with defeat, for example. But when it comes to poor race performance, women are more likely to blame it on a lack of ability, whereas men are more inclined to chalk it up to lack of effort. This self-doubt among women where sports performance is concerned is not surprising; after all, society has taught them in subtle ways that they are not good at athletics. If you don't agree, just compare the size of the crowds at boys' and girls' high-school basketball games.

Confidence is as important for success in multisport as physical ability. No matter how talented you are, if you don't believe you can win, you won't. I coached a young woman pro when she was one of the best in the country, and yet she always offered me reasons why she couldn't achieve her high goals. She frequently raised the issue of her limitations and failures. I put her on a confidence-building program. Every night she would use those few minutes in bed between turning the lights off and falling asleep to review and relive the biggest success of her day, no matter how small it seemed. It could simply be that she finished a tough workout feeling strong, or that she climbed one hill particularly well, or that one interval felt especially good. She would recapture that experience in her mind and go to sleep feeling good about her ability. That year she had her best season ever, winning a national championship and finishing fifth at the world championship.

Other ideas for improving confidence include keeping a "success log" in which you record the day's achievements. Athletes are unbeatable when they learn to "act as if" they were confident, no matter how insignificant and unsure they may feel. It may even help to take an acting class to develop this skill. You must believe in yourself if you are to succeed.

Diet

Many women triathletes and duathletes overly restrict their food intake. It is not unusual for women athletes to eat fewer than 2,000 calories per day, when in fact they may need up to 3,000. These restrictions mean that many important nutrients are limited. With an average of 5 milligrams of iron per 1,000 calories in the standard American diet, for example, most woman triathletes and duathletes probably consume about 10 mg of iron a day. However, they need about 15 mg per day.

To make matters worse, the vegetarian diets that are favored by many women athletes are even lower than the standard diet in absorbable iron. Exercise and menstruation further decrease iron levels. Becoming iron-deficient, or anemic, is a definite possibility under such circumstances. Owen Anderson, Ph.D., the publisher of *Running Research News,* estimates that 30 percent of women athletes have an iron deficiency. Such a condition results in early fatigue and low endurance. One study of high-school girls even linked low iron with an increase in running injuries.

Such problems are easily corrected by including red meat in the diet three or four times a week. If you are not a meat eater, add vitamin C–rich foods to your meals to improve iron absorption, and eat lots of beans and spinach. Should you become anemic, such a diet may still prove inadequate for correcting the situation. Your physician may recommend an iron supplement. However, do not take an iron supplement without the approval of your health care provider, as there are many possible complications.

Many women athletes also limit their intake of high-fat foods. Dietary fat is necessary for peak performance, however. A body deprived of essential fats is in danger of becoming run down and susceptible to illness due to a weakened immune system. If you are sick, injured, or tired, you can't perform at your best. Include fat in your diet daily from good sources such as nuts, nut spreads, avocados, canola oil, and olive oil. Continue to avoid saturated fat and trans fat, the type found in foods that have been "hydrogenated," such as snack foods and prepackaged meals. Chapter 16 provides more details on the athlete's diet.

OTHER FACTORS RELATED TO PERFORMANCE

A study at the University of Illinois showed that women who use oral contraceptives may have an advantage in endurance sports. During a period of long endurance sessions at low intensity, women taking birth-control pills showed an increase in growth hormone. They used significantly less carbohydrate and more fat for fuel than women who were not on the pill. This suggests that using oral contraceptives may improve a woman's capacity for burning fat, allow her to get into shape faster than she could without the pill, and extend her endurance range in races. No other studies are known to have confirmed this finding, so the results should be applied with some caution. If you are not currently using an oral contraceptive, but are considering it, talk with your health-care provider before starting. Don't take the pill only for race-performance reasons.

Women must be cautious not to overtrain, as it can cause menstrual dysfunction and associated medical problems such as osteoporosis and stress fractures. Bone density is known to peak, and then decrease, at about age 35. Overtraining may hasten the process, as it has been shown to reduce bone density. It is imperative that the female athlete determine the appropriate workload by building up to it rather than shooting high and working down. If you are not sure how to select a training load, err on the side of doing too little.

MASTERS

The world has changed a lot in the past 30 to 40 years—and it is the old "coots" who have changed the most. In the 1960s, age 40 meant one foot in the grave, at least as far as the sporting world was concerned. The medical community once advised anyone beyond that ancient age to slow down so as not to damage their hearts. Now "old timers" in their forties accomplish feats once considered practically impossible.

Take, for example, the Irish runner Eamonn Coghlan, who at age 41 became the first person over 40 to run a mile in less than 4 minutes. Then there is Kent Bostick. In 1996, at age 42, Bostick qualified for the U.S. Olympic cycling team by beating 28-year-old Mike McCarthy by nearly a second in the 4,000-meter pursuit on the track (Bostick qualified again for the 2000 Olympics at age 46). Dara Torres, at 41, put in an amazing performance at the 2008 Beijing Olympics, defeating swimmers less than half her age. In

2007, at age 43, Dave Wiens out-biked Floyd Landis to win the Leadville 100, then beat Lance Armstrong the following year. Marathoner Dean Karnazes was 44 in 2007 when he ran 50 marathons in 50 days.

These athletes are just the tip of the iceberg. There are hundreds more aging athletes in the world of endurance sports who are within seconds of their best performances of all time. Now that the baby boomers are well into their forties, we can expect to see the number of masters athletes swell to record proportions—and their times to keep dropping.

FORTY PHYSIOLOGY

Just because there are many fast masters out there, however, doesn't mean that you can stop the aging process. There's no denying that with increasing age there is a decline in performance. In fact, world records for running events seem to confirm that, on average, athletes slow down by about 1 percent per year after age 30. For a 10 km run, that translates into about a 14-second slowdown every year.

Scientists have studied the link between aging and physiological function since the 1930s. One inescapable conclusion has come from this research: Getting older means a reduction in the functioning of many systems in the human body. Aerobic capacity (VO_2max) is a case in point. You probably recall from an earlier chapter that aerobic capacity is a measure of how much oxygen the body uses to produce energy at a maximal workload. The higher one's aerobic capacity, the greater the potential for performance in an event like triathlon or duathlon. But studies show that starting at about age 20, aerobic capacity usually begins dropping, partly because maximum heart rate decreases. A lowered max heart rate means less oxygen delivery to the muscles, and therefore a lowered VO_2max. The usual rate of decline measured in the research is in the range of six to ten beats in the max heart rate per decade.

Similar results have come from studies on the aging pulmonary, nervous, muscular, thermal regulatory, immune, and anaerobic systems: The functional decreases begin sometime in the third or fourth decades of life, with the average losses in the range of 6 to 10 percent per decade. Compounding the problem is what appears to be a normal increase in body fat after the early twenties, which is obviously made worse by a sedentary lifestyle.

THE AGING MYTH

A little skepticism is a healthy thing when it comes to research. Most studies of aging are based on "cross-sectional" analysis. That means, for example, that a group of 30-year-olds and a similar group of 40-year-olds are tested for some parameter of fitness. The researchers base their findings on the assumption that the difference represents a normal amount of loss.

The alternative is "longitudinal" research, which involves following a group of subjects for several years and testing them regularly to see how they change. This method has many benefits, but there are few longitudinal studies of athletes. Such studies are rare in any case because of the large amount of time that is needed to gather the data.

Cross-sectional studies raise many questions. Who were the test subjects? Were the two groups similar enough that the older group can be seen as comparable to the younger group in every way except for age? In research on fitness, many studies define the subjects as "trained endurance athletes." This vague description is usually based on measures of training volume, such as years of activity, or hours trained in a week. Of course, one study's trained endurance athlete may be another's novice. The intensity of training is hard to quantify, but it is this factor that the researchers highlight in defining the groups. Since it appears that intensity is the key to maintaining race fitness, this is a crucial issue.

The few longitudinal studies that have been done show that when an athlete maintains training intensity while aging, aerobic capacity and other selected measures of fitness may decline by as little as 2 percent per decade. This rate of decline is roughly a third to a fifth of what sedentary subjects usually experience. Even those who maintain their health and exercise at low intensities experience the higher rate of decline.

The "normal" decline in performance of 6 to 10 percent per decade is probably more a result of self-imposed training and lifestyle limitations than of human physiology. Aging may actually account for only a fourth of the losses while disuse takes the bigger bite.

TRAINING IMPLICATIONS

The bottom line is that intense training keeps the heart, nerves, muscles, lungs, and other systems all working to their genetic potential. If you never rev your engine up to high speed, you will lose horsepower more rapidly than is necessary.

The following training guidelines will help masters athletes to keep their fitness high. Don't let all the statistics about aging discourage you: They represent averages and general trends, not limitations for individuals. You can even improve your performance as you age if you train smarter, eat right, and cultivate your mental skills.

Train Intensely

Build and maintain endurance, but give a higher priority to intense workouts, if you are a masters multisport athlete. This doesn't mean you must train anaerobically all of the time; rather, it means that your most intense sessions should be meticulously planned. Know exactly what it is you intend to achieve, and then run, ride, or swim with that purpose in mind. "Intense" doesn't mean "killer" efforts, intervals until you throw up, or even necessarily redlining. Intense workouts are those incorporating zones 4 and 5 (see Chapter 4). The intense workouts you use the most should put you in zone 4 for extended periods. Such training near the lactate threshold can be quite effective. Intense workouts should stress you without leaving you wasted. Always stop before reaching failure. Save the maximum efforts for races.

Use Intensity Sparingly

Do no more than three intense workouts in a week if you are a masters athlete. For example, you could do one intense swim, one bike ride, and one intense run weekly. Some masters should do only two. Observing how quickly you recover is the key to knowing how many is best. You should go into each intense workout feeling ready and eager. Devote the other days of the week to recovery and the development of skills and techniques like those discussed in Chapter 12.

Plan Frequent Rest

Train hard for two or three weeks, and then take a week to recover and rest. Table 7.2 may help you to schedule this rest. For those who need more frequent recovery, Table 14.1 is a better guide. Taking frequent R&R is the best way for the serious master to

TABLE 14.1

Weekly Training Hours by Period for Select Masters

PERIOD	WEEK	200	250	300	350	400	450	500	550	600	650	700
Prep	All	4.0	4.0	5.0	6.0	7.0	7.5	8.5	9.0	10.0	11.0	12.0
Base 1	1	4.0	5.0	6.0	7.0	8.0	9.0	10.0	11.0	12.0	12.5	14.0
	2	5.0	6.0	7.0	8.5	9.5	10.5	12.0	13.0	14.5	15.5	16.5
	3	5.5	6.5	8.0	9.5	10.5	12.0	13.5	14.5	16.0	17.5	18.5
	4	4.0	4.0	4.0	5.0	5.5	6.5	7.0	8.0	8.5	9.0	10.0
Base 2	1	4.0	5.5	6.5	7.5	8.5	9.5	10.5	12.5	12.5	13.0	14.5
	2	5.0	6.5	7.5	9.0	10.0	11.5	12.5	14.0	15.0	16.5	17.5
	3	5.5	7.0	8.5	10.0	11.0	12.5	14.0	15.5	17.0	18.0	19.5
	4	4.0	4.0	4.5	5.0	5.5	6.5	7.0	8.0	8.5	9.0	10.0
Base 3	1	4.5	5.5	7.0	8.0	9.0	10.0	11.0	12.5	13.5	14.5	15.5
	2	5.0	6.5	8.0	9.5	10.5	12.0	13.5	14.5	16.0	17.0	18.5
	3	6.0	7.5	9.0	10.5	11.5	13.0	15.0	16.5	18.0	19.0	20.5
	4	4.0	4.0	4.5	5.0	5.5	6.5	7.0	8.0	8.5	9.0	10.0
Build 1	1	5.0	6.5	8.0	9.0	10.0	11.5	12.5	14.0	15.5	16.0	17.5
	2	5.0	6.5	8.0	9.0	10.0	11.5	12.5	14.0	15.5	16.0	17.5
	3	4.0	4.0	4.5	5.0	5.5	6.5	7.0	8.0	8.5	9.0	10.0
Build 2	1	5.0	6.0	7.0	8.5	9.5	10.5	12.0	13.0	14.5	15.5	16.5
	2	5.0	6.0	7.0	8.5	9.5	10.5	12.0	13.0	14.5	15.5	16.5
	3	4.0	4.0	4.5	5.0	5.5	6.5	7.0	8.0	8.5	9.0	10.0
Build 3	1	5.0	6.0	7.0	8.5	9.5	10.5	12.0	13.0	14.5	15.5	16.5
	2	5.0	6.0	7.0	8.5	9.5	10.5	12.0	13.0	14.5	15.5	16.5
	3	4.0	4.0	4.5	5.0	5.5	6.5	7.0	8.0	8.0	8.5	10.0
Peak	1	5.0	5.5	6.5	7.5	8.5	9.5	10.5	11.5	13.0	13.5	14.5
	2	4.0	5.0	5.0	6.0	6.5	7.5	8.5	9.5	10.0	11.0	11.5
Race	All	4.0	4.0	4.5	5.0	5.5	6.5	7.0	8.0	8.5	9.0	10.0
Tran	All	4.0	4.0	4.5	5.0	5.5	6.5	7.0	8.0	8.5	9.0	10.0

ANNUAL HOURS

improve steadily. Adequate rest time means not only breaks from training every two or three weeks, but also taking one, two, or even three days of easy training between intense sessions. Masters may also improve more by allowing for more recovery time between intervals within a workout.

Strength Train Year-Round

Strength training can be done in the weight room, or on the bike, climbing hills. Masters who live in the flatlands will improve their hill strength by lifting weights year round. Aerobic training on flat terrain is insufficient to prevent the loss of muscle mass, especially after the age of 50. The advantage of weight training is that you can also work the upper body, which slows the loss of muscle mass above the waist.

Maintain Leg Speed

In cycling, masters athletes should concentrate on improving leg turnover rate until cadences of about 90 rpm, whether running or cycling, feel comfortable and come naturally. Count one leg's revolutions for a minute to check your cadence. You should find that this cadence makes you more efficient and reduces your risk of injury while also stimulating nervous-system maintenance. Include workouts such as strides, spin-ups, and isolated leg training throughout the year (see Appendices C and D).

Successful racing as a master means refusing to accept the loss of physical function as normal, but instead always setting challenging goals. You may need more recovery time, but you do not have to slow down your pace or lower your expectations. Redefine "over the hill" in terms of your workout, not your age.

GRAND MASTERS AND SENIORS

In the early days of triathlon, the 55–59 group was the oldest age group recognized in racing. It was rare that anyone over age 60 would even be at the race as a spectator, let alone competing. Now athletes in their sixties, seventies, and even eighties are competing at all distances, from sprint to Ironman, and their numbers are growing every year. Seniors such as Sister Madonna Buder, Harriet Anderson, Bob Scott, and Robert McKeague are role models for thousands of young, aspiring triathletes. They and others like them have taught us that age no longer means what it did a generation ago when the sport was in its infancy.

Everything described in the previous section on masters also applies to grand masters—only more so. Whereas forty-something athletes can still make training mistakes and discover that their bodies will still adapt and forgive them, athletes in their seventies or eighties at some point find out this is no longer the case. The older you are, the fewer mistakes you can make and still get away with it. This means getting the details dialed in exactly right for nutrition, rest and recovery, strength training, volume, intensity, equipment, and everything else that affects health and performance. Errors in judgment at these ages mean unusable joints, surgery, broken bones, and, at the very least, days lost to overwhelming fatigue.

The good news is that athletes who have reached these ages tend to be both patient and wise. They see triathlon as a lifestyle, not as something to be defeated and vanquished. They're in it for the long haul. Younger athletes could learn a lot from them. If science could figure out how to put a grand master's wisdom into the mind of a 25-year-old physical specimen, it would create the ultimate athlete.

How should the grand master and senior athlete train? To remain in top shape and continue racing, they especially need to keep challenging the muscular system. This means including strength training, hill work, and open-water swims in the training program on a regular basis, yet keeping such workouts widely spaced to allow time for recovery. It is especially important for them to continue their strength training program, as this will not only benefit their triathlon performance but also the quality of their lives in general. Research with 90-year-olds has found that their rate of improvement in strength is the same as that of 20-year-olds when they are put on a similar resistance training program.

Grand masters and senior athletes have well-honed swimming, cycling, and running skills; if they do not, the risk of injury is greatly magnified. It is never too late to learn good skills—focus on technique, if necessary, to reduce that risk, if you are a masters or grand masters athlete. In nutrition, you must emphasize alkaline-enhancing foods in the vegetable and fruit categories to minimize acidic body fluids and the loss of muscle and bone. See Table 16.4 for more details.

JUNIORS

If you are a teenager who has taken up the sport of triathlon or duathlon, you probably already participate in swimming or running programs at your school and see multisport as a challenging way to combine those sports with cycling. It's because of young athletes like you that the sport is experiencing such rapid change, especially in terms of race performances. For example, in the "old days" of triathlon back in the early 1980s, if a man could finish an Olympic-distance race in under two hours, he was almost certain to win. Today such a time may not even crack the top ten in a local event. Times are dropping rapidly as former junior athletes move up to the senior ranks. Multisport is more competitive now than ever before, in part because of all the young athletes coming on board. This development continues to progress at a rapid pace, thanks largely to the impact of triathlon's successful debut in the 2000 Sydney Olympics.

Triathlon and duathlon are not easy sports. They require hours of difficult training in different disciplines. The races aren't over in a few seconds, and there are no time-outs.

When the gun goes off to start a multisport race, you know you are in for a long effort. It takes serious commitment to training to be among the best in this sport.

If you are a junior, you are undoubtedly serious about multisport, since you have gone so far as to buy and read this book. That in itself is quite an accomplishment. You're probably wondering whether everything you have read so far applies to you. With some exceptions, it does. Let's examine the details of training for juniors.

HOW TO IMPROVE QUICKLY

The best way to advance in multisport, just as with school sports, is by working with a coach, especially one who lives close by. A good coach will help you progress by offering tips on technique, nutrition, race strategy, and sports psychology. These are all things you would undoubtedly figure out for yourself eventually, but a coach will speed up the learning process. He or she will also design a training program that fits your personal needs. This is an important benefit of having a coach, since triathlon and duathlon are individual, not team, sports. With a coach you will also develop more quickly because there will be fewer setbacks due to injury, burnout, or overtraining.

Another way to speed up your progress is by attending a multisport camp for juniors. USA Triathlon (USAT), the governing body of the sport in the United States, sponsors junior camps in different parts of the country staffed by top-level coaches and athletes. You will learn a lot about training, nutrition, technique, and racing by attending one of them during your school's summer vacation. If you are concerned about the expense of attending such a camp, look into the scholarships available through USAT. (For more information on the camps and scholarships, contact USAT at 719-597-9090 or visit www.usatriathlon.org.)

Triathlon clubs are also beneficial because they can provide juniors with support, expertise, racing experience, and the camaraderie of other juniors. Join a club if there is one in your region. Then ask the club to include juniors events at their sponsored races, if they don't already do so. They could add an extra wave with little difficulty. Sprint-distance races are best for older juniors (17–19), and even shorter distances can be arranged for younger juniors. USAT can provide guidance for your club in setting up such events.

On a slightly different note, you and your parents have probably come to realize that multisport is an expensive sport, with bike equipment leading the list of costly items. Don't be concerned with having the latest and greatest frame, wheels, and pedal system. Instead, concentrate on becoming the best motor and the most skilled rider in your group. When it's time to replace a bike you have outgrown, talk with older juniors about purchasing a bike they have outgrown. In the same way, see if younger athletes can use your old bike. Regardless of what you may read in the magazines or hear your friends say, the key to improvement is not equipment, but fitness.

TRAINING GUIDELINES

In 1996, Dr. Randy Wilber and his associates at the Olympic Training Center in Colorado Springs, Colorado, studied the physiologies of the U.S. junior triathlon team members. What they found was that these athletes were relatively weaker on the bike than they were in the swim or run. Especially noteworthy was that they became anaerobic on the bike at a relatively low 76 percent of their VO_2max for cycling, on average, while in swimming they went anaerobic at 83 percent, and in running at an outstanding 89 (girls) to 91 (boys) percent of VO_2max. This discrepancy was probably the result of the availability of programs in swimming and running at their schools. Schools simply do not have programs in cycling, unless it is a very brief program in bicycle safety. People tend to get good at what they work on, and the VO_2max scores reflected that principle. Fitness for one or even two sports does not "rub off" in another sport. No matter how good you are, there is always room for improvement somewhere. Your weakest sport is what you need to focus on when it's time to begin specializing in multisport.

Juniors under the age of 15 probably should not specialize in triathlon or duathlon. The best training at this age involves participating in your school's swimming and running programs and riding your bike in the summer. At about age 15, you may begin doing triathlon-specific workouts such as "bricks" (see Appendix E). You may also begin racing more frequently at this time. Until then, play a variety of sports. Swim, bike, and run, but also participate in team sports such as soccer and volleyball. Develop your sports skills and have fun.

When you begin serious multisport training, it's still a good idea to keep things in perspective. Remember that you are not yet an accomplished athlete; there is a lot of room for improvement, and steady progression is necessary if you are to eventually achieve your potential. Cyle Sage, a professional triathlete and coach to many juniors, offers the following tips to juniors and their coaches for maintaining a healthy perspective and steady growth.

Skills Before Fitness

Develop good technique before increasing mileage. Efficient and effective form ultimately means faster race times and less training time lost to injuries. Exercise caution with volume increases, as high mileage is more likely than high intensity to cause breakdowns from injury and burnout.

Be Patient

For juniors, the most important thing about racing is just the fact that you are participating. Just by going through the experience, you will be learning race strategy, especially pacing. Think of races as hard workouts where you get to observe and learn from more experienced athletes. The best adult athletes were seldom the best as juniors, and in fact, most were not even close to being the best. For example, did you know that Michael Jordan was cut from his junior-high-school basketball team?

Think Long Term

Rather than simply trying to beat other athletes in every workout and race, develop long-term, personal-improvement goals that focus on advancing to the next level of racing. Such a goal might be to run 10 km in less than 40 minutes by the time you turn 17, for example. Make realistic goals for each sport and begin working steadily toward them. This takes the pressure off of you to always be the best at the next race and allows you to focus on what is really important—steady progress.

Speed Before Endurance

Develop speed with drills and short, race-paced efforts, such as running strides (see Appendix D). These exercises will train your nervous system and muscles to develop more efficient and effective patterns of movement. Short, fast efforts done frequently are better for you now than long, slow endurance workouts are.

Form Before Weight

Improve total-body strength by doing light weight workouts in the gym. Stay with the Anatomical Adaptation (AA) weight phase (see Chapter 13) until you are 17. Concentrate more on perfecting form than on the amount of weight lifted. If you begin weight training at age 17, spend the first year doing only AA workouts. Be sure to include hip-extension work (leg press, squat) to strengthen these important large muscles.

Get a Physical

Before the start of each season, get a complete physical examination by your doctor. This is something even the pros do, and it will allow you and your coach, if you have one, to feel good about starting the year with a clean bill of health. If your school requires a physical to participate in sports, you can check this off.

Have Fun

Always remember why you race. It certainly isn't for money or to get dates. You are probably doing multisport for the personal challenge, for the enjoyment of having exceptional fitness, and, most of all, for fun. Keep that perspective. Learn to laugh at yourself, to accept your successes with humility, and to learn from your mistakes without complaining or offering excuses.

NOVICES

In the 1980s, multisport drew nearly all of its participants from injured runners, bored swimmers, and cyclists looking to expand their horizons. Today, people often come into the sport with no background at all in swimming, cycling, or running. This new breed of triathletes and duathletes is attracted by the challenge of combining two or three sports into one event, by the obvious fitness benefits of crosstraining, or simply by the lure of the sport after seeing a race such as the Hawaii Ironman on television.

Whatever your reason for accepting the challenge of multisport, it's important that you know the ingredients for success, especially those that are central to the sport. As with all sports, success in duathlon and triathlon, no matter how it's measured, is only as great as your preparation. Training must steel you to the specific demands of the goal event. For example, a hilly course requires training in the hills, and long races demand great aerobic endurance. In fact, endurance is the single most important requirement of the sport regardless of the race. If you can't go the distance, nothing else matters.

TRAINING TO GO THE DISTANCE

If pressed, most multisport athletes will admit that they like training more than racing. Races are merely the carrot on the stick that gets them out of bed at 5 A.M. for a swim, and into their running shoes as soon as they get home from work. Without races there would be no feeling of necessity or sense of urgency about workouts. Races give a focus and direction to training. Workouts, however, are the fun part. That's when you can drop all of the cares of the day and concerns for tomorrow, while living strictly in the present. Swimming, cycling, and running reduce life to its most basic elements—breathing and movement.

Workouts are also times when you may get together with training partners who share common interests. Having a group to train with makes the effort seem easier and boosts motivation. And there will certainly be times when motivation wanes. Even the best in the sport find that their desire to work out has highs and lows. This is not a sign of weakness, and may even have self-protection benefits, such as ensuring recovery. But missing too many workouts because of low enthusiasm means the erosion of fitness and race performance. It is at such times that training partners are beneficial. Find other individuals who are at a similar level of development for each sport, and schedule your week so you can regularly join them.

It is also possible to have too much motivation when you are new to the sport, and this is something that you must be careful to avoid. Compulsive training is likely to prevent you from achieving your goals. Working out excessively leads only to injury, illness, and overtraining—not to superior fitness. In Chapter 1 I presented an argument for training with moderation in a sport that appears, at least on the surface, to encourage extremes. Extreme training will not get you to the top echelons of the sport. At no time in your multisport career is a conservative approach to training more critical than in the early stages of your fitness development. Training with excessive volume and intensity at this time can only be counterproductive.

So how do you determine what is appropriate? Here are some tips that may provide guidance in your first year of multisport training.

Volume

Are there externally imposed limits on the amount of time you have available to train? For example, if you realistically examine your workday and all other daily commitments, you may find it possible to fit in only one hour a day for swimming, biking, or running. Perhaps you have even less free time. The weekends may then be the best time for longer workouts. Remember that winter brings fewer daylight hours and foul weather, further reducing training time.

Add up your available weekly hours using a conservative estimate, and multiply by 50 to find your projected annual training volume. By using 50 instead of 52, you are assuming that two weeks will be lost during the year to unavoidable illness, travel, or other commitments. The number you come up with includes all training time in addition to swimming, cycling, and running, such as weight lifting, cross-country skiing, and any other crosstraining. Round your annual hours off to the closest 50 hours.

Then go to Table 7.2 to find a suggested periodization plan for your volume. You may find that it is necessary to slightly increase the lighter training weeks or decrease the high-volume weeks on this table, if your restrictions are imposed more by available time than by your physical capacity for training and recovery. Remember that this table is merely a suggested guideline, not a requirement.

Periodization

In your first year of multisport, it's best to train primarily in the Transition and Base periods, as described in Chapters 3 and 7. This means you will focus on the development of aerobic endurance, force, technique (speed skills), and muscular endurance. These are the most important and basic components of triathlon and duathlon fitness and will take a year, possibly more, to hone. There is no reason to build power and anaerobic endurance, the other fitness components, before the basics are well established. If you have prior and recent experience in any of the three sports, you may make an exception for that sport. For example, if you have been running for several years, you may include high-intensity power and anaerobic endurance workouts in running, along with a complete periodization program in that sport. You would still limit your swimming and cycling workouts to the Transition- and Base-period guidelines.

Weekly Routines

There are endless possibilities for organizing your training week. Your training schedule will depend on the amount of time available for training; your work schedule; your prior experience in one or more of the sports; your ability to recover; your commitment to established group workouts (for example, when your masters swim team meets); the times when a pool or weight room is open; and numerous individual lifestyle issues. There is no standard way to arrange the week's workouts. Most new triathletes and duathletes find, however, that doing one workout a day and alternating the sports every three days, plus a weekly day off, produces good results. Such a pattern is illustrated in Table 14.2. This pattern provides adequate weekly time in each sport to create enough fitness to complete a sprint-distance or even an Olympic-distance race.

TABLE 14.2

Novice Training Schedule: One Workout per Day

	MON	TUE	WED	THUR	FRI	SAT	SUN
Triathlon	Swim	Bike	Run	Off	Swim	Bike	Run
Duathlon	Run	Bike	Run	Bike	Off	Run	Bike

Devoting a little more time to training each week, as suggested in Table 14.3, may produce better results. When doing two workouts in a day, you probably need at least 30 minutes in each workout to get a physiological benefit. Two very short workouts, unless they are put together into a combined workout (see Appendix E), have limited fitness value. Always remember that more workouts or training time is not always better, and may even result in setbacks due to injury.

TABLE 14.3

Novice Training Schedule: Some Two-a-Day Workouts

	MON	TUE	WED	THUR	FRI	SAT	SUN
Triathlon	Swim / Bike	Run	Swim / Bike	Off	Swim / Run	Bike	Run
Duathlon	Bike	Run / Bike	Run / Bike	Run / Bike	Off	Run	Bike

Weights

If you have only a few hours to train each week and it is difficult to fit everything in, weight workouts are the first ones to omit so that you may concentrate available time on swimming, biking, and running. Your greatest need at this stage of training is aerobic fitness. If you have time for the gym, and weight training doesn't compromise your sport-specific training, use only the Anatomical Adaptation (AA) phase (see Chapter 13). Concentrate on perfecting your technique with light weights. You will probably be surprised at how strong you become by doing just this. In the second full year of weight training, you can introduce the other strength building phases.

YOUR FIRST RACE

Several weeks or months prior to your first race, you began building fitness with short, slow workouts, and you gradually progressed to longer sessions at low effort mixed with shorter workouts at somewhat higher effort. In the first year, you will probably find that there isn't much speed variance between these effort levels. Your purpose in this early stage of training is to develop enough fitness to comfortably go the distance in each sport. In the last two to three weeks before your first race, your workouts should become increasingly specific to the event. This is the time to include combined workouts to prepare you for the exact demands of the race. These might include swim-bike, bike-run, and swim-bike-run workouts for a triathlon, and run-bike, bike-run, and run-bike-run workouts for a duathlon. In the last two or three weeks, you may reduce the training volume by 20 to 30 percent weekly to allow for the slightly higher efforts and stresses of these combined workouts.

It's wise to estimate how long you expect to take to finish the race, including each part of it. This estimate can guide you in determining the length of your longest single-sport workouts. You do not, however, need a goal time for your first race. The objective of this race is simply to finish comfortably with a smile on your face. Once you accomplish that challenge, and know what your capabilities are, you can begin to aim higher, setting realistic time goals for the next race. Every time you race, you will learn something that makes you a wiser, and ultimately more fit, athlete.

As with any sport, it's important to know the rules of multisport before competing. The essential rules of the sport are obvious: Proceed in order through the three legs of the event from start to finish. Along the course, however, there are a number of issues that may arise to cause a penalty or even disqualification. The three most common occur in the cycling leg. These rules are almost always discussed at the pre-race meeting. Let's quickly go over them.

When you are on the bike, including in the transition area if you are allowed to ride there, your helmet must be on *and buckled at all times.* In the excitement of the race, athletes will sometimes forget to buckle the helmet before mounting the bike, or will unbuckle it just before getting off. You may be penalized for this safety violation. Get into the habit of putting on and buckling your helmet first, and taking it off in the transition area only after you have dismounted.

Another common rule violation has to do with drafting on the bike. For an amateur triathlete it is illegal to ride behind or to the side of another rider in order to gain an advantage. The way to avoid this is to picture each bike rider within a box that extends 7 meters behind the leading edge of the front wheel and 1 meter to either side. Once you enter that space you have only a few seconds to pass or fall back. Lingering in that box may result in a penalty. Related to this rule is another called "blocking." When being overtaken by another rider, if you position your bike so as to impede his or her progress, you are blocking. The way to avoid this is to stay to the right side of the road at all times, and to pass on the left.

Race Week

In the final four to five days before the race, greatly reduce your training time while increasing your resting time. The tendency of new triathletes and duathletes is to "test" themselves in the last few days to make sure they are capable of going the distance. This is a sure way to ruin your first race. Trust your training, and take the time to rest.

Eat normally throughout this week, including the night before, by sticking with foods that are known to suit you. Don't experiment with unusual foods or supplements of any type. The time to experiment is in training several weeks before the race. When it comes to what we put in our stomachs, there is a lot of individual variation in tolerance and benefits. Use only what is known to work for you.

The day before the race, pick up the packet that includes your numbers and other information and attend the pre-race meeting. If possible, drive the bike and run courses by car to become familiar with the hills, road surfaces, and turns. Although it is unlikely that you will get off course, it has happened. The responsibility for knowing where to go is yours.

Race Morning

The morning of the race, eat a light breakfast at least two hours before you are supposed to start. Easily digested, low- to moderate-glycemic-index carbohydrate is probably best for this meal (see Chapter 16). Whatever you eat, it should be something you have previously tried with good results before a morning workout. Again, don't experiment on race morning.

Plan to arrive at the race an hour or so before the start to allow ample time for preparation. You will need to have your number marked on your body, pump up your tires, arrange everything you will need in the transition area, use the toilet several times, and warm up.

Race Site

Look around to see how others have arranged their transition stalls. Also notice exactly where your transition stall is in relation to the finish of the swim (triathlon) or first run leg (duathlon). If you are unsure where the first leg finishes, ask an official. Pick out easily identifiable landmarks to help guide you to your bike and equipment. When arranging items in your transition stall, keep in mind that good organization can shave minutes off your time. In fact, you can streamline and practice your transition routine in the weeks leading up to a race.

Keep the warm-up short. Ride just enough to make sure the bike is working well. Then, for a triathlon, swim for a few minutes, unless the water is cold. In that case, a short run and some upper-body exercises, such as a few push-ups and stretches, will have to do. You don't want to become hypothermic before starting. For a duathlon, run for a few minutes before the start.

Race Start

When your age-group wave is called to the starting line for an open-water-swim triathlon, line up to the side or at the back of the group. Staying away from the front and middle of the pack will help you avoid most of the turmoil at the start. In the middle of the group, it's not unusual to have goggles knocked off and athletes swimming over you. This is best avoided in your first race.

For a run-start duathlon, line up within your group based on the pace you expect to run. The fastest runners, those who will run in about the 6-minute range or faster, are in the front rows. The back rows are the slowest runners, those anticipating a 9-minute-or-so pace. Position yourself accordingly.

Your pace for the first few minutes of the race is critical to achieving your goal of finishing comfortably. The tendency is to go out considerably faster than you can maintain, and in the process build up a lot of lactic acid in your muscles and blood. This will come back to haunt you later in the race, severely slowing your pace. Continually remind yourself to start slowly regardless of what the others are doing.

Besides finishing the race, you also want to learn as much as you can about your new sport. The way to do this is to watch and listen throughout the day. Observe what the other racers do to warm up, how they start, what they do in the transition area, how they mount their bikes, what happens at the aid stations, how the course marshals direct you, and what you are instructed to do at the finish. Talk with other athletes and ask questions after the race. The more you learn in this first race, the faster you will progress in the sport.

Most of all, have fun! Don't take yourself or your results too seriously. Keep in mind why you are racing. You are not a pro attempting to make a living from the sport; you are doing this for enjoyment, health, and fitness, to challenge yourself physically and mentally, or some other personal reason.

In the days after the race, evaluate how you did and think about how you can improve your performance. Perhaps you started too fast, or your transitions were slow, or you didn't drink enough on the bike. You now have a good understanding of what it takes to do a triathlon or duathlon and can begin preparing for the next one with higher goals in mind.

ELITE ATHLETES

Elite endurance athletes are unique and gifted individuals. They have an amazing capacity for physical work and are blessed with an ability to improve fitness quickly as a result of this capacity. Most have an extreme work ethic that borders on obsession. In addition, they are highly motivated and dedicated to training and reaching their goals, which causes them to persevere through the most demanding workouts and extraordinary environmental conditions. It is because of such qualities, combined with genetic luck, that they have risen to the top one-tenth of 1 percent in sport.

These same physical and psychological talents, however, are also their worst enemies. It is not uncommon for elite athletes, especially those relatively new to the elite ranks, to drive themselves into an overtrained state with frequent regularity. Many never realize their full potential and soon leave the sport disheartened because their overzealous and unbridled training methods have led to burnout. This section explores how the elite multisport athlete can avoid this fate and steadily progress toward his or her innate fitness peak.

COACHING

For many, perhaps most, elite triathletes and duathletes, the best way to ensure steady growth and racing success is to train under the guidance of a knowledgeable and experienced coach. A coach with a good understanding of the scientific aspects of the sport interprets and applies the latest concepts and methods to meet the unique needs of the elite competitor. And by planning and managing training from a more objective point of view than the athlete can achieve, the wise coach counsels and directs the athlete's racing career toward the accomplishment of personal goals and dreams.

A good coach offers many skills and services above and beyond training design and implementation. He or she also helps the athlete clearly define goals and objectives, maintain a vision of the future, and cope with unusual psychological stress. The coach provides a sympathetic ear for concerns ranging from financial woes to interpersonal relationship problems. A coach with an extensive network of contacts may recruit others whose unique skills and services can assist with the athlete's development, such as doctors and other health-care providers, exercise physiologists, physical therapists, nutritionists, bike mechanics, and sports psychologists.

Two (or more) heads are better than one. When new challenges arise, as they often do, an experienced coach may offer fresh views on dealing with them. He or she often has a gut-level solution based on years of experience that might never have occurred to you. In addition, a good coach may even anticipate problems before they appear, and correct your course to avoid them altogether.

Having a coach in your corner lightens the burden of training and can transform your career from an often frustrating and solitary pursuit into a team effort. All of this means that you are able to put your entire energy and time into what you are already good at—training.

TRAINING

It's obvious that in order to compete in multisport, an athlete must work hard. The typical emerging elite athlete's approach is to always strive to do more—more volume, more intensity, or both, with the latter being the usual choice. However, coupling this approach with inadequate rest is an inevitable path to breakdown from illness, injury, or, most likely, overtraining. While at this level limited training is problematic, elite athletes must avoid overtraining at all costs.

The leading cause of overtraining is inadequate recovery time. The smart athlete knows how to balance the stresses of training with rest to promote gains in strength and speed. The second most common factor in overtraining among elite competitors is excessive volume. Increasing workout frequency and duration is a more probable cause of overtraining than excessive intensity in the absence of high volume. Periodization, as discussed in several previous chapters, is the best way to avoid overtraining, since a good periodization plan schedules rest, volume increases, and gradual step-ups of intensity in relation to the highest-priority races.

Other lifestyle factors can also contribute to overtraining in the elite athlete. These include poor diet, the demands of social and family life, occupational and academic demands, travel, and financial stresses. Notable on this list, and easily controlled, is poor diet, especially one dangerously low in protein and high in sugar (see Chapter 16). A less well-understood, psychological cause may be simply the monotony of training when an athlete grows tired of doing the same workouts day after day, week after week.

The mix of stresses and the impact they have in any given athlete's life are obviously highly individual matters. Just because a training partner easily handles a certain mix of physical and psychological stresses doesn't mean that you can. If you think you may be close to burnout because of too many stress factors in your life, it's important to reconsider your lifestyle and training. If possible, get some advice from a sports psychologist to figure out how to reduce the amount of stress. The solution may be just to bring your recovery practices into better alignment with the recommendations in this book and your own individual needs.

When you suspect overtraining, you must also consider whether other health factors may be at stake. Before deciding how to rectify the situation, get a full check-up with your physician and examine your diet objectively. Always maintain a close working relationship with your health-care provider or a full-service testing facility so that if your health changes in any way, your provider can assess them adequately. Every elite athlete should have a baseline blood test done during the winter months when his or her health and training status are known to be normal. This baseline test can be compared to later tests if you experience any problems, providing valuable information.

On the positive side, there are several training techniques that can lead to competitive racing form. The following are those that pertain strictly to the elite multisport athlete.

Multiple Daily Training Sessions

The athlete who wins the race is not always the one who trains with the most volume, yet many elite multisport competitors seem to approach training with such a belief. Peak race performance, however, always results from finding the optimal balance between workout stress and rest. At this level, training volume is not determined merely by how much time you have available, but rather by what it is you hope to achieve and how quickly recovery occurs. More is not always better. The athlete who is hungry to win and physically fresh as a result of being properly trained or even slightly undertrained will almost always beat another who is mentally and physically fatigued from chronic overreaching.

That said, it is also obvious that the best endurance athletes in the world typically employ a relatively high volume of training made up of multiple daily workouts. Training three or even four times a day is common among elite multisport athletes, although not universal. It's difficult to compete at the highest levels with a regimen limited to three or four swims, rides, and runs in a week for extended periods. This amount of training is even less adequate for the aspect of the sport that is your limiter. It may easily take five or six weekly sessions in your weakest sport to ensure achieving a level of performance on par with the competition. If weight training is a part of your training mix, this means seventeen to twenty sessions a week, averaging three to four a day. Although this may sound like a lot, it is the amount that is usually necessary to be competitive at the highest level of the sport.

How you ration the duration and intensity of those multiple daily sessions is critical to how steadily you improve and how well you avoid overtraining. The following are general guidelines for providing balance in a week of hard training. These do not apply to recovery weeks or to Peak-, Race-, or Transition-period weeks, all times in which optimal recovery is emphasized.

Breakthrough Workouts. Plan only one or two high-stress, breakthrough (BT) workouts (force, muscular endurance, anaerobic endurance, and power) per week for two of the three sports, but include two in the sport that is your limiter. This will result in four to six BT sessions each week.

You may find that grouping the BT sessions into two consecutive days, followed by at least one day of low-intensity training before the next two-day grouping, allows adequate stress and recovery. For example, the four to six high-stress workouts may be planned in a Wednesday-Thursday-Saturday-Sunday pattern, thus providing recovery on Friday, Monday, and Tuesday.

Aerobic Endurance Workouts. Include one or two aerobic endurance workouts in each sport weekly, as this is the most basic and necessary component of multisport competition. These workouts are best completed at a low level of intensity (zones 1 and 2) to allow for recovery prior to the next BT session.

Technique. Continue to refine your technique with weekly speed sessions in each sport. Doing swimming or cycling drills or running strides would be the focus at these times.

Ability Workouts. To make the best use of your time, you can combine two ability-related workouts into a single session. For example, in the Base periods, you can develop your bike force and endurance by doing a long ride on a hilly course. Or you could combine running anaerobic endurance and muscular endurance workouts into one session by doing anaerobic intervals followed by a threshold run. When combining abilities within a training session, the higher-intensity workout comes first and is followed by the more endurance-based workout.

Active Recovery. The primary purpose of all other sessions is active recovery. These sessions may include, for example, going for an easy spin on the bike or a relaxing swim. Active recovery is probably a better way for the elite athlete to recuperate than complete rest, as restoration is encouraged by the increased inflow of blood because it contains amino acids, glucose, hormones, and other components. Some elites, however, may find that a regular day off is necessary for psychological recovery. In any case, days when you are training at a low intensity must be seen as days when you are getting stronger, not as "wasted" workouts.

Table 14.4 provides an example of a week following these guidelines for an elite triathlete in the Base 3 period. The sessions are numbered each day to suggest an order that places stress earlier in the day. The easier sessions later in the day encourage recovery. When there are two or more BT sessions on a given day, a meal and rest separating them will bring the best results. A between-workout nap will further enhance the adaptive process. Realize that Table 14.4 offers just one way to arrange these sessions. There are many other options that are equally effective.

TABLE 14.4

Example of an Elite Triathlete's Base 3 Week

	MON	TUE	WED	THUR	FRI	SAT	SUN
Swim		2-Speed drills	2-Muscular endurance	3-Active recovery	2-Speed drills	2-Endurance	2-Active recovery
Bike	3-Endurance	3-Active recovery	3-Speed drills	1-Endurance & force		3-Speed drills	1-Muscular endurance
Run	1-Speed drills	1-Endurance	1-Muscular endurance	2-Active recovery	1-Speed drills	1-Endurance & force	
Weights	2-ME Phase						

Note: See Appendices B, C, and D for workout options for these session categories. Numbers indicate suggested workout order for a given day.

"Crash" Training

As I explained in Chapter 3, after a training stress is applied and the body is allowed to recover, fitness soon develops to a level somewhat higher than originally enjoyed. This process is known as "overcompensation." Recent studies show that when the training stresses are closely spaced for an extended period, followed by a long rejuvenation phase, the level of overcompensation is enhanced. This is known as "supercompensation." Such a risky flirtation with overtraining is sometimes called "crashing"—a descriptive if somewhat ominous name.

Two studies in the early 1990s explored supercompensation resulting from crash cycles. In 1992 a group of seven Dutch cyclists crashed for two weeks by increasing their training volume from a normal 12.5 hours per week to 17.5. At the same time, their intense training went from 24 to 63 percent of total training time. The immediate effect was a drop in all aspects of their fitness. But after two weeks of recovering, they realized a 6 percent improvement in power. In addition, their time trials improved by an average of 4 percent, and they produced less blood lactate at top speed compared with pre-crash levels. Not bad for two weeks of hard training.

A similar study in Dallas put runners through a two-week crash cycle with results similar to those of the Dutch study, and there was also an increase in aerobic capacities. Again, it took two weeks following the crash cycle for the test subjects to realize the gains. Further research suggests that a high-stress crash period and the ensuing supercompensation can result in an increase in blood volume, greater levels of hormones that cause muscle growth, and an improved ability to metabolize fat.

From the findings of these and other studies we can make three generalizations to guide a elite multisport athlete designing a crash cycle. The first is that, since it takes only about three weeks to produce overtraining in young, well-trained athletes, one must be careful not to make crash cycles too long, and they should probably be far shorter than that. In a study of elite rowers preparing for the world championship, three hours of daily training for three weeks produced overtraining. Second, large volume increases are generally not as effective as dramatic increases in intensity at producing supercompensation. One set of researchers doubled the weekly mileage of a group of well-trained runners for three weeks, and at another time doubled the number of miles that they ran at high intensity for three weeks. Following the high-volume phase, the endurance and running performance of the test subjects plateaued, but it improved following the increased-intensity period. Finally, studies report that it takes one-half to a full day of active recovery for every day spent crashing to realize the gains. Short crash cycles of, for example, five to seven days are best followed by an equal number of recovery days. Longer crash cycles, in the neighborhood of fourteen to twenty-one days, may be matched with fewer recovery days, about one-half day for every day of crashing.

Table 14.5 provides an example of a crash cycle for a triathlete. Bear in mind that this is only one way in which a crash cycle may be organized.

Be careful with crashing. The risk of overtraining rises dramatically during such a buildup. It's important that your fitness base (aerobic endurance, force, speed skills, and muscular endurance) is well established before attempting a crash cycle. If the typical signs of overtraining appear, such as a greatly changed resting heart rate or feelings of depression, cut back on the workload immediately. It is probably best not to attempt more than one crash cycle for each racing peak in the season. In addition, the last crash workout should probably be no closer to the goal race than two weeks.

TABLE 14.5

Five-Day "Crash" Cycle for an Elite Triathlete

		MON	TUE	WED	THUR	FRI	SAT	SUN
"CRASH" WEEK	Swim		2-Speed	1-Anaerobic endurance	3-Active recovery	2-Muscular endurance	1-Anaerobic endurance	Off
	Bike	2-Active recovery	1-Endurance	2-Muscular endurance	1-Anaerobic endurance	3-Active recovery	2-Muscular endurance	Off
	Run	1-Endurance			3-Active recovery	2-Muscular endurance	1-Anaerobic endurance	Off
RECOVERY WEEK	Swim	Off	2-Active recovery		2-Active recovery		2-Endurance	2-Active recovery
	Bike	Off	1-Active recovery	2-Active recovery		2-Active recovery	1-Endurance	
	Run	Off		1-Active recovery	1-Active recovery	1-Active recovery		1-Endurance

Note: See Appendices B, C, and D for workout options for these session categories. Numbers indicate suggested workout order for a given day.

Draft-Legal Training

The advent of draft-legal races is changing the way elite multisport athletes train. Preparation for these events differs from preparation for nondrafting races in several ways. The obvious difference is the increased importance of the ability to swim and run fast in the drafting format. If you are not among the leaders out of the water in a draft-legal event, the race may well be over for you, since you will miss getting in the draft with the top athletes. Moreover, following the cycling portion, several athletes will enter the second transition at the same time, which will mean that running performance will decide the race.

This doesn't mean that the bike leg in a draft-legal race is unimportant. It merely changes the emphasis of the total training volume slightly in the three sports and the manner in which the bike training is done. Also changed is the bike design and set-up. Instead of large seat-tube angles and long top tubes, criterium-style, draft-legal races favor bikes that are shorter, with small seat-tube angles. Such frames are rigid and responsive to match the demands of the faster pace and quicker speed changes of these events. The bike is adjusted in ways that make it more like the set-up that bicycle road racers use, with the saddle aft so that a plumb line dropped from the front of the knee (instead of the side of the knee, as for time trialing) intersects the pedal spindle. This allows the application of force to the pedal earlier in the downstroke than in a typical saddle-forward time trial set-up, in effect increasing the time per pedal stroke in which force is applied. It also improves your ability to pedal at a high cadence, which is beneficial when the pack's speed changes abruptly.

As for training, draft-legal racing requires frequent training with groups, especially in the Build and Peak periods, so that you can gain confidence when riding in a pack and improve your handling skills. If you are planning to race in a draft-legal event, it would be a good idea for you to ride with road racers on their weekly club rides. Many cycling clubs also hold weekly training races in the spring that they may allow you to enter without a USA Cycling license. Be careful, however, of criterium-style races held on courses with tight turns and large fields. The chances of a crash in such a race are high.

Draft-legal races also require an increased emphasis on anaerobic endurance and power. When you are in a small group chasing down a breakaway, or trying to stay away in a break, you must go deeply anaerobic and stay there for several minutes. The ability to tolerate high levels of lactate makes this possible. Also required is the ability to quickly produce power, especially on courses with many turns or short hills.

You also need to be able to time trial powerfully for short periods of time, such as 10 minutes, for those times when you come out of the water just behind the leaders and want to catch up with them. If, after about 10 minutes of chasing, you still haven't caught them, it's time to sit up and allow the pack to catch you. Your training should include such efforts to prepare you for these situations.

EXTENDING YOUR CAREER

Motivation is necessary for success at the highest level of sport, and it may determine who will place in the money on a given day. If you aren't mentally driven and absolutely in love with training and racing, there is little chance of a long and successful career in multisport. But high motivation is also a double-edged sword. Because of it, elite athletes will push through any formidable training session deemed important for producing faster races. This can lead to burnout, recurring injuries, and frequent overtraining. Such interruptions break patterns of training consistency and force a return to previous levels. Consistency is the single most important component for producing peak race fitness. Inconsistent training can result in poor race performances and even eventual abandonment of multisport. Promising careers sometimes end early when high motivation gets in the way of clear thinking.

Treat your body with respect—it's a fine instrument, not a blunt object. Avoid anything that has high risk and the potential to interfere with training stability. The starting point for optimal training and a long, successful career is paying close attention to recovery in order to balance stress. When rest is adequate, the problems of inconsistency diminish and you feel positive, confident, and eager to race.

Other than ensuring the timely inclusion of rest, the best way to prevent breakdown is to increase your training workload incrementally over a period of several weeks using a standard periodization scheme (see Chapters 3, 7, and 9). Sudden large increases in volume or intensity, such as the increases seen in crash training, must have predetermined time limits, and the body's responses must be carefully monitored when they are in progress. At the first sign that something is not right, such as unusual joint discomfort or inability to recover, you must decrease your workload even if you have not yet achieved your training goals. To continue is to risk an even larger setback.

If you want to extend your career in multisport, it is important for you to think and plan for the long term. It's easy to get caught up in preparing only for the next race, regardless of how insignificant that event may be to your stated, long-term goals. The athlete with training myopia sees every race as having equal importance and tries to attain peak fitness levels for each. This is physiologically, and perhaps even psychologically, impossible. Know what is important for your career, not only for this season but for the next three or four years. If you want a berth on the Olympic team, or Ironman placement, think in terms of steady, continual improvement. Keep the long-term goals uppermost in your mind when designing your Annual Training Plan and weekly workout patterns. As discussed earlier, this is where a wise and experienced coach is of great value.

THE TRAINING DIARY

A well-kept training log and journal will serve as a window into the vaults of information and experiences you've accumulated through training and racing.

—RAY BROWNING

THIS BOOK EMPHASIZES planning and managing your race preparation instead of training by impulse, which is all too common among endurance athletes. This methodical approach to training requires a constant feedback of information for effective decision-making. A well-kept training diary meets that need. Without a record of your workouts and racing experiences, you must rely on memory, which all too often is spotty. Your recollections of what you did a year ago, last month, or even yesterday may be exaggerated or minimized depending on your prerogative—either way, it will be of little help in shaping your training.

A diary is especially helpful to the self-coached, time-constrained triathlete or duathlete who must make every hour of training count. It's also a source of information about what has or hasn't worked in the past, the progress you are making, the need for recovery, how your body responds to a given workout, and how much recovery is necessary following breakthrough workouts and races. The training diary motivates as it builds confidence whenever you review obstacles you have overcome, whether these obstacles have involved foul weather, difficult workouts, high workload weeks, or days you've worked out even though you didn't feel up to it. Your confidence grows when you write down your successes and remember them later on. Successful workouts, personal racing bests, and goals accomplished should all be recorded for later inspiration.

In its simplest form, the diary is a log of workouts, races, goals, objectives, and distances covered. But it can also provide an early warning system for illness and injury, which generally give advance notification, if you are paying attention. Tracing the origins of these setbacks to the circumstances that may have caused them can help you avoid these same problems in the future. A diary is also a planning tool. Use it to schedule your training weeks based on the Annual Training Plan from Chapters 7 and 8.

A diary is not an end in itself. If you write down workouts, but never use the data, the diary's full potential to help you achieve peak racing fitness is not realized. A well-kept diary that is used effectively can be a vehicle to lead you on a journey of personal discovery. It may show you why things aren't going well, or why they are. By paying attention to it, you learn how long it takes to get into race shape following a certain routine. The possibilities are endless. The diary can help you remember and analyze past performance; it can give you the information you need to modify your training, diet, and other components of your plan; it can motivate you and build your confidence; it can help you plan; and it can hold you accountable. All of this sounds surprisingly similar to what a good coach does.

But be aware that there are also downsides to the training diary. It's possible to record too much data and then spend more time analyzing the data than you did creating it in workouts. Another drawback is that some diary keepers seem to have the compulsion to use it as a "scorecard." For example, athletes have been known to realize on the last day of the week that they are a few minutes or miles short of their diary-planned weekly volume, and so they head out the door to accumulate the missing numbers. Avoid the compulsion to use your diary in this way.

Where should you record all of the data? The mode you choose is likely to determine how diligent you are with record keeping. If you enjoy technology and detailed analysis, a computer-based software diary may be just what you need. After years of athletes asking about this option, I finally created one at www.TrainingPeaks.com. But if you don't think you will boot up the computer immediately following a workout, then an electronic diary is not for you. Choose a standard paper format instead.

Many elite athletes prefer to use a simple notebook in which they may record anything they want without being forced into a mold by a standard layout. Others design their own by laying out basic pages, and then making copies, which are kept in a loose-leaf notebook.

Appendix F offers a format that follows the one suggested in this chapter. You may copy it for your own use. Or you can purchase the spiral-bound *Triathlete's Training Diary* based on this format from VeloPress (www.velopress.com). You'll also find in Appendix F a Race Evaluation form, which is yet another tool that can give you insight on the effectiveness of your training when reviewed alongside a training diary.

WHAT TO RECORD

How should you train? There is unlimited information available to help you answer this question; the sources include magazines, books, television programs, Web sites, computer programs, videotapes, advertisements, and even training partners. Given that you are an individual with unique needs, however, how do you know which training concepts to keep and which to discard? The best way is to do what any good scientist does with something suspected of holding promise—experiment and observe. In this study, however, you are the only subject. What works for you, or doesn't, is all that matters when it comes to deciding what workout to do, when to rest, what to eat, and how to handle the many other details that define training. Think of your diary as the place where the ongoing experiment is recorded and observed. The more systematic you are in collecting the data, the greater the chance that you will learn the answers to your questions.

Although data is required to train scientifically, writing down too much is just as bad as not recording enough. If you have to wade through every minute detail of every workout, you will have a difficult time drawing conclusions. Record only what is important, but include anything you think you are likely to study. Your diary should be simple and succinct, or you won't use it for very long.

The following five categories provide a general framework for collecting information that may help you make daily decisions and analyze what you need to improve: morning warnings, basic log entries, physical notes, mental notes, and miscellaneous notes. Don't feel you have to record all of this. Only keep track of those items that you can quickly write down after a workout, and that you are likely to use later on. Figure 15.1 is a sample diary that will help you follow along.

MORNING WARNINGS

Following the collapse of the Berlin Wall, one of the administrators of the East German Olympic sports program came to the United States and spoke about the accomplishments of the Eastern Bloc athletes. Although banned drugs had apparently played a role in their success, he explained how the individual attention given to each athlete had contributed to the medal count. Each athlete's day began with a visit by a staff of professionals and a quick evaluation of readiness to train. This included medical and psychological evaluations that guided the coaches in refining the day's training plan. The purpose was to have the athlete do only what was appropriate that day—nothing more or less.

Wouldn't it be nice if you had such professional guidance every day? Since it's unlikely to happen, the next best option is to learn to make these decisions for yourself. One way to do that is to start each day with a self-evaluation of your physical and mental readiness. Every morning when you wake up, there are clues to indicate whether you are up to the workouts for that day. The problem is that most amateur athletes don't listen to them.

According to an Australian study, certain kinds of daily log entries may help athletes pay close attention to the clues. The researchers found that rating sleep quality, fatigue, psychological stress, and muscle soreness on a scale of 1 to 7, with 1 representing the best condition and 7 the worst, was highly predictive of readiness to train. All scores are subjective, but if you are honest, a rating of 5, 6, or 7 for any of these warning signs means

298 WEEK BEGINNING: 9/15/08   PLANNED WEEKLY HOURS/MILES: 11:30

Swim—9000 meters
Bike—75 miles
Run—26 miles

FIGURE 15.1

Sample of a
Training Diary

NOTES

Mon—A little tired after
a good weekend. Quads
sore from hills Saturday.
Strength—SM Phase. Easy
on legs.

Tue—Lots of 100s in MS.
Most ~1:30. A bit tired.
Run—steady tempo on trail.
Felt good.

NOTES

Wed—Swim form. Drills and
steady pace.
Bike—climb up S. Mtn in
zone 4. Kept RPM high.
A bit tired.

Thurs—Swim MS was
5 x 300. All about 5:00.
Good! Run—3 x 1 mile at
6:25-6:35 with 200 m
recoveries. Negative split each
of them.

MONDAY 9/15/08

[2] Sleep [4] Fatigue [1] Stress [3] Soreness

Resting heart rate 49   Weight 152¼

WORKOUT 1 □S □B □R [X] Other: Wts

Weather 80° clear

Route Rec center

Distance

Time :45   Total :45

Time by zone 1   2

3   4   5

WORKOUT 2 □S □B □R □Other:

Weather

Route

Distance

Time   Total

Time by zone 1   2

3   4   5

TUESDAY 9/16/08

[1] Sleep [3] Fatigue [2] Stress [4] Soreness

Resting heart rate 47   Weight 152½

WORKOUT 1 [X]S □B □R □Other:

Weather 77° clear

Route Rec center

Distance 2800 meters

Time 1:07   Total 1:52

Time by zone 1   2

3   4   5

WORKOUT 2 □S □B [X]R □Other:

Weather 86° clear

Route Pima Park trail

Distance 7.32 miles

Time 1:01   Total 2:53

Time by zone 1 25:10   2 24:50

3 11:00   4   5

WEDNESDAY 9/17/08

[2] Sleep [4] Fatigue [2] Stress [3] Soreness

Resting heart rate 48   Weight 152

WORKOUT 1 [X]S □B □R □Other:

Weather 75° cloudy

Route Rec center

Distance 1500 meters

Time :32   Total 3:25

Time by zone 1   2

3   4   5

WORKOUT 2 □S [X]B □R □Other:

Weather 88° clear, windy

Route S. Mountain

Distance 23.8 miles

Time 1:32   Total 4:57

Time by zone 1 28:15   2 27:45

3 6:10   4 28:30   5 1:20

THURSDAY 9/18/08

[3] Sleep [3] Fatigue [1] Stress [2] Soreness

Resting heart rate 50   Weight 151¹¹⁄₄

WORKOUT 1 □S □B [X]R □Other:

Weather 76° clear

Route Rec center

Distance 3100 meters

Time :57   Total 5:54

Time by zone 1   2

3   4   5

WORKOUT 2 □S □B [X]R □Other:

Weather 82° clear, gusty

Route SCC Mountain

Distance 9.6 miles

Time 1:12   Total 7:06

Time by zone 1 26:33   2 20:00

3 6:12   4 18:00   5 1:15

WEEK'S GOALS (Check off as achieved)

☑ *Emphasis on run with quality workouts on Tuesday and Thursday.*

☑ *Very easy recovery days Friday and Saturday.*

☑ *Go under 2:19 at Soma Qauerterman.*

FRIDAY   9 / 19 / 08

☑2 Sleep ☑2 Fatigue ☑2 Stress ☑4 Soreness

Resting heart rate *50*   Weight *151½*

WORKOUT 1 ☐ S ☒ B ☐ R ☐ Other:

Weather *83° cloudy*

Route *Fruit Loop*

Distance *18.5*

Time *1:02*   Total *8:08*

Time by zone **1** *45:30*   **2** *16:22*

3   **4**   **5**

WORKOUT 2 ☐ S ☐ B ☐ R ☐ Other:

Weather

Route

Distance

Time   Total

Time by zone **1**   **2**

3   **4**   **5**

SATURDAY   9 / 20 / 08

☑1 Sleep ☑1 Fatigue ☑1 Stress ☑2 Soreness

Resting heart rate *48*   Weight *151¾*

WORKOUT 1 ☒ S ☐ B ☐ R ☐ Other:

Weather *70° clear*

Route *Tempe Town Lake*

Distance *~1000 meters*

Time *16:00*   Total *8:24*

Time by zone **1**   **2**

3   **4**   **5**

WORKOUT 2 ☐ S ☒ B ☒ R ☒ Other: *Brick*

Weather *77° clear*

Route *Soma course*

Distance *B—9.5 mile   R—2 miles*

Time *:46*   Total *9:09*

Time by zone **1** *B-7, R-2*   **2** *B-6, R-3*

3 *B-4, R-3* **4** *B-12, R-37* **5** *B-2*

NOTES

Fri—Rode very easy. Nice day. A little sore in calves. Mostly just tight.

Sat—Worked out on race course. Swam at 7 a.m. to see shore at race time. Did pick-ups on bike and run. Feeling good!

SUNDAY   9 / 21 / 08

☑4 Sleep ☑2 Fatigue ☑3 Stress ☑1 Soreness

Resting heart rate *54*   Weight *151¾*

WORKOUT 1 ☐ S ☐ B ☐ R ☒ Other: *Race*

Weather *71° clear*

Route *Soma Quarterman*

Distance *S—1500 / B—40 km / R—10 km*

Time *2:17*   Total *11:26*

Time by zone **1** *B-0, R-0*   **2** *B-:01, R-0*

3 *B-:06, R-:02* **4** *B-:48, R-:33* **5** *B-:08, R-:06*

WORKOUT 2 ☒ S ☒ B ☒ R ☐ Other:

Weather *71° clear*

Route *Warm up and cool down*

Distance *S-100 / B-2m / R-1m*

Time *:19*   Total *11:45*

Time by zone **1** *B-4, R-5*   **2** *B-2, R-2*

3 *B-1, R-2* **4**   **5**

WEEKLY SUMMARY

	Time/Distance	Year to Date
Swim	3:23/9000 m	118:26/297 km
Bike	4:15/78.8 mi	140:16/2,642 mi
Run	3:18/26.12 mi	108:50/862 mi
Strength	:45	39:36
Other	0	18:24
Total	11:41	425:32

Soreness

NOTES *The week went just as planned. A lot of rest on Friday and Saturday.*

NOTES

Sun—Won my age group. All times faster than last year. Consistent training is really working! See Race Evaluation form for details.

that something is wrong and that you should reconsider the workload for that day. Three or more such warning flags are signs that you need a day off.

Your waking pulse and body weight are also fairly reliable indicators of readiness. Find your average waking pulse during a week when you are healthy and well rested. Anytime your heart rate is five or more beats above this number, take that as a warning. Be aware that a slightly elevated heart rate, by itself, is not reason enough to change your training plan for the day. Since heart rate can vary considerably for a long list of reasons, look for other warning flags to corroborate it before making modifications.

Another warning sign is your body weight dropping 2 pounds or more in 24 hours. This can signal a diet that does not match your caloric needs or excessive training. Be sure to weigh yourself under the same conditions each day, such as just after waking and using the toilet, but before drinking anything or eating breakfast. Short-term weight loss is a measure of fluid levels, so if your weight is down a pound from the previous day, the first thing you should do is drink water. A pint of water weighs about one pound. A study done in Oregon found that afternoon weight loss is a good indicator of overtraining and may be the first indicator that is easy to measure. (Refer to Chapter 11 for greater detail on overtraining.)

Forces other than training may affect your warning signs. These could include, for example, travel, work stress, relationship issues, financial problems, heat, humidity, and home responsibilities. It makes no difference what causes the warning signs. The bottom line is the same: You must reduce the training workload on the days that the warning signs indicate a problem.

BASIC LOG ENTRIES

Your basic log entries should be brief and easy to record and analyze. Include the workout date, the course or venue, distance and time, weather conditions, time of day, equipment used, and training partners. Also make note of the quality indicators of the workout, such as interval times, wattage, pace, or vertical feet gained. Note anything unusual. This might be a knee that felt "funny," or a slight headache.

PHYSICAL NOTES

During workouts, pay close attention to how you feel, and later, translate your thoughts into a number on a scale of 1 to 10, with 1 meaning you felt great, and 10 that you felt terrible (in which case, you probably won't have finished the workout). Just as with the warning signs, such a rating keeps you in tune with your body.

Also record heart rate data from your monitor. This may be how many minutes you were in each training zone. As the season progresses from the Prep to the Base and Build periods, the higher zones, such as 3, 4, and 5, should make up increasingly greater percentages of your total weekly volume if you are training for short-course races. For longer races volume will increase in zones 2 and 3. Exactly what those percentages are varies a great deal from one athlete to another and from one type of goal event to another. This kind of personal data is ripe for analysis.

You may also want to include other intensity-related workout data, such as peak heart rate achieved, average heart rate, and how much the heart rate dropped in the minute following the end of the workout. If you have the equipment to do so, record average power, maximum power, and lactate levels.

Another simple way of measuring training intensity, especially in the Build period, is to set the upper end of the range for your heart rate monitor for your lactate threshold (LT) (bottom of zone 5a) for each sport, and the lower end for the top of zone 1. Then record how much time you spent above LT and how much time at low effort each day. At the end of the week, add them up by sport and you'll have a good idea how much anaerobic training you are doing and how much active recovery you are allowing. Again, there are no established standards for these categories, so you will want to discover what works best for you by experimenting.

Women should record their menstrual periods to help them get a clear picture of how their cycle affects training and racing.

MENTAL NOTES

Most athletes think of training as a strictly physical activity and ignore what's happening with the mind and emotions. But sometimes feelings are the most telling aspect of training. For example, low motivation, as evidenced by diary comments such as, "I didn't feel like working out today," may signal overreaching, an early stage of overtraining. Again, noting and paying attention to these sometimes hormonally-dependent emotions keeps you in tune with the inner workings of the body. Don't ignore them.

In addition to physical development, workouts should provide training for mental skills that are necessary for successful racing. For example, how good are you at staying focused during a race? Do you find your pace dropping as your mind wanders? If so, work on concentration. Key workouts that simulate race effort, such as intervals and threshold workouts, are great for staying in tune with what your body is doing by continually running physical "checklists." Confidence, relaxation, attitude, and visualization may also need development. Record your daily accomplishments in these areas in your diary.

MISCELLANEOUS NOTES

Other training and racing elements you may include in your diary from time to time are travel; environmental factors, such as altitude and humidity; work hours or other work-related stresses; weight-training records; and family activities, such as vacations that impact training. You could also add comments on gears used in climbing a local, challenging hill; race information, including strategy, results, field size, and conditions; or the effects of different types of pre-race meals. The possibilities are endless, and limited only by what you find possibly important to your "experiment."

PLANNING WITH A DIARY

It can also be quite effective to use your training diary as a planning tool, although this is seldom done. At the end of each week, decide what you need to accomplish in the next week to attain your goals, based on the objectives on your Annual Training Plan, and write these steps down as weekly goals in your diary. For example, you may set a goal of improving your cycling hill strength by climbing 10 more minutes this week than you did last week. Or perhaps one of your annual objectives is to take a minute off of your 10 km running time by a certain point in the season. To accomplish that you will need to improve the quality of certain workouts, so a weekly goal may be to complete a certain number of mile repeats at LT pace. The idea is that your weekly goals should continue to bring you closer to the training objectives that are necessary to accomplish your season, race-related goals.

Once you know what you need to accomplish in the upcoming week, decide on the supporting workouts and the days on which you will do them. Chapter 8 provides guidance in making these decisions so that your recovery will be adequate. In these planning notes you can use a shorthand system of your own making, or use the workout codes suggested in Appendices B, C, D, and E. For example, for a planned workout you might jot down, "Run, 45, F3," meaning you would run for 45 minutes doing workout F3 (hill repeats, as described in Appendix D). Then, just before starting the training session, you can flip to the scheduled workout in the proper appendix to review the details. Always keep in mind that once you start a workout, it may become necessary to change it, depending on how you feel. Overtraining and injury start with an inability to pay attention to the body and a willful disregard for the future. If your body is telling you to slow down, listen carefully.

At first, the planning for each day may take 20 to 30 minutes. But as you get into the routine, it will take only 10 minutes or so. As far as your progress goes, this is the most important 10 minutes you will spend each week. Such weekly planning will do more to improve your racing than anything else you do, other than working out, eating right, and sleeping well.

USING A DIARY FOR ANALYSIS

Now that you have recorded all of this information, what do you do with it? The answer depends on your situation and experiences. If you are having a problem of some sort, you will look into the diary to see how the problem developed. For example, you may be seeking the cause of an injury, determining why you are chronically tired, or trying to find the cause of a poor race performance. The situation needing analysis might be about planning. For example, you might want to figure out what has or hasn't worked in the past when you were attempting to peak at the right time for an important race. There is an endless array of situations that you may need to delve into using a diary as you pursue multisport excellence. Keep your entries brief so that your analysis doesn't require sifting through excess verbiage, but include enough information to be helpful.

TRAINING ANALYSIS

When problems occur, as they invariably do, it is imperative that you take action to minimize their impact on training and do whatever is necessary to ensure your return to normal workouts as soon as possible. Injuries, illnesses, and overtraining are the most common obstacles for the multisport athlete. The roots of these problems are often found in some combination of excesses in training and lifestyle. Knowing the mistakes you made that caused the setback can help you prevent the same pattern from developing again.

For some multisport athletes, managing injuries is a way of life. Running is the sport most likely to produce recurring problems. Training excess isn't always the culprit. Injuries are sometimes related to training in shoes that are breaking down, or from running in shoes that just aren't right for you. Modern running-shoe design is quite technical and aims to control certain foot movements and encourage others. If you don't have the biomechanical or structural tendency that a particular pair of shoes was designed for, the shoes may cause injury. Keeping a record of how you have used your shoes may help you make such determinations. For example, keeping track of how many miles or hours a pair of running shoes have accumulated can be valuable when it comes to deciding when to replace them in order to prevent injury.

In the same way, recording changes that you make in your bike set-up, especially in saddle position, may prove helpful if a few weeks later a knee flares up. Perhaps the changes you made were the cause of the problem. How much did you move the saddle up or down, or fore and aft? Have you ever had it in that position before and experienced anything like this with your knee? Are you able to put it back in the exact same position it was before? Or did something change with your training, such as more hills in a high gear, that might have led to a problem?

Sometimes there are simply nagging questions that beg for answers. Have you done enough training of certain abilities, such as force development? Are you allowing adequate recovery between workouts? What workout sequences produce the best results for you? What taper procedure seems to work? How did you do in this race two years ago? Looking back through your diaries for recent years often provides answers and new directions in training.

RACE ANALYSIS

Competitions are ripe for analysis. Why did your race not meet expectations? Was there any particular aspect of it that was especially strong or weak? How about pacing, hills, transitions, endurance, refueling, strategy, tactics, focus, and confidence? The answers to such questions often come from examining race results that indicate splits and group rankings and by comparing current results with previous performances on the same course. Take a close look at each race and write down your observations while they're still fresh in your mind. Figure 15.2 is a sample evaluation; you'll find the Race Evaluation form for your own use in Appendix F.

RACE EVALUATION FORM

Race name: *Soma Quarterman*

Date and start time: *9/21/08   7 a.m.*

Location: *Tempe*

Type/distance: *Olympic / S—1500 / B—40K / R—10K*

Key competitors: *Bob Smith, Sam Strout*

Weather: *71°   Clear at start, 82° at finish*

Course conditions: *S—Calm, B—Good roads, R—Flat and fast*

Race goal: *Go under 2:19*

Race strategy: *S—Steady, B—Zone 4, R—Zone 4 and move up*

Warm-up description: *10-min. run, 10-min. swim with short pick-ups to start.*

Start-line arousal level: Very low   Low   Moderate   (High)   Very high

Results (place, time, splits, etc.): *1st place age group! S—28:00, T1-:03, B-1:03, T2-:02, R-:41, Finish-2:17*

What I did well: *I followed race strategy exactly, and it worked!*

What I need to improve: *Need to go out faster at start of swim.*

Aches/pains afterward: *Calves tight and a bit sore.*
Massage therapy.

Other comments: *My training has gone very well for the last 6 weeks.*

FIGURE 15.2

Sample Race
Evaluation

Days on which you felt great, especially if they were race days, deserve special analysis. Examine the preceding days to determine what may have led to this high point. Perhaps it was a certain pattern of workouts, a period of rest, the elimination of some lifestyle stress, or a dietary change. In the same way, consider what was going on leading up to a particularly bad day. What may have caused this? If you can identify trends, you are one step closer to knowing the secret of what does and doesn't work for you. Reproducing the positive forces while minimizing the negative is valuable for race peaking.

ANALYSIS SOFTWARE

Computer software is now available to help you analyze the data you download from devices such as power meters, heart rate monitors, GPS devices, and accelerometers. The manufacturers of these training tools nearly always include such software with the purchase of the device. Some of these are quite basic but others are fairly complex.

The problem with most software that comes in the box with a new device is that it was designed by a company that may make excellent hardware but knows little about software. Unfortunately, the manufacturer also does not usually know what's important in training. Training analysis software designed by knowledgeable athletes in a software-focused company is usually better than what came in the box.

One of the best software analysis tools is called "WKO+" and is available online at TrainingPeaks.com. I admit I'm rather partial, as I've played a small role in its development and use it to analyze all of my clients' training and racing data. It's a powerful tool for the serious athlete and makes analysis simple for almost any training device you own. It's great for analyzing heart rate, power, and pacing data regardless of your device's manufacturer.

No matter what software you use, the key question you want answered has to do with your progress toward race goals—"Am I improving?" If the software doesn't help you figure this out easily, then it is useless. The software should be capable of performing several key functions:

- It should be able to track your time in each heart rate, power, and pace zone by workout and for the entire season.
- It should allow you to change your zones, especially in power and pacing, as your fitness changes.
- It should provide a way for you to quickly compare similar workouts.
- You should be able to record changes in pace or power relative to body weight.
- There should be an easy way to track improvements in workout pace or power for similar workouts.
- You should be able to track your capacity for handling greater training stress.
- It should be possible for you to use the data to gauge the level of fatigue you can manage without breaking down.
- A graphic or metric should be provided that shows how your fitness is progressing.
- There should be a way to determine when you are ready to race.

Even if you decide to use software to help you interpret your training data, it can still be incredibly useful to keep a diary. If the hard-copy approach provided here doesn't work for you, there are plenty of electronic formats that might suit you better. Regardless, a diary helps you see the big picture by keeping all the details in focus, both the hard data and the subjective feedback. When used effectively, it serves as an excellent tool for planning your steps, motivating you, and diagnosing your problems. It also provides a personal history of training and racing accomplishments. A well-kept diary ranks right up there with training, rest, and nutrition when it comes to developing a competitive edge.

FUEL

Some days you want broccoli, other days
Hostess Ding Dongs. Don't ask me why.
—SCOTT TINLEY

HOW AND WHAT should you eat to maximize performance now and for many healthy years to come? The possibilities are nearly endless—and endlessly confusing: the Zone diet, the South Beach diet, the Atkins diet, Dr. Phil's diet, the vegetarian diet . . . the list goes on and on. In fact, it seems that whenever you open the daily newspaper, you find that more nutrition research is making headlines, with the findings touted as major breakthroughs. The problem is, these studies are often contradictory.

Loren Cordain, professor of exercise and sport science at Colorado State University in Fort Collins, Colorado, believes that the answers are to be found in the distant past when Mother Nature shaped our ancestors with the hard facts of evolution. He points out that modern-day endurance athletes already have a lifestyle that closely replicates that of the Old Stone Age (Paleolithic) men and women of 10,000 to 120,000 years ago. His studies reveal that these prehistoric "athletes" probably burned more than 3,000 calories a day as they went about the many tasks of staying alive in a demanding environment. The men would often spend their days tracking and hunting animals at a steady clip, and then carry the carcasses back to camp. Cordain estimates that they may have often run and jogged 10 miles in one day—hauling about a 25-pound load for part of the trek. The women were also active, as they carried children while gathering vegetables and other foodstuffs. Life was hard, but they met the challenge.

Cordain, author of *The Paleo Diet,* points out that the genetic changes evolution brought still shape our dietary needs today, 2 million years after humans first appeared as a separate genus in the anthropological record. He believes that since evolution is a slow and steady process requiring tens, if not hundreds, of thousands of years to produce even small changes, our space-age bodies are still best adapted to the diet of our Stone Age ancestors. The foods our predecessors ate for millennia are still the optimal fuels, since we long ago developed the mechanics, chemistry, and gut to process them. So what did Paleolithic people eat?

By comparison with people today, Paleolithic people ate a simple diet consisting primarily of fruits, vegetables, and lean meats and organs from wild game. They supplemented these foods with nuts, seeds, berries, and eggs. There were no grains or dairy foods. Saturated fats were low. Products from very lean animals accounted for most of the calories, perhaps 40 to 50 percent, Cordain estimates. But these animals were not fattened on corn in feedlots or growth-enhanced with drugs, so the meat was far different from what we usually find in our local supermarket. Today, for example, a cut of USDA prime beef contains 560 percent more saturated fat than the same amount of meat from wild game such as elk, which is similar to what our ancestors ate.

Stone Age people ate far less carbohydrate than is commonly recommended now, and what carbohydrate they did eat released its energy slowly. With the exception of rare and infrequent honey finds, they ate no foods that were calorically dense and nutritionally empty. Their foods were fresh and high in fiber, vitamins, and minerals. Their only fluid was water.

Despite the absence of food pyramids and recommended daily allowances, our Paleolithic ancestors did not suffer from the diet- and lifestyle-induced diseases we now experience: heart disease, hypertension, diabetes, and some types of cancers. It appears that, on average, they most likely died in their thirties or forties, usually from accidents or acute illnesses for which there were no cures. Although we don't know exactly what the long-term effects of their diet might have been, we do know that many people still following a Stone Age existence in remote areas today live into their sixties, seventies, and even eighties. These modern-day hunter-gatherers are not plagued by the aforementioned lifestyle diseases. Apparently, they are doing something right.

Today many people assume that Stone Age people were small in stature; however, this is a misconception. Research reveals that men and women of 25,000 years ago were about the same size as we are. The men averaged 5 feet 11 inches, and the women were about 5 feet 6 inches. Over 2 million years, stature had gradually increased to these dimensions. In fact, it wasn't until the advent of agriculture about 10,000 years ago that humans lost physical stature not to be regained until the early twentieth century. It appears that something about the dietary change produced smaller people.

With the new agrarian lifestyle also came higher infant mortality rates, a reduced life span, iron deficiency, and bone disorders such as osteoporosis and dental cavities. Modern people are still afflicted with many of these same disorders.

In only 10,000 years—fewer in most parts of the world—agriculture reshaped our diets and our health. While a hundred centuries may seem like a long time, it's really not in the context of nearly 2 million years of man's time as a genus on earth. If human existence were represented by 24 hours, farming would have been around for only the last 8 minutes, far too little time for the body to have adapted to the diets that are most prevalent today. Modern men and women have bodies meant for a diet that is different from what most of us now eat.

So what should you eat? The short answer is to eat the same foods that our ancestors ate for nearly 2 million years: lean meats, preferably from wild game or free-range animals, plus fish, poultry, and shellfish; fresh vegetables and fruits that are in season and close to their natural state; and nuts, seeds, and dried fruit in small amounts. Those foods that are newest, and especially those that are highly processed, should be eaten in the smallest amounts. Now let's take a look at the details of Mother Nature's training table.

FOOD AS FUEL

Times change. Fifty years ago, endurance athletes were advised to avoid starchy foods such as bread and potatoes and to eat more vegetables and meats instead. In the 1970s, a dietary shift away from protein, with an increase in carbohydrates, especially starches, began. The 1980s brought concerns for fat in the diet, and low-fat and fat-free foods boomed. Now, the pendulum seems to be swinging in the other direction, with the realization that certain fats are beneficial and that some carbohydrates are deleterious in large quantities.

The crux of your daily dietary decisions is the relative mix of the four macronutrients you consume. Those nutrients are protein, fat, carbohydrate, and water. How much of each you include in your diet has a great deal to do with how well you train and race.

PROTEIN

The word "protein" is derived from the Greek word *proteios*, meaning "first" or "of primary importance." That's fitting because determining macronutrient balance begins with protein intake.

Protein has a checkered history in the world of athletics. Greek and Roman competitors believed that the strength, speed, and endurance qualities of animals could be gained by merely eating their meat. Lion meat was in great demand. In the 1800s, protein was considered the major fuel of exercise, so athletes in that period also ate prodigious quantities of meat. In the early part of the twentieth century, scientists came to understand that fat and carbohydrate provide most of our energy for movement. By the 1960s, athletic diets began to change, reflecting this shift in knowledge. In fact, little attention was paid to the role of protein in sports fuel throughout most of the 1970s and 1980s. That changed in the 1990s as more research was done on this almost forgotten macronutrient.

Protein plays a key role in health and athletic performance. It is necessary to repair muscle damage, maintain the immune system, manufacture hormones and enzymes, and replace red blood cells that carry oxygen to the muscles, and it produces perhaps 10 percent of the energy needed for long or intense workouts and races. It also stimulates the secretion of glucagon, a hormone that allows the body to use fat for fuel more efficiently.

Protein is so important to the athlete's diet that it may determine the outcome of races. For example, a study of Olympians by the International Center for Sports Nutrition in Omaha, Nebraska, compared the diets of medalists and nonmedalists. The only significant difference was that the winners ate more protein than those who did not win a medal.

Performance is so dependent on dietary protein because the body is unable to produce all it needs from scratch. And, unlike carbohydrate and fat, protein is not stored in the body at fuel depot sites for later use. It is used to meet immediate needs, such as those listed above, and any excess is converted to carbohydrate or fat.

Dietary protein is made up of 20 amino acids usable by the human body as building blocks for replacing damaged cells. Most of these amino acids are readily produced when a need arises, but there are nine that the body cannot manufacture. These "essential" amino acids must come from the diet for all of the protein-related functions to continue normally. If your diet is lacking in protein, your body is likely to break down muscle tissues to satisfy the areas of greater need, thus resulting in muscle wasting. This is evidenced in a 1988 study of the 7-Eleven cycling team. During the Tour de France that year it was discovered that the circumferences of the riders' thighs had decreased during three weeks of racing. After studying their diets, the team doctor determined that they were protein deficient.

The body's demand for protein is quite high, as there is a lot of turnover. Approximately 20 percent of your body weight is protein. About two-thirds of a pound of this protein is replaced every day. At least a fourth of this daily requirement must come from your diet, with the remainder produced by recycling.

Unfortunately, there is not general agreement within the field of nutrition research regarding the recommended protein intake for endurance athletes. The U.S. Recommended Daily Allowance (RDA) for protein is 0.013 ounces per pound of body weight (0.8 grams per kilogram) daily, but that intake is likely far too low for an athlete. Peter Lemon, a noted protein researcher at Kent State University in Ohio, suggests that athletes consume about 0.020 to 0.022 ounces of protein per pound of body weight each day (1.2–1.4 g/kg). During a period of heavy weight lifting, such as in the MS phase described in Chapter 13, Lemon recommends 0.028 ounces per pound (1.8 g/kg). The American Dietetic Association suggests a high-end protein intake of 0.032 ounces per pound (2.0 g/kg) each day, and a 1997 nonscientific survey of sports scientists from around the world found they suggested a rather broad range of 0.020 to 0.040 ounces per pound (1.2–2.5 g/kg) for endurance athletes daily. Applying these recommendations for a 150-pound multisport athlete, the possible range, excluding the U.S. RDA, would be 3 to 6 ounces of protein each day. Table 16.1 shows how much protein there is in common foods.

So much for numbers and generalizations. How much protein do you need? Are you getting enough? One way to determine this is to evaluate your physical and mental well-being. For example, here are some indicators that you may need more protein in your diet:

- Frequent colds or sore throats
- Slow recovery after workouts
- An irritable demeanor
- Poor response to training (slow to get in shape)
- Slow fingernail growth and easily broken nails
- Thin hair or unusual hair loss
- Chronic fatigue
- Poor mental focus
- Sugar cravings
- Pallid complexion
- Cessation of menstrual periods

Note that none of these indicators is sure-fire proof of the need for more protein, as each may have other causes. A dietary analysis by a registered dietitian, or by the use of a computer software program such as Diet Balancer, may help you make the

TABLE 16.1

Protein Content of Common Foods

FOOD (3.5 oz./100 g)	PROTEIN (oz.)	(g)
Animal sources		
Sirloin steak, broiled	1.05	30
Chicken breast	1.05	30
Swiss cheese	1.01	29
Pork loin	0.92	26
Hamburger	0.92	26
Cheddar cheese	0.85	24.5
Tuna	0.82	23
Haddock	0.82	24
Venison	0.73	21
Cottage cheese, low-fat	0.43	12
Whole egg	0.42	12
Egg white	0.36	10
Milk, skim	0.12	3
Plant sources		
Almonds, dried	0.71	20
Tofu, extra-firm	0.39	11
Bagel	0.38	11
Kidney beans	0.30	9
Rye bread	0.29	8
Cereal, corn flakes	0.28	8
Refried beans	0.22	6
Baked beans	0.17	5
Hummus	0.17	5
Soy milk	0.10	3
Brown rice, cooked	0.09	2.5
Tomato, red	0.03	1

determination if you have concerns. Increasing your protein intake to see how it affects you is another simple option. Even at 30 percent of daily calories, the amount often recommended in popular diets, such as "the Zone," it's unlikely that you will eat too much protein. The excess, if any, will be converted to glycogen or fat and stored. Such high-protein diets pose no health risk for otherwise healthy individuals so long as plenty of water is consumed each day to help with the removal of nitrogen, a by-product of protein metabolism.

Animal foods are the most efficient and effective way to get the nine essential amino acids, as, ounce for ounce, they are richer in protein than plant sources and provide all of the proteins in their proper ratios. Animal sources also provide B vitamins and minerals such as highly absorbable iron and zinc, which are lacking in plant foods (see Table 16.2). Vegetable protein is of lower quality because it's not as digestible, and it always lacks one

TABLE 16.2

Iron Content of
Common Foods

FOOD (3.5 oz./100g)	IRON (mg)
Heme (up to 15% absorption)	
Canned clams	27.90
Beef liver, braised	6.77
Sirloin steak, broiled	3.36
Canned tuna	3.19
Hamburger, broiled	2.44
Boston Blade, roasted	1.60
Chicken breast, roasted without skin	1.03
Pork loin, broiled	0.81
Manhattan clam chowder	0.77
Turkey breast, roasted without skin	0.46
Non-heme (up to 5% absorption)	
Dried sulfured peaches	4.06
Oatmeal, instant	3.57
Spinach, raw	2.71
Swiss chard, raw	2.26
Dried figs	2.23
Lentils, cooked	1.11
Green pea soup	0.78

or more of the essential amino acids. It takes large quantities of plant food and smart combining of foods to meet your protein needs on a vegetarian diet.

Many people think of hamburger, bacon, sausage, luncheon meats, and hot dogs when they decide to eat more protein. These foods and certain other protein sources, such as cheese and whole milk, are high in saturated fat, which is closely linked to heart disease in research. Such foods are best eaten infrequently and in small amounts. Better animal sources of protein are lean meats from wild game or free-ranging cattle, seafood, poultry, and egg whites. Such foods and others high in protein should be eaten throughout the day, however, not simply consumed in one meal.

FAT

In the 1980s, Western society created such a terrifying specter of dietary fat that many multisport athletes, even to this day, see fat as the enemy and try to eliminate all types of it entirely from their diet. Indeed, there are some types of fat that should be kept at low levels. These are the saturated fats (found in prodigious quantities in feedlot cattle) and the trans-fatty acids, the human-made fats found in many highly processed foods and called "hydrogenated" on the label. Hydrogenated fats lead to artery clogging just as the saturated variety does.

But don't confuse these "bad" fats with all types of fat. There are, in fact, many health benefits associated with eating fat. Good fats can prevent dry, scaly skin and dull, brittle hair, for example. More importantly, fat helps to maintain a regular menstrual cycle in women and prevent colds and other infections common to serious athletes. It assists with the manufacture of hormones, such as testosterone and estrogen, and nerve and brain cells, and is important for carrying and absorbing the vitamins A, D, E, and K. Fat is also the body's most efficient source of energy: Every gram of fat provides nine calories, compared with four each for a grams of protein or carbohydrate. You may find that eating more fat improves your long-term recovery and capacity to train at a high level, if you previously have kept your fat intake low.

After three decades of believing that high-carbohydrate eating is best for performance, sports nutritionists now believe there is compelling evidence that eating more fat may be good for endurance athletes, especially in very long events such as an Ironman-distance race. Several studies reveal that eating a diet high in fat causes the body to preferentially use fat for fuel, and that eating a high-carbohydrate diet results in the body relying more heavily on limited stores of muscle glycogen for fuel. Theoretically, even the skinniest triathlete has enough fat stored to last for 40 hours or more of low-intensity exercise without refueling, but only enough carbohydrate for about 3 hours, at most.

A study at the State University of New York illustrates the benefits of fat. Researchers had a group of runners include a higher-than-usual percentage of fat in their diets for one week to see how it would affect their performance and VO_2max. The high-fat diet consisted of 38 percent fat and 50 percent carbohydrate calories for one week. The second week, the researchers had the runners include a greater amount of carbohydrates in their diets. In the high-carbohydrate diet, 73 percent of their calories came from carbs and 15 percent from fat. At the end of each week the subjects were tested for maximum aerobic capacity and instructed to run to exhaustion on a treadmill. On the high-fat diet, their VO_2max was 11 percent greater than when they were on the high-carb diet. Also, on the high-fat diet, they lasted 9 percent longer on the run to exhaustion.

A 1994 study conducted by Tim Noakes, author of *The Lore of Running*, along with his colleagues at the University of Cape Town in South Africa, found that after cyclists ate a diet consisting of 70 percent fat for two weeks, their endurance at a low intensity improved significantly compared with cycling after a diet high in carbohydrates for two weeks. At high intensities, there was no difference in the performances. Fat did just as well as carbohydrate.

Other research has shown that our greatest fears associated with dietary fat—increased risk of heart disease and weight gain—do not occur when people eat a diet high in what might be called "good" fats. The good fats are the "monounsaturated" and "omega-3" types and were plentiful in our Stone Age ancestors' diets. They include the oils and spreads of almonds, avocados, hazelnuts, macadamia nuts, pecans, cashews, and olives. Other good sources are the oils of coldwater fish such as tuna, salmon, and mackerel. The red meat of wild game also provides significant amounts of monounsaturated and omega-3 fats.

The bottom line on fat is to select the leanest cuts of meat (wild game, if possible) and trim all the visible fat from the meat; include seafood and poultry; eat low- or non-fat dairy in small quantities; avoid hydrogenated, trans-fatty acids in packaged foods; and regularly include monounsaturated fat in your diet. Eating 20 to 30 percent of your calories from fat, with an emphasis on the good fats, is not harmful, and may actually be helpful for training and racing.

CARBOHYDRATES

The overly zealous athlete who learns that carbohydrates are important for performance often overeats carbs at the expense of protein and fat—and his or her health. A day in the life of such a person may include a breakfast of cereal, toast, and orange juice; a bagel as a mid-morning snack; a baked potato with vegetables for lunch; sports bars or pretzels in the afternoon; and pasta with bread for supper. Not only is such a diet excessively high in starch, with an overemphasis on wheat, but it is also likely to produce dangerously low protein and fat levels. Such a dietary plan could be improved by replacing the cereal with an egg-white omelet and including fresh fruit, topping the potato with tuna, snacking on mixed nuts and dried fruit, adding shrimp to the pasta, and dipping the bread in olive oil as Italians do.

When you eat a high-carbohydrate meal or snack, the pancreas releases insulin to regulate the level of blood sugar. That insulin stays in the blood for up to two hours, just in time for another high-carbohydrate snack, during which time it has other effects, such as preventing the body from utilizing stored fat, converting carbohydrate and protein to body fat, and moving fat in the blood to storage sites. This may explain why, despite serious training and eating a "healthy" diet, some athletes are unable to lose excess body fat.

Some carbohydrates enter the bloodstream more quickly than others, producing an exaggerated blood-sugar response and rapidly bringing about all of the negative aspects of high insulin described above. These easily digested carbohydrates are high on the glycemic index—a food rating system developed for diabetics. Foods low on the glycemic index produce a less dramatic rise in blood sugar and help you avoid the cravings for more sugary food that come with eating high-glycemic carbohydrates. Table 16.3 lists some common foods that are high, moderate, low, and very low on the glycemic-index scale.

How a carbohydrate food is prepared and the other foods it is eaten with affects its glycemic-index rating. Adding fat to a sugary food lowers its rating. An example of this

TABLE 16.3

Glycemic Index of Common Foods

VERY LOW (LESS THAN 30%)	LOW (30–50%)		MODERATE (50–80%)	
Barley	Apple	Kiwifruit	All-Bran cereal	Bread, white
Beans, kidney	Apple juice	Oranges	Apricots	Corn chips
Beans, soy	Apple sauce	Pasta (whole wheat)	Bagels	Corn, sweet
Cherries	Beans, baked	Pears	Bananas	Cornmeal
Grapefruit	Beans, black	Peas, black-eyed	Barley	Couscous
Lentils	Beans, lima	Peas, split	Beets	Crackers
Milk	Beans, pinto	Rye	Black bean soup	Doughnuts
Peaches	Chocolate	Tomato soup	Bread, pita	Ice cream
Peanuts	Grapefruit juice	Yogurt, fruit	Bread, rye	Mango
Plums	Grapes		Bread, wheat	Muesli

is ice cream that has a moderate glycemic-index rating despite the presence of high sugar. In the same way, adding fat, protein, or fiber to a meal that includes a high- or moderate-glycemic-index carbohydrate reduces the meal's effect on your blood sugar levels and turns it into a "time-release food capsule."

Notice in Table 16.3 that many of the foods with moderate to high glycemic-index ratings are the ones we have typically thought of as "healthy" and therefore eaten in the largest amounts. These include the starchy foods—cereal, bread, rice, pasta, potatoes, crackers, bagels, pancakes, and bananas. No wonder so many endurance athletes are always hungry and have a hard time losing excess body fat. Their blood sugar levels are routinely kept at high levels between workouts, causing regular cascades of insulin. Not only does high insulin negatively impact food cravings and body weight, it is also associated with such widespread health problems as high blood pressure, heart disease, and diabetes. When you feel a habitual craving for sweets and starches between meals, eat some protein. That usually cures it.

It is necessary to replenish carbohydrate stores in the muscles and liver during long and intense training sessions and races. That's why sports drinks and gels are used during exercise. In the 30 minutes immediately following a breakthrough session, high-glycemic-index carbohydrates and insulin are beneficial. This is the time to use a commercial recovery drink or food. Combining protein with a high-glycemic-index food has been shown in a few studies to effectively boost recovery. Otherwise, sports drinks, gels, and soft drinks should be avoided. Other high- and moderate-glycemic-index foods should be consumed in moderation.

If you have been following the high-carb principle in your diet, it may well be time for a change. Experiment with making small changes in your diet to switch to more moderate- to low-glycemic-index foods. The high-carbohydrate diet you have been following may be causing your body to rely more heavily on glycogen with an associated increase in blood lactate levels, reducing your use of fat as a fuel for exercise.

MODERATE (50–80%) (continued)		HIGH (80% OR HIGHER)	
Muffins	Potatoes, sweet	Bread, French	Rice, instant
Oat bran	PowerBar	Corn flakes	Rice Krispies
Oatmeal	Pumpkin	Grapenuts flakes	Rice, white
Orange juice	Raisins	Molasses	Tapioca
Pea soup	Rice, brown	Parsnips	Tofu frozen dessert
Pineapple	Rye crisps	Pasta (rice)	
Popcorn	Soft drinks	Potatoes, baked	
Potato chips	Taco shells	Potatoes, instant	
Potatoes, boiled	Watermelon	Rice cakes	
Potatoes, mashed	Yams	Rice Chex	

WATER

Many multisport athletes don't drink enough fluids, which leaves them perpetually on the edge of dehydration. In this state, recovery is compromised and the risk of illness rises. Drinking throughout the day is one of the simplest yet most effective means of boosting performance for such athletes. Since sports drinks and most fruit juices are high to moderate on the glycemic index, the best fluid replacement between workouts is water.

A 150-pound (68 kg) adult loses just over half a gallon (2 liters) of body fluids a day just by living, not including swimming, cycling, and running. Up to half of this loss is through urine, at the rate of about 1.5 to 2 ounces (30 milliliters) per hour. Heavy training or a hot and humid environment can increase the loss to 2 gallons (8 liters) daily through heavy sweating.

The human thirst mechanism works well, but unfortunately we often ignore it. By the time we pay attention to thirst, dehydration may already be well underway. Following prolonged and intense training or racing, it may take an athlete 24 to 48 hours to rehydrate if the thirst is never fully quenched. In contrast, a dog will drink up to 10 percent of its body weight immediately following exercise, replacing all lost body fluids at once. It's important to pay attention to your thirst level and drink water throughout the day to quench it regardless of your training load.

SIDEBAR 16.1

Are You Really Overtrained?

Low dietary intake of the mineral iron may be the most common nutritional deficiency for serious multisport athletes, especially women. Unfortunately, it goes undetected in most.

A 1988 university study of female high school cross-country runners found 45 percent had low iron stores. In the same study, 17 percent of the boys were low. Other research conducted on female college athletes showed that 31 percent were iron deficient. Up to 80 percent of women runners were below normal iron stores in a 1983 study.

Commonly accepted, although still debated, causes of iron depletion include high-volume running, especially on hard surfaces; too much anaerobic training; chronic intake of aspirin; travel to high elevation; excessive menstrual flow; and a diet low in animal food products. Athletes most at risk for iron deficiency, in order, are runners, women, endurance athletes, vegetarians, those who sweat heavily, dieters, and those who have recently donated blood.

The symptoms of iron deficiency include loss of endurance, chronic fatigue, high exercise heart rate, low power, frequent injury, recurring illness, and an attitude problem. Since many of these symptoms are the same as in overtraining, the athlete may correctly cut back on exercise, begin feeling better, and return to training, only to find an almost immediate relapse. In the early stages of iron depletion, performance may show only slight decrements, but additional training volume and intensity cause further declines. Many unknowingly flirt with this level of "tired blood" frequently.

If a deficiency is suspected, what should you do? Once a year have a blood test to determine your healthy baseline levels of serum ferritin, hemoglobin, reticulocytes, and haptoglobin. This should be done during the Transition, Prep, or early Base training period when training volume and intensity are low. This blood test should be done in a fasted state with no exercise for fifteen hours prior. Your health-care provider will help you understand the results. Then, if the symptoms of low iron appear later in the season, a follow-up test may support or rule this out as the culprit. Your blood indicators of iron status may be "normal" based on the reference range, but low in relation to your baseline. Many exercise scientists believe that even this obvious dip may adversely affect performance.

Should the blood test indicate an abnormally low iron status, an increased dietary intake of iron is necessary. You may want to have a registered dietitian analyze your eating habits for adequate iron consumption. The RDA for women and teenagers is 15 mg per day. Men should consume 10 mg. Endurance athletes may need more. The typical North American diet contains about 6 mg of iron for every 1,000 calories eaten, so a female athlete restricting food intake to 2,000 calories a day while exercising strenuously can easily create a low-iron condition in a few weeks.

Dietary iron comes in two forms—heme and non-heme. Heme iron is found in animal meat. Plant foods are the source of non-heme iron. Very little of the iron you eat is absorbed by the body regardless of source, but heme iron has the best absorption rate, at about 15 percent. Up to 5 percent of non-heme iron is taken up by the body. So the most effective way to increase iron status is by eating meat, especially red meat. Humans probably developed this capacity to absorb iron from red meat as a result of our omnivorous, hunter-gatherer origins. Plant sources of iron, although not very available to the human body due to their accompanying phytates, are raisins, leafy green vegetables, dates, dried fruits, lima beans, baked beans, broccoli, baked potatoes, soybeans, and Brussels sprouts. Other sources are listed in Table 16.2.

Iron absorption from any of these foods, whether plant or animal, is decreased if they are accompanied at meals by egg yolk, coffee, tea, wheat, or cereal grains. Calcium and zinc also reduce the ability of the body to take up iron. Including fruits, especially citrus fruit, in meals enhances iron absorption.

Don't use iron supplements unless under the supervision of your health-care provider. Some people are susceptible to iron overload, a condition called hemochromatosis, marked by toxic deposits in the skin, joints, and liver. Other symptoms, including fatigue and malaise, may mimic iron deficiency and overtraining. Also note that ingesting iron supplements is the second leading cause of poisoning in children. Aspirin is first.

DIET AND PERFORMANCE

How the macronutrients—protein, fats, carbohydrates, and water—are mixed into your diet has a lot to do with how well you train and race and how healthy you are.

Several recent human and animal studies examining the effects of diet on performance have found that increased dietary fat enhances endurance and aerobic capacity. The benefit seems to increase as the duration of the exercise lengthens. During short, high-intensity efforts, there appears to be no significant difference, although most studies find a slight advantage for high-carbohydrate intake in such events.

One of the downsides of eating a high-carbohydrate, low-fat diet is a greater production of lactic acid by the muscles during exercise and even at rest. This is probably the result of the body not burning as much fat, but instead using carbohydrate preferentially for fuel when it is abundantly available. Carbohydrate seems to reduce the body's fat-utilization processes.

Additionally, several studies have found the rather surprising result that the risk of coronary heart disease increases with a high-carbohydrate, low-fat diet, compared with a more moderate intake of both nutrients that emphasizes monounsaturated and polyunsaturated fats. These risk-factor shifts include lowered HDL ("good") cholesterol, increased LDL ("bad") cholesterol, and elevated triglyceride levels. There is still much to be learned about the interaction of diet and health.

A diet exceptionally low in fat has also been shown to depress testosterone levels. Testosterone is an important hormone that assists with rebuilding tissues broken down by exercise. When fat was increased in research subjects' diets, testosterone production increased.

Eating fat in its natural state—for example, in lean meats, plants, nuts, seeds, and natural oils—appears to have no deleterious effect on health. Many cultures live quite well on high-fat diets based on such foods. The problem with the standard American diet is that much, if not most, of the dietary fat is saturated, hydrogenated, altered, processed, or artificial. Eating fat is not a problem unless its chemical structure has been changed by food producers.

The foods you eat day in and day out have long-term implications for your health, of course, but the foods you choose to eat immediately before a race have a direct effect on how well you do in the event. It seems a waste to train for weeks for a certain race and then to blow it by eating inappropriate foods as the race approaches. When preparing for a high-intensity event, such as a sprint- or Olympic-distance race, your diet should change a bit as the race day approaches. In general, you should be eating a diet that is moderate in fats with fats making up in the neighborhood of 30 percent of total calories, but for two or three days prior to the race, you should switch to carbohydrate loading. On the morning of a short-course race, your pre-race meal could include up to 200 calories for every hour until race time, depending on your body size and what you can tolerate. So if you eat three hours before starting your warm-up, 600 calories is about the top end. Most of these calories, for events that take about two hours or less to complete, should come from low- to moderate-glycemic-index carbohydrates. Small amounts of protein may be included. You may benefit from including more fat in this meal if you are competing in a longer event.

DIET, AGING, AND MUSCLE

It's apparent that as we grow older, we tend to lose muscle mass. Although this loss is slowed somewhat by weight lifting and vigorous aerobic exercise, it still happens, and as a result, athletes in their sixties typically have considerably less muscle mass than they had in their forties.

Now there is research that shows why. As we age, nitrogen, an essential component of muscle protein, is given up by the body at an increasing rate, so that at some point it is being depleted faster than it can be taken in. This is due to a gradual change in kidney function that produces an acidic state in the blood. With a net loss of nitrogen, muscles cannot be maintained. Essentially, we are peeing off our muscles as we pass the half-century mark in life. This same acidic state also leaches calcium from the bones, resulting in osteoporosis for many, especially women, with advanced age.

The key to reducing, or even avoiding, this situation is to lower the blood's acidity level and increase its alkalinity. Simply consuming more protein isn't the answer, as that actually increases the acidity level. There are studies demonstrating that taking a potassium bicarbonate supplement daily for as few as 18 days can increase the blood's alkaline level by balancing nitrogen in the body. While it can be purchased relatively inexpensively in laboratory supply shops, potassium bicarbonate is not currently available as an over-the-counter supplement, and there are no long-term studies of its effects on health. There is some evidence that it may contribute to irregular electrocardiogram (ECG) readings, so supplementation is not advised at this time.

But there is also a natural way of achieving this same result through diet by eating foods that naturally increase the blood's alkalinity—that is, fruits and vegetables. Fats and oils have a neutral effect on blood acid. In other words, they do not make it either more acidic or more alkaline. All other foods, including grains, meats, nuts, beans, dairy, fish, and eggs, increase the blood's acidity. If your diet is high in these foods but low in fruits and vegetables, you can expect to lose muscle mass and bone calcium as you age.

A study by T. Remer and F. Manz ranked foods in terms of their effect on blood acidity and alkalinity. They found, for example, that among the foods they studied, Parmesan cheese had the most acidic effect, and therefore contributed the most to a loss of nitrogen and ultimately muscle mass. The food they found to have the greatest alkaline effect, thus reducing nitrogen and muscle loss the most, was the humble raisin. Among vegetables, spinach was the most alkaline food. So it turns out that Popeye was right.

Table 16.4 ranks a sampling of the common foods (per 100-gram portions) that Remer and Manz studied and lists their effect on alkalinity and acidity. The higher a food's positive acidic ranking, the more likely it is to contribute to a loss of muscle mass and bone-mineral levels. The more negative the food's alkaline ranking, the more beneficial the effect is on these measures.

TABLE 16.4

Acidity and Alkalinity of Common Foods

ACID FOODS (+) (3.5 oz./100 g)		ALKALINE FOODS (−) (3.5 oz./100 g)	
Grains		**Fruits**	
Brown rice	+12.5	Raisins	−21.0
Rolled oats	+10.7	Black currants	−6.5
Whole wheat bread	+8.2	Bananas	−5.5
Spaghetti	+6.5	Apricots	−4.8
Corn flakes	+6.0	Kiwifruit	−4.1
White rice	+4.6	Cherries	−3.6
Rye bread	+4.1	Pears	−2.9
White bread	+3.7	Pineapple	−2.7
		Peaches	−2.4
Dairy		Apples	−2.2
Parmesan cheese	+34.2	Watermelon	−1.9
Processed cheese	+28.7		
Hard cheese	+19.2		
Gouda cheese	+18.6	**Vegetables**	
Cottage cheese	+8.7	Spinach	−14.0
Whole milk	+0.7	Celery	−5.2
		Carrots	−4.9
		Zucchini	−4.6
Legumes		Cauliflower	−4.0
Peanuts	+8.3	Potatoes	−4.0
Lentils	+3.5	Radishes	−3.7
Peas	+1.2	Eggplant	−3.4
		Tomatoes	−3.1
Meats, Fish, Eggs		Lettuce	−2.5
Trout	+10.8	Chicory	−2.0
Turkey	+9.9	Leeks	−1.8
Chicken	+8.7	Onions	−1.5
Eggs	+8.1	Mushrooms	−1.4
Pork	+7.9	Green peppers	−1.4
Beef	+7.8	Broccoli	−1.2
Cod	+7.1	Cucumber	−0.8
Herring	+7.0		

BODY WEIGHT MANAGEMENT

Many triathletes want to know how to lose weight to improve climbing on the bike and running in general. There's little doubt that being lighter means climbing and running faster. A pound of excess body weight takes about 2 watts to get up a hill on a bike and costs about 2 seconds a mile when running. So dropping 10 pounds of excess flab means you'll ride up a hill 7 to 10 percent faster and run a 5 km about a minute faster than you are now. Those are significant improvements in performance that would otherwise take months of hard training to accomplish.

This is not to say that all triathletes should lose weight. Many are already lean enough, but how can you tell if you're in the correct range? You really can't base your evaluation just on weight—200 pounds may sound heavy, but if a 200-pound athlete was 7 feet tall, he would be very skinny. A better way to think about your body weight is to compare it with height. Determine your weight-to-height ratio by dividing your weight in pounds by your height in inches. Competitive male triathletes are generally about 2.1 to 2.3 pounds per inch. High-performance women triathletes are usually in the range of 1.8 to 2.0.

If your ratio is above this range, how can you get it closer to the "ideal"? Unfortunately, there have been few studies of serious athletes that looked at this question. One group of researchers, however, has examined the issue in an interesting way. They compared eating less to exercising more to see which was more effective in helping athletes drop excess body fat.

The scientists had six endurance-trained men create a 1,000-calorie-per-day deficit for seven days by either exercising more while maintaining their caloric intake or eating less while keeping exercise the same. With 1,000 calories of increased exercise daily—comparable to running an additional 8 miles or so each day—the men averaged 1.67 pounds of weight loss in a week. The subjects eating 1,000 fewer calories each day lost 4.75 pounds on average for the week.

So, according to this study, the old adage that "a calorie is a calorie" doesn't hold true. At least in the short term, restricting food intake appears to have a greater return *on the scales* than increasing training workload does.

Notice that I said "on the scales." The reduced-food-intake group in this study unfortunately lost a greater percentage of muscle mass than the increased-exercise group did. That is an ineffective way to lose weight. If the scales show you're lighter, but you have less muscle to create power, the trade-off is not a good one.

How can you reduce calories and yet maintain muscle mass? Unfortunately, that question hasn't been answered for athletes. One study did address it for sedentary women, however, and the conclusions may be applicable to athletes.

In 1994, Italian researchers had 25 women eat only 800 calories a day for 21 days. Ten ate a relatively high-protein, low-carbohydrate diet. Fifteen ate a low-protein, high-carbohydrate diet. Both groups were restricted to 20 percent of calories from fat. The two groups lost similar amounts of weight, but there was a significantly greater loss of muscle for the women on the high-carbohydrate, low-protein diet.

So if cutting calories is a more effective way to lose weight than increasing training workload, it appears that the protein content of the diet must be kept at near normal levels. This assumes that you're eating adequate protein before starting the diet, which many athletes aren't. If your protein intake is already low, typically less than about 20 percent of total calories, then dieting will negatively affect training quality and you are likely to lose muscle mass.

It seems that when trying to lose those last few pounds of excess fat, cutting calories is more effective than increasing exercise volume. But a quality source of protein should be included in every meal. The best time in the season to lose weight is during the Base period. The closer you get to your A-priority race, the more detrimental calorie-cutting will be to your recovery and performance.

PERIODIZATION OF DIET

The optimal diet for peak performance must vary with the athlete just as the optimal training protocol must vary from person to person. We can't all eat the same things in the same relative amounts and reap the same benefits. Where your ancestors originated on the planet, and what they ate over the past 100,000 years or so, affect what you should eat now.

So the bottom line is that you must discover what mix of foods works best for you. If you have never experimented with this, don't automatically assume you have found it already. You may be surprised at what happens when you make changes at the training table. A word of caution: Make changes gradually, and allow at least three weeks for your body to adapt to a new diet before passing judgment based on how you feel and your performance in training. It usually takes two weeks for someone to adapt to dietary changes before seeing any results. During the adaptation period, you may feel lethargic and train poorly. For this reason, changes in diet are best done in the Transition and Prep periodization cycles early in the season. Also, be aware that as you age, changes may occur in your body chemistry requiring further shifts in diet.

That said, an optimal diet to enhance training, racing, and recovery involves not only eating moderate amounts of the macronutrients, but also varying the mix of these foods throughout the year. In other words, diet should cycle just as training does within a periodization plan. Protein serves as the anchor for the diet and stays relatively constant throughout the year, whereas the intake of fats and carbohydrates will rise and fall alternately. Figure 16.1 illustrates this "see-saw" effect of the periodized diet. Note that the numbers used in this figure are merely an example, and the dietary mix right for you may vary considerably.

THE FIVE STAGES OF RECOVERY

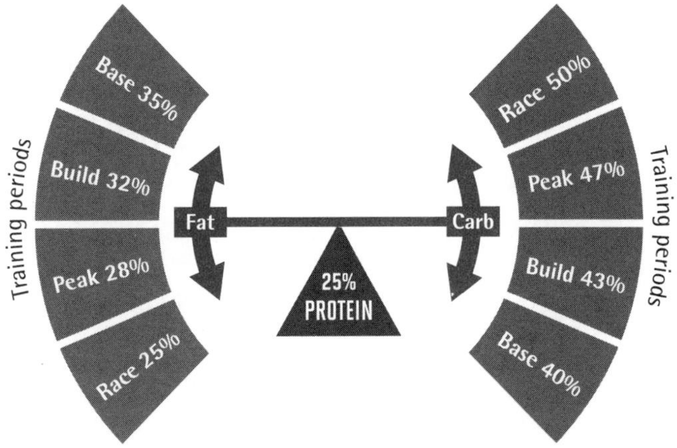

In the Paleo diet, it may sound as if carbo-hydrates are the "bad guy" in an endurance athlete's diet. On the contrary, eating carbo-hydrates is necessary for high levels of perfor-mance. But the timing of carbohydrate intake is critical to success. In fact, if your carb in-take is timed correctly, you can actually cut back a bit on the amount and take in a wider variety of nutrient-dense foods. Those foods can in turn help you recover faster and per-form at a higher level.

Note: Exact percentages will vary depending on the triathlete.

FIGURE 16.1

The Dietary
Periodization
"Seesaw"

The key is to accept that your workouts are the central events of each day, and that the types of foods you eat are determined by when those workouts take place. This is likely a fairly easy notion to acquire since, as a serious athletes, you probably already have a "training is life, everything else is just the details" way of seeing the world.

Each workout has five feeding times linked with it. I call these "stages."

Stage 1: Before the Workout

The goal of this stage is to store sufficient carbohydrate to get you through the workout. This is especially important for early-morning sessions. For the perfect fuel, eat 200 to 400 calories, primarily from a moderate-glycemic-index, carbohydrate-rich food, two hours before the workout. Of course, few are willing to get up at 3 A.M. just to eat before a 5 A.M. masters swim session. Instead, take a bottle of your favorite sports drink or a couple of gel packets with 12 ounces of water to the workout. Ten minutes before the warm-up begins, start taking in your "breakfast." This isn't quite as good as eating a real breakfast two hours beforehand, but it's far better than training on a low fuel tank.

Stage 2: During the Workout

For an hour or less of training, water is all you need, assuming you refilled the tank in Stage 1. For longer workouts you also need carbohydrates, and the amount you should take in increases with the length of the workout. It could be as little as 120 calories or as much as 500 calories of carbs per hour, depending not only on workout length but also on body size, workout intensity, and your personal experience.

These carbohydrates should be mostly in the form of liquids from a high-glycemic-index source. The best choice is your favorite sports drink. You could also use gels, chased immediately by lots of water. The longer the workout, the more important the carbohydrates are for top performance and good recovery later. It's usually a good idea

Recovery Drink

You can buy a commercial product for this type of refueling, but they are expensive. Make your own recovery drink with this simple list of ingredients.

16 oz. fruit juice

1 banana

3–5 tbsp. glucose (such as Carbo-Pro, available at sportquestdirect.com), depending on body size

2–3 tbsp. protein powder (egg or whey sources are best)

2–3 pinches of salt

Consuming this drink during the 30-minute, post-workout window is critical for recovery. It should be your highest priority after a hard workout. If the workout lasted less than an hour and was low intensity, omit this stage.

for a liquid fuel source to include sodium, especially if it's hot and you sweat heavily. The research is less than overwhelming on the benefits of other ingredients, including potassium, magnesium and protein. Include them if you want to. If you pay careful attention as you train and experiment with your nutrition, you can develop a sense of the type of carbohydrate that works best for you and the amount you need for different workouts.

Stage 3: Immediately After the Workout

This and the next stage are the key times in the day for taking in carbohydrate. When athletes say that eating in stages leaves them hungry or fatigued, it's nearly always because they don't take in enough carbohydrates in stages 3 and 4.

Your goal now is to replace the carbohydrate used during the workout. In the first 30 minutes or so after a workout, your body is several hundred times more sensitive to carbohydrate and will readily store more than at any other time of the day. The longer you wait to refuel, the less likely you are to completely refill the gas tank. Take in three to four calories per pound of body weight, mostly from high-glycemic-index carbohydrate, in this stage.

Stage 4: As Long as the Workout Lasted

Continue to focus your diet on carbohydrates, especially from moderate- to high-glycemic-index sources, for a time period equal to the amount of time you were working out. Take in some protein as well. You may be ready to eat a meal in Stage 4 if the workout was long. Now is the time to eat starches such as pasta, bread, bagels, cereal, rice, corn, and other foods rich in fast-absorbing glucose to facilitate the recovery process. Perhaps the perfect foods to eat at this time are potatoes, sweet potatoes, yams, and bananas, since they also have a net alkaline-enhancing quality that reduces body acidity following workouts. Raisins are a great snack food for Stage 4. Eat until satisfied. If you feel full after only a small meal, try eating several smaller meals during this period.

Stage 5: Until the Next Workout

Usually, by the time Stage 5 comes around, you will be at work, back in class, spending time with your family, mowing the grass, or doing whatever it is you do when not training or racing. Although this part of your day may look ordinary to the rest of the world, it really isn't. You can still focus on nutrition for long-term recovery.

This is the time when many athletes get sloppy with their diets. The most common mistake is to continue to eat stage 3 and 4 foods that are low in nutrient value and high in starch and sugar. Such foods are great for immediate recovery but not effective for building up long-term nutritional stores. The most nutrient-dense foods are vegetables, fruits, and lean protein from animal sources, especially seafood. Snack on nuts, seeds, and berries. All of these foods are rich in vitamins, minerals, and other trace elements necessary for health, growth, and recovery.

Avoid processed foods that come in packages, including those with labels that say "healthy." They aren't, and that even includes foods invented by sports nutrition scientists. They are still several million years behind nature in producing nutritious chow. Just eat *real* food in Stage 5.

Pareto and Perfection

Vilfredo Pareto was an Italian economist of the late nineteenth and early twentieth centuries who discovered that 80 percent of the land in Italy was owned by 20 percent of the population. Experts in other fields soon discovered that this "80-20 Rule" also applied to their areas of study. For example, 80 percent of the productivity in a business is typically generated by 20 percent of the employees. Schoolchildren spend 80 percent of their time with 20 percent of their friends. Investors find that 80 percent of their income comes from 20 percent of their stock. The 80-20 Rule is also known as the "Pareto Principle."

His rule also applies to your diet. The Pareto Principle says that you don't need to eat perfectly. Stage 5 of recovery is often viewed as being quite restrictive, since your diet must be focused on fruits, vegetables, and lean protein. The 80-20 Rule tells us that it's okay to occasionally eat a cookie, a slice of pizza, a piece of bread, or even a bit of pasta in Stage 5—so long as this makes up less than 20 percent of your food intake. In other words, it's perfectly acceptable to cheat a little. Just make sure that 80 percent of the calories on your plate is nutrient-dense, and you will be healthy, lean, fit, and fast. You can thank Vilfredo for that.

If you are doing two or three workouts in a day, you may not get to Stage 5 until late in the day. Also, Stage 4 may replace Stage 1 with closely spaced workouts. That's not a problem.

That's all there is to it—a simple way of organizing your day into five stages of eating to ensure adequate recovery and optimal health. You can find more details on this topic in my book *The Paleo Diet for Athletes.*

FUELING THE IRONMAN

There are seven situations that may lead to a poor Ironman performance, or even a failure to finish the race:

- Inadequate training
- Overtraining with an inadequate taper
- An overly aggressive pacing strategy, especially on the bike
- Heat intolerance
- Excessive dehydration
- Glycogen depletion
- Excessive dilution of sodium

The first four situations should be addressed in your training program by matching your workouts to the demands of the event and your specific needs; by following a periodization plan that allows for periodic rest; by cutting back on training far enough in advance of the race to recover; by learning to hold back early on the bike; and by training in the heat. The last three are fueling issues. Let's examine them.

Your pre-race fueling strategy must ensure that you will have plenty of water and carbohydrates as well as undiluted sodium stores throughout the event. If any one of these is slighted, just finishing can be a problem. They are closely related.

The sports drink you use on the bike and run is the starting point for your fueling plan. This, of course, is largely decided by the race organizers who will provide fluids at the aid stations, so you must adapt to this product in your training. Start the bike leg with enough sports drinks of your own choosing already on the bike for the first couple of hours or so. This might be an MCT-spiked drink (see "Ergogenic Aids" on the following pages) with greater caloric density than a regular sports drink like Gatorlode or Metabolol Endurance. Whatever you decide to use, practice with it in your longest workouts to make sure the product or specific mix agrees with you.

Maintenance of your body's glycogen stores actually starts months in advance of the race when you "teach" your body to spare glycogen and use more fat for fuel. This is done by eating a diet during your Ironman training that favors fat intake and limits carbohydrate, especially from high-glycemic-index sources, in stages 2, 3, and 4. In the last three days before the race, it still may be wise to increase your intake of fruits and vegetables while cutting back on fat. Commercial liquid meals, such as Ensure, may work well the day before the race, as you eliminate much of the fiber in your diet. Try it first for a low-priority race. The point of these dietary principles is to ensure that you use glycogen sparingly but have plenty of it on board.

The morning of the race, eat breakfast at least three hours before the starting time, including about 200 to 300 calories for each hour remaining before the race begins, depending on your body size and experience. Take in mostly liquid meals such as Ensure. It's best to keep your fiber intake low on race morning. In a 1984 Ironman-distance race, Japanese researchers found that those who ate the most calories at breakfast ran the fastest marathons.

During the bike and run portions of the race, you will need to take in as many calories as you can. The type and amount of calories you consume during these segments are things that you must determine in training. Start this process by using about 300 to 400 calories per hour on the bike. Modify this amount either up or down depending on what you learn. Most athletes discover that using mostly liquid feedings helps prevent stomach shutdowns. The faster you race, the more useful this advice may be. The slower you race, the more likely you are to tolerate solid foods along with the liquids. You may want to set your wristwatch to beep every 10 to 15 minutes or so as a reminder to take in fuel.

Low concentrations of sodium, a condition called hyponatremia, is one of the biggest challenges you will face as an endurance athlete. It's estimated that 30 percent of Hawaii Ironman finishers have dangerously low concentrations of sodium in their blood. When sweating profusely, as in Kona in October, it's possible to lose up to a liter of body fluids an hour. And since a liter of sweat contains 2 to 3.5 grams of sodium, a total of 24 to 42 grams could be lost in a twelve-hour race. This does not present a problem unless you drink plain water throughout the race. Drinking a sports drink and/or liquid fuel source that includes sodium as an ingredient will help you maintain a healthy concentration of sodium in your blood while racing or working out.

Early signs of hyponatremia include bloating around the elastic waistband of your shorts and around or just above your ankles, where the tops of your socks are; nausea or vomiting; or headache, muscle cramps, weakness, slurred speech, or disorientation. In extreme cases there may be seizures or coma. Athletes have died of hyponatremia.

The use of aspirin, ibuprofen, acetaminophen (for example, Tylenol), or other anti-inflammatories may increase the risk of hyponatremia, so it's best not to use these

TABLE 16.5

Recommended Sources of Sodium for Ironman

FOOD	SERVING/HR.
Sunshine Bavarian Sourdough Pretzels	2 pretzels
Baked Rold Gold Hard Sourdough Pretzels	2–3 pretzels
Snackwell Wheat Crackers	15 crackers
Premium Fat-Free Saltine Crackers	20 crackers
Protein 21 Bar	2 bars
Balance Bar	4 bars
PowerBar	5–6 bars
PowerGel	10 packets
Clif Bar	4 bars
Clif Shot	20 packets

products during the race. It's probably also wise to avoid such medications in the last 48 hours before racing.

Race nutrition is so critical to Ironman-distance racing that you must give it considerable attention. You developed and wrote down an Annual Training Plan to prepare your training for the race; create a nutrition plan with just as much attention to detail.

NUTRITION FOR IRONMAN RACING

On race day, your digestive system may react to your excitement about the race. To reduce the likelihood of an in-race stomach shutdown prior to, during, or immediately following an Ironman-distance race, it may be useful for you to take certain steps that have been shown to be helpful for experienced athletes who are focused on fast times or race placement. If your goal is simply to finish the race, then the pacing instructions here will be too aggressive for you, though the refueling suggestions may still be effective.

You may need to modify this plan to fit your body size, previous race-nutrition experience, and personal food likes and dislikes. You should refine the plan you adopt weeks or even months ahead of your Ironman race by experimenting in workouts, first in bricks and long sessions, then in C-priority races, and, finally, in B-priority races. Don't do anything on race day that you have not done successfully many times before. Determine how many calories you will take in during the race and the strategy for doing so. As points of reference, in an 11- to 12-hour Ironman you will burn roughly 6,500 to 7,000 calories, and in a 9-hour Ironman you will use about 8,000 calories. Approximately half of these calories come from glycogen (storage form of carbohydrate), and most of these must be replaced during the race.

Gastric problems are a leading cause of poor performances and DNFs (did not finish) in Ironman-distance races. If your stomach shuts down during the race, you either (1) went out too fast—using poor pacing strategy or control, (2) ate too much solid food, (3) have not taken in enough water, or (4) are becoming hyponatremic (low blood sodium concentration). The following is intended to prevent these occurrences.

Prior to Race Day

Reduce your food intake as your training volume tapers during the late Peak and Race periods. Eat "normal" foods during this period. Do not experiment with anything new.

Day Before the Race

Before you head out to view the swim course at race time, eat a big breakfast with an emphasis on moderate- to low-glycemic-index carbohydrates. Eat a large lunch when you next become hungry, again emphasizing moderate to low-glycemic-index foods. Have a moderately sized dinner that is "normal" food for you, but with limited fiber intake. For dinner, focus on moderate- to low-glycemic-index foods. Make sure you pay close attention to your thirst throughout the day.

Race-Day Breakfast

Four to five hours prior to the race start, take in 800 to 1,500 calories from moderate- to low-glycemic-index foods, depending on your body size and experience. You will have rehearsed this already during bricks and long workouts or before C- and B-priority races. Stick with the foods that have worked for you before.

If you have a nervous stomach, use liquid or semisolid foods. Options may include Ensure, 1 medium banana (100 calories), a bagel with a tablespoon of nut butter (250 calories), 1 cup of unsweetened applesauce mixed with 1 ounce of protein powder (200 calories), 1 jar of baby food (100–200 calories), 1 packet of instant oatmeal (100–200 calories); 1 cup of instant pudding (100–300 calories), or 1 can of tomato soup (200 calories). A good breakfast mix could include 4 cans of Ensure, a banana, and a bagel with nut butter (1,350 calories).

After eating breakfast, either go back to bed or relax with some light stretching that focuses on hips, glutes, and low back.

Pre-Race

Snack before the race, but eat no more than 200 calories per hour during the last three hours before start time. Stick with liquids or semisolid foods. To soothe your stomach, think calming thoughts or listen to calming music—do not stress yourself out. When apprehensions appear, recall previous successes in training and racing. Eat something such as a sports bar with a sports drink 1 to 1.5 hours before the race start. In the last hour before the race, eat and drink nothing except water. This prevents exercise-induced hypoglycemia early in the race. Ten minutes before the race start, take in as much sports drink as you feel comfortable with.

Swim

Carry a plastic bottle of the sports drink into the water so you can drink until the race start. At the gun, toss the bottle. To conserve energy, do not go anaerobic at the start of the swim—hold back.

Bike

Mentally divide the bike portion of the race into fourths. The first quarter is about fueling for the day; the second quarter is focused on an even, steady pace; the third quarter is when you should gain time if you held back in the first quarter; and the final quarter is a time to ride strongly but steadily.

Aim for 300 to 400 calories per hour on the bike, adjusting up or down based on your size, training, racing experience, and tolerance for food intake. Carry most of your calories with you on the bike, and get water and sports drink at aid stations. Rely more on drinks and less on solid food throughout the race. If you have any special nutritional requirements, make sure that you have backup sources in your transition and special-needs bags. Consider starting the bike leg with your bike loaded with a little more nutrition than you need for the entire ride.

For fluids, depending on your caloric needs and anticipated race duration, carry two or three 20-ounce bottles with about 750 calories of fluid in each, along with gels. A 750-calorie bottle may be made up by mixing your favorite sports drink to a normal concentration and then adding Carbo-Pro (if you mix this the day before, refrigerate it). Chase each mouthful from the 750-calorie bottle with two or three mouthfuls of water that you get from aid stations. If you are using any solid foods on the bike (not recommended for sub-12-hour goal times), drink only *water* with them.

Take in some sodium on the bike from drinks, foods, and supplements. Let heat, humidity, body size, and your experience dictate the amount. Above all, remember to take in calories! If your experience in racing has been that your mind wanders and you forget to eat and drink, then set your watch to beep every 15 minutes as a reminder.

Bike Miles 1–30. Begin sipping a sports drink right away out of T1 and continue for 20 minutes. Start liquid feedings after 20 minutes. The key to this leg is to hold yourself back. Set your heart rate monitor to beep at the bottom of your zone 3. You should not hear the beep for the first 30 miles on the bike. If you do, you are going too hard and the chances of digestive problems later on rise. This first quarter should feel like the slowest part of the bike leg, relative to terrain and wind. Your heart rate zone readings should be the lowest of the four portions of the bike leg.

Bike Miles 31–60. The goal of the second quarter is to maintain a steady effort at goal Ironman-distance bike pace. Ride steadily and predominantly in zone 2. Remember that only the fittest athletes, generally elites with very fast bike portions, will be able to tolerate sustained periods of zone 3 riding. You would be well advised to ride *under* the intensity of your toughest race simulation rides. Maintain your feeding and fluids schedule.

Bike Miles 61–90. If you are feeling good, consider increasing the speed and/or effort, but only slightly. This is where you can move up through the field. You may be experiencing cardiac drift by now, so pay more attention to how you feel and less to your heart rate monitor. Stay focused. Regardless of the cause, you should *slow down immediately* when faced with stomach issues, no matter what your time or pacing goals are. You will more than make up for the time that you lose with an improved run split. Trying to push through stomach issues doesn't work.

Bike Miles 91–112. Continue to take in fuel, although you may not feel like it. Your effort should feel like zone 2—steady to moderately hard—regardless of what your heart rate monitor says.

Run

Gauge your effort out of T2 based on how you feel, not on your heart rate or pace. Use the latter as secondary markers of intensity, if used at all. Divide the run into three parts.

Part 1 has to do with finding a comfortable pace and level of effort. Part 2 is a time to run steadily and cautiously. In Part III, you may push your pacing limits if you feel like it.

Run Minutes 1–20. Run easily the first 20 minutes, getting in as many liquid calories as you can tolerate. Aim for about 200 calories during this time based on your training and previous race experience.

Run 21 Minutes to Mile 18. Resist the temptation to pick up the pace. Save it for the last 8 miles. Take in gel and water, sports drink, or cola at every aid station (do not take gels with sports drink or cola, however). When using gels, immediately take in at least 6 ounces of water for each packet to avoid dehydration. Get in about 200 calories per hour—more, if possible, if you've practiced eating at a higher rate in training runs (up to 400–500 calories per hour). Calories may be in the form of gels, cola, or sports drink.

Run Mile 18 to Finish. If you've come to mile 18 feeling good and you can pick up the pace, you will gain a lot of time on your competitors who went out too fast. Smart pacing and refueling prior to mile 18 will pay off now. Continue to take in sports drinks or gels with water (6 ounces minimum per packet of gel).

Immediate Post-Race Period

Remove all heat stress as soon as possible. Continue moving around for 5 to 10 minutes after crossing the finish line and begin drinking fluids, especially those with sodium, carbohydrates, and protein. Eat any foods that appeal to you, but avoid fiber and spicy foods. Eat and drink as much as you feel like taking in. Do not drink only water, though, as this may exacerbate hyponatremia.

Parting Thoughts

Scott Molina, a legendary triathlete, once said, "When you feel good, eat." Translation: When you feel good during the race, don't hammer; rather, take advantage of this time to get more fuel onboard. Another thought, this one from Ryan Bolton, winner of Ironman USA: "When your attitude about the race changes, take in some fuel." Translation: Feeling sorry for yourself or angry at the wind is potentially a sign of low blood sugar. Eat.

ANTIOXIDANT SUPPLEMENTS

Generally it's a good idea to meet your nutritional needs with real foods and only use food supplements sparingly. Scientists and supplement designers just aren't as smart as nature when it comes to deciding what to include and what to leave out of something you may be consuming on a regular basis. Real food provides everything needed for health and fitness. Adding lots of pills and potions to your diet is usually a waste of money. There is one exception that I recommend: antioxidant supplements. Here's why.

During the process of metabolizing food and oxygen for exercise, free radicals are released that cause damage to healthy cells. This process can be compared with the rusting of metal—a breakdown caused by oxidation. Hard training produces large numbers of free radicals that threaten your health and ability to recover following workouts.

One study measuring the by-products of free radical damage in highly trained athletes, moderately trained athletes, and a sedentary group found that the highly trained athletes had the highest levels of damage, while the moderately trained subjects had the least. The sedentary group was in the middle. A little exercise appears to be a healthy thing when it comes to free radicals, but extensive exercise or none at all causes problems.

In recent years, studies have shown that vitamins C and E reduce this damage and prevent upper respiratory infections associated with extreme physical exertion by combining with the free radicals to stop the oxidative process. The research typically uses large doses of each of these micronutrients, usually hundreds of times the RDA. The exact amounts needed have not been determined yet, as variables such as age, sex, diet, body composition, size, and training load are involved. Recommended daily intakes based on these studies generally fall into the range of 400 to 800 IU (international units) of vitamin E and 300 to 1,000 milligrams of vitamin C.

The problem is that in order to get even the lowest of these dosages you would have to eat all of these foods daily: 15 asparagus spears, 31 avocados, 4 cups of broccoli, 33 peaches, 30 prunes, 12 ounces of tomato juice, 17 cups of spinach, and one-quarter cup of wheat germ. While it's true that serious athletes tend to eat more than average citizens, they seldom eat enough of the right foods to come even close to these amounts. A 1989 study of triathletes who competed in the national championship, the Hawaii Ironman, or the Alabama Double Ironman found that as a group they had inadequate caloric intakes and poor food selection resulting from rigorous training schedules and limited time for eating. All of this means that it is unlikely that many multisport athletes are getting in adequate levels of vitamins C and E from food alone.

One option is to take a vitamin and mineral supplement containing a variety of nutrients, but these seldom provide vitamins C and E in large enough quantities. You may need to supplement your diet with individual dosages—especially of vitamin E, which is difficult to obtain in sufficient quantities even from a nutrient-dense Paleo diet. It appears that dosages of individual supplements should be taken with meals twice a day for best results.

Vitamin C has a low level of risk at levels of 300 to 1,000 milligrams, but high dosages of vitamin E can cause problems for those who are deficient in vitamin K. Those on blood-thinning medications or high doses of pain relievers should also be cautious with vitamin E. Check with your health-care provider before starting supplementation with either vitamin C or E.

ERGOGENIC AIDS

Several years ago, university researchers asked a group of elite athletes, "If you could take a pill that would ensure a gold medal in the next Olympics, but you would die within five years, would you take it?" The overwhelming answer, surprisingly, was yes.

Such attitudes have led athletes to experiment with anabolic steroids, erythropoietin (EPO), amphetamines, and other dangerous and banned ergogenic aids. Some have consequently died in their quest for athletic excellence. Others have simply wasted their money on products that have no benefit beyond a placebo effect. Many of these substances have not withstood scientific investigation.

There is no magic pill that will guarantee an Olympic medal or even a better-than-average performance. Training and a good diet are still the most important components of athletic excellence. There are, however, a few products that go beyond a normal diet and that science has generally found effective. Realize, however, that in the scientific study of almost any substance, there are often contradictory results. Also, not all ergogenic aids have the same benefits for everyone. Individualization applies here just as it does in training. Some of these products are discussed later in this chapter.

First, however, let's look at ways to evaluate any ergogenic substance to determine whether it's worth a try. There are five questions to ask concerning any product that claims to aid performance:

1. *Is it legal?* Products are often promoted to athletes despite the fact that they contain a banned substance. There have been many instances of blind trust resulting in a disqualification or worse for an elite athlete. To check on a specific product, call the U.S. Olympic Committee's Drug Hotline at (800) 233-0393, or for a list of banned substances go to http://multimedia.olympic.org/pdf/en_report_542.pdf.

2. *Is it ethical?* Only you can answer this question. Some believe that sport must be conducted in its purest form with absolutely no artificial assistance. But once we begin to ponder such ergogenic aids as carbohydrate loading or vitamin and mineral supplements, it becomes clear that it is difficult to draw a line in the sand.

3. *Is it safe?* Studies on the effects of various sports aids are often limited to a few weeks, as most subjects don't want to donate their entire lives to science. Such short periods of observation may not produce the observable effects that might occur with long-term use. It is also possible that using multiple substances simultaneously or in combination with common medications may produce undesirable side effects. Finally, another complication is that government safety regulations for supplements are more lenient than those for food products. Finally, it's always a good idea to check with your physician before supplementing, since your individual health or your family history may affect your decision about how to proceed.

4. *Is its use supported by the research?* There may be an isolated study on a product that shows evidence of a possible benefit, but does the bulk of the literature agree? To search the scientific journals for studies, point your browser at the government's PubMed Web site www.ncbi.nlm.nih.gov/PubMed/, and search on the substance of interest. You'll be presented with a list of archived studies and their abstracts. Have fun reading the list—it could be a thousand or more items long. Better yet, ask a knowledgeable and trusted coach, trainer, registered dietitian, or medical professional for insights on the product in question.

5. *Will it help in my race?* Even if a product is generally supported by the research, it may not work for you. Not all ergogenic aids benefit all people in all events. There are many individual differences that may affect the use of a given product. It may not work well for you because of some combination of your age, sex, health status, medications used, and years of experience in the sport. Some aids have been shown to provide a benefit for short events, such as the 100-meter dash, but not for events lasting several hours.

Below you will find a summary of some ergogenic aids that are generally thought to be safe and effective for athletes in swimming, cycling, and running. Before trying these substances or any other dietary supplement, it's a good idea to talk with your health care provider. Diabetes, hypertension, and any number of other medical conditions may present reasons you shouldn't use one or more of these supplements. They are not free of side effects. It's also a good idea to try out a product in training before using it in a race.

CAFFEINE

No ergogenic aid is more commonly used by athletes than caffeine. Although a cup of coffee doesn't sound too sinister, the International Olympic Committee (IOC) has determined that in sufficient quantities, caffeine unfairly aids performance, and it is therefore banned in high amounts. As of this writing, however, the IOC is considering lifting the ban on caffeine at all levels of intake.

Numerous scientific studies of caffeine's effects over the past 20 years have produced many contradictions. Most have shown benefits for long-distance endurance athletes. A British study, however, found no benefits for marathon runners, but significant aid for milers. The majority of studies have suggested that caffeine helps only in events lasting longer than 90 minutes; others have shown improvement in 60- and even 45-minute competitions.

The author of one study concluded that caffeine causes a complex chemical change in the muscles that stimulates more forceful contractions during a longer period of time than would occur without it. However, most researchers have found that caffeine simply spares muscle glycogen during endurance exercise. Glycogen is an energy source stored in the muscles. When glycogen runs low, the athlete is forced to slow down or stop. Anything that causes the body to conserve this precious fuel, as caffeine appears to do, allows an athlete to maintain a fast pace for a longer time period. For example, a study of cyclists reported a 20 percent improvement in time to exhaustion following two cups of coffee one hour before testing. The beneficial effects peak at about one hour after consumption and seem to last for three to five hours.

The IOC's banned limit would prohibit anything more than about six to eight 5-ounce cups of coffee in an hour, depending on the athlete's size. While that's quite a bit to drink, it's certainly possible. It's interesting to note that some recent research suggests that caffeine at the illegal level actually has a negative effect on performance.

Most studies find that 1.4 to 2.8 milligrams of caffeine per pound of body weight taken an hour before exercise benefits most subjects engaged in endurance exercise. That's about two or three cups of coffee for a 154-pound person. Athletes have also been known to use other products high in caffeine before and during competition. Table 16.6 lists the caffeine content of common products.

While caffeine may seem a safe and effective aid, be aware that there are possible complications. Most studies have shown it to have a diuretic effect on nonexercisers, although one using athletes found little increased fluid loss during exercise. In people not familiar with caffeine, it may bring on anxiety, muscle tremors, gastrointestinal cramps, diarrhea, upset stomach, and nausea. These are not good things to experience before a race. Caffeine also inhibits the absorption of thiamine, a vitamin needed for carbohydrate metabolism, as well as several minerals, including calcium and iron.

BEVERAGE (6 oz./180 ml)	CAFFEINE (mg)
Drip coffee	180
Instant coffee	165
Percolated coffee	149
Brewed tea	60
Mountain Dew	28
Chocolate syrup	24
Coca-Cola	23
Pepsi Cola	19

TABLE 16.6

Caffeine Content of Common Products

If you normally have a cup or two of coffee in the morning, you will probably have no side effects if you do the same before a race. It appears that the benefits are no different for non-coffee drinkers or for regular users. If you don't drink coffee, but are considering using it before a competition, try it several times before workouts to see how it affects you.

BRANCHED-CHAIN AMINO ACIDS

During intense workouts and those lasting longer than about three hours, the body turns to protein to provide fuel. Protein can thus supply as much as 10 percent of the energy requirement in endurance sports. Three essential amino acids—out of the eight that must be present in the diet because they cannot be synthesized by the human body—make up about a third of the muscle tissue. These are leucine, isoleucine, and valine. Collectively they are called branched-chain amino acids (BCAAs).

Several studies have shown that supplementing the diet with BCAAs can enhance endurance performance in several ways:

- BCAAs seem to help to maintain the immune system following exhaustive workouts and races, reducing the likelihood of overtraining. Thus they have the potential to aid recovery.
- BCAAs may help to maintain muscle mass, power, and endurance during exhaustive, multiday endurance events such as bicycle stage races or crash training (see Chapter 14).
- BCAAs may help to reduce central nervous system fatigue, thus enabling an athlete to maintain speed late in a race.
- BCAAs may promote the use of fat for fuel while conserving glycogen.

BCAA capsules may be purchased in health food stores and drugstores. They should come in a dark bottle to protect them from light, and the label should list each of the individual amino acids preceded by an "L," as in "L-valine." This ensures adequate absorption.

There are four times in the training season to use BCAAs—during the maximum strength (MS) phase, in the Build and Peak training periods, before long and intense races, and while training intensely at high altitudes. Here are guidelines for supplementing with BCAA capsules:

- Take about 35 milligrams of BCAA daily for each pound (0.45 kg) of body weight, but only at the times indicated above. A 150-pound (68 kg) athlete would take 5,250 milligrams, or about 5 grams daily. A 120-pound athlete could consume 4,200 milligrams, or about 4 grams a day.
- One or two hours before an MS workout, a high-intensity workout in the Build or Peak periods, or an A-priority race, take one-half of your daily dose. Then one or two hours before bedtime the same day, take the other half.

The only potential negative side effect of taking BCAAs has to do with imbalances in the dietary intake of amino acids. When you eat meat, all of the amino acids are present in the proper ratios; excessive supplementation with BCAAs may upset this balance. Some scientists and nutritionists are concerned that this may have long-term health implications.

MEDIUM-CHAIN TRIGLYCERIDES

Medium-chain triglycerides (MCTs) are processed fats that are metabolically different from other fats in that they are quickly absorbed by the digestive system and aren't readily stored as body fat. Studies have shown that use of MCT can improve endurance and late-race speed in long races such as a half-Ironman or Ironman.

In a study at the University of Cape Town in South Africa, six experienced cyclists rode two hours at about 73 percent of maximum heart rate. Immediately after this steady, low-intensity ride, they time trialed 40 kilometers at maximum effort. They did this three times on different days using a different drink for each attempt. One drink was a normal carbohydrate sports drink. Another was an MCT-only beverage. A third ride used a sports drink spiked with MCT.

With the MCT-only drink their average 40 km time was 1:12:08, and with the carbohydrate sports drink it was 1:06:45. With the mixed MCT-carbohydrate beverage their average time was 1:05:00—a significant improvement. The study's authors believed that the MCT spared glycogen during the two-hour steady ride, allowing the riders to better utilize carbohydrate during the more intense time trial.

Consuming an MCT/sports drink mix may benefit your performance late in races that last three hours or longer. You can create a similar drink for yourself by mixing 16 ounces of your favorite sports drink with four tablespoons of MCT. You can purchase liquid MCT at most health food stores. There are no known side effects for MCT used in this manner.

CREATINE

Creatine is one of the most recent additions to the ergogenics field, having its first known usage in athletics in 1993. Since then, the number of creatine studies has steadily increased, but a lot of questions remain unanswered.

Creatine is a substance found in dietary meat and fish, but it can also be created in the liver, kidneys, and pancreas. It is stored in muscle tissue in the form of creatine phosphate, a fuel used mostly during maximum efforts of up to about 15 seconds and, to a lesser extent, in intense efforts lasting a few minutes.

The amount of creatine made by the human body is not enough to boost performance, but scientists have found that certain types of performance can be enhanced through supplementation with creatine for a few days preceding an event. In order to get an adequate amount of creatine from the diet, an athlete would have to eat up to 5 pounds of rare meat or fish daily. Supplementation appears to be quite effective in increasing stored creatine.

A few years ago, scientists from Sweden, Britain, and Estonia studied the effect of creatine supplements on a group of runners. They tested the runners in a 4,000-meter interval workout (four intervals of 1,000 meters each) at maximum effort to obtain a baseline time, and then, following a creatine-loading period, tested them again in the same event. The creatine-supplemented subjects improved their total 4,000-meter times by an average of 17 seconds, while the athletes in the control group, who took only a placebo, slowed by 1 second. The relative advantage the creatine users experienced increased as the workout progressed—they experienced less fatigue and were faster at the end. Be aware, however, that a few other studies using swimmers and cyclists found no performance enhancement from creatine supplementation in repeated short, anaerobic efforts.

There is still not a lot known about creatine supplementation, but the benefits are probably greatest for maximizing the gains from brief exercise bouts, such as interval and hill-repeat workouts. Some users believe that it decreases body fat, but it may only appear that way because creatine may cause total body weight to increase due to water retention, as fat stays the same. This would skew the results of certain forms of body-fat testing. Also, creatine does not directly build muscle tissue. Instead it provides the fuel so that more power training is possible within a given workout, thus stimulating fast-twitch muscle-fiber growth.

The data on creatine use by endurance athletes is inconclusive. If you decide to use it, the best time to supplement is during the Maximum Strength weight-training phase and the higher-intensity Build period of training. Athletes who are low in force and power stand to benefit the most at these times. About 20 to 30 percent of those who take creatine experience no measurable physiological changes. Vegetarians may realize a greater gains from creatine use than meat-eating athletes because they typically have low levels.

Most studies have used very large dosages, such as 20 to 30 grams of creatine a day, taken in 4 to 5 doses over a period of 4 to 7 days. The average for 18 studies was 19 grams per day for 5 days. One found the same muscle gain levels, however, on as little as 3 grams daily for 30 days. After loading, muscle creatine levels can be maintained at high levels for up to 7 additional weeks with 2 to 7 grams taken daily. Dissolving the creatine in water and drinking it with grape or orange juice seems to improve absorption.

According to scientists who have studied creatine, there is little health risk with supplementation because the creatine is passively filtered from the blood and puts no extra workload on the kidneys; however, the longest study has lasted only a few weeks, so the effects of long-term use are unknown. Scientists do know that once you stop short-term use, natural production of creatine resumes. The only well-established side effect is the addition of 2 or 3 pounds of extra body weight during the loading phase, probably largely from water retention, which quickly disappears. A greater concern is that creatine may give you a false positive in a urine test for kidney problems. There have also been anecdotal accounts of muscle spasm and cramping in power athletes using creatine on a long-term basis. This problem may be caused by a lowered concentration of magnesium in the muscles. Talk with your health care provider before using creatine.

FINAL THOUGHTS

The supplement industry in the United States is not closely regulated by the government, so product purity may be an issue for any supplement, especially if you purchase it from an unscrupulous manufacturer. An analysis of a widely advertised category of dietary supplements found unidentifiable impurities in most of the products. Buy only from reputable companies whose products are well established in the marketplace.

Also, it is unknown how the ergogenic aids described here may interact if used in combination with each other, with other supplements, or even with many of the medications commonly used by athletes, such as ibuprofen or aspirin. It's always a good idea to talk with your health care provider before taking any supplement, all the more so if you are also taking a prescribed or over-the-counter medication.

When using an ergogenic aid, it's important that you assess the benefits, if any, for your performance. Try one at a time, and keep careful notes in your training diary. Not only does using several aids concurrently increase your risk of side effects or problems, it also clouds the issue of which one provided the performance gain. In addition, you should always be skeptical of claims that you will experience faster race times as a result of supplementation. Was it really the pill, or was it the placebo effect? Look at these claims and studies with a critical eye. Taking the time to understand what helps you and what doesn't will ultimately lead to your best races.

In the final analysis, training and diet provide 99.9 percent of the impetus for performance improvements. Supplements offer only a small benefit. If your training and diet are less than desirable, there is no reason to add any ergogenic supplement to the mix.

EPILOGUE

This book was a great challenge. It was not my first but certainly was the most difficult to write, owing to the complexity of multisport. Although it's rather long for a training book, there is still much that was omitted. The most glaring void is perhaps in the area of mental skills. Initially a chapter was planned for this topic, but was eliminated along with a chapter of frequently asked questions in favor of holding down the book's size. If you want to fully develop your ability as a triathlete or duathlete, I highly recommend learning more about the psychology of training and racing. Such mental skills as motivation, confidence, focus, visualization, and positive thought habits are every bit as important as swim, bike, and run workouts for the athlete who is approaching his or her peak potential. See the "References and Recommended Reading" section for books on mental training.

The trouble with writing a book is that it is a snapshot of what is believed to be true at a given point in time. Even though I've been coaching multisport athletes for more than twenty years, there has never been a season in which I didn't change something based on new information or experience. I expect that at some point down the road, I may well disagree with a concept strongly supported on these pages. To do otherwise means never growing.

In fact, during the nine months it took to initially write this book, I refined methods and concepts related to my training system. That was due primarily to the difficulty of trying to put on paper what you think you understand. The third edition includes many other significant changes to my training methodology.

Writing a book teaches you how much you don't know. For me that meant constantly returning to the scientific literature to check facts and conclusions. One of my coaching associates read the manuscript from a technical viewpoint and frequently and correctly suggested that I support or clarify some point that seemed obvious to me. Such challenges were often difficult to answer, but the ensuing thought-provoking discussions and research review gave many of the thoughts expressed here much firmer foundations.

In the Preface, I explained that the book's purpose is to take the guesswork out of training by giving the serious multisport athlete a scientifically based system and set of tools for implementing purposeful training. I hope that this goal has been realized, and that your race performance and enjoyment of the sport are better for having read *The Triathlete's Training Bible.*

APPENDIX A
ANNUAL TRAINING PLAN TEMPLATE

Athlete:

Annual hours:

Seasonal goals:

1.

2.

3.

Training objectives:

1.

2.

3.

4.

5.

Wk#	Mon	Race	PRI	Period	Hours	Weights	SWIM							BIKE							RUN						
							Endurance	Force	Speed Skills	Muscular Endurance	Anaerobic Endurance	Power	Testing	Endurance	Force	Speed Skills	Muscular Endurance	Anaerobic Endurance	Power	Testing	Endurance	Force	Speed Skills	Muscular Endurance	Anaerobic Endurance	Power	Testing
01																											
02																											
03																											
04																											
05																											
06																											
07																											
08																											
09																											
10																											
11																											
12																											
13																											
14																											
15																											
16																											
17																											
18																											
19																											
20																											
21																											
22																											
23																											
24																											
25																											
26																											
27																											
28																											
29																											
30																											
31																											
32																											
33																											
34																											
35																											
36																											
37																											
38																											
39																											
40																											
41																											
42																											
43																											
44																											
45																											
46																											
47																											
48																											
49																											
50																											
51																											
52																											

APPENDIX B
SWIM WORKOUTS

The following are basic swim sets that may be combined in various ways into one swim session. For example, after the warm-up, you may start with a speed skill set, followed by an anaerobic endurance set and then an endurance set before cooling down.

Endurance Sets

E1. Recovery. Swim 10 to 20 minutes or more in Zone 1 concentrating on technique. Do this as a workout following a BT bike or run workout to speed recovery, or as a swim session cool-down. (Periods: All)

E2. Extensive Endurance Intervals. Swim intervals that take 6 to 12 minutes in Zones 2 and 3. Recover after each for 10 to 15 percent of the work-interval time. Total work-interval distance may match the distance of the swim portion of your next A- or B-priority race. A variation on this set is to recover with a 25- to 50-meter/yard drill or kick. Example: 4 x 500 meters/yards in 7 minutes, 30 seconds, leaving every 8 minutes, 15 seconds. Or swim long and steady in Zone 2, especially in open water. (Periods: All)

E3. Intensive Endurance Intervals. Swim intervals that take 3 to 5 minutes to complete. Intensity is mostly Zone 3. Recover after each for about 5 to 10 percent of the preceding work-interval time. Total interval time may match the distance of the swim portion of your next A- or B-priority race. Example: 5 x 400 meters in 3:00, leaving every 3:20. (Periods: Prep, Base 1, Base 2, Base 3)

Force Sets

F1. Open Water. Swim in a river, lake, or the ocean with alternating sets against and with the current. Swim each set against the current at near-maximal effort without breaking form, taking 20 to 30 strokes (each arm) in each set. Recover by swimming with the current for 60 to 90 seconds. Complete three to eight of these sets. Do this only with a partner or group. Example: 5 x 30 strokes with 1-minute recovery intervals. (Periods: Base 2, Base 3, Build 1, Build 2)

F2. Paddles. Swim any set other than warm-up or cool-down using paddles. When first beginning to use paddles, start with small ones, use them only on Endurance sets, and do no more than 15 percent of the total workout distance with them. Over the course of several weeks, increase the size of the paddles used. Don't do more than 50 percent of a workout with them, and never increase both paddle size and total distance using them within a workout at the same time. (Periods: Base 2, Base 3, Build 1)

F3. Drag Sets. Do any set other than warm-up and cool-down wearing a drag suit, T-shirt, or carpenter's apron with pockets. Initially, limit these to endurance sets, adding drag to higher-intensity sets gradually. (Periods: Base 2, Base 3, Build 1)

Speed Skills Sets

(Remember that "speed skills" as used here doesn't mean fast velocity but rather the ability to move effectively.)

S1. Drill Sets. Within a workout, usually near the beginning, include drills that help correct technique flaws (see Chapter 12 for drill descriptions). Practice the drills in repeats each made up of fewer than 30 strokes (each arm) before stopping to rest, and evaluate your technique for 10 to 20 seconds. This is about 50 to 100 meters/yards per repeat. Repeat one drill for no more than 150 strokes (each arm), about 250 to 500 meters/yards, before going to a new drill or set. (Periods: All)

S2. Fin Sets. Do any set, other than warm-up and cool-down, wearing fins. Fins are especially helpful when doing some drills in order to maintain body position on top of the water. (Periods: All)

S3. Speed Reps. Early in a workout, do fast repeats, with each about 30 strokes or fewer (each arm). The pace should be Zone 5b or 5c, but don't sacrifice form for speed. Focus on technique on each repeat. Recover for 30 to 60 seconds between repeats. You must be well recovered to train the nervous system and muscles to work efficiently. Doing speed reps in a fatigued state will only drill in poor technique. Limit a set of speed reps to 150 strokes (each arm). Example: 6 x 50 meters/yards in 40 seconds, leaving every 90 seconds. (Periods: All)

Muscular Endurance Sets

M1. Long Cruise Intervals. Swim work intervals of a distance that takes 6 minutes or more, with recovery intervals approximately one-fourth as long. Intensity is Zone 4 to 5a. The total work-interval distance for a set may equal the swim distance of the next A- or B-priority race. Example: 4 x 400 meters/yards in 6:00, leaving every 7:30. (Periods: Base 2, Base 3, Build 1, Build 2, Peak)

M2. Short Cruise Intervals. Swim intervals that take 3 to 5 minutes to complete. Intensity is Zones 4 to 5a. Recover after each for about 15 percent of the preceding work-interval time. Total work-interval time may match the distance of the swim portion of your next A- or B-priority race. Example: 8 x 200 meters in 3:00, leaving every 3:30. (Periods: Base 2, Base 3, Build 1, Build 2, Peak)

M3. Threshold. Swim 12 to 20 minutes in Zones 4 and 5a without stopping. Example: 1,200 meters/yards in 18:00. (Periods: Base 3, Build 1, Build 2, Peak)

Anaerobic Endurance Sets

A1. AE Intervals. Complete work intervals of 3- to 5-minute duration with recoveries that are about half of the work-interval time. Intensity is Zone 5b. The combined work-interval duration may equal the anticipated time of your next sprint- or Olympic-distance race. Recovery intervals may be gradually reduced to 25 percent of the work interval during the Build period as fitness improves. Example: 5 x 300 meters/yards in 4:30, leaving every 6:45. (Periods: Build 1, Build 2, Peak)

A2. Lactate Tolerance Reps. Swim repeats of 30-second to 2-minute duration at Zone 5c effort with recoveries that are 1 minute, up to twice as long in order to clear lactate before the next repeat. Greatest improvement comes from gradually lengthening the repeats while holding effort/pace constant. Total volume of lactate tolerance reps for one swim session is 3 to 12 minutes. Example: 5 x 100 meters/yards in 1:20, leaving every 2:30. (Periods: Build 2, Peak)

Power Sets

P1. Sprints. Swim a distance that takes 10 to 30 seconds at maximal (Zone 5c) effort. Recover after each for two to three times as long as the work interval. Be careful with sprints, as the tendency is to allow form to break down as the effort escalates. Power sprints should be done early in the workout in order to maintain optimal swim technique. One variation of this workout is to do the sprints with paddles, but only if there is no tendency for shoulder injury. Use small paddles initially. The total combined time of sprint work intervals within a set may be 1 to 6 minutes. Example: 12 x 25 meters/yards in 15 seconds leaving every 45 seconds. (Periods: Build 1, Build 2, Peak, Race)

Test Workouts

T1. Broken Kilometer. After a standard warm-up, swim 10 x 100 meters/yards at maximal effort with 10-second recovery intervals. Time the entire set, including recovery intervals, with a running clock from the start of the first 100 to the end of the tenth. Subtract 90 seconds (for recovery intervals) to produce a test "score." This test may be done at the end of each four-week period to gauge progress. (Periods: Base 1, Base 2, Base 3, Build 1, Build 2, Peak)

T2. Time Trial. Following a standard warm-up, swim 1,000 meters/yards at race effort, as described in Chapter 5. Record the time of the swim and your finishing heart rate in your log. This test may be done at the end of each four-week training period as a measure of progress. (Periods: Base 1, Base 2, Base 3, Build 1, Build 2, Peak)

APPENDIX C
BIKE WORKOUTS

Endurance Workouts

E1. Recovery. Done in Zone 1 using the small chainring on a flat course with a comfortably high cadence. Do these in the Prep period as the primary aerobic workout and the day after a BT workout in all other periods. An indoor trainer or rollers may be used for these at any time of the year, especially if flat courses are not available. Crosstraining is also beneficial for recovery in the Preparation, Base 1, and Base 2 periods. An excellent time to do a recovery ride is in the evening on a day when you have done intervals, weights, a hard group workout, hills, or a race. Spinning for 15 to 30 minutes on rollers or a trainer hastens recovery for most experienced riders. Novices benefit more by taking the time off. These workouts are not scheduled on the Annual Training Plan, but are an integral part of training throughout the season. (Periods: All)

E2. Extensive Endurance. Used for aerobic maintenance and endurance training. Stay primarily in Zones 1 and 2 on a rolling course with small grades up to 4 percent. Remain seated on the uphill portions to build greater strength while maintaining a comfortably high cadence. Can be done with a disciplined group or on an indoor trainer by shifting through the gears to simulate rolling hills. In the Base periods, riding steadily in Zone 2 for 20 to 90 minutes or more is quite effective for developing aerobic endurance. Crosstraining is an option during Preparation and Base 1. (Periods: All)

E3. Intensive Endurance. Develops aerobic endurance while stressing muscular endurance. Ride a rolling course with small hills and gear selections (race gearing) that take you into Zone 3 frequently for a few minutes at a time. Remain seated on the hills. Accumulate 10 to 30 minutes or more of Zone 3 time in this manner within a ride. A variation on this workout is to run 15 to 20 minutes immediately after the ride, especially when in the early stages of training for an Ironman or half Ironman. Intensive Endurance is an excellent workout during the Base period, but should seldom, if ever, be included in the other periods. (Periods: Base 1, Base 2, Base 3)

Force Workouts

F1. Moderate Hills. Select a course that includes several moderately steep hills of up to about 6 percent grade that take 2 to 5 minutes to climb. Stay seated on all hills, pedaling from the hips with little or no rocking of the upper body. Cadence at 60 rpm or higher. Stay in Zones 1–5a on this ride. On a trainer, hills are simulated by placing a 5- to 7-inch riser under the front wheel and selecting resistances and gears that force a slowing of cadence. (Periods: Base 2, Base 3)

F2. Long Hills. Ride a course including several long grades of up to 8 percent that take 6 or more minutes to climb. Stay seated on most hills, standing only to rest muscles and get up short, steep rises. Cadence at 60 rpm or higher on climbs. Go no higher than Zone 5a. Concentrate on bike position and smooth pedaling with minimal movement of the upper body. Simulate this workout on an indoor trainer with an 8- to 10-inch block under the front wheel and higher resistances and gears. (Periods: Base 3, Build 1)

F3. Hill Reps. Warm up thoroughly. Then on a steep hill of 6 to 8 percent grade that takes 30 to 60 seconds to climb, do three to eight repeats with 2 to 4 minutes of recovery between them. Intensity may climb to Zone 5b several times. Recover into Zone 1 with easy spinning while descending and at the bottom. Climb in the saddle, holding the handlebar tops with minimal upper body movement. Maintain a cadence of at least 60 rpm. Stop the workout if you cannot maintain at least 60 rpm in your easiest gear or if your knees hurt. Do this workout no more than twice per week with at least 48 hours between them. Do not do this workout if you have knee problems. (Periods: Build 1, Build 2, Peak)

Speed Skills Workouts

S1. Spin-ups. On a downhill or on an indoor trainer set to light resistance, for 1 minute gradually increase cadence to maximum. Maximum is the cadence you can maintain without bouncing. As the cadence increases, allow your lower legs and feet to relax—especially the toes. Hold your maximum for as long as possible. Recover for at least a minute, and repeat several times. These are best done with a handlebar computer that displays cadence. Heart rate and power ratings have no significance for this workout. (Periods: Prep, Base 1, Base 2, Base 3)

S2. Isolated Leg. With light resistance on a trainer or downhill, do 90 percent of work with one leg while the other is "along for the ride." Spin with a higher than normal cadence. Change legs when fatigue begins to set in. You can also do this on a trainer with one foot out of the pedal and resting on a stool, while the other works. Focus on eliminating "dead" spots at top and bottom of the stroke. Heart rate and power ratings have no significance for this workout. (Periods: Base 1, Base 2, Base 3)

S3. Jumps. Within an Endurance ride include several 8- to 12-second, maximum-effort sprints with a high cadence rather than a high gear. Alternate in and out of saddle. These can be done with another rider or with a group. Power/RPE should be Zone 5c Heart rate is not a good indicator. Allow at least 2 minutes' recovery between jumps. (Periods: Build 1, Build 2, Peak, Race)

Muscular Endurance Workouts

M1. Tempo. After warm-up, on a mostly flat course or on an indoor trainer, ride in Zone 3 for an extended time without recovery. Avoid roads with heavy traffic and stop signs. Stay in an aerodynamic position throughout. Start with 10 to 20 minutes of Zone 3 work and build to 50 to 60 minutes or more by adding 10 minutes or so each week. Cadence is at the low end of your comfort range. This workout may be done two or three times weekly. (Periods: Base 2, Base 3)

M2. Cruise Intervals. On a relatively flat course or an indoor trainer, complete three to five work intervals that are of 6- to 12-minute duration. Build to Zone 4 and 5a on each work interval. If training with a heart rate monitor, the work interval starts as soon as you begin pedaling hard—not when Zone 4 is achieved. Recover for 2 or 3 minutes after each. Recovery should be in Zone 1 or 2. The first workout should total about 20 minutes of work intervals. Stay relaxed, aerodynamic, and closely listen to your breathing. Cadence is at the low end of your comfort range. A variation that develops greater strength is shifting every 30 seconds between your "normal" gear and a higher gear (lower cadence). (Periods: Base 3, Build 1, Build 2, Peak)

M3. Hill Cruise Intervals. Same as M2 cruise intervals, except done on a long, low grade such as 2 to 4 percent, or into a strong headwind. Stay in the aero position and work on a smooth stroke with minimal upper body motion. A variation on this workout is to shift between a "normal" and a higher gear (lower cadence) every 30 seconds to build even greater strength. These are good if muscular endurance and force are both limiters. (Periods: Build 1, Build 2, Peak)

M4. Crisscross Threshold. On a mostly flat course with little traffic and no stops, ride 20 to 40 minutes in Zones 4 and 5a. Once Zone 4 is attained, gradually build effort to the top of Zone 5a, taking about 2 minutes to do so. Then gradually back off and slowly drop back to the bottom of Zone 4, taking about 2 minutes again. Continue this pattern throughout the ride. Complete two or three cruise interval workouts before doing this workout. Cadence is at the low end of your comfort range. (Periods: Build 1, Build 2, Peak)

M5. Threshold. On a mostly flat course with little traffic and no stops, ride 20 to 40 minutes nonstop in Zones 4 and 5a. Stay relaxed, aerodynamic, and closely listen to your breathing throughout. Cadence is at the low end of your comfort range. A variation involves shifting between a "normal" gear and a higher gear every minute or so to develop strength. Don't attempt a threshold ride until you've completed at least four cruise interval workouts. This workout should definitely be included in your training. (Periods: Build 2, Peak)

Anaerobic Endurance Workouts

A1. Group Ride. Ride how you feel. If tired, sit in or break off and ride by yourself. If fresh, ride hard, going into Zone 5b several times. (Periods: Build 1, Build 2, Peak)

A2. AE Intervals. After a good warm-up, on a mostly flat course with no stop signs and light traffic, do five work intervals of 3- to 6-minute duration each. Build to Zone 5b on each. Cadence is at the high end of your comfort range. Recover to Zone 1 for the same time as the preceding work interval. (Periods: Build 1, Build 2, Peak)

A3. Pyramid Intervals. The same as AE intervals, except the work intervals are 1, 2, 3, 4, 4, 3, 2, 1 minutes building to Zone 5b. The recovery after each is equal to the preceding work interval. Complete one or two of these sets. (Periods: Build 1, Build 2, Peak)

A4. Hill Intervals. Following a thorough warm-up, go to a 6 to 8 percent hill that takes 3 to 4 minutes to go up and do five climbs. Stay seated with cadence at 60 rpm or higher. Build to Zone 5b on each climb. Recover to Zone 1 by spinning down the hill and at the bottom for a total of 3 to 4 minutes, depending on how long the climb is. (Periods: Build 2, Peak)

A5. Lactate Tolerance Reps. Done on a flat or slightly uphill course or into the wind. After a long warm-up and several jumps, perform four to eight repetitions of 90 seconds to 2 minutes each. Intensity is Zone 5c. The total of all work intervals should not exceed 12 minutes. Recovery intervals are 2.5 times as long as the preceding work interval. For example, after a 2-minute rep, recover for 5 minutes. Build to this workout, conservatively starting with 6 minutes total and adding 2 minutes weekly. Cadence is at the high end of your comfort range. Do this workout no more than once a week and recover for at least 48 hours after. Do not do this workout if you are in the first two years of training for triathlon. (Periods: Build 2, Peak)

A6. Hill Reps. After a good warm-up, go to a 6 to 8 percent hill and do four to eight reps of 90 seconds each. The first 60 seconds are seated, building to Zone 5b just as in AE intervals, with a cadence of at least 60 rpm. With about 30 seconds remaining on the climb, shift to a higher gear, stand, and drive the bike to the top, attaining Zone 5c. Recover completely for 4 minutes after each rep. Do not do this workout if you are in the first two years of training for cycling. (Periods: Build 2, Peak)

A7. AE Intervals + Threshold. Combine A2 and M5 into one workout by completing the AE intervals and then riding 20 minutes of threshold. This is an excellent workout for simulating the stresses of racing. (Periods: Build 2, Peak)

Power Workouts

P1. Sprints. Following a warm-up, do six to nine 30-second sprints in a big gear with a very high cadence. Stand for the first 10 seconds while increasing the cadence to 90 rpm or higher. Then sit for 20 seconds and maintain the cadence in the same gear. Recover for 3 to 5 minutes after each sprint. (Periods: Build 1, Build 2, Peak, Race)

P2. Hill Sprints. Early in the workout, after a good warm-up, go to a hill with a 4 to 6 percent grade. Do six to nine sprints of 20 seconds each with a very high cadence. Use a flying start for each sprint, taking 10 seconds to build speed on the flat approach. Climb the hill in the saddle for 10 seconds, applying maximal force to the pedals with a high cadence. Recover for 3 minutes after each sprint. Power/RPE should be Zone 5c. Heart rate is not a good indicator of exertion for this workout. (Periods: Build 2, Peak)

Test Workouts

T1. Aerobic Time Trial. This is best on an indoor trainer with a rear-wheel computer pickup or on a CompuTrainer or Electronic Trainer. May also be done on a flat section of road, but weather conditions will have an effect. After a warm-up, ride 5 miles with heart rate 9 to 11 beats below lactate threshold heart rate. Use a standard gear without shifting. Record time. The conditions of this workout must remain constant from one test to the next. This includes the amount of rest since the last BT workout, the length and intensity of the warm-up, the weather if on the road, and the gear used during the test. As aerobic fitness improves, the time should decrease. (Periods: Base 1, Base 2, Base 3)

T2. Time Trial. After a 15- to 30-minute warm-up, complete a 10 km time trial on a flat course. Go 5 km out, turn around, and return to the start line. Mark your start and turn for later reference. Look for faster times as your anaerobic endurance and muscular endurance improve. In addition to time, record average power/heart rate and peak power/heart rate. Keep the conditions the same from one time trial to the next as in the aerobic time trial. Any gear may be used and you may shift during the test. (Periods: Build 1, Build 2, Peak)

APPENDIX D
RUN WORKOUTS

Endurance Workouts

E1. Recovery. Done in Zone 1 on a flat, soft course such as a park or golf course. Check cadence several times by counting right-foot strikes for 20 seconds and attempting to achieve 28 to 30. Do this run in the Prep period as the primary aerobic workout, and the day after a BT workout in all other periods. A treadmill may be used for these at any time of the year, especially if flat courses are not available. Crosstraining is also beneficial for recovery in the Preparation, Base 1, and Base 2 periods. Novices recover faster by taking the time off. These workouts are not scheduled on the Annual Training Plan, but are an integral part of training throughout the season. (Periods: All)

E2. Extensive Endurance. Used for aerobic maintenance and endurance training. Stay primarily in Zones 1 and 2 on a rolling course with small grades up to 4 percent. Can be done with a disciplined group or on a treadmill with gradient control to simulate rolling hills. Check cadence, aiming for 28 to 30 right-foot strikes in 20 seconds. In the Base periods, running steadily in Zone 2 for 20 to 90 minutes or more is quite effective for developing aerobic endurance. Crosstraining is an option during Preparation and Base 1. (Periods: All)

E3. Intensive Endurance. Develops aerobic endurance while stressing muscular endurance. Run a rolling course with small hills that take you into Zone 3 frequently for a few minutes at a time. Check cadence, aiming for 28 to 30 right-foot strikes in 20 seconds. Accumulate 10 to 30 minutes or more of Zone 3 time in this manner within a run. This is an excellent workout during the Base period, but should seldom, if ever, be included in the other periods. (Periods: Base 1, Base 2, Base 3)

Force Workouts

F1. Moderate Hills. Select a course that includes several moderately steep hills of up to about 6 percent grade that take 2 to 5 minutes to run up. Maintain a "proud" posture—head up and back straight—while going up the hills. Stay in Zones 1-5a. Can also be done on a treadmill. (Periods: Base 2, Base 3)

F2. Long Hills. Run a course including several long grades of up to 8 percent that take 6 or more minutes to ascend. Maintain a proud posture. Go no higher than Zone 5a. Concentrate on proud posture while getting a full extension on the drive leg on each stride. Simulate this workout on a treadmill. (Periods: Base 3, Build 1)

F3. Hill Reps. Warm up thoroughly. Then on a steep hill of 6 to 8 percent grade that takes 30 to 60 seconds to run up, do three to eight repeats with 2 to 4 minutes of recovery between them. Intensity may climb to Zone 5b several times. Recover into Zone 1 while jogging and walking to the bottom. Maintain a proud posture. Stop the workout if your knees hurt. Do this workout no more than twice per week with at least 48 hours between them. Do not do this workout if you have knee problems. (Periods: Build 1, Build 2, Peak)

Speed Skills Workouts

S1. Strides. On a very slight, soft downhill such as in a park, run 20 seconds at 95 percent effort (RPE 5c) four to eight times. Relax face and fingers while running with a proud posture and quick cadence. A variation on this workout is to count your right-foot strikes for 20 seconds, with a goal of 30 to 32. Another variation is to run these barefoot, but only if the grass is free of sharp objects and there are no breaks in the skin on your feet. Heart rate has no significance for this workout. (Periods: All)

S2. Pickups. Within an endurance run, insert several 20-second accelerations to faster than 5 km race pace. Heart rate is not a good indicator of intensity for these. Maintain a proud posture and quick cadence. Recover for several minutes between these pickups. (Periods: Base 1, Base 2, Base 3, Build 1, Build 2, Peak, Race)

Muscular Endurance Workouts

M1. Tempo. Warm up first. On a mostly flat course or treadmill, run in Zone 3 for an extended time without recovery. Maintain a proud posture and quick cadence. Start with 10 to 15 minutes and build to 30 to 45 minutes or more by adding 5 minutes each week. This workout may be done two or three times weekly. (Periods: Base 2, Base 3)

M2. Cruise Intervals. On a relatively flat course or treadmill, complete three to five work intervals that are of 6- to 12-minute duration. Build to Zones 4 and 5a on each work interval. If training with a heart rate monitor, the work interval starts as soon as you begin running with high effort—not when Zone 4 is achieved. Recover for 2 or 3 minutes after each. Recovery should be into Zone 1 or 2. A variation is to run cruise intervals on the track with 1- to 2-mile work intervals. Stay relaxed and proud with a quick cadence while closely monitoring your breathing. (Periods: Base 3, Build 1, Build 2, Peak)

M3. Hill Cruise Intervals. Same as M2 cruise intervals, except done on a long, low grade such as 2 to 4 percent, or into a strong headwind. Maintain a proud posture and quick cadence. These are good if muscular endurance and force are both limiters. (Periods: Build 1, Build 2, Peak)

M4. Crisscross Threshold. On a mostly flat course, run 15 to 30 minutes in Zones 4 and 5a. Once Zone 4 is attained, gradually build effort to the top of Zone 5a, taking about 2 minutes to do so. Then gradually back off and slowly drop back to the bottom of Zone 4, taking about 2 minutes again. Continue this pattern throughout the run. Complete 2 or 3 cruise interval workouts before doing this workout. (Periods: Build 1, Build 2, Peak)

M5. Threshold. On a mostly flat course, run 15 to 30 minutes nonstop in Zones 4 and 5a or at a pace about 30 seconds per mile slower than 10 km running race pace. Keep a proud posture and quick cadence while listening to your breathing throughout. Don't attempt a threshold run until you've completed at least four cruise interval workouts. (Periods: Build 2, Peak)

Anaerobic Endurance Workouts

A1. Group Run. Run with others of similar ability. Treat this like a "controlled" race. Gradually increase the tempo until you are running in Zones 4 and 5a. Throw in periodic surges that take you into Zone 5b. (Periods: Build 1, Build 2, Peak)

A2. AE Intervals. On the track, run three to five work intervals that take 3 to 6 minutes to complete, achieving Zone 5b on each. Jog (don't walk) for half the distance of the preceding work interval for recovery. For example, run 4 x 800 meters with 400-meter recoveries. These may also be run on the road using time, instead of distance, for duration. Recoveries in this case are equal to the time of the work intervals. Run these on soft surfaces, not on concrete. (Periods: Build 1, Build 2, Peak)

A3. Surge Intervals. Warm up well. Then on a fixed-distance course, such as 10 km, run 2 minutes to Zone 5b and recover for 1 minute by jogging. Run 1 minute to Zone 5b and recover for 30 seconds, and 30 seconds to Zone 5b and recover for 30 seconds. Repeat this pattern for the entire distance before cooling down. (Periods: Build 1, Build 2, Peak)

A4. Hill Intervals. Following a thorough warm-up, go to a 6 to 8 percent hill that takes 3 to 4 minutes to go up and do three to five climbs. Run with a proud posture and powerful toe-off. Build to Zone 5b on each. Recover to Zone 1 by jogging and walking down the hill and at the bottom for a total of 3 to 4 minutes. Complete at least two or three A1 and F2 workouts before doing this one. (Periods: Build 2, Peak)

A5. Lactate Tolerance Reps. After a long warm-up, on a track or other soft surface, run a distance that takes 30 seconds to 2 minutes at maximum speed. The total of all work intervals should not exceed 12 minutes. Recovery intervals are 2.5 times as long as the preceding work interval. For example, after a 2-minute rep, recover for 5 minutes. Build to this workout conservatively, starting with 6 minutes total and adding 2 minutes weekly. Do this workout no more than once a week and recover for at least 48 hours after. Do not do this workout if you are in the first two years of run training. (Periods: Build 2, Peak)

A6. Hill Reps. After a good warm-up, go to a 6 to 8 percent hill and do three to six reps of 90 seconds each. In the first 60 seconds build to Zone 5b just as in AE intervals. With about 30 seconds remaining on the hill, increase the effort, attaining Zone 5c by the top. Recover completely for at least 4 minutes after each rep. Do not do this workout if you are in the first two years of training for running. Recover for at least 48 hours following this run. (Periods: Build 2, Peak)

A7. AE Intervals + Threshold. Combine A2 and M5 into one workout by completing the AE intervals and then running a fixed distance, such as 2 miles, or a fixed time, such as 20 minutes, in Zones 4 and 5a. This is an excellent workout for simulating the effort required in the run portion of an Olympic-distance triathlon. (Periods: Build 2, Peak)

Power Workouts

P1. Sprints. On a track or other soft surface, following a thorough warm-up, do four to eight 20- to 30-second sprints at maximum effort—RPE Zone 5c. Emphasize proud posture and quick cadence. Don't try to "muscle" it. Recover by walking and jogging for 3 to 5 minutes after each sprint. (Periods: Build 1, Build 2, Peak, Race)

P2. Hill Sprints. Early in the workout, after a good warm-up, go to a hill with a 4 to 6 percent grade. Do four to eight sprints of 20 seconds each. Use a flying start for each sprint, taking 10 seconds to build speed on the flat approach. Run up the hill for 10 seconds, emphasizing good technique. Recover by walking and jogging for 3 to 5 minutes after each sprint. Power/RPE should be Zone 5c. Heart rate is not a good indicator of exertion for this workout. (Periods: Build 2, Peak)

P3. Plyometrics. After a good warm-up, include several bounding, jumping, and skipping exercises on grass, track, or another soft surface. Do only 30 to 50 landings broken into three to five sets within the first workout, depending on your ability to tolerate lower-leg stress. Over the next 6 to 8 weeks, build to 80 to 100 landings within three to five sets. There are several possibilities. For example, on a hill exaggerate knee lift and vertical bounce. Or, on a flat surface, run strides, exaggerating float time with each step. Other exercises include single-leg and double-leg hops, skipping for distance rather than height, and squat jumps. (Periods: Base 2, Base 3)

Test Workouts

T1. Aerobic Time Trial. This is best on a track. May also be done on a flat section of road. Extreme weather conditions will skew the results, so seek out days when the temperatures are moderate and there is little wind. After a warm-up, run 1 mile with heart rate 9 to 11 beats below lactate threshold heart rate. Record time. The conditions of this workout must remain constant from one test to the next. This includes the amount of rest since the last BT workout, the length and intensity of the warm-up, the weather, and the shoes (racing or training) used during the test. As aerobic fitness improves, the time should decrease. (Periods: Base 1, Base 2, Base 3)

T2. Time Trial. After a 10- to 20-minute warm-up, complete a 1.5-mile, maximum-effort time trial on a track or road course. Look for faster times as your race fitness improves. In addition to time, record average heart rate and peak heart rate. Keep the conditions the same from one time trial to the next as in the aerobic time trial. Your VO_2max may be estimated using Table D.1. (Periods: Build 1, Build 2, Peak)

Estimation of
VO$_2$max Based on
1.5-Mile Run Test

TIME (MIN.:SEC.)	EST. VO$_2$MAX
7:30 and under	75
7:31–8:00	72
8:01–8:30	67
8:31–9:00	62
9:01–9:30	58
9:31–10:00	55
10:01–10:30	52
10:31–11:00	49
11:01–11:30	46
11:31–12:00	44
12:01–12:30	41
12:31–13:00	39
13:01–13:30	37
13:31–14:00	36
14:01–14:30	34
14:31–15:00	33
15:01–15:30	31
15:31–16:00	30
16:01–16:30	28
16:31–17:00	27
17:01–17:30	26
17:31–18:00	25

APPENDIX E
COMBINED WORKOUTS

Endurance Workouts

E1. Extensive Endurance Brick. Complete a long ride on a rolling course, staying in Zones 1 and 2. Then transition to a long run on a mostly flat course, also staying in Zones 1 and 2. The total time for this brick may vary from 2 to 6 hours. One week the run portion may be longer, and the next the bike is emphasized. Duathletes may run first as a warm-up. (Periods: Base 2, Base 3, Build 1, Build 2)

E2. Intensive Endurance Brick. Ride long on a rolling course with more than half of the time in Zones 2 and 3 accumulating as much Zone 3 as possible. Then transition to a long run, also primarily in Zones 2 and 3. The emphasized portion of this workout may vary from week to week by alternately lengthening the bike or the run. This is an especially good workout when preparing for a half-Ironman-distance race. Duathletes may run first slowly, building intensity to Zone 3 by the end of the first run. (Periods: Base 3, Build 1, Build 2)

Force Workouts

F1. Hill Brick. Ride and/or run on a hilly course at intensities ranging from Zones 1 to 5a. On the bike, stay in the saddle on most climbs to build hip extension force. This can be a relatively short brick broken into bike and run portions that are 30 to 60 minutes long, or, in preparation for a hilly race, treat it more as an intensive endurance brick done on a hilly course with higher intensities due to the hills. Duathletes may run first. (Periods: Base 3, Build 1, Build 2)

Speed Skills Workouts

S1. Pre-Race Brick. The day before an A- or B-priority race, complete a combined workout, including a 30-minute bike and a 15-minute run. During each leg of the workout include three to five accelerations to slightly faster than race pace with long recoveries. The start-finish area of the race is a good venue for this workout. Tighten all bolts on your bike following this workout. (Periods: Build 1, Build 2, Peak, Race)

S2. Transition #1 Practice. At the pool or other swimming venue, set your bike up on a trainer. Swim several race-pace sets and then transition to the bike for 5 minutes at race intensity. Repeat this three to five times. Emphasis should be placed on making T1 as efficient and quick as possible. (Periods: Peak, Race)

S3. Transition #2 Practice. At the running track or other handy venue, set your bike up on a trainer. After a warm-up, ride 5 minutes at race pace and then transition to running for 3 to 5 minutes at race pace. Repeat this three to five times. Emphasis should be placed on making T2 as efficient and quick as possible. (Periods: Peak, Race)

Muscular Endurance Workouts

M1. Tempo Brick. Bike 60 to 90 minutes, including a 10 km to 20 km time trial on a course similar to that of your next A- or B-priority race. Ride the time trial at an intensity similar to or slightly greater than that planned for your next important race. Then transition to a 15- to 45-minute run at goal race pace depending on the length of your next race. Duathletes may run first for 20 to 30 minutes, building to planned race intensity by the end. (Periods: Build 2, Peak)

Anaerobic Endurance Workouts

A1. Bike Intervals Brick. Ride a flat to rolling course. After warming up, do three to five work intervals each of about 2 km to 5 km so that the shortest is at least 2 minutes and the longest takes no more than 6 minutes. Intensity is the same or slightly greater than that anticipated for the next A- or B-priority race. Recover for a time equal to half of the preceding work-interval time. For example, after a 6-minute work interval, recover for 3 minutes. Transition to a run of about half the duration of the bike portion (for example, if you rode for 60 minutes, run for 30). Include 10 to 20 minutes of steady state in Zones 4 to 5a. Duathletes may run first primarily as a warm-up. (Periods: Build 2, Peak)

A2. Run Intervals Brick. Take your indoor bike trainer to a track. Run for 10 to 20 minutes in Zones 1 to 3 to warm up. Then, on the bike trainer, ride for 5 to 10 minutes, achieving Zones 4 or 5a the last minute or so. Change into running shoes and complete two to four work intervals that last 2 to 4 minutes, with intensity rising into Zone 5b on each. Recovery intervals are half the duration of the previous work interval. Return to the bike and again ride 5 minutes or so, building to Zones 4 or 5a. Repeat this pattern one to three more times before cooling down for 10 minutes or so on the bike. Aim for about 20 minutes or 3 miles of total work-interval time for running. (Periods: Build 2, Peak)

APPENDIX F
RACE EVALUATION FORM, DIARY PAGES

RACE EVALUATION FORM

Race name:

Date and start time: _____

Location: _____

Type/distance: _____

Key competitors: _____

Weather: _____

Course conditions: _____

Race goal: _____

Race strategy: _____

Warm-up description:

Start-line arousal level: Very low   Low   Moderate   High   Very high

Results (place, time, splits, etc.): _____

_____

What I did well: _____

_____

What I need to improve: _____

_____

Aches/pains afterward: _____

_____

Other comments: _____

WEEK BEGINNING   **PLANNED WEEKLY HOURS/MILES:**

NOTES _____

_____
_____
_____
_____
_____
_____
_____
_____
_____
_____
_____
_____
_____
_____
_____
_____

MONDAY   /   /

☐ Sleep   ☐ Fatigue   ☐ Stress   ☐ Soreness

Resting heart rate   Weight

WORKOUT 1   ☐ S   ☐ B   ☐ R   ☐ Other:

Weather

Route

Distance

Time   Total

Time by zone   1   2

3   4   5

WORKOUT 2   ☐ S   ☐ B   ☐ R   ☐ Other:

Weather

Route

Distance

Time   Total

Time by zone   1   2

3   4   5

TUESDAY   /   /

☐ Sleep   ☐ Fatigue   ☐ Stress   ☐ Soreness

Resting heart rate   Weight

WORKOUT 1   ☐ S   ☐ B   ☐ R   ☐ Other:

Weather

Route

Distance

Time   Total

Time by zone   1   2

3   4   5

WORKOUT 2   ☐ S   ☐ B   ☐ R   ☐ Other:

Weather

Route

Distance

Time   Total

Time by zone   1   2

3   4   5

NOTES _____

_____
_____
_____
_____
_____
_____
_____
_____
_____
_____
_____
_____
_____
_____
_____
_____

WEDNESDAY   /   /

☐ Sleep   ☐ Fatigue   ☐ Stress   ☐ Soreness

Resting heart rate   Weight

WORKOUT 1   ☐ S   ☐ B   ☐ R   ☐ Other:

Weather

Route

Distance

Time   Total

Time by zone   1   2

3   4   5

WORKOUT 2   ☐ S   ☐ B   ☐ R   ☐ Other:

Weather

Route

Distance

Time   Total

Time by zone   1   2

3   4   5

THURSDAY   /   /

☐ Sleep   ☐ Fatigue   ☐ Stress   ☐ Soreness

Resting heart rate   Weight

WORKOUT 1   ☐ S   ☐ B   ☐ R   ☐ Other:

Weather

Route

Distance

Time   Total

Time by zone   1   2

3   4   5

WORKOUT 2   ☐ S   ☐ B   ☐ R   ☐ Other:

Weather

Route

Distance

Time   Total

Time by zone   1   2

3   4   5

WEEK'S GOALS (Check off as achieved)

☐ _____
☐ _____
☐ _____

FRIDAY	/ /

☐ Sleep ☐ Fatigue ☐ Stress ☐ Soreness

Resting heart rate _____ Weight _____

WORKOUT 1 ☐ S ☐ B ☐ R ☐ Other: _____

Weather _____

Route _____

Distance _____

Time _____ Total _____

Time by zone 1 _____ 2 _____

3 _____ 4 _____ 5 _____

WORKOUT 2 ☐ S ☐ B ☐ R ☐ Other: _____

Weather _____

Route _____

Distance _____

Time _____ Total _____

Time by zone 1 _____ 2 _____

3 _____ 4 _____ 5 _____

SATURDAY	/ /

☐ Sleep ☐ Fatigue ☐ Stress ☐ Soreness

Resting heart rate _____ Weight _____

WORKOUT 1 ☐ S ☐ B ☐ R ☐ Other: _____

Weather _____

Route _____

Distance _____

Time _____ Total _____

Time by zone 1 _____ 2 _____

3 _____ 4 _____ 5 _____

WORKOUT 2 ☐ S ☐ B ☐ R ☐ Other: _____

Weather _____

Route _____

Distance _____

Time _____ Total _____

Time by zone 1 _____ 2 _____

3 _____ 4 _____ 5 _____

NOTES _____

_____
_____
_____
_____
_____
_____
_____
_____
_____
_____
_____
_____
_____
_____
_____

SUNDAY	/ /

☐ Sleep ☐ Fatigue ☐ Stress ☐ Soreness

Resting heart rate _____ Weight _____

WORKOUT 1 ☐ S ☐ B ☐ R ☐ Other: _____

Weather _____

Route _____

Distance _____

Time _____ Total _____

Time by zone 1 _____ 2 _____

3 _____ 4 _____ 5 _____

WORKOUT 2 ☐ S ☐ B ☐ R ☐ Other: _____

Weather _____

Route _____

Distance _____

Time _____ Total _____

Time by zone 1 _____ 2 _____

3 _____ 4 _____ 5 _____

WEEKLY SUMMARY

	Time/Distance	Year to Date
Swim		
Bike		
Run		
Strength		
Other		
Total		

Soreness _____

_____

NOTES _____

_____
_____
_____
_____
_____

NOTES _____

_____
_____
_____
_____
_____
_____
_____
_____
_____
_____
_____
_____
_____
_____
_____
_____

GLOSSARY

Adaptation. Refers to the body's ability to adjust to various demands placed on it over a period of time.

Aerobic. In the presence of oxygen; aerobic metabolism utilizes oxygen. Below the anaerobic-intensity level.

Aerobic capacity. The body's maximal capacity for using oxygen to produce energy during maximal exertion. Also known as VO_2max.

Agonistic muscles. Muscles directly engaged in a muscular contraction.

Anaerobic. Literally, "without oxygen." Exercise that demands more oxygen than the heart and lungs can supply. The intensity of exercise performed above the lactate threshold.

Anaerobic endurance. The ability resulting from the combination of speed skills and endurance, allowing the athlete to maintain a high speed for an extended period of time while anaerobic.

Anaerobic threshold (AT). When aerobic metabolism no longer supplies all the need for energy, energy is produced anaerobically; indicated by an increase in lactic acid. Sometimes referred to as lactate threshold.

Antagonistic muscles. Muscles that have an opposite effect on movers, or work against other muscles, by opposing their contraction. For example, the triceps is an antagonistic muscle for the biceps.

Base period. The period during which the basic abilities of endurance, speed skills, and force are emphasized.

Bonk. A state of extreme exhaustion mainly caused by the depletion of glycogen in the muscles.

Breakthrough (BT). A workout intended to cause a significant, positive, adaptive response. These generally require 36 or more hours to adequately recover.

Build period. The specific preparation mesocycle during which high-intensity training in the form of muscular endurance, speed endurance, and power are emphasized, and endurance, force, and speed skills are maintained.

Cadence. Revolutions or cycles per minute of the swim stroke, pedal stroke, or running stride.

Capillary. A small vessel located between arteries and veins in which exchanges between tissue and blood occur.

Carbohydrate loading (glycogen loading). A dietary procedure that elevates muscle glycogen stores by emphasizing carbohydrate consumption.

Cardiorespiratory system. Cardiovascular system and lungs.

Cardiovascular system. Heart, blood, and blood vessels.

Central nervous system. Spinal cord and brain.

Circuit training. Selected exercises or activities performed rapidly in sequence; used in weight training.

Concentric contraction. The shortening of a muscle during contraction. (See "Eccentric contraction.")

Cool-down. Low-intensity exercise at the end of a training session.

Criterium. A multilap race held on a short course.

Crosstraining. Training for more than one sport during the same period of time.

Drafting. Swimming, biking, or running behind others in order to reduce effort.

Drops. The lower portion of turned-down handlebars.

Duration. The length of time of a given workout.

Eccentric contraction. The lengthening of a muscle during contraction. For example, slowly setting down a heavy, handheld weight. (See "Concentric contraction.")

Endurance. The ability to persist, to resist fatigue.

Ergogenic aid. A substance, device, or phenomenon that can improve athletic performance.

Fartlek. Swedish for "speed play," or an unstructured, interval-type workout.

Fast-twitch fiber (FT). A muscle fiber characterized by fast contraction time, high anaerobic capacity, and low aerobic capacity, all making the fiber suited for high-power activities.

Force. The strength evident in a muscle or muscle group while exerting against a resistance.

Free weights. Weights not part of an exercise machine (i.e., barbells and dumbbells).

Frequency. The number of times per week that one trains.

Glucose. A simple sugar.

Glycemic index. A system of ranking carbohydrate foods based on how quickly they raise the blood's glucose level.

Glycogen. The form in which glucose (sugar) is stored in the muscles and the liver.

Growth hormone. A hormone secreted by the anterior lobe of the pituitary gland that stimulates growth and development.

Hammer. A fast, sustained effort.

Hamstring. Muscle on the back of the thigh that flexes the knee and extends the hip.

Hoods. On drop handlebars, the covers of the brake handles.

Individuality, principle of. The theory that any training program must consider the specific needs and abilities of the individual for whom it is designed.

Intensity. The qualitative element of training referring to effort, velocity, maximum strength, and power.

Interval training. A system of high-intensity work marked by short but regularly repeated periods of hard exercise interspersed with periods of recovery.

Isolated leg training (ILT). Pedaling with one leg to improve technique.

Lactate. Formed when lactic acid from the muscles enters the bloodstream.

Lactate threshold (LT). The point during exercise of increasing intensity at which blood lactate begins to accumulate above resting levels. Sometimes referred to as anaerobic threshold.

Lactic acid. A by-product of the lactic acid system resulting from the incomplete breakdown of glucose (sugar) in the production of energy.

Long, slow distance (LSD) training. A form of continuous training in which the athlete performs at a relatively low intensity for a long duration.

Macrocycle. A period of training including several mesocycles; usually an entire season.

Mash. To push a big gear.

Mesocycle. A period of training generally two to six weeks long.

Microcycle. A period of training of approximately one week.

Muscular endurance. The ability of a muscle or muscle group to perform repeated contractions for a long period of time while bearing a load.

Overload, principle of. A training load that challenges the body's current level of fitness.

Overreaching. Training above the workload that would produce overtraining if continued long enough.

Overtraining. Extreme fatigue, both physical and mental, caused by extensively training at a workload higher than that to which the body can readily adapt.

Peak period. The mesocycle during which volume of training is reduced and intensity is proportionally increased, allowing the athlete to reach high levels of fitness.

Periodization. The process of structuring training into periods.

Power. The ability resulting from force and speed skills.

Preparation (Prep) period. The mesocycle during which the athlete begins to train for the coming season; usually marked by the use of crosstraining and low workloads.

Progression, principle of. The theory that the workload must be gradually increased accompanied by intermittent periods of recovery.

Quadriceps. The large muscle in front of the thigh that extends the lower leg and flexes the hip.

Race period. The mesocycle during which the workload is greatly decreased, allowing the athlete to compete in high-priority races.

Rating of perceived exertion (RPE). A subjective assessment of how hard one is working.

Recovery. A period of training when rest is emphasized.

Recovery interval. The relief period between work intervals within an interval workout.

Repetition. The number of times a task, such as a work interval or lifting a weight, is repeated.

Repetition maximum (RM). The maximum load that a muscle group can lift in one attempt. Also called "one-repetition maximum" (1RM).

Session. A single practice period that may include one or more workouts.

Set. A group of repetitions.

Slow-twitch fiber (ST). A muscle fiber characterized by slow contraction time, low anaerobic capacity, and high aerobic capacity, all making the fiber suited for low-power, long-duration activities.

Specificity, principle of. The theory that training must stress the systems critical for optimal performance in order to achieve the desired training adaptations.

Speed skills. Within the context of this book, the ability to move the body in ways that produce optimum performance. For example, the ability to turn the cranks quickly and efficiently on the bike.

Tapering. A reduction in training volume prior to a major competition.

Tops. The portion of the handlebar closest to the stem.

Training. A comprehensive program intended to prepare an athlete for competition.

Training zone. A level of intensity based on a percentage of some measure, such as heart rate or power, of the individual's capacity for work.

Transition (Tran) period. The mesocycle during which the workload and structure of training are greatly reduced, allowing physical and psychological recovery from training and racing.

Ventilatory threshold (VT). The point during increasing exertion at which breathing first becomes labored. Closely corresponds with lactate threshold.

VO_2max. The capacity for oxygen consumption by the body during maximal exertion, also known as aerobic capacity and maximal oxygen consumption. Usually expressed as liters of oxygen consumed per kilogram of body weight per minute (ml/kg/min).

Volume. A quantitative element of training, such as miles or hours of training within a given time. The combination of duration and frequency.

Warm-up. The period of gradually increasing intensity of exercise at the start of a training session.

Work interval. High-intensity efforts separated by recovery intervals.

Workload. Measured stress applied in training through the combination of frequency, intensity, and duration.

Workout. A portion of a session that is focused on a specific aspect of training, such as power.

REFERENCES AND RECOMMENDED READING

Alter, M. J. *Sport Stretch.* Champaign, IL: Human Kinetics, 1998.

American College of Sports Medicine. "Antioxidants and the Elite Athlete." Proceedings of panel discussion, May 27, 1992, Dallas, TX.

American Dietetic Association. "Nutrition and Physical Fitness and Athletic Performance." *Journal of the American Dietetics Association* 87 (1987): 933–939.

Anderson, B. *Stretching.* Bolinas, CA: Shelter Publications, 1980.

Anderson, O. "Carbs, Creatine & Phosphate: If the King Had Used These Uppers, He'd Still Be Around Today." *Running Research News* 12, no. 3 (1996): 1–4.

———. "German Study Confirms Major Shifts in Intensity Work Far Better Than Big Upswings in Mileage." *Running Research News* 12, no. 9 (1996): 1–5.

———. The Search for the Perfect Intensity Distribution. *Cycling Research News* 1, no. 10 (2004): 1, 4–10.

———. "Things Your Parents Forgot to Tell You about Tapering." *Running Research News* 11, no. 7 (1995): 1–8.

Appell, H. J., et al. "Supplementation of Vitamin E May Attenuate Skeletal Muscle Immobilization Atrophy." *International Journal of Sports Medicine* 18 (1997): 157–160.

Armsey, T. D., and G. A. Green. "Nutrition Supplementation: Science vs. Hype." *The Physician and Sports Medicine* 25, no. 6 (1997): 77–92.

Astrand, P. O., and K. Rohdahl. *Textbook of Work Physiology.* New York: McGraw-Hill, 1977.

Atwater, A. E. "Gender Differences in Distance Running." In P. R. Cavanagh, ed., *Biomechanics of Distance Running.* Champaign, IL: Human Kinetics, 1990.

Balaban, E. P., et al. "The Frequency of Anemia and Iron Deficiency in the Runner." *Medicine and Science in Sport and Exercise* 21 (1989): 643–648.

Balsam, P. D. "Creatine Supplementation Per Se Does Not Enhance Endurance Exercise Performance." *Acta Physiologica Scandinavica* 149, no. 4 (1993): 521–523.

Bemben, D. A., et al. "Effects of Oral Contraceptives on Hormonal and Metabolic Responses during Exercise." *Medicine and Science in Sport and Exercise* 24, no. 4 (1992): 434–441.

Bernhardt, G. *Training Plans for Multisport Athletes.* Boulder, CO: VeloPress, 2000.

Billat, V. L., et al. "Physical and Training Characteristics of Top-Class Marathon Runners." *Medicine and Science in Sports and Exercise* 33, no. 12 (2001): 2089–2097.

Blomstrand, E., et al. "Administration of Branched Chain Amino Acids during Sustained Exercise—Effects on Performance and on Plasma Concentrations of Some Amino Acids." *European Journal of Applied Physiology* 63, no. 2 (1991): 83–88.

Bompa, T. *From Childhood to Champion Athlete.* Toronto, ON: Veritas Publishing, 1995.

———. *Periodization of Strength.* Toronto, ON: Veritas Publishing, 1993.

———. "Physiological Intensity Values Employed to Plan Endurance Training." *New Studies in Athletics* 3, no. 4 (1988): 37–52.

———. *Theory and Methodology of Training.* Dubuque, IA: Kendall/Hunt Publishing, 1994.

Bonen, A., and A. Belcastro. "Comparison of Self-Selected Recovery Methods on Lactic Acid Removal Rates." *Medicine and Science in Sports and Exercise* 8 (1976): 176–178.

Borg, G. *An Introduction to Borg's RPE-Scale.* Ithaca, NY: Movement Publications, 1985.

Bouchard, C., and G. Lortie. "Heredity and Endurance Performance." *Sports Medicine* 1 (1984): 38–94.

Brenner, I.K.M. "Infection in Athletes." *Sports Medicine* 17, no. 2 (1994): 86–107.

Broker, J. P., and R. J. Gregor. "Cycling Biomechanics." In E. Burke, ed., *High-Tech Cycling.* Champaign, IL: Human Kinetics, 1996.

Brown, C., and J. Wilmore. "The Effects of Maximal Resistance Training on the Strength and Body Composition of Women Athletes." *Medicine and Science in Sports and Exercise* 6 (1974): 174–177.

Brunner, R., and B. Tabachnik. *Soviet Training and Recovery Methods.* Pleasant Hill, CA: Sport Focus Publishing, 1990.

Brzycki, M. "Strength Testing—Predicting a One-Rep Max from Reps to Fatigue." *Journal of Physical Education, Recreation and Dance* 64 (1993): 88–90.

Budgett, R. "Overtraining Syndrome." *British Journal of Sports Medicine* 24 (1990): 231–236.

Bull, Stephen J. *Sports Psychology: A Self-Help Guide.* Marlborough, UK: Crowood Press, 2000.

Bunt, J. C., et al. "Sex and Training Differences in Human Growth Hormone Levels during Prolonged Exercise." *Journal of Applied Physiology* 61 (1986): 1796.

Burke, E. *High-Tech Cycling.* Champaign, IL: Human Kinetics, 1996.

———. *Serious Cycling.* Champaign, IL: Human Kinetics, 1995.

Burke, L. M., and R.S.D. Read. "Dietary Supplements in Sport." *Sports Medicine* 15 (1993): 43–65.

Butts, N. K., B. A. Henry, and D. Mclean. "Correlations between VO_2Max and Performance Times of Recreational Triathletes." *Journal of Sports Medicine and Physical Fitness* 31, no 3 (1991): 339–344.

Cade, J. R., et al. "Dietary Intervention and Training in Swimmers." *European Journal of Applied Physiology* 63 (1991): 210–215,

Cavanagh, P. R., and D. J. Sanderson. "The Biomechanics of Cycling: Studies of the Pedaling Mechanics of Elite Pursuit Riders." In E. Burke, ed., *Science of Cycling.* Champaign, IL: Human Kinetics, 1986.

Cavanagh, P. R., et al. "A Biomechanical Comparison of Elite and Good Distance Runners." *Annals of the New York Academy of Sciences* 301 (1977): 328–345.

Cedaro, R. (ed.). *Triathlon: Achieving Your Personal Best.* New York: Facts on File, 1993.

Cerra, F. B., et al. "Branched-Chain Amino Acid Supplementation during Trekking at High Altitude." *European Journal of Applied Physiology* 65 (1984): 394–398.

Child, J. S., et al. "Cardiac Hypertrophy and Function in Masters Endurance Runners and Sprinters." *Journal of Applied Physiology* 57 (1984): 170–181.

Clark. "Red Meat: To Eat or Not to Eat." *National Strength and Conditioning Association Journal* 15 (1993): 71–72.

Clement, D. B., et al. "Branched-Chain Metabolic Support: A Prospective, Randomized Double-Blind Trial in Surgical Stress." *Annals of Surgery* 199, no. 3 (1984): 286–291.

Cohen, J., and C. V. Gisolfi. "Effects of Interval Training in Work-Heat Tolerance in Young Women." *Medicine and Science in Sport and Exercise* 14 (1982): 46–52.

Conley, D. L., and G. Krahenbuhl. "Running Economy and Distance Running Performance of Highly Trained Athletes." *Medicine and Science in Sports and Exercise* 12, no. 5 (1980): 357–360.

Conley, D. L., et al. "Following Steve Scott: Physiological Changes Accompanying Training." *The Physician and Sports Medicine* 12, no. 1 (1984): 103–106.

Cordain, L. Department of Exercise and Sport Science, Colorado State University, Fort Collins, CO. 1998. Personal communication with author.

———. *The Paleo Diet.* New York: Wiley, 2002.

Cordain, L., and J. Friel. *The Paleo Diet for Athletes.* Emmaus, PA: Rodale, 2005.

Cordain, L., R. W. Gotshall, and S. B. Eaton. "Evolutionary Aspects of Exercise." *World Review of Nutrition and Dietetics* 81 (1997): 49–60.

Costill, D. "Predicting Athletic Potential: The Value of Laboratory Testing." *Sports Medicine Digest* 11, no. 11 (1989): 7.

Costill, D., et al. "Adaptations to Swimming Training: Influence of Training Volume." *Medicine and Science in Sports and Exercise* 23 (1991): 371–377.

Costill, D. L., et al. "Effects of Repeated Days of Intensified Training on Muscle Glycogen and Swimming Performance." *Medicine and Science in Sport and Exercise* 20 (1988): 249–254.

Coyle, E. F., et al. "Cycling Efficiency Is Related to the Percentage of Type I Muscle Fibers." *Medicine and Science in Sports and Exercise* 24 (1992): 782.

Cunningham, D. A., et al. "Cardiovascular Response to Intervals and Continuous Training in Women." *European Journal of Applied Physiology* 41 (1979): 187–197.

Daniels, J. "Physiological Characteristics of Champion Male Athletes." *Research Quarterly* 45 (1989): 342–348.

Daniels, J., et al. 1984. "Interval Training and Performance." *Sports Medicine* 1 (1984): 327–334.

David, A. S., et al. "Post-Viral Fatigue Syndrome: Time for a New Approach." *British Medical Journal* 296 (1988): 696–699.

Davis, J. M. "Carbohydrates, Branched-Chain Amino Acids, and Performance—the Central Fatigue Hypothesis. *International Journal of Sport Nutrition* 5 (1995): S29–S38.

Deuster, P. A., et al. "Nutritional Survey of Highly Trained Women Runners." *American Journal of Clinical Nutrition* 45 (1986): 954–962.

deVries, H. A. "Effects of Various Warm-up Procedures on 100-Yard Times of Competitive Swimmers." *Research Quarterly* 30 (1959): 11–20.

DiCarlo, L. J., et al. "Peak Heart Rates during Maximal Running and Swimming: Implications for Exercise Prescription." *International Journal of Sports Medicine* 12 (1991): 309–312.

Dill, D., et al. "A Longitudinal Study of 16 Champion Runners." *Journal of Sports Medicine* 7 (1967): 4–32.

Dimsdale, J, et al. "Postexercise Peril: Plasma Catecholamines and Exercise." *Journal of the American Medical Association* 251 (1984): 630–632.

Doherty, M. "The Effects of Caffeine on the Maximal Accumulated Oxygen Deficit and Short-Term Running Performance." *International Journal of Sports Nutrition* 8, no. 2 (1998): 95–104.

Dragan, I., and I. Stonescu. *Organism Recovery Following Training.* Bucharest, Romania: Sport-Turism, 1978.

Drinkwater, B. L., ed. *Female Endurance Athletes.* Champaign, IL: Human Kinetics, 1986.

Drinkwater, B. L. "Women and Exercise: Physiological Aspects." *Exercise and Sports Sciences Reviews* 12 (1984): 21–51.

Drinkwater, B. L., et al. "Bone Mineral Content of Amenorrheic and Eumenorrheic Athletes." *New England Journal of Medicine* 311 (1984): 277–281.

Driver, H. S., et al. "Prolonged Endurance Exercise and Sleep Disruption." *Medicine and Science in Sports and Exercise* 26, no. 7 (1994): 903–907.

Droghetti, P., et al. "Noninvasive Determination of the Anaerobic Threshold in Canoeing, Cross-Country Skiing, Cycling, Roller and Ice Skating, Rowing and Walking." *European Journal of Applied Physiology* 53 (1985): 299–303.

Dufaux, B., et al. "Serum Ferritin, Transferrin, Haptoglobin, and Iron in Middle- and Long-Distance Runners, Elite Rowers, and Professional Racing Cyclists." *International Journal of Sports Medicine* 2 (1981): 43–46.

Dunbar, C. C., et al. "The Validity of Regulating Exercise Intensity by Ratings of Perceived Exertion." *Medicine and Science in Sports and Exercise* 24 (1992): 94–99.

Dutto, D. J., and J. M. Cappaert. "Biomechanical and Physiological Differences between Males and Females during Freestyle Swimming." *Medicine and Science in Sports and Exercise* 26, no. 5 (1994): S1098.

Eaton, S. B. "Humans, Lipids, and Evolution." *Lipids* 27, no. 1 (1992): 814–820.

Eaton, S. B., and M. Konner. "Paleolithic Nutrition: A Consideration of Its Nature and Current Implications." *The New England Journal of Medicine* 312, no. 5 (1985): 283–289.

Eaton, S. B., and D. A. Nelson. "Calcium in Evolutionary Perspective." *American Journal of Clinical Nutrition* 54 (1991): 281S–287S.

Eaton, S. B., M. Shostak, and M. Konner. *The Paleolithic Prescription.* New York: Harper & Row, 1989.

Ekblom, B. "Effect of Physical Training in Adolescent Boys." *Journal of Applied Physiology* 27 (1969): 350–353.

Elliott, Richard. *The Competitive Edge.* Mountain View, CA: TAFNEWS Press, 1991.

Ericsson, K. A., R. T. Krampe, and S. Heizmann. "Can We Create Gifted People?" *CIBA Foundation Symposium* 178 (1993): 221–231.

Evans, M. *Endurance Athlete's Edge.* Champaign, IL: Human Kinetics, 1997.

———. *Triathlete's Edge.* Champaign, IL: Human Kinetics, 2003.

Evans, W., et al. "Protein Metabolism and Endurance Exercise." *The Physician and Sports Medicine* 11, no. 7 (1983): 63–72.

Farber, H. W., et al. "The Endurance Triathlon: Metabolic Changes after Each Event and during Recovery." *Medicine and Science in Sports and Exercise* 23, no. 8 (1991): 959–965.

Faria, I. E. "Applied Physiology of Cycling." *Sports Medicine* 1 (1984): 187–204.

Farrell, P. A., et al. "Enkephalins, Catecholamines, and Psychological Mood Alterations: Effects of Prolonged Exercise." *Medicine and Science in Sports and Exercise* 19 (1987): 347.

Fitzgerald, L. "Exercise and the Immune System." *Immunology Today* 9, no. 11 (1988): 337–339.

Francis, K. T., et al. "The Relationship between Anaerobic Threshold and Heart Rate Linearity during Cycle Ergometry." *European Journal of Applied Physiology* 59 (1989): 273–277.

Freeman, W. *Peak When It Counts.* Mountain View, CA: TAFNEWS Press, 1991.

Freund, B. J., et al. "Glycerol Hyperhydration: Hormonal, Renal, and Vascular Fluid Responses." *Journal of Applied Physiology* 79 (1995): 2069–2077.

Friel, J. *The Cyclist's Training Bible*, 4th ed. Boulder: VeloPress, 2009.

Fry, R. W., et al. "Biological Responses to Overload Training in Endurance Sports." *European Journal of Applied Physiology* 64, no. 5 (1992): 335–344.

Fry, R. W., et al. "Overtraining in Athletes: An Update." *Sports Medicine* 12, no. 1 (1991): 32–65.

Fry, R. W., et al. "Periodization and the Prevention of Overtraining." *Canadian Journal of Sports Science* 17 (1992): 241–248.

Gibbons, E. S. "The Significance of Anaerobic Threshold in Exercise Prescription." *Journal of Sports Medicine* 27 (1987): 357–361.

Gibbons, T. P., et al. "Physiological Responses in Elite Junior Triathletes during Field Testing." *Medicine and Science in Sports and Exercise* 28, no. 5 (1996): SA756.

Gleeson, M. "Biochemical and Immunological Markers of Overtraining." *Journal of Sports Science and Medicine* 1 (2002): 31–41.

Goedecke, J. H., et al. "Effects of Medium-Chain Triaclyglycerol Ingested with Carbohydrate on Metabolism and Exercise Performance." *International Journal of Sports Nutrition* 9, no. 1 (1999): 35–47.

Goforth, H. W., et al. "Simultaneous Enhancement of Aerobic and Anaerobic Capacity." *Medicine and Science in Sports and Exercise* 26, no. 5 (1994): 171.

Goldspink, D. F. "The Influence of Immobilization and Stretch on Protein Turnover of Rat Skeletal Muscle." *Journal of Physiology* 264 (1977): 267–282.

Gonzalez, H., and M. L. Hull. "Bivariate Optimization of Pedaling Rate and Crank-Arm Length in Cycling." *Journal of Biomechanics* 21, no. 10 (1988): 839–849.

———. "Multivariable Optimization of Cycling Biomechanics." *Journal of Biomechanics* 22, nos. 11 and 12 (1989): 1151–1161.

Graham, T. E., and L. L. Spriet. "Caffeine and Exercise Performance." *Sports Science Exchange* 9, no. 1 (1996): 1–6.

Graham, T. E., et al. "Metabolic and Exercise Endurance Effects of Coffee and Caffeine Ingestion." *Journal of Applied Physiology* 85, no. 3 (1998): 883–889.

Grandjean, A. C. "Diets of Elite Athletes: Has the Discipline of Sports Nutrition Made an Impact?" *Journal of Nutrition* 127, no. 5 (1997): 874S–877S.

Green, D. R., et al. "An Evaluation of Dietary Intakes of Triathletes: Are RDAs Being Met?" *Brief Communications* 89, no. 11 (1989): 1653–1654.

Guezennec, C. Y., et al. "Increase in Energy Cost of Running at the End of a Triathlon." *European Journal of Applied Physiology* 73, no. 5 (1996): 440–445.

Guilland, J. C., et al. "Vitamin Status of Young Athletes Including the Effects of Supplementation." *Medicine and Science in Sport and Exercise* 21 (1989): 441–449.

Hagberg, J. M. "Physiological Implications of the Lactate Threshold." *International Journal of Sports Medicine* 5 (1984): 106–109.

Hamilton, N., et al. "Changes in Sprint Stride Kinematics with Age in Masters Athletes." *Journal of Applied Biomechanics* 9 (1993): 15–26.

Harr, E. *Triathlon Training in Four Hours a Week.* Emmaus, PA: Rodale Sports, 2003.

Harris, R. C., et al. "Elevation of Creatine in Resting and Exercised Muscle of Normal Subjects by Creatine Supplementation." *Clinical Science* 83, no. 3 (1992): 367–374.

Hawley, J. A., and W. G. Hopkins. "Aerobic Glycolytic and Aerobic Lipolytic Power Systems: A New Paradigm with Implications for Endurance and Ultra-Endurance Events." *Sports Medicine* 20 (1995): 321–327.

Hawley, J. A., et al. "Effects of Ingesting Varying Concentrations of Sodium on Fluid Balance during Exercise." *Medicine and Science in Sport and Exercise* 28, no. 5 (1996): S350.

Heath, G. A. "Physiological Comparison of Young and Older Endurance Athletes." *Journal of Applied Physiology* 51, no. 3 (1981): 634–640.

Heath, G. W., et al. "Exercise and the Incidence of Upper Respiratory Tract Infections." *Medicine and Science in Sports and Exercise* 23 (1991): 152.

Heath, G. W., et al. "Exercise and Upper Respiratory Tract Infections: Is There a Relationship?" *Sports Medicine* 14, no. 6 (1992): 353–365.

Heil, D. P., et al. "Cardiorespiratory Responses to Seat-Tube Angle Variation during Steady-State Cycling." *Medicine and Science in Sports and Exercise* 27, no. 5 (1995): 730–735.

Hemmert, M. K., et al. "Effect of Plasma Volume on Exercise Stroke Volume in Normally Active and Endurance-Trained Men." Paper presented at the American College of Sports Medicine annual meeting, 1985.

Hendy, H. M., and B. J. Boyer. "Specificity in the Relationship between Training and Performance in Triathlons." *Perception and Motor Skills* 81, no. 3 (1995): 1231–1240.

Hermiston, R. T., and M. E. O'Brien. "The Effects of Three Types of Warm-Up on the Total Oxygen Cost of a Short Treadmill Run." In A. W. Taylor, ed., *Training: Scientific Basis and Application.* Springfield, IL: Charles C. Thomas, 1972.

Hickson, R. C., et al. "Potential for Strength and Endurance Training to Amplify Endurance Performance." *Journal of Applied Physiology* 65 (1988): 2285–2290.

Hickson, R. C., et al. "Strength Training Effects on Aerobic Power and Short-Term Endurance." *Medicine and Science in Sports and Exercise* 12 (1980): 336–339.

Hoffman-Goetz, L., and B. K. Peterson. "Exercise and the Immune System: A Model of the Stress Response." *Immunology Today* 15, no. 8 (1994): 382–387.

Holly, R. G., et al. "Stretch-Induced Growth in Chicken Wing Muscles: A New Model of Stretch Hypertrophy." *American Journal of Physiology* 7 (1980): C62–C71.

Hooper, S. L., and L. T. MacKinnon. "Monitoring Overtraining in Athletes: Recommendations." *Sports Medicine* 20, no. 5 (1995): 321–327.

Hooper, S. L., et al. "Hormonal Responses of Elite Swimmers to Overtraining." *Medicine and Science in Sports and Exercise* 25 (1993): 741–747.

Hooper, S. L., et al. "Markers for Monitoring Overtraining and Recovery." *Medicine and Science in Sports and Exercise* 27, no. 1 (1995): 106–112.

Hopkins, W. G. "Advances in Training for Endurance Athletes." *New Zealand Journal of Sports Medicine* 24, no. 3 (1996): 29–31.

Horowitz, J. F., et al. "Pre-Exercise Medium-Chain Triglyceride Ingestion Does Not Alter Muscle Glycogen Use during Exercise." *Journal of Applied Physiology* 88, no. 1 (2000): 219–225.

Hortobagyi, T., et al. "Effects of Simultaneous Training for Strength and Endurance on Upper- and Lower-Body Strength and Running Performance." *The Journal of Sports Medicine and Physical Fitness* 31 (1991): 20–30.

Houmard, J., and R. Johns. "Effects of Taper on Swim Performance." *Sports Medicine* 17 (1994): 224–232.

Houmard, J., et al. "The Effect of Warm-Up on Responses to Intense Exercise." *International Journal of Sports Medicine* 12, no. 5 (1991): 400–403.

Houmard, J., et al. "The Effects of Taper on Performance in Distance Runners." *Medicine and Science in Sports and Exercise* 26, no. 5 (1994): 624–631.

Houmard, J. A., et al. "Testosterone, Cortisol, and Creatine Kinase Levels in Male Distance Runners during Reduced Training." *International Journal of Sports Medicine* 11 (1990): 41.

Howe, M.J.J., W. Davidson, and J. A. Sluboda. "Innate Talents: Reality or Myth?" *Behavior and Brain Science* 21, no. 3 (1998): 399–407.

Hu, F. B., et al. "Dietary Fat Intake and the Risk of Coronary Heart Disease in Women." *New England Journal of Medicine* 337, no. 21 (1997): 1491–1499.

Huddle, P., and R. Frey. *Triathlon: Starting Out.* Oxford, UK: Meyer & Meyer Sport, 2003.

International Dance and Exercise Association. "Antioxidants: Clearing the Confusion." *IDEA Today,* September 1994, 67–73.

Ivy, J. L., et al. "Muscle Respiratory Capacity and Fiber Type as Determinants of the Lactate Threshold." *Journal of Applied Physiology* 48 (1980): 523–527.

Jackson, S. A., and M. Csikszentmihalyi. *Flow in Sports.* Champaign, IL: Human Kinetics, 1999.

Janssen, P.G.J.M. *Training, Lactate, Pulse Rate.* Oulu, Finland: Polar Electric Oy, 1987.

Jansson, E., and L. Kaijser. "Effect of Diet on Muscle Glycogen and Blood Glucose Utilization during a Short-Term Exercise in Man." *Acta Physiologica Scandinavica* 115, no. 3 (1982): 341–347.

Jeukendrup, A. E., et al. "Physiological Changes in Male Competitive Cyclists after Two Weeks of Intensified Training." *International Journal of Sports Medicine* 13, no. 7 (1992): 534–541.

Johnston, R. E., et al. "Strength Training for Female Distance Runners: Impact on Economy." *Medicine and Science in Sports and Exercise* 27, no. 5 (1995): S47.

Kanter, M. M. "Free Radicals, Exercise, and Antioxidant Supplementation." *International Journal of Sport Nutrition* 4 (1994): 205–220.

Karvonen, J. "Importance of Warm-Up and Cool Down on Exercise Performance." *Medicine in Sports Training and Coaching.* Dasel, Germany: Karger, 1992.

Keast, D., et al. "Exercise and the Immune Response." *Sports Medicine* 5 (1988): 248–267.

Keul, J., et al. *Energy Metabolism of Human Muscle.* Baltimore: University Park Press, 1972.

Kirwan, J. P., et al. "Physiological Responses to Successive Days of Intense Training in Competitive Swimmers." *Medicine and Science in Sport and Exercise* 20 (1988): 255–259.

Knuttgen, H. G., et al. "Physical Conditioning through Interval Training with Young Male Adults." *Medicine and Science in Sports* 5 (1973): 220–226.

Kokkonen, J., and S. Lauritzen. "Isotonic Strength and Endurance Gains through PNF Stretching." *Medicine and Science in Sports and Exercise* 27, no. 5 (1995): S127.

Koltyn, K. F., P. J. O'Connor, and W. P. Morgan. "Perception of Effort in Female and Male Competitive Swimmers." *International Journal of Sports Medicine* 12 (1991): 427–429.

Korkia, D. S., et al. "An Epidemiological Investigation of Training and Injury Patterns in British Triathletes." *British Journal of Sports Medicine* 28 (1994): 191–196.

Koutedakis, Y. "Seasonal Variation in Fitness Parameters in Competitive Athletes." *Sports Medicine* 19 (1995): 373–392.

Koutedakis, Y., R. Budgett, and L. Faulmann. "Rest in Underperforming Elite Competitors." *British Journal of Sports Medicine* 24 (1990): 248–252.

Kovacs, E.M.R., et al. "Effect of Caffeinated Drinks on Substrate Metabolism, Caffeine Excretion and Performance." *Journal of Applied Physiology* 85, no. 2 (1998): 709–715.

Kraemer, W. J., et al. "Compatibility of High-Intensity Strength and Endurance Training on Hormonal and Skeletal Muscle Adaptations." *Journal of Applied Physiology* 78, no. 3 (1995): 976–989.

Kuipers, H., and H. A. Keizer. "Overtraining in Elite Athletes: Review and Directions for the Future." *Sports Medicine* 6 (1988): 79–92.

Kuipers, H., et al. "Comparison of Heart Rate as a Non-Invasive Determination of Anaerobic Threshold with Lactate Threshold when Cycling." *European Journal of Applied Physiology* 58 (1988): 303–306.

Lambert, E. V., et al. "Enhanced Endurance in Trained Cyclists during Moderate-Intensity Exercise following Two Weeks Adaptation to a High-Fat Diet." *European Journal of Applied Physiology* 69 (1994): 287–293.

Lambert, E. V., et al. "Nutritional Strategies for Promoting Fat Utilization and Delaying the Onset of Fatigue during Prolonged Exercise." *Journal of Sports Science* 15, no. 3 (1997): 315–324.

Lapachet, R. A., et al. "Body Fat and Exercise Endurance in Trained Rats Adapted to a High-Fat and/or High-Carbohydrate Diet." *Journal of Applied Physiology* 80, no. 4 (1996): 1173–1179.

Laughlin, T., and J. Delves. *Total Immersion.* New York: Simon & Schuster, 1996.

Leake, C. N., and J. E. Carter. "Comparison of Body Composition and Somatotype of Trained Female Triathletes." *Journal of Sports Science* 9, no. 2 (1991): 125–135.

Legwold, G. "Masters Competitors Age Little in Ten Years." *The Physician and Sports Medicine* 10, no. 10 (1982): 27.

Lehmann, M., et al. "Overtraining in Endurance Athletes: A Brief Review." *Medicine and Science in Sports and Exercise* 25, no. 7 (1993): 854–862.4.

Lehmann, M. P., et al. "Training-Overtraining: An Overview and Experimental Results in Endurance Sports." *Journal of Sports Medicine and Physical Fitness* 37, no. 1 (1997): 7–17.

Lehmann, M. P., et al. "Training-Overtraining: Influence of a Defined Increase in Training Volume vs. Training Intensity on Performance, Catecholamines and Some Metabolic Parameters in Experienced Middle- and Long-Distance Runners." *European Journal of Applied Physiology* 64 (1992): 169–177.

Lemon, P.W.R. "Is Increased Dietary Protein Necessary or Beneficial for Individuals with a Physically Active Lifestyle?" *Nutrition Reviews* 54, no. 4 (1996): S169–S175.

———. "Protein and Amino Acid Needs of the Strength Athlete." *International Journal of Sports Nutrition* 1 (1991): 127–145.

Loehr, J. *Mental Toughness Training for Sports.* New York: Stephen Greene Press, 1982.

———. *The New Mental Toughness Training for Sports.* New York: Penguin Books, 1995.

Lynch, J. *Creative Coaching.* Champaign, IL: Human Kinetics, 2001.

———. *Running Within.* Champaign, IL: Human Kinetics, 1999.

———. *Thinking Body, Dancing Mind.* New York: Bantam Books, 1992.

———. *The Total Runner.* Upper Saddle River, NJ: Prentice Hall, 1987.

Lynch, J., and C. A. Huang. *Working Without, Working Within.* New York: Tarcher & Putnam, 1998.

MacDougal, J. D., et al. "The Time Course for Elevated Muscle Protein Synthesis following Heavy Resistance Exercise." *Canadian Journal of Applied Physiology* 20, no. 4 (1995): 480–486.

MacIntyre, J. G. "Growth Hormone and Athletes." *Sports Medicine* 4 (1987): 129.

MacLaren, C. P., et al. "A Review of Metabolic and Physiologic Factors in Fatigue." *Exercise and Sports Science Review* 17 (1989): 29.

Maglischo, E. *Swimming Faster.* Mountain View, CA: Mayfield, 1982.

Malarkey, W. B., et al. "The Influence of Age on Endocrine Responses to Ultraendurance Stress." *Journal of Gerontology* 48, no. 4 (1993): M134–139.

Malwa, R. M. "Growth and Maturation: Normal Variation and Effect of Training." In C. V. Gisolfi and D. R. Lamb, eds., *Perspectives in Exercise Science and Sports Medicine: Youth, Exercise and Sport.* Carmel, IN: Benchmark Press, 1989.

Marcinik, E. J., et al. "Effects of Strength Training on Lactate Threshold and Endurance Performance." *Medicine and Science in Sports and Exercise* 23, no. 6 (1991): 739–743.

Martin, D. E., and P. N. Coe. *Better Training for Distance Runners.* Champaign, IL: Human Kinetics, 1997.

———. *Training Distance Runners.* Champaign, IL: Leisure Press, 1991.

Matzen, L. E., et al. "Different Short-Term Effects of Protein and Carbohydrate Intake on TSH, GH, Insulin and Glucagon." *Scandinavian Journal of Clinical and Laboratory Investigation* 50, no. 11 (1990): 801–805.

Maughan, R. J. "Creatine Supplementation and Exercise Performance." *International Journal of Sports Nutrition* 5 (1995): 94–101.

Mayhew, J., and P. Gross. "Body Composition Changes in Young Women and High Resistance Weight Training." *Research Quarterly* 45 (1974): 433–440.

McArdle, W., F. Katch, and V. Katch. *Exercise Physiology.* Baltimore: Williams & Wilkins, 1996.

McCarthy, J. P., et al. "Compatibility of Adaptive Responses with Combining Strength and Endurance Training." *Medicine and Science in Sports and Exercise* 27, no. 3 (1995): 429–436.

McMurtrey, J. J., and R. Sherwin. "History, Pharmacology and Toxicology of Caffeine and Caffeine-Containing Beverages." *Clinical Nutrition* 6 (1987): 249–254.

Messier, S. P., and K. J. Cirillo. "Effects of a Verbal and Visual Feedback System on Running Technique, Perceived Exertion, and Running Economy in Female Novice Runners." *Medicine and Science in Sports and Exercise* 21, no. 2 (1989): S80.

Milne, C. "The Tired Athlete." *New Zealand Journal of Sports Medicine* 19, no. 3 (1991): 42–44.

Mora, J. *Triathlon 101.* Champaign, IL: Human Kinetics, 1999.

Morgan, D. W., et al. "Effect of Step-Length Optimization on the Aerobic Demand of Running." *Journal of Applied Physiology* 77 (1994): 245.

Morgan, D. W., et al. "Effects of a Prolonged Maximal Run on Running Economy and Running Mechanics." *Medicine and Science in Sports and Exercise* 21, no. 2 (1989): S26.

Mujika, I., and S. Padilla. "Creatine Supplementation as an Ergogenic Aid for Sports Performance in Highly Trained Athletes: A Critical Review." *International Journal of Sports Medicine* 18, no. 7 (1997): 491–496.

Muoio, D. M., et al. "Effect of Dietary Fat on Metabolic Adjustments to Maximal VO_2 and Endurance in Runners." *Medicine and Science in Sports and Exercise* 26 (1994): 81–88.

Nagao, N., et al. "Energy Intake in the Triathlon Competition by Means of Cluster Analysis." *Journal of Sports Medicine and Physical Fitness* 31, no. 1 (1991): 62–66.

Nelson, A. G., et al. "Consequences of Combining Strength and Endurance Training Regimens." *Physical Therapy* 70 (1990): 287–294.

Nelson, A. G., et al. "Muscle Glycogen Supercompensation Is Enhanced by Prior Creatine Supplementation." *Medicine and Science in Sports and Exercise* 33, no. 7 (2001): 1096–1100.

Nelson. M. E., et al. "Diet and Bone Status in Amenorrheic Runners." *American Journal of Clinical Nutrition* 43 (1986): 910–916.

Nemoto, I., et al. "Branched-Chain Amino Acid (BCAA) Supplementation Improves Endurance Capacities and RPE." *Medicine and Science in Sports and Exercise* 28, no. 5 (1996): S219.

Newby-Fraser, P. *Peak Fitness for Women.* Champaign, IL: Human Kinetics, 1995.

———. Personal communication with author, 1998.

Newham, D. J., et al. "Muscle Pain and Tenderness after Exercise." *Australian Journal of Sports Medicine and Exercise Science* 14 (1982): 129–131.

Nieman, D. C., et al. "Infectious Episodes in Runners before and after the Los Angeles Marathon." *Journal of Sports Medicine and Physical Fitness* 30 (1990): 316–328.

Niles, R. "Power as a Determinant of Endurance Performance." Unpublished study at Sonoma State University, 1991.

———. *Time-Saving Training for Multisport Athletes.* Champaign, IL: Human Kinetics, 1997.

Nissen, S. L., and R. L. Sharp. "Effect of Dietary Supplements on Lean Mass and Strength Gains with Resistance Exercise: A Meta-Analysis." *Journal of Applied Physiology* 94, no.2 (2003): 651–659.

Noakes, T. D. "Implications of Exercise Testing for Prediction of Athletic Performance: A Contemporary Perspective." *Medicine and Science in Sports and Exercise* 20, no. 4 (1988): 319–330.

———. *The Lore of Running.* Champaign, IL: Leisure Press, 1991.

Noakes, T., et al. "Effects of a Low-Carbohydrate, High-Fat Diet Prior to Carbohydrate Loading on Endurance Cycling Performance." *Clinical Science* 87 (1994): S32–S33.

Nose, H., et al. "Involvement of Sodium Retention Hormones during Hydration in Humans." *Journal of Applied Physiology* 65 (1988): 325–331.

O'Brien, C., et al. "Glycerol Hyperhydration: Physiological Responses during Cold-Air Exposure." *Journal of Applied Physiology* 99 (2005): 515–521.

Okkels, T. "The Effect of Interval- and Tempo-Training on Performance and Skeletal Muscle in Well-Trained Runners." *Twelfth European Track Coaches Congress,* Acoteias, Portugal, 1983, 1–9.

Orlick, T. *Psyched to Win.* Champaign, IL: Leisure Press, 1992.

———. *Psyching for Sport.* Champaign, IL: Leisure Press, 1986.

O'Toole, M. L. "Prevention and Treatment of Injuries to Runners." *Medicine and Science in Sports and Exercise* 24, no. 9 (1992): S360–363.

O'Toole, M. L., and P. S. Douglas. "Applied Physiology of Triathlon." *Sports Medicine* 19, no. 4 (1995): 251–267.

O'Toole, M. L., et al. "Fluid and Electrolyte Status in Athletes Receiving Medical Care at an Ultradistance Triathlon." *Clinical Journal of Sports Medicine* 5, no. 2 (1995): 116–122.

O'Toole, M. L., et al. "Overuse Injuries in Ultraendurance Triathletes." *American Journal of Sports Medicine* 17 (1989): 514–518.

Parizkova, J. "Body Composition and Exercise during Growth and Development." *Physical Activity: Human Growth and Development* (1974).

Pate, R. R., and J. D. Branch. "Training for Endurance Sport." *Medicine and Science in Sports and Exercise* 24, no. 9 (1992): S340–343.

Pate, R. R., et al. "Cardiorespiratory and Metabolic Responses to Submaximal and Maximal Exercise in Elite Women Distance Runners." *International Journal of Sports Medicine* 8, no. S2 (1987): 91–95.

Pendergast, D. R., et al. "A Perspective on Fat Intake in Athletes." *Journal of the American College of Nutrition* 19, no. 3 (2000): 345–350.

Peters, E. M., et al. "Anti-Oxidant Nutrient Supplementation and Symptoms of Upper Respiratory Tract Infections in Endurance Athletes." *Medicine and Science in Sports and Exercise* 26, no. 5 (1993): S218.

Peyrebrune, M. C., et al. "The Effects of Oral Creatine Supplementation on Performance in Single and Repeated Sprint Training." *Journal of Sports Science* 16, no. 3 (1998): 271–279.

Phinney, S. D., et al. "The Human Metabolic Response to Chronic Ketosis with Caloric Restriction and Preservation of Submaximal Exercise Capabilities with Reduced Carbohydrate Oxidation." *Metabolism* 32 (1983): 769–776.

Pollock, M., et al. "Effect of Age and Training on Aerobic Capacity and Body Composition of Master Athletes." *Journal of Applied Physiology* 62, no. 2 (1987): 725–731.

Pollock, M., et al. "Frequency of Training as a Determinant for Improvement in Cardiovascular Function and Body Composition of Middle-Aged Men." *Archives of Physical Medicine and Rehabilitation* 56 (1975): 141–145.

Remer, T., and F. Manz. "Potential Renal Acid Load of Foods and Its Influence on Urine pH." *Journal of the American Dietetic Association* 95, no. 7 (1995): 791–797.

Reuter, B. H., and G. Wright. "Overuse Injury Prevention in Triathletes." *Strength and Conditioning* 18, no. 6 (1996): 11–14.

Richardson, A. B., and J. W. Miller. "Swimming and the Older Athlete." *Clinical Sports Medicine* 10, no. 2 (1991): 301–318.

Riegel, P. "Athletic Records and Human Endurance." *American Scientist* 69 (1981): 285–290.

Roberg, R. A. "Glycerol Hyperhydration to Beat the Heat?" 1998, *Sportscience,* www.sportsci.org/traintech/glycerol/rar.htm.

Robinson, S. "Temperature Regulation in Exercise." *Pediatrics* 32 (1963): 691–702.

Rogers, M. A., et al. "Decline in VO_2Max with Aging in Masters Athletes and Sedentary Men." *Journal of Applied Physiology* 68, no. 5 (1990): 2195–2199.

Romanov, N. S., with J. Robson. *Dr. Nicholas Romanov's Pose Method of Running.* Coral Gables, FL: PoseTech Press, 2002.

Romijn, J. A., et al. "Regulation of Endogenous Fat and Carbohydrate Metabolism in Relation to Exercise Intensity and Duration." *American Journal of Physiology* 265 (1993): E380.

Rushall, B. *Psyching in Sport: The Psychological Preparation for Serious Competition in Sport.* London: Pelham Books, 1979.

Rushall, B. S. "A Tool for Measuring Stress Tolerance in Elite Athletes." *Applied Sport Psychology* 2 (1990): 51–66.

———. "Some Psychological Considerations for U.S. National Swimming Teams." *American Swimming,* February-March (1994): 8–12.

Sale, D. G., and D. MacDougall. "Specificity in Strength Training: A Review for the Coach and Athlete." *Canadian Journal of Applied Sport Sciences* 6 (1981): 87–92.

Sale, D. G., et al. "Comparison of Two Regimens of Concurrent Strength and Endurance Training." *Medicine and Science in Sports and Exercise* 22, no. 3 (1990): 348–356.

Schatz, M. P. "Easy Hamstring Stretches." *Physician and Sports Medicine* 22, no. 2 (1994): 115–116.

Schena, F. "Branched-Chain Amino Acid Supplementation during Trekking at High Altitude." *European Journal of Applied Physiology* 65 (1992): 394–398.

Schneider, D. A., et al. "Ventilatory Threshold and Maximal Oxygen Uptake during Cycling and Running in Triathletes." *Medicine and Science in Sports and Exercise* 22, no. 2 (1990): 257–264.

Schumacher Y. O., and P. Mueller. "The 4000-m Team Pursuit Cycling World Record: Theoretical and Practical Aspects." *Medicine and Science in Sports and Exercise* 34, no. 6 (2002): 1029–1036.

Seals, D. R., et al. "Endurance Training in Older Men and Women." *Journal of Applied Physiology* 57 (1984): 1024–1029.

Seiler, K. S., and G. O. Kjerland. "Quantifying Training Intensity Distribution in Elite Endurance Athletes: Is There Evidence of an Optimal Distribution? *Scandinavian Journal of Medicine and Science in Sports* 18, no. 2 (2008): 212–220.

Shangold, M. M., and G. Mirkin, eds. *Women and Exercise: Physiology and Sports Medicine.* Philadelphia: F. A. Davis, 1988.

Sharp, N.C.C., and Y. Koutedakis. "Sport and the Overtraining Syndrome." *British Medical Journal* 48, no. 3 (1992): 518–533.

Shasby, G. B., and F. C. Hagerman. "The Effects of Conditioning on Cardiorespiratory Function in Adolescent Boys." *Journal of Sports Medicine* 3 (1975): 97–107.

Simon, J., et al. "Plasma Lactate and Ventilation Thresholds in Trained and Untrained Cyclists." *Journal of Applied Physiology* 60 (1986): 777–781.

Simonson, J. C., et al. "Dietary Carbohydrate, Muscle Glycogen, and Power Output during Rowing Training." *Journal of Applied Physiology* 70 (1991): 1500–1505.

Sleamaker, R., and R. Browning. *Serious Training for Serious Athletes.* Champaign, IL: Leisure Press, 1996.

Sleivert, G. G., and D. S. Rowlands. "Physical and Physiological Factors Associated with Success in the Triathlon." *Sports Medicine* 22, no. 1 (1996): 8–18.

Sleivert, G. G., and H. A. Wenger. "Physiological Predictors of Short-Course Triathlon Performance." *Medicine and Science in Sports and Exercise* 25, no. 7 (1993): 871–876.

Somer, E. *The Essential Guide to Vitamins and Minerals.* New York: HarperCollins, 1992.

Speechly, D. P., S. R. Taylor, and G. G. Rogers. "Differences in Ultra-Endurance Exercise in Performance-Matched Male and Female Runners." *Medicine and Science in Sports and Exercise* 28 (1996): 359–365.

Stahl, A. B. "Hominid Dietary Selection before Fire." *Current Anthropology* 25, no. 2 (1984): 151–168.

Steed, J. C., et al. "Ratings of Perceived Exertion (RPE) as Markers of Blood Lactate Concentration during Rowing." *Medicine and Science in Sports and Exercise* 26 (1994): 797–803.

Steinacker, J. M., et al. "Training of Rowers before World Championships." *Medicine and Science in Sports and Exercise* 30, no. 7 (1998): 1158–1163.

Stone, M., et al. "Overtraining: A Review of the Signs, Symptoms, and Possible Causes." *Journal of Applied Sport Sciences* 5, no. 1 (1991): 35–50.

Stone, M. H., et al. "Health- and Performance-Related Potential of Resistance Training." *Sports Medicine* 11, no. 4 (1991): 210–231.

Svedenhag, J., and B. Sjodin. "Physiological Characteristics of Elite Male Runners In- and Off-Season." *Canadian Journal of Applied Sport Sciences* 10, no. 3 (1985): 127–133.

Taimura, A., and M. Sugahara. "Effect of Fluid Intake on Performance, Body Temperature, and Body Weight Loss during Swimming Training." *Medicine and Science in Sport and Exercise* 28, no. 5 (1996): S940.

Thomas, D. Q., et al. "Changes in Running Economy and Mechanics during a Submaximal 5-Km Run." *Journal of Strength and Conditioning Research* 9, no. 3 (1995): 170–175.

Thompson, P. D., et al. "The Effects of High-Carbohydrate and High-Fat Diets on the Serum Lipid and Lipoprotein Concentrations of Endurance Athletes." *Metabolism* 33 (1984): 1003–1010.

Thorland, W. G., et al. "Strength and Anaerobic Responses of Elite Young Female Sprint and Distance Runners." *Medicine and Science in Sports and Exercise* 19: 56–61.

Tipton, C. M., et al. "The Influence of Physical Activity on Ligaments and Tendons." *Medicine and Science in Sports and Exercise* 7 (1975): 165–175.

Toussaint, H. M. "Differences in Propelling Efficiency between Competitive and Triathlon Swimmers." *Medicine and Science in Sports and Exercise* 22, no. 3 (1990): 409–415.

Toussaint, H. M., and A. P. Hollander. "Energetics of Competitive Swimming: Implications for Training Programs." *Sports Medicine* 18 (1994): 384.

Toussaint, H. M., et al. "Effect of Triathlon Wetsuit on Drag during Swimming." *Medicine and Science in Sports and Exercise* 21 (1989): 325.

Town, G., and T. Kearney. *Swim, Bike, Run.* Champaign, IL: Human Kinetics, 1994.

Ungerleider, S. *Mental Training for Peak Performance.* Emmaus, PA: Rodale Sports, 1996.

Urhausen, A., et al. "Blood Hormones as Markers of Training Stress and Overtraining." *Sports Medicine* 20 (1995): 251–276.

Vanderburgh, H., and S. Kaufman. "Stretch and Skeletal Myotube Growth: What Is the Physical to Biochemical Linkage?" In K. Borer et al., eds., *Frontiers of Exercise Biology.* Champaign, IL: Human Kinetics, 1983.

VanHandel, P. J. "Planning a Comprehensive Training Program." *Conditioning for Cycling* 1, no. 3 (1991): 4–12.

———. "The Science of Sport Training for Cycling, Part I." *Conditioning for Cycling* 1, no. 1 (1991): 8–11.

———. "The Science of Sport Training for Cycling, Part II." *Conditioning for Cycling* 1, no. 2 (1991): 18–23.

———. "Specificity of Training: Establishing Pace, Frequency, and Duration of Training Sessions." *Bike Tech* 6, no. 3 (1987): 6–12.

Vanzyl, C. G., et al. "Effects of Medium-Chain Triglycerides Ingestion on Fuel Metabolism and Cycling Performance." *Journal of Applied Physiology* 80, no. 6 (1996): 2217–2225.

Venkatraman, J. T., et al. "Influence of the Level of Dietary Lipid Intake and Maximal Exercise on the Immune Status in Runners." *Medicine and Science in Sport and Exercise* 29, no. 3 (1997): 333–344.

Vogt, M., et al. "Effects of Dietary Fat on Muscle Substrates, Metabolism, and Performance in Athletes." *Medicine and Science in Sports and Exercise* 35 no. 6 (2003): 952–960.

Wakayoshi, K., et al. "Does Critical Swimming Velocity Represent Exercise Intensity at Maximal Lactate Steady State?" *Medicine and Science in Sports and Exercise* 25, no. 5 (1993): S366.

Wallin, D., et al. "Improvement of Muscle Flexibility: A Comparison between Two Techniques." *The American Journal of Sports Medicine* 13, no. 4 (1985): 263–268.

Walsh, R. M., et al. "Impaired High-Intensity Cycling Performance Time at Low Levels of Dehydration." *International Journal of Sports Medicine* 15 (1994): 392–398.

Wells, C. L. *Women, Sport, and Performance: A Physiological Perspective.* Champaign, IL: Human Kinetics, 1991.

Weltman, A. *The Blood Lactate Response to Exercise.* Champaign, IL: Human Kinetics, 1995.

Weltman, A., et al. "The Effects of Hydraulic Resistance Strength Training in Pre-Pubertal Males. *Medicine and Science in Sports and Exercise* 18 (1986): 629–638.

Weltman, A., et al. "Endurance Training Amplifies the Pulsatile Release of Growth Hormone: Effects of Training Intensity." *Journal of Applied Physiology* 72 (1992): 2188.

Wemple, R. D., et al. "Caffeine vs. Caffeine-Free Sports Drinks: Effects on Urine Production at Rest and during Prolonged Exercise." *International Journal of Sports Medicine* 18 (1997): 40–46.

Weston, A. R., et al. "Skeletal Muscle Buffering Capacity and Endurance Performance after High-Intensity Interval Training by Well-Trained Cyclists." *European Journal of Applied Physiology* 75 (1997): 7–13.

Williams, K. R. "Relationship between Distance Running Biomechanics and Running Economy." In P. R. Cavanagh, ed., *Biomechanics of Distance Running.* Champaign, IL: Human Kinetics, 1990.

Williams, W. *Ergogenics Edge.* Champaign, IL: Human Kinetics, 1994.

Wilmore, J., and D. Costill. *Physiology of Sport and Exercise.* Champaign, IL: Human Kinetics, 1994.

Wilmore, J., et al. "Is There Energy Conservation in Amenorrheic Compared with Eumenorrheic Distance Runners?" *Journal of Applied Physiology* 72 (1992): 15–22.

Zatsiorsky, V. M. *Science and the Practice of Strength Training.* Champaign, IL: Human Kinetics, 1995.

INDEX

ABOUT THE AUTHOR

Joe Friel is the founder and president of Training Bible Coaching, with endurance coaches around the world who learn and apply the coaching philosophy and methods described in this book. Training Bible Coaching's athletes include recreational and elite triathletes, duathletes, cyclists, mountain bikers, runners, and swimmers.

Joe has an extensive background in coaching, having trained endurance athletes since 1980. His clients have included novices, elite amateurs, and professionals. The list includes an Ironman Triathlon winner, USA and foreign national champions, world championship competitors, and an Olympian.

As well as *The Triathlete's Training Bible,* Joe is the author of *The Cyclist's Training Bible, Cycling Past 50, Precision Heart Rate Training* (co-author), *The Mountain Biker's Training Bible , Going Long: Training for Ironman-Distance Triathlons* (co-author), *The Paleo Diet for Athletes* (co-author), *Your First Triathlon,* and *Total Heart Rate Training.* He is the editor of the VeloPress series Ultrafit Multisport Training. He holds a master's degree in exercise science and is a USA Triathlon and USA Cycling–certified elite coach. He helped to found the USA Triathlon National Coaching Commission and served two terms as chair.

Joe is also a columnist for *Inside Triathlon* and *VeloNews* magazines and writes feature stories for other international magazines and websites. His opinions on matters related to training for endurance sports are widely sought and have been featured in such publications as *Runner's World, Outside, Triathlete, 220, Women's Sports & Fitness, Men's Fitness, American Health, Masters Sports, Walking, Bicycling,* the *New York Times,* and even *Vogue.*

He conducts yearly seminars and camps on training and racing for endurance athletes and provides consulting services to corporations in the fitness industry and to national governing bodies.

As an age-group competitor, he is a former Colorado State Masters Triathlon Champion and a Rocky Mountain region and Southwest region duathlon age-group champion, has been named to several All-American teams, and has represented the United States at the world championships. He also competes in USA Cycling bike races.

Joe Friel may be contacted through his website at trainingbible.com.